Jorma Larimo, DSc
Editor

Market Entry and Operational Decision Making in East-West Business Relationships

Market Entry and Operational Decision Making in East-West Business Relationships has been co-published simultaneously as *Journal of East-West Business*, Volume 13, Numbers 1/2/3 2007.

Pre-publication
REVIEWS,
COMMENTARIES,
EVALUATIONS . . .

"A VERY IMPORTANT AND TIMELY PUBLICATION PRESENTED FROM THE EUROPEAN PERSPECTIVE. The discussion focusing on regionalization decisions should be particularly interesting to many researchers. At the same time, the broader internationalization research included in this publication contributes to and supplements the existing body of literature on internationalization."

George Tesar, PhD, MBA, BSME
Professor of Marketing
and International Business Emeritus
Umeå School of Business
Umeå University, Umeå, Sweden

Professor of Marketing Emeritus
University of Wisconsin-Whitewater

Market Entry
and Operational
Decision Making
in East-West
Business Relationships

Market Entry and Operational Decision Making in East-West Business Relationships has been co-published simultaneously as *Journal of East-West Business*, Volume 13, Numbers 1/2/3 2007.

Monographic Separates from the *Journal of East-West Business*™

For additional information on these and other Haworth Press titles, including descriptions, tables of contents, reviews, and prices, use the QuickSearch catalog at http://www.HaworthPress.com.

Market Entry and Operational Decision Making in East-West Business Relationships, edited by Jorma Larimo, DSc (Vol. 13, No. 1/2/3, 2007). *Analysis of case studies on companies in Central and Eastern Europe exploring entry and marketing strategies of multinational companies.*

Expansion or Exodus: Why Do Russian Corporations Invest Abroad?, edited by Kari Liuhto, PhD, (Vol. 11, No. 3/4, 2005). *An examination of how and why Russian corporations invest outside the country and why most of that money remains abroad as the growth and performance of these companies increases at an accelerated rate.*

Marketing Challenges in Transition Economies of Europe, Baltic States and the C.I.S., edited by Gopalkrishnan R. Iyer, PhD, and Lance A. Masters, PhD (Vol. 5, No. 1/2, 1999). *"This book is a practical presentation of the problems that Central and Eastern Europe countries have had in changing from a command economy to a market economy. This book helps provide a much-needed analysis of why the good intentions of western governments and firms as well as transition economy governments and firms have not had more success in changing to a market economy." (James E. Littlefield, Professor of Marketing, Virginia Polytechnic Institute, Blacksburg, Virginia)*

Enterprise Restructuring and Foreign Investment in the Transforming East: The Impact of Privatization, edited by Val Samonis (Vol. 4, No. 1/2, 1998). *"This impressive volume represents a significant contribution to the rapidly growing literature on private sector development in transition economies." (Peter Cornelius, PhD, Chief International Economist, Deutsche Bank Research, Frankfurt, Germany)*

Marketing in Central and Eastern Europe, edited by Jan Nowak (Vol. 3, No. 1, 1997). *"Identify[ies] the methodological requirements for doing effective marketing research in the countries of Central and Eastern Europe." (Journal of Economic Literature)*

East-West Business Relationships: Establishment and Development, edited by Jarmo Nieminen (Vol. 1, No. 4, 1996). *"Recommended as first-rate reading for all those interested and involved in east-west business transactions and direct investment in eastern European countries." (Adam Gwiazda, PhD, Professor of International Economics, Gdansk University, Poland)*

The Central and Eastern European Markets: Guideline for New Business Ventures, edited by Petr Chadraba (Vol. 1, No. 3, 1995). *"An interesting collection of strategies and approaches to rapidly evolving markets in central and Eastern Europe." (George Tesar, PhD, Professor of Marketing, University of Wisconsin-Whitewater)*

Market Entry and Operational Decision Making in East-West Business Relationships

Jorma Larimo, DSc
Editor

Market Entry and Operational Decision Making in East-West Business Relationships has been co-published simultaneously as *Journal of East-West Business*, Volume 13, Numbers 1/2/3 2007.

International Business Press®
An Imprint of The Haworth Press, Inc.

Published by

The International Business Press®, 10 Alice Street, Binghamton, NY 13904-1580 USA

The International Business Press® is an imprint of The Haworth Press, Inc., 10 Alice Street, Binghamton, NY 13904-1580 USA.

Market Entry and Operational Decision Making in East-West Business Relationships has been co-published simultaneously as *Journal of East-West Business*™, Volume 13, Numbers 1/2/3 2007.

The development, preparation, and publication of this work has been undertaken with great care. However, the publisher, employees, editors, and agents of The Haworth Press and all imprints of The Haworth Press, Inc., including The Haworth Medical Press® and Pharmaceutical Products Press®, are not responsible for any errors contained herein or for consequences that may ensue from use of materials or information contained in this work. With regard to case studies, identities and circumstances of individuals discussed herein have been changed to protect confidentiality. Any resemblance to actual persons, living or dead, is entirely coincidental.

The Haworth Press is committed to the dissemination of ideas and information according to the highest standards of intellectual freedom and the free exchange of ideas. Statements made and opinions expressed in this publication do not necessarily reflect the views of the Publisher, Directors, management, or staff of The Haworth Press, Inc., or an endorsement by them.

Library of Congress Cataloging-in-Publication Data

Market entry and operational decision making in East-West business relationships / Jorma Larimo, editor.
    p. cm.
    "Market Entry and Operational Decision Making in East-West Business Relationships has been co-published simultaneously as Journal of East-West Business, Volume 13, Numbers 1/2/3 2007."
    Includes bibliographical references and index.
    ISBN-13: 978-0-7890-3543-1 (hard cover : alk. paper)
    ISBN-10: 0-7890-3543-X (hard cover : alk. paper)
    ISBN-13: 978-0-7890-3544-8 (soft cover : alk. paper)
    ISBN-10: 0-7890-3544-8 (soft cover : alk. paper)
    1. International business enterprises–Europe, Eastern. 2. Export marketing–Europe, Eastern. 3. Business planning–Europe, Eastern. 4. Investments, Foreign–Europe, Eastern. 5. Europe, Eastern–Foreign economic relations. I. Larimo, Jorma.
HD2844.7.M37 2007
382.0947–dc22
                                                                                    2006029101

The HAWORTH PRESS Inc.

Abstracting, Indexing & Outward Linking

PRINT *and* ELECTRONIC BOOKS & JOURNALS

This section provides you with a list of major indexing & abstracting services and other tools for bibliographic access. That is to say, each service began covering this periodical during the the year noted in the right column. Most Websites which are listed below have indicated that they will either post, disseminate, compile, archive, cite or alert their own Website users with research-based content from this work. (This list is as current as the copyright date of this publication.)

Abstracting, Website/Indexing Coverage . . . . Year When Coverage Began

- *(IBR) International Bibliography of Book Reviews on the Humanities and Social Sciences (Thomson)*
  <http://www.saur.de> 2006

- *(IBZ) International Bibliography of Periodical Literature on the Humanities and Social Sciences (Thomson)*
  <http://www.saur.de> 2001

- ***ABI/INFORM Complete (ProQuest)***
  <http://www.proquest.com> 2006

- ***ABI/INFORM Global (ProQuest)***
  <http://www.proquest.com> 2001

- ***ABI/INFORM Research (ProQuest)***
  <http://www.proquest.com> 2001

- ***Academic Search Premier (EBSCO)***
  <http://www.epnet.com/academic/acasearchprem.asp> 2006

- ***Business Source Complete (EBSCO)* 2006

- ***Business Source Premier (EBSCO)*
  <http://www.epnet.com/adademic/bussourceprem.asp> 2006

- ***MasterFILE Premier (EBSCO)***
  <http://www.epnet.com/government/mfpremier.asp) 2006

- *BEFO <http://www.fiz-technik.de/en_db/d_befo.htm>* 2005

- *British Library Inside (The British Library)*
  <http://www.bl.uk/services/current/inside.html>. 2006
- *EBSCOhost Electronic Journals Service (EJS)*
  <http://ejournals.ebsco.com>. 2001
- *EconLit & Journal of Economic Literature (EconLit,*
  on CD-ROM, and eJel) 1995
- *Elsevier Eflow-D <http://www.elsevier.com>.* 2006
- *Elsevier Scopus <http://www.info.scopus.com>* 2005
- *Entrepreneurship Research Engine*
  <http://research.kauffmann.org> 2005
- *Environmental Sciences and Pollution Management (Cambridge*
  Scientific Abstracts)
  <http://www.csa.com> 2006
- *FirstSearch Electronic Collections Online (OCLC)*
  <http://www.oclc.org/electroniccollections/> 2006
- *GEOBASE (Elsevier) <http://www.elsevier.com>* 1995
- *Google <http://www.google.com>.* 2004
- *Google Scholar <http://scholar.google.com>* 2004
- *Guide to Social Science & Religion in Periodical Literature*
  <http://nplguide.com> 1995
- *Haworth Document Delivery Center*
  <http://www.HaworthPress.com/journals/dds.asp> 1995
- *Hospitality & Tourism Index (EBSCO)* 2006
- *Index Guide to College Journals* 1999
- *Index to Periodical Articles Related to Law*
  <http://www.law.utexas.edu>. 1995
- *Internationale Bibliographie der geistes- und*
  sozialwissenschaftlichen Zeitschriftenliteratur. . . See IBZ
  <http://www.saur.de>. 2001
- *Journal Quality List, 23rd Edition <http://www.harzing.com>* . . . 2006
- *JournalSeek <http://www.lexisnexis.com>* 2006
- *Lexis.com <http://www.lexisnexis.com>* 2006
- *LexisNexis Academic Universe <http://www.lexisnexis.com>* 2005
- *Links@Ovid (via CrossRef targeted DOI links)*
  <http://www.ovid.com>. 2005
- *Management & Marketing Abstracts <http://www.pira.co.uk/>* . . . 1995
- *NewJour (Electronic Journals & Newsletters)*
  <http://gort.ucsd.edu/newjour> 2006
- *Nexis.com <http://www.lexisnexis.com>* 2006
- *OCLC ArticleFirst <http://www.oclc.org/services/databases/>* . . . 2006
- *Operations Research/Management Science.* 1995

(continued)

- *Ovid Linksolver (OpenURL link resolver via CrossRef targeted DOI links) <http://www.linksolver.com>* 2005
- *Personnel Management Abstracts* 1997
- *ProQuest 5000 International <http://www.proquest.com>* 2001
- *Referativnyi Zhurnal (Abstracts Journal of the All-Russian Institute of Scientific and Technical Information–in Russian) <http://www.viniti.ru>* 1995
- *Risk Abstracts (Cambridge Scientific Abstracts) <http://csa.com>* 2006
- *Scopus (See instead Elsevier Scopus) <http://www.info.scopus.com>* 2005
- *SwetsWise <http://www.swets.com>* 2002
- *zetoc (The British Library) <http://www.bl.uk>* 2004

Bibliographic Access

- *Cabell's Directory of Publishing Opportunities in Management <http://www.cabells.com>*

- *MediaFinder <http://www.mediafinder.com/>*

- *Ulrich's Periodicals Directory: International Periodicals Information Since 1932 <http://www.Bowkerlink.com>*

Special Bibliographic Notes related to special journal issues (separates) and indexing/abstracting:

- indexing/abstracting services in this list will also cover material in any "separate" that is co-published simultaneously with Haworth's special thematic journal issue or DocuSerial. Indexing/abstracting usually covers material at the article/chapter level.
- monographic co-editions are intended for either non-subscribers or libraries which intend to purchase a second copy for their circulating collections.
- monographic co-editions are reported to all jobbers/wholesalers/approval plans. The source journal is listed as the "series" to assist the prevention of duplicate purchasing in the same manner utilized for books-in-series.
- to facilitate user/access services all indexing/abstracting services are encouraged to utilize the co-indexing entry note indicated at the bottom of the first page of each article/chapter/contribution.
- this is intended to assist a library user of any reference tool (whether print, electronic, online, or CD-ROM) to locate the monographic version if the library has purchased this version but not a subscription to the source journal.
- individual articles/chapters in any Haworth publication are also available through The Haworth Document Delivery Service (HDDS).

As part of
Haworth's
continuing
committment
to better
serve our
library
patrons, we
are proud to
be working
with the
following
electronic
services:

AGGREGATOR SERVICES

EBSCOhost

Ingenta

J-Gate

Minerva

OCLC FirstSearch

Oxmill

SwetsWise

FirstSearch

Oxmill Publishing

SwetsWise

LINK RESOLVER SERVICES

1Cate (Openly Informatics)

CrossRef

Gold Rush (Coalliance)

LinkOut (PubMed)

LINKplus (Atypon)

LinkSolver (Ovid)

LinkSource with A-to-Z (EBSCO)

Resource Linker (Ulrich)

SerialsSolutions (ProQuest)

SFX (Ex Libris)

Sirsi Resolver (SirsiDynix)

Tour (TDnet)

Vlink (Extensity, *formerly Geac*)

WebBridge (Innovative Interfaces)

Gold Rush

$S \cdot F \cdot X$

SerialsSolutions

TOUR

Market Entry and Operational Decision Making in East-West Business Relationships

CONTENTS

Foreword   xiii

Introduction   1

The Emergence and Success Factors of Fast Internationalizers:
Four Cases from Estonia   11
Tiia Vissak

First Mover Advantages in Central and Eastern Europe:
A Comparative Analysis of Performance Measures   35
Kristian Jakobsen

Internationalization of the Biggest Finnish and Swedish Retailers
in the Baltic States and Russia   63
Jorma Larimo
Ari Huuhka

Trade and Market Liberalisation in Eastern Europe:
The Effects on the FDI Location Decisions of Italian Firms   93
Antonio Majocchi
Roger Strange

In-Store Shopping Behavior: A Cross-Cultural Comparison
in Italy, France and Poland   115
    Donata Vianelli
    Christian Dianoux
    Tomasz Domanski
    Jean Luc Herrmann

Regionalization in Central and Eastern Europe: Searching
for Regiocentric Orientations in MNC Strategies   143
    Arnold Schuh

The Interconnections of Regional and Domestic Cluster
Development Processes: Using the Example of Estonian Wood
and Forest Industries   167
    Tonu Roolaht

Local Heroes, Regional Champions or Global Mandates?
Empirical Evidence on the Dynamics of German MNC
Subsidiary Roles in Central Europe   191
    Stefan Eckert
    Frank Rossmeissl

The Impact of the Change from Partial to Full Foreign
Ownership on the Internationalization of Foreign
Subsidiaries: Four Estonian Cases   219
    Tiia Vissak

The Role of Cooperation and Innovation in Reducing
the Likelihood of Export Withdrawals: The Case
of the Estonian Wood Sector   243
    Ele Reiljan

Index   263

ABOUT THE EDITOR

Jorma Larimo, DSC, is currently Professor of International Marketing at the University of Vaasa in Vaasa, Finland. He is also the Responsible Director of the Graduate School in International Business (FIGSIB) in Finland and has the position of a Docent at the Turku School of Economics in Finland. He has received his doctoral degree in Marketing at the University of Vaasa. In addition to several visiting lecturer and doctoral degree evaluation committee membership roles in Finland, he has acted in respective roles also, e.g., in Sweden, Denmark, the Netherlands, Estonia, Russia, and Australia. Furthermore, he has been a member of evaluation committees for Professorships, both in Finland and in the USA. He is the Finnish representative in the board of the European International Business Academy (EIBA) and a member in the editorial board of *Management International Review* (MIR).

His studies have been published in several international journals such as *Journal of Business Research, Journal of International Business Studies, Management International Review, Journal of Euromarketing, Journal of East-West Business, Journal for East European Management Studies, European Business Review*, and *Asian Business & Management*. His research focuses on the export and internationalization behavior, strategies, and performance of small and medium-sized companies; foreign direct investment and divestment behavior and strategies; international joint venture strategies and performance; and on entry and marketing strategies in Central Eastern and Eastern Europe.

Foreword

The paper by Tiia Vissak aims to study the internationalization process of Estonian fast internationalizers and the reasons why they succeeded in entering several markets not only in Europe, but also in Asia and/or America. It is based on four Estonian cases: the first (TEA) from IT/publishing and the other three from biotechnology.

For many Estonian firms, internationalization has been almost inevitable: the small home market (a population of 1.35 million and a GDP per capita of about 6300 EUR) clearly does not offer them enough growth opportunities. It has not been easy for these companies to internationalize as after the dissolution of the Soviet Union, Estonia's relationship with Russia worsened, some other former member states faced serious economic crises and Estonian managers lacked contacts and knowledge of foreign markets in the West. Still, some companies, despite being small and relatively young, managed to internationalize faster than others: for instance, enter some markets outside their own continent quickly. Four such companies–TEA, Asper Biotech, Mikromasch and Quattromed–were selected for this paper.

From the case study evidence it can be concluded that all the four companies have been relatively successful in foreign markets despite their young age (TEA was founded in 1988, the others in 1998 or 1999) and smallness (they still have only 15-50 employees and their turnover is below 2 million EUR): they have already entered some countries outside Europe: TEA has been active in China, Indonesia, India, Japan and some Arabic countries, Asper Biotech has entered Japan, Korea, the USA, Canada, Australia, Taiwan, Hong Kong, Kuwait, Singapore and China, Mikromasch has sold its products to the USA, Taiwan, Israel, Japan, China, Hong-Kong, Singapore, Australia and New Zealand while

[Haworth co-indexing entry note]: "Foreword." Kaynak, Erdener. Co-published simultaneously in *Journal of East-West Business* (The Haworth Press, Inc.) Vol. 13, No. 1, 2007, pp. xxiii-xxxv and: *Market Entry and Operational Decision Making in East-West Business Relationships* (ed: Jorma Larimo) The Haworth Press, Inc., 2007, pp. xiii-xxv. Single or multiple copies of this article are available for a fee from The Haworth Document Delivery Service [1-800-HAWORTH, 9:00 a.m. - 5:00 p.m. (EST). E-mail address: docdelivery@haworthpress.com].

xiii

Quattromed has exported to Canada, the USA and Japan. Moreover, Mikromasch managed to establish foreign subsidiaries in Spain, the USA and Russia relatively soon after its establishment. TEA also had a subsidiary in Russia for a short period, but it decided to close it down; now it is considering opening one or two in China.

It is also important to note the case firms did not have considerable (financial) resources. In addition, in the quickly developing biotechnology and IT/publishing sectors, market conditions could be hardly considered stable. On the other hand, it can be assumed that the smallness of the Estonian home market and the unstable situation in these sectors have pushed the case firms fast to foreign markets. The role of managers and owners cannot be underestimated, either: the case firms were globally oriented almost from the beginning.

In the internationalization of the four companies, network relationships have been very important. Quattromed was the only firm with some foreign capital and it benefited to some extent from it–it obtained two business areas from its Finnish minority owner and it hopes to increase its presence in Asia in the near future–but other network relationships also had a clear positive role. The other three case firms have also co-operated with universities or other educational institutions and several companies in Estonia and abroad. Similarly to market selection, the selection of co-operation partners has not been determined by the countries' distance from Estonia: for instance, Asper Biotech has done research with partners outside Europe while Quattromed has found two distributors in the USA. The firms also tend to export to those countries where they have managed to establish beneficial network relationships. For the above-mentioned two companies, network relationships have also been very useful in receiving international grants: in Estonia, it is quite hard to find local financing. So, for growth, co-operation with foreign companies, universities and research institutes is almost obligatory. Due to their intense co-operation, Asper Biotech and Quattromed have also managed to receive some support from the EU funds. The former has also involved some venture capital.

In addition to financing and market entry, co-operation has been very useful in technology and product development. From the four companies, two have even managed to earn awards for their products: Asper Biotech and Quattromed have received the Estonian PricewaterhouseCoopers Gene Technology Award. TEA also managed to develop some unique products. In addition, the case firms consider flexibility, the existence of several patents, high potential demand and loyal customers as their major strengths. In other words, in addition to co-operation, unique resources and capabilities seem to have a very important role in the case firms' internationalization process. Still, managers should keep in mind that internationalization does not always succeed and co-operation may also sometimes fail. There is also no guarantee that the demand on such products will grow or at least remain the same. Thus, markets, customers and co-operation partners should be selected with great care and the organization's and its surrounding environment's specific characteristics should be taken into account when making decisions how to internationalize.

The choice of entry timing is perceived to be an important strategic decision for firms that choose to engage in foreign direct investments. In the study by Kristian Jakobsen analyzes the performance implications of entry timing choices in Central and Eastern Europe (CEE). The role of emerging and transition economies as a field of interest has grown considerably over the last two decades. Both because these economies play an increasing role in the global economy, but also because they allow us to study economic phenomena in different structural or institutional settings. It is the object of this study to derive managerial implications for investing in emerging and transition economies, but also to critically reexamine the relationship between entry timing and performance.

What makes emerging markets particularly suitable for studying the relationship between entry timing and performance is the scale of industry restructuring that has taken place in recent years. These settings offer a large number of observations from virtually every possible industry. CEE in particular offers another important feature; the close proximity to Western Europe ensured plenty of actual and potential entrants. It is our view that a sample of CEE firms offers the best possibility to study the impact of entry timing on performance in a competitive environment.

The author conducted the study based on a cross sectional survey of firms in Poland, Hungary and Lithuania. We use OLS regression analysis for a comparative study on three different performance measures. The first measure of performance is market share, which in previous studies have received overwhelming support. For comparison we use two unique measures for perceived performance. Our results support that order of entry is positively associated with market share, however we found no support that order of entry is positively related to the management's perception of performance. Our results are supportive of recent studies, both in emerging markets and in general.

They further advance the study of entry timing by analyzing the role of early mover advantages. We adopt a contingency approach and show that early mover advantages are fairly consistent across industries. The results indicated that the role of early mover advantages is significantly larger for acquisition stile entry modes than for greenfields and Joint Ventures.

The results were not consistent for all three countries. Our results indicated that early movers are adversely affected by demand shocks. This suggests that the relationship between early entry and performance may largely be a trade off between risk and return.

The author discovered a tendency for strong firms to enter early in utilities related industries, whereas they would tend to be late movers in the financial sector. This may suggest that when the possibility of pre-emption is high, firms are forced to rush to the market. On the other hand, when this is not the case and when uncertainty is high, they will prefer to wait.

The managerial implication of our study is that managers should not rush to market in the hope of achieving advantages that may not materialize. Management should carefully consider whether the potential advantages are enduring. Evidence of superior market share for first movers is very strong, which suggest that firms that can leverage a high market share to improved performance may do well to pursue a first mover strategy. If this is not the case, it may often be better to adapt a wait and see or an early follower strategy. Results from recent studies may also be good news for firms that have not yet entered and are afraid they have forfeited their chance. The opportunities are still there!

During the past ten years there have been many changes in the Central Eastern European and Eastern European retail markets due to the economic and political transformations and the international retailers' intensified activities. The article by Larimo and Huuhka has analyzed the international behavior of three Finnish retailers–Stockmann, the S Group, and the K Group, and two Swedish retailers, ICA and IKEA, in the Baltic and Russian markets. Their expansion to these markets has been motivated by factors related to both their domestic markets (push factors: for example small size, low and limited growth) and the attractiveness of their target markets (pull factors: for example high market growth, low to moderate levels of competition). They have also benefited from the cultural and geographic closeness of the target markets.

All the Finnish and Swedish retailers have a significant role in their fields in the Baltic States. Thus far only Ahold (ICA-Ahold), and Schwarz Group (Lidl chain) are the only European world class food retailers that have been interested in the Baltic markets which are relatively smaller and thus less attractive than the much bigger Central Eastern European or Russian markets. In the near future also Swedish Hennes & Mauritz and KappAhl or other big western clothing retailers might enter the Baltic and/or Russian markets.

Those international retailers who had entered into the Baltic States and, especially, into Russia with modern formats had significant first-mover advantages due to factors like low to moderate levels of competition and the good availability of premium locations. The competition will increase. Still in the mid 1990s large international retailers showed very low levels of interest in entering into Russia. In ten years Russia's attractiveness for international retail operations has increased significantly. Among the 250 world's biggest retailers in 2004, a total of 53 were operating in the Central Eastern European market; eight of them in the Baltic States and twelve of them in Russia. Russia will certainly attract more international retailers in the future, since it has been estimated that by the year 2020 Russia will become Europe's biggest food retail market, worth nearly 450 billion USD.

Russia's retail structure is excepted to sensibly change in the future due to the continuing penetration of modern formats operated by both domestic and international retailers. At present the share of modern retail formats is clearly lower in Russia than in general in the Central Eastern European markets. However, in Moscow and St. Petersburg the retail structural change has been faster than elsewhere in Russia.

In order to succeed in the highly dynamic Russian markets, international retailers have to be prepared to take substantial risks and to face several potential problems, caused by factors like the country's uncertain legal system and the high level of bureaucracy. Moreover, difficulties may arise because of the local tax systems or from the processes of obtaining building permissions for large-scale retail outlets. Furthermore, the experiences of the case companies demonstrate that it is crucial to set up cooperation and distribution networks with right partners, since it can often be hard to find good local suppliers. Evidence shows that the time needed for profitable operations seems to be longer than in the Western European countries. So far, retailers entering into Russia with gradual and long-term expansion strategies seem to have been the most likely to succeed in this highly evolving market. However, since the markets are changing fast and the competition increases all the time, the stepwise/gradual progress is becoming more difficult.

The question of why multinational companies (MNCs) choose to locate in one region rather than another has been an important topic in IB research for many years, but has recently received even more attention. Such increased attention is well-merited as firms' location decisions may well influence their modes of entry, their choice of foreign partner in joint ventures, and the subsequent performance of their foreign affiliates.

The paper by Majocchi and Strange presents the results of the first econometric investigation of the locational determinants of Italian firms in Eastern Europe. Italian firms have been very active investors in the CEE countries, and their investments have had substantial impacts upon the domestic economies. Our results broadly confirm the findings of previous studies of MNE location, in that we find that local market size and market growth, labor availability, the quality of infrastructure and agglomeration economies are all important determinants. But the Eastern European setting has also enabled us to break new theoretical ground in testing for the effects of various types of liberalization. We find that both the extent of trade liberalization and the extent of market liberalization are important influences upon the location decision. If, and it is a question of 'if' because there are disadvantages as well as advantages from increased inward investment flows, the CEEC governments wish to attract further (Italian) foreign investment, then further liberalization of the domestic economies should be a policy priority.

From a managerial perspective, it has been alleged that Italian small and medium-sized firms often pursue international expansion strategies that rely heavily on chance. Yet our results clearly show that, on average, such firms–which make up the bulk of our sample–take into account a range of relevant factors, and act in a rational economic manner, when choosing country locations for the FDI projects. These firms were not lured simply by the promise of low labor costs or by the most populous markets but were aware of, and responded to, a variety of location-specific factors.

The paper by Vianelli, Dianoux, Domanski, and Herrmann analyses in-store shopping behavior by comparing three countries: Italy, France and Poland. The main purpose is to find out if these countries, which were once considered representative of Western and of Eastern Europe respectively, today are moving toward homogenization in the buying process. In fact the analysis of in-store consumer shopping behavior is one of the most critical aspects to be taken into consideration regarding decisions related to the development of a standardized distribution format versus an adapted one.

The research has been conducted with referring to the household goods retailing industry (interior decoration, accessories, and so on), with the objective of highlighting the existing differences between consumers in different countries regarding the in-store behavior and consumer logistic, putting in to evidence socio-cultural outcomes, consumer involvement and the perception of the store atmosphere. For this product category retail internationalization appears to be particularly critical: at a global level, where Ikea is the leading retailer and the European market accounts for 49,30% of the sector's overall value, the home furnishing retail sector reveals in 2004 a year-on-year growth of 5,7%, a positive trend that is predicted to continue through 2009. Nevertheless, for the countries considered in the research, the analysis of the local distribution systems still points out the existence of some differences which can have a significant impact on in-store behavior. In Italy the specialized independent retailers represent the most diffused household goods store format. In France about 50% of the product is sold through hypermarkets and store atmosphere is considered particularly important in managerial decisions. The Polish distribution system, which has changed dramatically during the last decade, is characterized by a very large supply of this product category by international hypermarkets such as Carrefour, Casino, Leclerc, Auchan, Real and Tesco, extending their usual offers of this product category, mostly due to the relative weakness of Polish specialized retailers at the moment of arrival.

Evaluating the results obtained in the present analysis, a significant number of aspects should be pointed out in relation to the standardization/adaptation decision. In general French and Polish consumers give more importance to store atmosphere if compared with the Italian ones. From a managerial perspective, they requires more attention in relation to the definition of atmosphere design.

The fact that Polish consumers reveal high brand involvement and a high sensitivity to external and internal sources of information (external and in-store advertising, seller's advice, etc.), has to convince retailers about the importance, in particular to this country, of developing marketing actions that can reinforce brand value and can influence consumer behavior providing a continuous stream of information both outside and inside the store. Furthermore, the exploratory behavior that characterizes the Polish sample requires particular attention to the price/quality ratio. The strategy of retailers should be clear and precise, also for price positioning.

The French consumers are similar to the Polish in how they are influenced, but the French are strongly involved in the doing of shopping itself and a retailer can facilitate, improve and emotionally enrich the shopping experience. The retail manager has to adopt a wide atmosphere approach, taking into account the multiple physical and social dimensions and interactions of the store environment.

In the Italian context, there is a strong presence of consumers not recognizing the role of store atmosphere. Hence for a retail manager it is not important to emphasize store atmosphere, especially in its emotional perspective, but vice versa try to improve the characteristics of the store mainly with functional solutions that can simplify the shopping activity.

In general results indicate that ignoring cross-cultural differences can lead retailing companies to centralize and homogenize operations and marketing, resulting in declining profitability instead of increasing efficiency.

The paper by Arnold Schuh examines based on an explorative case study design if and how regionalization concepts have actually been implemented by foreign MNCs in CEE. The findings show that regionalization is absolutely a meaningful management concept in the context of CEE. Managers active in the region primarily associate an organizational structuring principle with it. However, when the strategic dimension of regionalization is addressed, i.e., the reaping of integration benefits based on a high degree of homogeneity within a group of countries, opinions vary–and also the actual implementation in international business practice. It has to be understood that in order to gain transnational integration benefits different approaches are available and used. In all the MNCs studied many integration measures, especially on the level of processes and standards, could be identified, but it was mostly the vertical, unidirectional type of integration initiated by the center and directed at individual subsidiaries in the region. This procedure when applied in a successive form to all subsidiaries in the region will result in a high degree of transnational integration too (e.g., same IT processes, risk management standards, corporate identity features, sales approach). However, the integration does not originate from perceived commonalities in the region but is a pure strategy and processes transfer from the center, and that is the major difference. Even the model case of regionalization in our sample, the consumer goods producer Henkel CEE, is not exclusively pursuing regionalization. Managements of MNCs are assessing and comparing the benefits of different forms of transnational integration at the business, function or brand level and based on the analysis choose national, sub-regional, regional and global solutions. Country groupings by non-geographic criteria such as market stage (sub-clusters of advanced vs. emerging markets) are also very common. In order to implement a regional strategy it is necessary to have a regional structure in place, mostly a regional headquarters or regional management center. The existence of a regional headquarters is, however, no guarantee that the company follows a regionalization strategy.

The economic clusters have an important position as facilitators of development. Companies participating in the cluster benefit from integrated value creation processes along with several synergies. In the Nordic area, the cluster cooperation in wood and forest industries is expanding from Scandinavian countries to the Baltic region and Russia. According to Tonu Roolaht these cluster enlargements offer new opportunities in terms of forest resources and economic considerations, including labour costs. However, these new regions also have emerging local clusters and network relationships between wood and forest companies. The local companies benefit from technology transfers, financial support and market access provided within regional clusters. Yet, it is also possible that dominant actors in the regional cluster replace local value-adding processes with roundwood and paperwood exports in order facilitate production in more developed Nordic countries.

This conclusion about the Estonian wood and forest sector suggests the need to strive towards a medium-term balance between regional (or global) intra-corporate coordination and local arrangements that benefit both parties and preserve the integrity of the local cluster. In that sense, the management practice concerning local relationships within the regional cluster should aim at integrating local development interests into the regional framework rather than at facilitating the confrontation that clearly favours regional relationships over the development of interests in the local community.

In order to establish corporate policy that would take into account all development levels, the corporate management could use the following stepwise positioning idea: (1) Determine the company's position on the global market; (2) Determine the company's position in key regions; (3) Determine the company's position in local clusters.

This strategic positioning process could be aided by a detailed plotting of value-adding processes and supplier-distributor partnerships. Therefore, this global-regional-local view also helps us to further understand the structure of the company's supply network and operations.

In terms of implications for government policy, export and business promotion measures for the wood and forest sector could be directed specifically to further processing initiatives that take advantage of modern technologies. This policy would help to reinforce corporate interests in supporting the development of local production capabilities. Another field of support that needs further attention concerns joint research and development initiatives on the local as well as the international level. This measure should facilitate the distribution of certain development functions to local companies as well as technology transfers to the new business region.

In this article, Eckert and Rossmeissl focus on the development of the role of foreign subsidiaries in Central Europe (CE). We define a subsidiary's role as a three-dimensional construct, consisting of a subsidiary's tasks, its value chain activities and their respective geographical scope. We analyze how subsidiary's host country, subsidiary's task, subsidiary's mode of ownership and subsidiary's mode of foreign market entry influence the development of a subsidiary's role. Based on standardized questionnaires from 99 subsidiaries from the Czech Republic, Hungary, and Poland, we find evidence for the influence of subsidiary's host country, task, and mode of market entry on the development of its role.

When considering subsidiaries in CE, it seems especially important to differentiate between "market proximity seeking-subsidiaries" and subsidiaries where this task is not considered important. Greenfield subsidiaries tend to be market proximity seekers. Those market proximity seekers tend to operate a smaller number of value chain activities. Corresponding to the strategic relevance of the market proximity seeking-task these activities focus on the downstream end of the value chain. The geographical scope of market proximity seekers' value chain activities is often restrained to the national level, but tends to be incrementally enlarged over time comprising other countries from the same region.

The number of value chain activities that acquired subsidiaries perform is (on average) higher than compared to greenfields. Other tasks such as efficiency seeking and strategic asset seeking seem to be more important regarding this mode of market entry. For a considerable portion of efficiency seekers as well as for strategic asset seekers activities from the upstream end of the value chain are upgraded to global scale over the course of time.

For CE countries attempting to attract foreign direct investment our findings imply that the role of foreign subsidiaries in CE corresponds to their environment. Larger countries with a bigger domestic market are in charge of a natural advantage compared to smaller countries concerning the attraction of market proximity-seeking subsidiaries. Moreover, market proximity seeking-subsidiaries in larger markets seem to have a bigger chance of expanding the geographical scope of their most important value chain activities, namely marketing, sales, and customer services. However, concerning the allocation of activities from the upstream end of the value chain and concerning the expansion of the geographical scope of these activities efficiency-seeking subsidiaries as well as strategic asset seeking subsidiaries may be superior to "market proximity seeking-subsidiaries." Therefore, when a country aims to support its national economic development through spill-over-effects from MNC's subsidiaries it may not be sufficient to rely on "natural advantages" such as market size.

The most important implication for the management of MNCs is that there still seems to be potential for expansion or restructuring concerning MNC's activities in CE. CE subsidiaries often are constrained concerning their value chain activities to the national market of the host country. This means that MNCs either should consider entering other Central or East European markets or if they are already present there, it may be reasonable to consider a restructuring of activities in these countries: Value chain activities which have been tailored to the local markets may be redesigned to serve a larger region called Central Europe, Central and Eastern Europe, or even Europe.

This paper by Tiia Vissak aims to study how host country firms' internationalization has been impacted by their foreign owners' achievement of full ownership if the companies were not fully foreign-owned at first. It is based on four Estonian cases: two–Hansabank Group and SEB Eesti Ühispank–from banking and two–Wendre and Krenholm Group–from the textiles industry.

In the theoretical literature, there is no consensus whether in multinational networks, subsidiaries are reaching more important roles and a higher decision-making freedom (especially if they are innovative, have strong economic results and/or their managers are actively trying to reach higher autonomy in the parent company's network) or multinationals are, in general, reducing their subsidiaries' autonomy. Different authors have also not reached consensus on whether foreign ownership quickens or slows down host country firms' internationalization and which are the other main factors influencing this process. There is also a lack of evidence on how some multinationals' aim to achieve full ownership would impact their subsidiaries' internationalization.

The paper demonstrated that (full) foreign ownership can both inhibit and quicken companies' internationalization. Hansabank has managed to increase its presence in Latvia, Lithuania, Russia and enter Finland and it has also benefited from servicing its parent company's foreign customers in Estonia, SEB Eesti Ühispank has only entered Russia and that happened before becoming foreign-owned; moreover, it sold a bank in Latvia soon after, but it has also become to service some of its parent company's foreign customers and manage one of its owner's investment funds. Wendre has also mostly benefited from being foreign-owned: due to the owner's personal contacts and investments, the firm has become able to export to a large number of countries and establish a plant in China. For Krenholm, foreign ownership has not brought as many benefits as it was initially hoped: it has not been able to solve its financial difficulties and its number of employees has decreased considerably. Still, it has managed to establish subsidiaries in Sweden, Germany and the UK and export to many countries, including the USA. In addition to getting easier access to foreign markets, the firms have benefited in terms of technology, additional capital, foreign market knowledge, improved image or management know-how. Three enterprises have grown considerably, only Krenholm's turnover and a number of employees have decreased.

Foreign owners' success in obtaining full ownership in their companies has also impacted some case firms' strategies: for instance, their management changed. In Wendre, the former shareholder and managing director left soon after that because he had a different view about the firm's future and he did not agree to buy most of the raw material from the full owner's other subsidiaries. Hansabank's chairman of the board (and also a minor shareholder) decided to leave at once because he did not feel it was "his" bank any longer, but it is still a bit too early to tell how it would impact the bank's strategy in addition to intensified communication between the bank and the head office and an increase of the bank's operations in Russia. Krenholm's general manager left more than three years after the firm became fully foreign-owned. He complained that in the last year, when the firm' financial results worsened, the owners did not give him enough decision-making autonomy. The new management has considerably reduced the firm's number of employees but they have not improved the results yet. In addition, they have had to face problems with trade unions. Ühispank's general manager left two years after SEB obtained full ownership, but a change in the bank's strategy was probably not the reason as this bank has not been as autonomous in its decision-making in Hansabank.

As the results are mixed and the number of case companies is small, it is hard to offer any strict suggestions to the managers of (fully) foreign-owned companies. It seems that in some corporations, control over subsidiaries' actions has increased and the managers' activities toward achieving higher decision-making autonomy may not be approved. In some others, on the other hand, such activities could be appreciated. It should be also kept in mind that there does not seem to be a clear connection between decision-making autonomy, the share of foreign ownership and the level of a company's internationalization: both strictly and loosely controlled firms may succeed and fail in their internationalization and other activities. So, managerial decisions should be made taking in mind the organization's, its owner's and surrounding environment's specific characteristics.

The study by Ele Reiljan focuses on identifying the influence of cooperative and innovative activities on reducing the likelihood of withdrawals from the foreign markets in the case of Estonian wood sector enterprises. The analysis is based on the results of "Wood Sector Survey 2005" and "Community Innovation Survey 2001." In addition to the previously mentioned databases, aggregated data of the Estonian manufacturing industry is used for characterizing the developments that have taken place in the Estonian wood sector.

The discussion in the theoretical part of this study indicated that there are three groups of reasons behind export withdrawals–lack of international experience, change in strategy, and poor performance or increase in production costs. Cooperation and innovation have direct and indirect effects on firms' international activities and can help them overcome several problems that may otherwise lead to export withdrawals.

The analysis suggested that about 40% of the Estonian wood sector firms have faced export withdrawals. The main reason behind such developments in international markets is the termination of cooperation contracts with the existing partners. Lack of knowledge as a motivation was rated as the least important one.

The results indicate that Estonian wood sector firms have intensified their innovative activities, especially in the field of introducing new products. The need to introduce new products may, among other things, be determined by enhanced competitiveness in international markets. This kind of reasoning is supported by the low share of export withdrawals in the case of innovative firms, and especially in the case of those firms that have carried out product innovations.

On the other hand, our analysis of the influence of cooperative activities on the likelihood of export withdrawals provided mixed results. The share of withdrawals is relatively high both in the case when the firm cooperates with other subsidiaries, customers and suppliers and when it does not. However, the withdrawals are more characteristic of those enterprises that perceive cooperation as having low importance. Conversely, cooperative activities with competitors and other firms belonging to the wood industry present an opposite situation.

Erdener Kaynak

Introduction

This special issue of *Journal of East-West Business*, "Market Entry and Operational Decision Making in East-West Business Relationships" includes ten recent studies focusing on various aspects of the theme of the special issue. The Eastern expansion of the European Union in May 2004 has further increased the interest towards this geographic area. Some of the articles in this special issue focus on entry and marketing strategies of Western multinational companies (MNCs) in Central and Eastern Europe (CEE). Topics covered include choices of location for foreign direct investments, first mover advantages, entry behavior of retailing companies, dynamics in subsidiary operations, and degree of regional standardization of MNC operations in CEE.

The rest of the articles will focus on the development of industry clusters, decision-making autonomy, and internationalization of CEE based firms. The articles analyze the role of Western MNCs in the development of the clusters as well as the fast internationalizers, role of Western companies in the internationalization of CEE based firms, and the role of cooperation and innovation reducing likelihood of export withdrawals. Some of the articles in the special issue cover the whole CEE, whereas some articles will have a more specific focus concentrating on Estonia, Hungary, Lithuania, Poland, and/or Russia.

The paper by Tiia Vissak aims to study the internationalization process of Estonian fast internationalizers and the reasons why they succeeded in entering several markets not only in Europe, but also in Asia and/or America. For many Estonian firms, internationalization has been almost inevitable: the small home market clearly does not offer them enough growth opportunities. However, it has not been easy for these companies to internationalize as after the dissolution of the Soviet Un-

[Haworth co-indexing entry note]: "Introduction." Larimo, Jorma. Co-published simultaneously in *Journal of East-West Business* (The Haworth Press, Inc.) Vol. 13, No. 1, 2007, pp. 1-9; and: *Market Entry and Operational Decision Making in East-West Business Relationships* (ed: Jorma Larimo) The Haworth Press, Inc., 2007, pp. 1-9. Single or multiple copies of this article are available for a fee from The Haworth Document Delivery Service [1-800-HAWORTH, 9:00 a.m. - 5:00 p.m. (EST). E-mail address: docdelivery@haworthpress.com].

Available online at http://jeb.haworthpress.com
doi:10.1300/J097v13n01_01

ion, Estonia's relationship with Russia worsened, some other former states faced serious economic crises, and Estonian managers lacked contacts and knowledge of foreign markets in the Western Europe and North America.

The article starts with a review of the existing traditional internationalization, born global, foreign direct investment and network literature and brings out the differences between traditional (slowly, gradually internationalizing) and fast internationalizers (including born globals). Based on the literature review, the author develops a conceptual framework, demonstrating the role of network relationships, business environment and companies' unique resources and capabilities on the emergence and further development of such enterprises. Then, after a methodology section, four cases (three from biotechnology, one from IT/publishing) are introduced.

All four companies have been relatively successful in forging markets despite their young age and smallness. All four companies have entered several European countries–as well as some countries outside Europe–mainly China, Japan, USA, and Canada. The results show that in the internationalization of the four case companies, network relationships have been very important. In one case the Finnish minority owner helped the internationalization. In the three other cases the companies had co-operated with universities or other educational institutions and with several companies in Estonia and abroad.

Businesses entering early into new markets are believed to attain crucial competitive advantages over later entrants. However, this contention receives only mixed support in the empirical literature, in part because performance is measured in different ways. In the study by Kristian Jakobsen the author reexamines the performance difference between early movers and followers entering new geographical markets. He contrasts market share with two other measures of firm performance that are based on the managers' perception of their own performance relative to own prior expectations and relative to industry standards.

The empirical part of the study is based on a sample of 528 foreign entrants mainly in manufacturing, financial services, trade and distribution, and other services sectors. Of the entries 224 were in Hungary, 200 in Poland, and 104 in Lithuania. The investing companies were mainly from various European countries (141 from Germany and 80 from the Nordic countries). The author uses an OLS regression analysis to estimate the relationship between the dependent variables (market share, industry performance, and satisfaction with performance) and the independent variables.

In line with earlier studies he found a positive relationship between order of entry and market share (VanderWerf & Mahon 1997). However, he did not find positive relationship between order of entry and performance. He found general support for early mover advantages in Hungary and Poland, but a strongly negative relationship for Lithuania, suggesting that early entry is a trade off between risk and return.

Overall, the results suggest that the factors that explain performance vary considerably depending on how the performance is measured. According to the results the length of time the firm has been in the market, the firm's human resource activities, and transfer of technology were determinants of firm performance. The managerial implications of the study recommend that managers should not rush to market in the hope of achieving advantages that may not materialize. Managers should carefully consider whether the potential advantages are enduring

The political changes, together with the economic growth, have made the Eastern European emerging markets increasingly attractive for international retailers. Based on the rankings done by A.T. Kearney based on the economic and political risks, the level of retail saturation, and the differences between GDP growth and retail growth Russia has been during the last few years one of the most attractive emerging markets. Also Latvia and Lithuania have been among the top 20 emerging markets recently. Furthermore, it is estimated that by the year 2020 Russia will become Europe's biggest food retail market, worth nearly 450 billion USD. Among the 250 world's biggest retailers in 2004, a total of 53 were operating in the Central Eastern European market; eight of them in the Baltic States and twelve of them in Russia.

The article by Jorma Larimo and Ari Huuhka analyzes why, where, when and how the eastward expansion of the biggest Finnish and Swedish food and non-food sector retailers has taken place. The penetration of modern formats and the level of competion is still at a relatively low level, especially in the Russian market. Although retailing in the Baltic States and Russia has became more competitive and international, due to the introduction of efficient modern formats by international and domestic retailers, the majority of goods are still distributed through traditional forms of retailing, such as marketplaces, kiosks and other small-scale retail outlets.

The article shows that the case companies have expanded first, from their small and saturated domestic markets, to culturally and geographically close target markets. Furthermore their internationalization has developed from less intensive operation modes towards more intensive modes. The case companies display a great variation in the market and operation strategies used to enter the four target markets. The Finnish Stockmann company has been one of the pioneers in the Baltic and Russian markets. During the years especially two other case companies–the K Group from Finland and IKEA from Sweden–have gained strong market positions in Eastern Europe; the former in the Baltic food sector and the latter in the Russian (and also in some other CEE) markets. IKEA has even been one of the biggest foreign investors in Russia with several mega-mall center projects.

Russsia's retail structure is expected to sensibly change in the future due to the continuing penetration of modern formats operated by both domestic and international retailers. In order to succeed in the highly dynamic Russian markets, international retailers have to be prepared to take substantial risks and to face several potential problems caused by factors like the country's uncertain legal system and the high level of bureaucracy. Moreover, difficulties may arise because of the local tax systems or from the processes of obtaining building permissions for large-scale retail outlets. Evidence shows that the time needed for profitable operations seems to be longer than in the Western European countries. So far, retailers entering into Russia with gradual and long-term expansion strategies seem to have been the most likely to succeed in this highly evolving market.

The question why multinational companies (MNCs) choose to locate in one region rather than another has been an important topic in international business research for many years, but has recently received even more attention. The paper by Antonio Majocchi and Roger Strange presents the results of an econometric investigation of the location determinants of Italian firms in Central and Eastern Europe. Italian firms have been very active investors in the CEE countries. The empirical part of the study is based on 272 Italian firms which had made investments in various Central and Eastern European Countries between 1990 and 2003. Over half of the investments were made in Poland, and a further quarter in Slovenia and Bulgaria combined. The authors use conditional logit model as the methods of analysis.

The results broadly confirm the findings of previous studies, but the authors also find that both trade liberalization and market liberalization are important influences on the location decision. If the CEE governments wish to attract further (Italian) foreign investment, then further liberalization of their domestic economies should be a policy priority. From the managerial perspective, it has been alleged that Italian small and medium-sized firms often pursue international expansion strategies that rely heavily on chance. Yet the results of the study clearly show that, on average, such firms–which made up the bulk of their sample–take into account a range of relevant factors, and act in a rational economic manner, when choosing country locations for the FDI projects. These firms were not lured simply by the promise of low labor costs or by the most populous markets, but were aware of, and responded to, a variety of location-specific factors.

The analysis of consumer shopping behavior is one of the most critical aspects which has to be taken into consideration in a context of retailing internationalization, where managers need to define the degree to which international firms can standardize or adapt their strategies in foreign markets. The aim of the research by Donata Vianelli, Christian Dianoux, Tomasz Domanski, and Jean Luc Herrmann is to analyze and point out the main cross-cultural differences regarding in-store behavior comparing three countries: Italy, France and Poland.

The empirical part of the study was realized by means of direct interviews out of a sample of 201 units for France, 332 units for Italy, and 212 units for Poland, composed of women of various ages, mainly involved in house-keeping activities. The data elaboration applied descriptive statistics and processing data with factor and cluster analysis.

The results show that Polish consumers reveal high brand involvement and a high sensitivity to external and internal sources of information, has to convince retailers about the importance, in particular to this country, of developing marketing actions that can reinforce brand value and can influence consumer behavior providing a continuous stream of information both outside and inside the store. Furthermore, the explanatory behavior that characterizes the Polish sample requires particular attention to the price/quality ratio. The strategy of retailers should be clear and precise, also for price positioning.

The French consumers are similar to the Polish in how they are influenced, but the French are strongly involved in the doing of shopping itself and a retailer can facilitate, improve, and emotionally enrich the shopping experience. The retail manager has to adopt a wide atmosphere approach, taking into account the multiple physical and social dimensions and interactions of the store environment. In the Italian context, there is a strong presence of consumers not recognizing the role of store atmosphere. Hence, for a retail manager it is not important to emphasize store atmosphere especially in its emotional perspective, but vice versa try to improve the characteristics of the store mainly with functional solutions that can simplify the shopping activity.

In general results indicate that ignoring cross-cultural differences can lead retailing companies to centralize and homogenize operations and marketing, resulting in declining profitability instead of increasing efficiency.

Regional players among the MNCs operating in Central and Eastern Europe have to decide if they should regard their businesses as a collection of individual markets or as a homogeneous region. The purpose of the study by Arnold Schuh is to examine if and how regionalization concepts have actually been implemented by foreign MNCs in CEE. The analysis focuses on the preconditions for the emergence of a regional strategy, on the identification of the main areas of regional integration, and the relationship between strategy and organizational structure.

The character of the study is explorative. The author used a two-step process in the longitudinal data collection from the selected six case companies. By using a longitudinal case study approach a better insight is gained on how regional strategies have emerged during the internationalization process of the firm and, if they have emerged, in which way they have manifested themselves in business decisions. The results showed that, surprisingly, only one of the six case companies–the consumer goods manufacturer Henkel CEE–has pursued a regionalization strategy that fits the theoretical conception of the study. Henkel CEE formulates comprehensive strategies for the whole region and co-ordinates and controls the business in 29 countries as 100% owner of the local subsidiaries in CEE and CIS. The regional scope of the mandate had been constantly extended in the past years due to the success and accumulated competence of Henkel CEE. Corporate goals and strategic trust for the region are mutually negotiated between corporate and regional headquarters. In no other of the five case companies such a high degree of regional integration could be found.

The findings raise new questions about the regionalization construct with regard to the operationalization of regionalization, the relationship between strategy and structure, and its applicability to services.

The regional clusters have an important position in the modern world. One of the most prominent clusters in the Nordic area (Scandinavia, Baltic region and Russia) has been formed in the wood and forest industries. The aim of the study by Tonu Roolaht is to investigate the dual impact of regional clusters on the development of local clustering and networking ties. In this respect the positive impact in terms of technology transfers, financial support and market access are analysed alongside potentially more detrimental aspects, such as replacing local value-adding processes with roundwood and paperwood exports and limiting the international marketing options of the acquired producers.

The empirical part of the study is mainly based on interview data of four case companies, two of which are sawmilling companies, one pulp and sack paper producer, and one manufacturer of windows and doors. The case data material is supplemented limitedly with survey data.

The case evidence indicates that Nordic companies from Finland, Sweden, and Denmark have played a considerable role in the development of the Estonian wood and forestry sector as s domestic cluster. The results also indicate that regional clustering has several positive influences on the development of local/domestic wood and forest clusters in terms of technology transfer and foreign market access, but dominant intra-corporate networks can also lead to centralised operations that set a lower value on local supply chain relationships.

In the paper by Stefan Eckert and Frank Rossmeissl the authors analyze the influence of a subsidiary's external environment, of its task and of its mode of ownership and its mode of market entry on the development of its role for the case of German subsidiaries in Central Europe. They define a subsidiary's role as a three-dimensional construct, consisting of a subsidiary's tasks, its value chain activities and its respective geographical scope.

The empirical part of the study is based on 99 German subsidiaries from the Czech Republic, Hungary, and Poland. In correspondence to the study of Williams (1998) their findings highlight the importance to differentiate between greenfield subsidiaries and acquisitions when analyzing or discussing the development of the role of foreign subsidiaries located in Central Eastern European countries. Furthermore, in line with a number of several earlier studies, the authors found that the influence of a subsidiary's host country was a determinant of the development of its role. Supporting to Birkinshaw (1996) the authors were able to demonstrate the effect of a subsidiary's task on its role development.

They also found that Greenfield subsidiaries tended to be market proximity seekers whereas in the case of acquisitions this task often does not seem to be a major task. Market proximity seekers–no matter whether it regards geographical or psychic market proximity–tend to operate a smaller number of value chain activities. Corresponding to the relevance of the market proximity seeking task these activities focus on the downstream end of the value chain. On the contrary, acquired subsidiaries performed on average higher number of value chain activities than subsidiaries established using greenfield form of investment. Other tasks, such as efficiency seeking and strategic asset seeking, seemed to be more important in acquired subsidiaries.

The paper by Tiia Vissak aims to study how host country firms' internationalization has been impacted by their foreign owners' achievement of full ownership if the companies were not fully foreign-owned at first. It starts with a review of the existing traditional internationalization literature: the Uppsala model, the innovation-related internationalization models and the Finnish model. Then it reviews other research streams: born global, foreign direct investment (FDI) and network literature and the literature on subsidiary roles. A conceptual framework is developed.

The empirical part of the study is based on interview data in four Estonian cases–two from banking and two from the textiles industry. Some of the current literature indicates that in parent companies' networks, the roles of subsidiaries are expanding and managers should be especially active in order to achieve larger decision-making autonomy from the multinational. Some authors have shown that the opposite might be true.

The case studies showed that full foreign ownership can both inhibit and quicken companies' internationalization. In addition to getting easier access to foreign markets, the firms had benefited in terms of technology, additional capital, foreign market knowledge, improved image or management know-how. Three of the case companies had grown considerably whereas in one company the turnover and number of employees had decreased clearly in the last years. The case evidence showed that there was no clear pattern in terms of decision-making autonomy in the four case firms after the parent companies achieved full ownership. Thus, in summary the author concludes that managerial decisions should be made taking in mind the organization's, its owner's, and surrounding environment's specific characteristics.

The literature focusing on export withdrawals indicates that there are three groups of reasons behind export withdrawals: lack of international experience, change in strategy, and poor performance or increase in production costs. Cooperation and innovation have direct and indirect effects on firms' international activities and can help them to overcome several problems that may otherwise lead to export withdrawals. The study by Ele Reiljan concentrates on analyzing the role played by innovation and cooperation in the likelihood of Estonian wood industry enterprises' export withdrawals.

The empirical part of the study is based on two surveys. The first survey carried out by the Estonian Statistical Office provided information about innovative and co-operative activities of the Estonian enterprises in the period 1998-2000. The second survey was carried out by a research group to which the author of the article belonged. The survey included information about withdrawals of 65 Estonian wood companies from international markets and the main reasons for them.

The data obtained from two different databases show that about 40% of the Estonian wood sector firms have withdrawn from (some of) their foreign markets. The results indicate that Estonian wood sector firms have intensified their innovative activities, especially in the field of introducing new products. The need to introduce new products may, among other things, be determined by enhanced competitiveness in international markets. This kind of reasoning was supported by the low share of export withdrawals in the case of innovative firms, and especially in the case of those firms that had carried out product innovations. On the other hand, the analysis of the influence of co-operative activities on the likelihood of export withdrawals provided mixed results. The share of withdrawals was relatively high both in the case when the firm co-operated with other subsidiaries, customers and suppliers, and when it did not. However, the withdrawals were more characteristic of those enterprises that perceived co-operation as having low importance. Conversely, co-operative activities with competitors and other firms belonging to the wood industry presented an opposite situation.

Jorma Larimo

The Emergence and Success Factors of Fast Internationalizers: Four Cases from Estonia

Tiia Vissak

SUMMARY. This paper aims to study the internationalization process of Estonian fast internationalizers and the reasons why they succeeded in entering several markets not only in Europe, but also in Asia and/or America. It starts with a review of the existing traditional internationalization, born global, foreign direct investment and network literature and brings out the differences between traditional (slowly, gradually internationalizing) and fast internationalizers (including born globals). Based on the literature review, it develops a conceptual framework, demonstrating the role of network relationships, business environment and companies' unique resources and capabilities on the emergence and further development of such enterprises. Then, after a methodology section, four cases (three from biotechnology, one from IT/publishing) are introduced. After the discussion of the results, some managerial and research implications are drawn. doi:10.1300/J097v13n01_02 *[Article copies available for a fee from The Haworth Document Delivery Service: 1-800-HAWORTH. E-mail address: <docdelivery@haworthpress.com> Website: <http://www.HaworthPress.com> © 2007 by The Haworth Press, Inc. All rights reserved.]*

Tiia Vissak is Senior Researcher, Faculty of Economics and Business Administration, University of Tartu, Narva Road, 4-A211, 51009, Tartu, Estonia (E-mail: tiia.vissak@ut.ee).

[Haworth co-indexing entry note]: "The Emergence and Success Factors of Fast Internationalizers: Four Cases from Estonia." Vissak, Tiia. Co-published simultaneously in *Journal of East-West Business* (The Haworth Press, Inc.) Vol. 13, No. 1, 2007, pp. 11-33; and: *Market Entry and Operational Decision Making in East-West Business Relationships* (ed: Jorma Larimo) The Haworth Press, Inc., 2007, pp. 11-33. Single or multiple copies of this article are available for a fee from The Haworth Document Delivery Service [1-800-HAWORTH, 9:00 a.m. - 5:00 p.m. (EST). E-mail address: docdelivery@haworthpress.com].

KEYWORDS. Born globals, internationalization, Estonia, case study

INTRODUCTION

For many Estonian firms, internationalization–the process of increasing involvement in international operations (Welch and Luostarinen 1988, p. 36)–has been almost inevitable: the small home market (a population of 1.35 million and a GDP per capita of about 6300 EUR) clearly does not offer them enough growth opportunities. It has not been easy for these companies to internationalize as after the dissolution of the Soviet Union, Estonia's relationship with Russia worsened, some other former member states faced serious economic crises and Estonian managers lacked contacts and knowledge of foreign markets in the West. Still, some companies, despite being small and relatively young, have managed to internationalize faster than others: for instance, enter some markets outside their own continent quickly. Unfortunately, such enterprises have not received as much attention in the general internationalization literature as larger and slowly internationalizing corporations. There still has not been considerable empirical research examining the factors that drive the superior international performance of these young, highly entrepreneurial firms (Autio, 2005; Bell, Crick & Young, 2004; Knight & Cavusgil, 2004) within specific industries, business or geographical clusters (Jones, 2001). There are even fewer publications about such companies originating from Central and Eastern Europe (Rialp, Rialp & Knight, 2005).

This paper aims to study the internationalization process of Estonian fast internationalizers and the reasons why they succeeded in entering several markets not only in Europe, but also in Asia and/or America. It starts with a review of the existing traditional internationalization, born global, foreign direct investment and network literature, as they have attempted to explain at least some aspects of (early/rapid) internationalization; and the born-global phenomenon and a contemporary understanding of internationalization should be reached by integrating multiple theoretical perspectives (Autio, 2005; Jones & Coviello, 2005; Madsen & Servais, 1997). After the literature review, a conceptual framework is developed. Then, following a methodology section, four cases–TEA, Asper Biotech, Mikromasch and Quattromed–are introduced. After the discussion of the results, some managerial and research implications are drawn.

LITERATURE REVIEW

This section at first introduces some *earlier approaches to internationalization*: the Uppsala, innovation-related internationalization and Finnish models. Then it shows how the process has been understood in the born global literature and which explanations network and foreign direct investment (FDI) studies offer to this phenomenon.

The *Uppsala (or the U- or the internationalization process) model* (Johanson & Vahlne, 1977, 1990; Johanson & Wiedersheim-Paul, 1975; Vahlne & Johanson, 2002) assumes that internationalization is usually a long, slow and incremental process driven by experiential market knowledge. The acquisition of knowledge is gradual. Consequently, companies pass through steps from no regular export activities to export via independent representatives/agents, overseas sales and production/manufacturing subsidiaries. They first begin exporting to neighboring countries or the comparatively well-known and similar ones, and after that, try to enter farther markets. The U-model also states that large or resourceful firms or those with considerable experience in similar markets can internationalize more easily, especially if market conditions are stable.

Innovation-related internationalization (I-) models also propose that, in general, foreign market expansion is incremental and dependent on an enterprise's experiential learning and uncertainty regarding the decision to internationalize (Morgan & Katsikeas, 1997). On the other hand, unlike the U-model, this model states that besides knowledge, several other internal and external (f)actors, like other firms, government agencies, top managers, the companies' competitive advantages and general economic conditions, impact internationalization (for an overview, see Bilkey, 1978). For instance, foreign-owned firms may internationalize differently than locally-owned ones: the headquarters might take the initial decision to start exporting and organize sales through a global marketing network (Wiedersheim-Paul, Olson & Welch, 1978).

The authors of the *Finnish model* (Gabrielsson, Kirpalani and Luostarinen (2002) have also called it the target country internationalization process model) agree with the U- and I- models that at first, firms tend to penetrate closest countries. As they gain confidence, they might start seeking more distant markets and change the method of operating: for instance, establish foreign subsidiaries (Welch & Luostarinen, 1988), especially in geographically close countries (Nieminen, Larimo & Springer, 2001). On the other hand, the authors of this model have also paid attention to other aspects of internationalization. For example, they imply that inward internationalization (like imports and inward FDI) might precede and influence the development of outward activities and vice versa (Korhonen, 1999). In addition, the model shows that a firm does not inevitably have to move to the last step of development: the reverse of the process, or de-internationalization, may occur at any of the stages (Welch & Luostarinen, 1988). This may be followed again by advancing steps: in other words, re-internationalization (Luostarinen, 1994).

Although the three above-mentioned models have received considerable support in the literature (for an overview of such studies, see, for example, Vissak, 2003), there is also some evidence that the internationalization process of some enterprises may be quite different. So, some *approaches* concentrating on or *explaining* at least some aspects of *early, fast internationalization* have emerged.

The literature on *born globals/fast internationalizers* has gathered much support, although there is still no agreement how to define "born globals." For instance, according to Kuivalainen, Saarenketo and Puumalainen (2005), true born globals are those firms that internationalize during the first three years since their establishment, enter five or more foreign countries and earn at least 25 percent of turnover from abroad. Gabrielsson, Sasi and Darling (2004), in turn, have emphasized that these firms should be able to generate at least a half of total sales from outside their own continent maximum after 15 years since starting their operations. As there is still no consensus in the literature, this paper uses a less strict term, "fast internationalizers."

The literature implies that some companies view the world as their marketplace (McDougall, Oviatt & Shrader, 2003) and thus "leapfrog" into internationalization despite being young and small, having constrained resources, most volatile markets and, by definition, little or no experience in any country (Oviatt & McDougall, 1994): some firms even enter foreign countries before they have sold anything on their domestic markets (Bell, 1995; Chetty & Campbell-Hunt, 2004). Consequently, the U- or I-models cannot fully explain the internationalization of such firms. Moreover, these companies do not necessarily own foreign assets: FDI is not a requirement. Instead of establishing sales or production subsidiaries, they may participate in a large number of networks and relations like strategic alliances to use foreign resources such as manufacturing capacity or marketing (Oviatt & McDougall, 1994; Rasmussen and Madsen, 2002). Thus, some enterprises may not complete the internationalization process as it was viewed in the U- and I-models although, in some cases (for instance, see Hashai & Almor,

2004), a gradually increased commitment to foreign markets has been observed even in the case of born globals.

The emergence of born globals has been explained by the increasing role of niche markets, global networks and alliances, specialized and customized products; shorter product life cycles, larger domestic and international competition, homogenization of buyer preferences around the world, more elaborate capabilities of people, including those of the founders/entrepreneurs, advances in process and communication technology and inherent advantages of small companies, including quicker response time, flexibility and adaptability (Chetty & Campbell-Hunt, 2004; Coviello & Munro, 1995; Knight, 2001; Knight & Cavusgil, 1996, 2004; Moen & Servais, 2002; Rennie, 1993; Rialp, Rialp & Knight, 2005). Some other factors have also influenced the emergence of these firms: the background of their managers (Bell, Crick & Young, 2004; Chetty & Campbell-Hunt, 2004; Roolaht, 2002) or founders (including family background, education, entrepreneurial orientation, prior experience from living abroad and having had internationally oriented jobs), country characteristics (Autio, 2005; Knight, 2001; Madsen & Servais, 1997; McAuley, 1999), firm size, unique resources, financial strength, R&D spending, reputation, network partners (Moen & Servais, 2002; Zahra & George, 2002) and (foreign) ownership (Bell, Crick & Young, 2004; Roolaht, 2002). It has been found that born globals are generally the firms which, in contrast to organizations that evolve gradually from domestic firms to multinationals, begin with a proactive international strategy (Autio, 2005; Oviatt & McDougall, 1994; Rasmussen and Madsen, 2002). In other words, their top management has a desire and commitment to export from the beginning. The companies, which have small domestic markets (Madsen & Servais, 1997), compete on value (mainly quality, technology and product design), those which are extremely flexible and pro-active (Bell, Crick & Young, 2004; Moen & Servais, 2002; Rasmussen and Madsen, 2002) and have a strong customer orientation, may belong to this category as well (McKinsey & Co, 1993). They may be able to compensate the lack of a broad resource base by using a narrow but critical set of skills. Internationally experienced managers may also allow them to effectively compete in a broader domain (Wolff & Pett, 2000). According to Rialp, Rialp and Knight (2005), more and more countries and industries will witness an increasing emergence and further development of knowledge- and/or service-intensive born globals against more traditionally oriented exporting companies in the near future.

The authors of the *network approach* have stated that an enterprise's internationalization means establishing and developing business relationships in networks in other countries (Johanson & Mattson, 1988). They have demonstrated that through network relationships, a firm can increase its ability to innovate and develop its technology (Håkansson & Snehota, 2000), identify international opportunities, establish credibility (Oviatt & McDougall, 2005), acquire brands, skills and local market knowledge (Adarkar et al., 2001; Gabrielsson, Sasi & Darling, 2004) without necessarily having experience on a certain market (Eriksson et al., 1998). Moreover, not only direct partners, but also the ones of their partners affect a firm's behavior (Ford, 1998). The existing relationships can be used as bridges to other networks (Johanson & Vahlne, 1990). This, in turn, can be crucial for a firm's *internationalization*. As a result, a typical internationalization sequence has changed from gradual expansion to expansion in leaps by joining the nets (Hertz, 1996), although network relationships can sometimes also inhibit this process (Ford 1998). Still, many firms may enter a market directly with their own manufacturing unit (Björkman & Eklund, 1996) and not start from exporting as the U- and I-models suggest. In any case, the internationalization process of any firm cannot be seen in isolation; it can only be analyzed by understanding its environmental conditions and actual relationships (Madsen & Servais, 1997).

Substantial *research* has been made *on relationships between FDI and host country exports*. Several authors have shown that foreign subsidiaries are usually more international (at least, they export more) than locally owned firms. This is caused by the following two reasons (Blomström, 1990; Dunning, 1994; Lauter & Rehman, 1999; Roolaht, 2002; Simoneti, Rojec & Rems, 2001): (1) subsidiaries have better business contacts abroad, higher management and marketing skills, superior technology, greater general know-how and the right to use their parents' brand names; (2) the owners can help them to set up a distribution network, follow industrial norms, safety standards and consumer tastes; deal with product design, packaging, distribution, servicing and shaping a new product image.

Based on the above discussion, a table with two distinct internationalization types can be developed (see Table 1). Compared to traditional internationalizers, fast internationalizers (including born globals) enter foreign markets more quickly; they can use several entry modes from the start and begin their internationalization from farther countries without having any operations in closer ones, including the home market. These firms are also able to create network relationships fast and use

TABLE 1. Two Types of Internationalization

	A traditional internationalizer	A fast internationalizer
Market selection	Home market first, other markets later (gradual entry from closest to more distant markets)	Many markets fast; their distance does not matter (the home market does not have to be entered first)
Pace of internationalization	Slow, gradual both in terms of market selection and entry modes	Very fast (at once or only a couple of years after establishment) regarding both market selection and entry modes
Entry modes	Exports first, marketing and production subsidiaries later	Subsidiaries may be established even before exporting
Triggers of internationalization	Experiential market knowledge (especially in the U-model), other firms, top managers, the companies' competitive advantages and general economic conditions	A small home market, network relationships (for instance, with foreign owners), short product life cycles, large competition, unique resources, products and capabilities, global orientation, new (internationally experienced) managers or owners
The approaches studying them	the U-model, the I-models; to some extent, the Finnish model and other streams of literature	The born-global literature; to some extent, the network approach and the FDI literature and other research streams

them extensively for foreign market entry. Moreover, they may possess some unique resources and capabilities. These factors should considerably speed up their internationalization process.

Figure 1 brings out some factors influencing the emergence and further development of fast internationalizers. Based on the literature review, it can be concluded that the latter should emerge and flourish if their (business) environment is favorable, the firms are able to develop some unique resources and capabilities, their managers are globally oriented and the companies have been able to create useful network relationships with domestic and foreign partners. Naturally, these factors are inter-related (for instance, a firm's ability to develop unique resources and capabilities should depend on its surrounding environment and both may influence the enterprise's attractiveness for potential network partners; the partners, in turn, may help them to develop their capabilities further and so on). These factors are further discussed after presenting some case study evidence from Estonia.

METHODOLOGY

This paper is based on case studies as by combining previously developed theories with new empirically derived insights (Yin, 1994), this

FIGURE 1. The Emergence and Further Development of Fast Internationalizers: A Conceptual Framework

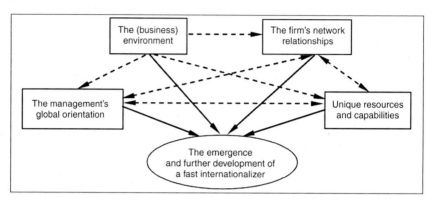

approach is especially appropriate in new topic areas. Its application can result in transcending the local boundaries of the investigated cases, capturing new layers of reality and developing novel, testable and empirically valid theoretical and practical insights (Eisenhardt, 1989; Ghauri, 2004; Tsoukas, 1989; Stuart et al., 2002; Voss, Tsikriktis & Frohlich, 2002). Case research is capable of discovering true causal relationships (Hillebrand, Kok & Biemans, 2001) and creating thick descriptions and rich understandings (Gibb Dyer & Wilkins, 1991) of phenomena in their natural settings (Dubois & Gadde, 2002; Yin, 1994). Moreover, the researcher can go far beyond a cross-sectional snapshot of a process and understand how and why things happen as they do (Miles & Huberman, 1994; Stuart et al., 2002; Yin, 1994). This method also enables to conduct research in a country where the sample base is too small to justify using statistical generalization (Chetty, 1996).

In this paper, multiple case study approach was used. There is no ideal number of cases in this approach. According to Eisenhardt (1989), a study of 4-10 cases usually works well. With fewer than four cases, theory is difficult to generate, and with more than ten cases, the volume of data is difficult to cope with. Gummesson (2003), on the other hand, claims that anything from one case to several, even hundreds, can be justified depending on the research purpose and questions.

This paper is based on four cases. As the number is small, it can be assumed that if not these, but any other four enterprises had been selected, the results might have been different. On the other hand, case studies are not always supposed to provide statistical generalizations. Even with such a small number of cases, theoretical generalization can be made: when it is possible to formulate logical conclusions in support of causal relationships, it may be concluded that these causal relationships also hold for cases that are structurally similar (Hillebrand, Kok & Biemans, 2001). Such generalizations could be made even from one case (Stuart et al., 2002), but a larger number of cases should augment external validity and help to guard against observer bias (Voss, Tsikriktis & Frohlich, 2002), confirm or refute the findings of the first case or to investigate whether the findings of the first case could be expanded to slightly different situations (Hillebrand, Kok & Biemans, 2001). For these reasons, in this paper, the multiple-case approach was preferred.

By treating each case as an individual study, rather than a sampling unit, the focus shifts to choosing the case or cases that are best suited for investigating the theory. Each of them should complement the others by examining the findings under various conditions or by addressing different aspects of the overall theory. The goal is that together the set of studies will provide rich support for the theory (Johnston, Leach & Liu, 1999; Miles & Huberman, 1994) rather than it is representative of the whole population (Chetty, 1996).

To increase the findings' generalizability, four case companies (see also Tables 2 and 3) were selected that belonged to different owners and did not have similar products. Still, they all had some common characteristics: they were (and still are) quite small but they internationalized quickly, they entered some markets outside Europe relatively soon after establishment, they have actively created network relationships and their products have a relatively high added value: in other words, they present a good illustration to the framework presented on Figure 1.

To increase the validity and reliability in studying these firms' internationalization, several public data sources were used, including newspapers and journals, the firms' homepages and annual reports. Although personal interviews were not conducted, the data were sufficient to provide relatively rich case descriptions.

CASE DESCRIPTIONS

Case 1. Mrs. Silva Tomingas established *TEA* Language Center–one of the first Estonian private enterprises and the first private language center–on July 4th 1988. She registered the trademark TEA in 1990 in

TABLE 2. An Overview of the Case Companies

	TEA (1988)	Asper Biotech (1998)	Mikromasch (1998)	Quattromed (1999)
Areas of operation	A language center (dictionaries, courses, a web portal)	Genotyping services, soft- and hardware	Industrial application of micro mechanical devices	Molecular diagnostics, functional genomics, proteomics
Turnover, million EUR	1.7	1.0	0.8	0.6
Employees	50	25	15	29
Founders/ owners	Mrs. Silva Tomingas	2 local scientists; since 2001, their firms, another Estonian and 3 venture capitalists	5 Estonian researchers	4 local scientists; since 2002, FIT Biotech (Finland), 22.4%; the founders and a local manager
Quality indicators	Several ministries of education have approved its publications	ISO 9001, ISO 9001:2000	The products have been used by many scientists in Estonia and abroad	ISO 15189:2003
Interna- tiona- lization	Has exported to over 40 countries in Europe, Arabia and Asia; in 1994-1998 had a sales subsidiary in Russia	Japan, Korea, the USA, France, Norway, Italy, Spain, Finland, Canada, Australia, Holland, the Czech Republic, Taiwan, Germany, Hong Kong, the UK, Sweden, Denmark, Ireland, Cyprus, Israel, Lithuania, Belgium, Kuwait, Poland, Singapore, Japan, China and Switzerland; export share 90%	Several European, Asian and other countries (a 15% market share in the world); a logistics center Spain, a sales office in the USA and a production subsidiary in Russia	Finland, Sweden, Canada, Italy, the UK, Portugal, the USA, Japan and Germany
Research partners	European developers of software solutions and related services	Universities and research centers in Europe, Asia and America	Universities and research centers in Europe, Asia and America	Universities, research centers and other partners in Estonia and abroad
Distributors	Several distributors in Europe and Asia	Several distributors in Europe and one in America	Several distributors in Europe, Asia and some elsewhere	Several distributors in Europe, one in America

the whole Soviet Union. In 1991, Mrs. Tomingas established TEA Publishers as TEA Language Center's daughter company due to a lack of high quality foreign language textbooks in Estonia.

Mrs. Tomingas bought her first computer at the end of 1988 in order to create her customers' database and compile language learning materials. In 1995, TEA became one of the first companies in Estonia that sold its dictionaries on hard disks. In 1999, the firm started selling them on CD-ROMs (since 2000, with pronunciation control) and developed a technical solution for using its dictionaries in a mobile phone (in 2000, a

TABLE 3. The Factors Affecting the Internationalization of the Case Companies

	TEA	Asper Biotech	Mikromasch	Quattromed
The business environment	Very dynamic	Very dynamic	Very dynamic	Very dynamic
The management's orientation	Global; plans to expand even more to Asia: for instance, open one or two subsidiaries in China	Global; plans to establish a daughter company in the USA	Global; plans to develop new products, suitable for mass production for many markets	Global; plans to increase its exports considerably
Network relationships	Very important both for research and distribution (see also Table 2)	Very important both for research and distribution	Very important both for research and distribution	Very important both for research and distribution; the foreign owner is also very important
Unique strengths (resources and capabilities)	A large number of partners, advanced technological solutions, experience in teaching languages and publishing teaching materials	Flexibility, advanced technology, adjusting to clients' needs, offering sound scientific support; several patents	Core technological competence, several partners in Estonia and abroad, several trademarks and well-known customers	Motivated and professional team, loyal customers, proprietary technology, modern laboratory facilities, several patents and licenses
International development	Very fast (see also Table 2)	Very fast	Very fast	Very fast

WAP version was added; it was among the first ones in the world). In 2004, TEA participated in developing a language portal where users can get access to their dictionaries for a moderate fee.

In 2003, the firm's turnover was 0.8, and in 2004, 0.9 million EUR. For 2005, an increase to 1.7 million EUR was expected. TEA Publishers has become one of Estonia's leading publishers of economics dictionaries and foreign language textbooks. Its publications have been endorsed not only by Estonia's Ministry of Education and Research, but such ministries in several foreign countries as well. In addition to textbooks, TEA publishes books on art, handicraft, music, and also some stories for children. Over 2000 people attend TEA's language courses each year (some of them foreigners interested in learning Estonian). The firm also participates in organizing foreign trips for language learners.

Network relationships have been very important for the company. Already at the end of 1988, Mrs. Tomingas managed to start a partnership with a language school in Torrance, California. In 1992, TEA's co-operation with several German and British publishers began: TEA was the first Estonian company that started importing their books. TEA also co-operates with several Russian publishers; Estonia's largest mobile operator EMT; a well-known French developer of software solutions and related services for foreign language learning Auralog and several other firms like Richard Lewis Communications (UK; a provider of training and support in cross culture and language skills development), Saint George International (offering English language courses in London), Colchester Institute (UK; offering several language and other courses), EF International Language Schools (offering its services in over 50 countries and having schools in 14 countries); and Aspect (a provider of educational programs and services to students from over 100 countries worldwide).

In 1994, TEA established a sales subsidiary in Russia (it decided to close it in 1998, but managed to retain some useful contacts). In 1995, the firm participated at the Baltic Book Fair for the first time and managed to sell some publishing rights to Latvian and Lithuanian publishers. At the same year, it went to the Frankfurt Book Fair and also sold some publishing rights. The following fairs were even more beneficial. In 2000, the firm hired a Chinese-speaking project manager to enter Chinese-speaking markets (in 2001, a TV show in China started where people could learn English using TEA's books). In the same year, it also sold publishing rights to India and Japan and a year later, to Indonesia. In total, its books have been sold to more than 40 and publishing rights to over 25 foreign countries, including some in Arabia. TEA plans to expand further, especially in Asia. In 2005 it announced of its plans to open a publishing subsidiary and maybe also a language school in China. TEA also wants to pay more attention to information technology, offer more products on CD-ROMs and online. The firm has over 50 foreign co-operation partners: both publishers and multimedia production companies. This is a large number taking into account that the firm only has about 50 employees.

Case 2. Asper Biotech is a leading Estonian biotechnology company. It offers custom genotyping services, software, hardware and consumables. Since its start of operations in 1999 with four scientists, it has grown to become the biggest bio-technology exporter in Estonia. Its annual turnover is approaching 1 million EUR. Currently, the company employs about 25 people. The enterprise introduced the ISO 9001 quality control system in 2000 and upgraded to ISO 9001:2000 in 2003. The whole lab process work as well as management is controlled by the system. The R&D projects in 1999 and 2000 resulted in a technological ability to start servicing clients. Simultaneously, the results of the development projects were published in major international scientific journals like *Nature* and *PNAS*. This was an important step for validation of the technology platform for international clients.

Already in 2001, the firm opened sales channels in the USA and Asia. In 2002, Deloitte and Touche included it into the "Fast 50 Technology Companies in Central Europe" list (from 12000 enterprises, Asper Biotech was 4th; in three years, its turnover grew by 1550 percent). At the same year, it also received the Estonian Gene Technology Prize from PriceWaterhouseCoopers. A year later, Asper Biotech started to promote its products actively in Western Europe and the USA (it also tried to enter Japan, but without as much success as it initially planned). Its number of clients doubled.

The company has succeeded in creating several long-lasting partnerships–for instance, with the Estonian Genome Centre, Stanford University, Columbia University, Baylor College of Medicine, Sunergia Medical (all from the USA), International Cancer Research Centre (France) and GoodGene (South Korea)–and client relationships. Together with its partners, the firm has developed and launched a number of DNA tests for cancer, ophthalmic disease and hereditary hearing loss-related research. The list of DNA tests is constantly expanding, especially in the area of ophthalmic research. Asper Biotech owns a semi-exclusive license for ABCR gene related ophthalmic disease diagnostics.

The company has also been active in involving venture capital (for instance, from SEAF CEE Growth Fund LLC and Baltics Small Equity Fund LLC) and state support (from the Estonian Export Agency and the Estonian Innovation Foundation). It has been also involved in various grant applications: for instance, of 26 applications to the FP6 (Sixth Framework Program of the EU), six were accepted. Asper Biotech plans to enter the diagnostic and personalized medicine market in the near future.

Case 3: Mikromasch, a leading Estonian nanotechnology company, dedicated to development and industrial application of micro mechanical devices–pressure sensors, optic alignment chips, microbolometers, SPM (scanning probe microscopy) probes and calibration standards–was founded in 1998 by five Estonian private researchers with backgrounds in physics and microelectronics. They possessed core competence in silicon technology (they all had graduated the Moscow Institute of Electronic Technology) and wanted to leverage this in the form of a company. The founders themselves invested the means needed to start the firm and today it is funded by reinvested profit. By 2004, its number of employees grew to 15. The company has an annual turnover of about 0.8 million EUR, and almost all profits are reinvested into R & D. It has registered several trademarks, some of them internationally: in the EU, USA and Japan. Mikromasch has achieved a 15 percent market share in the world. The firm has several well-known customers: for instance, Seiko, Jeol, SI, Olympus and Biersdorf. The majority of clients are found in the researcher and scientist community (for instance, metrology institutes), but approximately 40 percent of the customer stock consists of the worldwide chemical, bio- and polymer industry. Some microelectronics manufacturers are also among the company's customers. Its products have been used in several scientific experiments in Denmark, Germany, Switzerland, Holland, UK, France, Greece, Romania, Poland, Russia, Israel, Canada, USA, Australia, Japan, China, Korea, Mexico, Brazil and other countries and the results have been published in international journals. The company's representatives actively participate in international trade fairs and exhibitions in Europe and on other continents. During the next three years, the firm plans to double its turnover by introducing new products on the market. Its largest market is the USA. Although the EU countries and Japan are also important markets for the company, it plans to achieve even higher success is the American market. So, it tries to find some more partners in distribution and for franchise.

The firm has contracts with two distributors in Germany, three in France, one in Italy, one in Sweden, one in Switzerland and Austria, one in Benelux countries, four in Taiwan, one in Israel, one in Japan, one in China and Hong-Kong, one in Singapore and one in Australia and New Zealand. In addition, it has established a logistics center in Madrid that maintains stock of products in the EU, and a sales office in Portland, USA that is responsible for the USA, Canada and Mexico. It also has an online store. The headquarters provides centralized marketing assistance for these activities. In addition, it has acquired a small company Silicon-MDT, a Russian manufacturer of commercial silicon cantilevers and calibration gratings for Scanning Probe Microscopy (it has 10 employees). Silicon-MDT has made a number of custom structures for national universities, research centers, scientific laboratories, and hi-tech companies. All of its products are currently manufactured and developed in co-operation with Mikromasch and distributed under its own trademark.

The firm hopes that they can help to create a good infrastructure for nanotechnology projects in Estonia by participating in the Estonian Nanotechnology Competence Centre, established in December 2004 by Mikromasch, Tartu University, Evikon MCI, Maico Metrics and NexTech Supply from Estonia and K-TEK International (US distributor for Mikromasch; the companies have co-operated since 1998) and the University of North Carolina at Chapel Hill from the USA. The main orientations of the centre are nanotools, materials research techniques, and nanometrology. Through the centre, Mikromasch hopes to develop new innovative products, suitable for mass production. The company is constantly expanding its knowledge and production capabilities to advance in previously unreachable fields.

Case 4: Quattromed, active in molecular diagnostics (applications for detecting and genotyping bacterial and viral pathogens of sexually transmitted diseases and viruses to Estonian medical institutions) and functional genomics and proteomics (offering products and services for biochemical and functional characterization of proteins for research institutions worldwide), was established by four scientists in 1999 as a spin-off company of the University of Tartu. Only three years later, its export share was about 50 percent. In 2002, Quattromed involved a Finnish biotechnology company FIT Biotech (they also have their own development laboratory with 11 researchers in Tartu and another one in Thailand; in total, the firm has 40 employees) with 22.4% share (FIT Biotech also has an option to obtain the remaining shares of Quattromed, up to 100 %, until 2006). In 2003, Quattromed received the Estonian PricewaterhouseCoopers Gene Technology Award. A year later, the enterprise received the ISO 15189:2003 certificate. Quattromed has the only accredited molecular diagnostics laboratory in Estonia. It diagnoses 16 different pathogenic microorganisms. Currently it employs 29 professionals with academic degrees in laboratory medicine, molecular biology and business administration. Its annual turnover is 0.6 million EUR, but this should increase in the future as the enterprise obtained two additional business areas from FIT Biotech in June 2005: latex allergen testing and production of monoclonal antibodies. These areas were launched in November 2005. Through the deal, Quattromed hopes to develop a strong competitive advantage in the growing Asian markets. In the near future, it also plans to move into drug discovery and development. The firm currently has customers in Finland (a partner ABCELL), Sweden, Canada, Italy (it collaborates with BTG BiotecGen), Germany (BIODATA Medizintechnik and VitaMed), Portugal, the UK, the USA and Japan. It is also a shareholder of the Tartu Biotechnology Park. The firm has seven patent applications, two trademarks and over twenty technology licenses.

Quattromed pays a lot of attention not only to R&D, but also to marketing, customer relations, logistics and quality management. Marketing was difficult at first as there were many offers and competition was strong. Fermentas, a Lithuanian company with experience from the Soviet period and representations in more than 50 countries, became its first retailer. By now Quattromed has also established a distribution network of some special sales companies in other parts of the world. The firm's home page in English has contributed to increasing sales. For instance, Abcam, a retailer from Great Britain (it also has an office in the USA) contacted Quattromed after seeing its home page and now does most of the marketing. Novus Biologicals (a supplier of antibodies from the USA), Biofellows OY (a Finnish distributor of bioreagents) and STAB VIDA (a Portuguese genomics and proteomics company) are also among its distributors. Quattromed also co-operates with several local partners: over 30 healthcare institutions, Estonian Business School, Estonian Biocentre, Institute of Molecular and Cell Biology of the University of Tartu, National Institute of Chemical Physics and Biophysics to transfer valuable know-how and technologies to the market. It belongs to the Estonian Biotechnology Association and the European Federation of Hightech SMEs. Quattromed has received financing to its R&D activities from the Estonian Innovation Foundation, the Estonian Technology Agency and Enterprise Estonia. It has also received some support from EU programs. In addition, it belongs to the CONNECT network created for supporting technology-intensive companies through seminars and consultations. In 2005, the University of Tartu and Quattromed submitted a provisional patent application in the USA to protect a technology that accelerates the production process of therapeutic proteins and other biological substances in mammalian cells from 10-12 to 2-3 months.

DISCUSSION

From the case study evidence it can be concluded that all the four companies have been relatively successful in foreign markets despite their young age: they have already entered some countries outside Europe. TEA has been active in China, Indonesia, India, Japan and some Arabic countries, Asper Biotech has entered Japan, Korea, the USA, Canada, Australia, Taiwan, Hong Kong, Kuwait, Singapore and China, Mikromasch has sold its products to the USA, Taiwan, Israel, Japan, China, Hong-Kong, Singapore, Australia and New Zealand while Quattromed has exported to Canada, the USA and Japan. Compared to the earlier approaches to internationalization, these four firms have not followed the traditional route: instead of starting from nearest markets, they have quickly gone to several farther countries. Moreover, Mikromasch managed to establish foreign subsidiaries in Spain, the USA and Russia relatively soon after its establishment: faster than the earlier internationalization approaches would have predicted (TEA also had a subsidiary in Russia for a short period, but it decided to close it down; now it is considering opening one or two in China). Thus, the companies can be called fast internationalizers and they also had at least some characteristics of born globals.

Such a fast internationalization process cannot be explained by the exceptions of the U-model: all the case firms were young and small (they still have only 50 or fewer employees) and did not have considerable (financial) resources. In addition, in the quickly developing biotechnology and IT/publishing sectors, market conditions could be hardly considered stable. On the other hand, it can be assumed that the smallness of the Estonian home market and the unstable situation in these sectors have pushed the case firms fast to foreign markets. The role of managers and owners cannot be underestimated, either: the case firms were globally oriented almost from the beginning and they were very active in developing unique resources and capabilities.

In the internationalization of the four companies, network relationships have been very important. Quattromed was the only firm with some foreign capital and it benefited to some extent from it–it obtained two business areas from FIT Biotech and it hopes to increase its presence in Asia in the near future–but other network relationships also had a clear positive role. The other three case firms have also co-operated with universities or other educational institutions and several companies in Estonia and abroad. Similarly to market selection, the selection of co-operation partners has not been determined by the countries' psychic distance: for instance, Asper Biotech has done research with partners outside Europe while Quattromed has found two distributors in the USA. The firms also tend to export to those countries where they have managed to establish beneficial network relationships. For the above-mentioned two companies, network relationships have also been very useful in receiving international grants: in Estonia, it is quite hard to find local financing. So, for growth, co-operation with foreign companies, universities and research institutes is almost obligatory: otherwise it is not possible to receive international grants. Due to their intense co-operation, Asper Biotech and Quattromed have also managed to receive some support from the EU funds. The former has also involved some venture capital.

In addition to financing and market entry, co-operation has been very useful in technology and product development. From the four companies, two have even managed to earn awards for their products: Asper Biotech and Quattromed have received the Estonian PricewaterhouseCoopers Gene Technology Award. TEA also managed to develop some unique products. In addition, the case firms consider flexibility, the existence of several patents, high potential demand and loyal customers as their major strengths. In other words, unique resources and capabilities seem to have a very important role in the case firms' internationalization process. If they manage to get additional funding, find a sufficient number of suitable employees and additional co-operation partners and acquire some more experience in their areas, they may all grow substantially in the future.

CONCLUSIONS AND IMPLICATIONS

The paper demonstrated that if a company has actively participated in local and international networks (for instance, involved foreign owners or co-operated with research institutions), developed some unique resources and capabilities and constantly searched for new (international) growth opportunities and its business environment pushes or pulls it to foreign markets, it may internationalize much faster than the earlier internationalization approaches (the U-, I, and, to some extent, the Finnish model) would have predicted. It may enter far markets almost in the moment of its establishment and establish foreign subsidiaries before it has obtained substantial exporting experience: in other words, develop at least some characteristics of born globals. Thus, there was some support to the network literature, the literature on born globals/fast internationalizers and research on relationships between FDI and host country exports. Moreover, there was also some support to the framework developed on Figure 1: all the mentioned factors clearly played a role in the fast international development of the four case firms.

The results also agreed with the idea from the born global literature that in fast internationalization, a firm's smallness does not necessarily have to be a problem: it may even be a bonus (for instance, Asper Biotech considered smallness and resulting flexibility as one of its main strengths), but in this case, network relationships may be especially important. The four case enterprises have managed to co-operate with several distributors and research institutions both in Estonia and abroad. Such international partnerships have also been important for receiving research grants (although competition is very strong in this area and even very good projects do not always get support) and developing innovative products and services. Still, managers should keep in mind that internationalization does not always succeed and co-operation may also sometimes fail. There is also no guarantee that the demand on the firm's products will keep growing or at least remain the same. Thus, markets, customers and co-operation partners should be selected with great care and the organization's and its surrounding environment's specific characteristics should be taken into account when making decisions how to internationalize.

This paper covered only some issues of the internationalization of Estonian fast internationalizers and it was based only on four cases. Some other subjects should be still studied. For instance, it would be useful to examine a larger number of cases and include some companies that have completely failed in their internationalization after the initial fast expansion: it seems that the current internationalization literature mainly concentrates on success, not failures.

It might be also interesting to compare different countries, firms and industries to understand which factors are more important in determining a company's success or failure in internationalization and if these factors depend on the location of a specific firm (for example, if networks are more important in doing business in Asia or unique products in America). The roles of specific managers and development of business environments clearly also need more attention in the international business literature. The new cases might go deeper than those presented in this paper and include extensive interview material, but some survey evidence might also be useful for making more general conclusions about internationalizing in some specific countries, regions or industries. This would help to provide more specific managerial implications.

REFERENCES

Adarkar, A., Adil, A., Ernst, D., & Vaish, P. (2001). Emerging market alliances: must they be win-lose. In M. R. Czinkota & I. A. Ronkainen (Eds.), *Best practices in international business* (pp.142-158). Fort Worth: Harcourt College Publishers.

Autio, E. (2005). Creative tension: the significance of Ben Oviatt's and Patricia McDougall's article 'Toward a theory of international new ventures.' *Journal of International Business Studies, 36* (1), 9-19.

Bell, J. (1995). The internationalization of small computer software firms: a further challenge to "stage" theories. *European Journal of Marketing, 29* (8), 60-75.

Bell, J., Crick, D., & Young, S. (2004). Small firm internationalization and business strategy: An exploratory study of 'knowledge-intensive' and 'traditional' manufacturing firms in the UK. *International Small Business Journal, 22* (1), 23-56.

Bilkey, W. J. (1978). An attempted integration of the literature on the export behavior of firms. *Journal of International Business Studies, 9* (1), 33-46.

Björkman, I., & Eklund, M. (1996). The sequence of operational modes used by Finnish investors in Germany. *Journal of International Marketing, 4* (1), 33-55.

Blomström, M. (1990). *Transnational corporations and manufacturing exports from developing countries.* New York: United Nations.

Chetty, S. (1996). The case study method for research in small- and medium-sized firms. *International Small Business Journal, 15* (1), 73-85.

Chetty, S., & Campbell-Hunt, C. (2004). A strategic approach to internationalization: a traditional versus a "born-global" approach. *Journal of International Marketing, 12* (1), 57-81.

Coviello, N. E., & Munro, H. J. (1995). Growing the entrepreneurial firm: networking for international market development. *European Journal of Marketing, 29* (7), 49-61.

Dubois, A. & Gadde, L.-E. (2002). Systematic combining: an abductive approach to case research. *Journal of Business Research, 55* (7), 553-560.

Dunning, J. H. (1994). Re-evaluating the benefits of foreign direct investment. *Transnational Corporations, 3* (1), 23-51.

Eisenhardt, K. M. (1989). Building theories from case study research. *Academy of Management Review, 14* (4), 532-550.

Eriksson, K., Johanson, J., Majkgård, A., & Sharma, D. D. (1998). Time and experience in the internationalization process. In A. Majkgård (Ed.), *Experiential knowledge in the internationalization process of service firms* (pp. 185-217). Uppsala: Department of Business Studies.

Ford, D. (1998). Two decades of interaction, relationships and networks. In P. Naudé & P. Turnbull (Eds.), *Network dynamics in international marketing* (pp. 3-15). Oxford: Elsevier.

Gabrielsson, M., Kirpalani, V. H. M., & Luostarinen, R. (2002). Multiple channel strategies in the European personal computer industry. *Journal of International Marketing, 10* (3), 73-95.

Gabrielsson, M., Sasi, V. & Darling, J. (2004). Finance strategies of rapidly-growing Finnish SMEs: born internationals and born globals. *European Business Review, 16* (6), 590-604.

Ghauri, P. (2004). Designing and conducting case studies in international business research. In R. Marschan-Piekkari, & C. Welch (Eds.), *Handbook of qualitative research methods for international business* (pp. 109-124). Cheltenham, UK: Edward Elgar.

Gibb Dyer, W. Jr., & Wilkins, A. L. (1991). Better stories, not better constructs, to generate better theory: a rejoinder to Eisenhardt. *Academy of Management Review, 16* (3), 613-619.

Gummesson, E. (2003). All research is interpretive. *Journal of Business & Industrial Marketing, 18* (6/7), 482-492.

Håkansson, H., & Snehota, I. (2000). The IMP perspective: assets and liabilities of business relationships. In J. N. Sheth & A. Parvatiyar (Eds.), *Handbook of relationship marketing* (pp. 69-94). London: Sage.

Hashai, N. & Almor, T. (2004). Gradually internationalizing 'born global' firms: an oxymoron? *International Business Review, 13* (4), 465-483.

Hertz, S. (1996). The dynamics of international strategic alliances. *International Studies of Management & Organization, 26* (2), 104-130.

Hillebrand, B., Kok, R. A. W., & Biemans, W. G. (2001). Theory-testing using case studies: a comment on Johnston, Leach, and Liu. *Industrial Marketing Management, 30* (8), 651-657.

Johanson, J., & Mattson, L.-G. (1988). Internationalization in industrial systems–a network approach. In N. Hood & J.-E. Vahlne (Eds.), *Strategies in global competition* (pp. 287-314). London: Croom Helm.

Johanson, J., & Vahlne, J.-E. (1977). The internationalization process of the firm: a model of knowledge development and increasing foreign market commitments. *Journal of International Business Studies, 8* (1), 23-32.

Johanson, J., & Vahlne, J.-E. (1990). The mechanism of internationalisation. *International Marketing Review, 7* (4), 11-24.

Johanson, J., & Wiedersheim-Paul, F. (1975). The internationalization of the firm: four Swedish cases. *Journal of Management Studies, 12* (3), 305-322.

Johnston, W. J., Leach, M. P., & Liu, A. H. (1999). Theory testing using case studies in business-to-business research. *Industrial Marketing Management, 28* (3), 201-213.

Jones, M. V. (2001). First steps in internationalisation. Concepts and evidence from a sample of small high-technology firms. *Journal of International Management, 7* (3), 191-210.

Jones, M. V., & Coviello, N. E. (2005). Internationalisation: conceptualising an entrepreneurial process of behaviour in time. *Journal of International Business Studies, 36* (3), 284-303.

Knight, G. A. (2001). Entrepreneurship and strategy in the international SME. *Journal of International Management, 7* (3), 155-171.

Knight, G. A., & Cavusgil, S. T. (1996). The born global firm: a challenge to traditional internationalization theory. In S. T. Cavusgil, & T. K. Madsen (Eds.), *Advances in international marketing: export and internationalizing research–enrichment and challenges* (pp. 11-26). Greenwich: JAI Press.

Knight, G. A., & Cavusgil, S. T. (2004). Innovation, organizational capabilities, and the born-global firm. *Journal of International Business Studies, 35* (2), 124-141.

Korhonen, H. (1999). *Inward-outward internationalization of small and medium enterprises.* Doctoral dissertation No. A-147, Helsinki School of Economics, Helsinki.

Kuivalainen, O., Saarenketo, S., & Puumalainen, K. (2005). International pathways revisited: towards a longitudinal analysis of knowledge-intensive SMEs. In E. J. Morgan, & F. Fai (Eds.), *The 32nd Annual AIB UK Chapter Conference 'Innovation, Change and Competition in International Business,'* [CD-Rom]. Bath: University of Bath.

Lauter, G. P., & Rehman, S. S. (1999). Central and East European trade orientation and FDI flows: preparation for EU membership. *International Trade Journal, 13* (1), 35-52.

Leonard-Barton, D. (1990). A dual methodology for case studies: synergistic use of a longitudinal single site with replicated multiple sites. *Organization Science, 1* (3), 248-266.

Luostarinen, R. (1994). *Research for action: internationalization of Finnish firms and their response to global challenges.* Forssa: UNU Wider.

Madsen, T. K., & Servais, P. (1997). The internationalization of born globals: an evolutionary process? *International Business Review, 6* (6), 561-583.

McAuley, A. (1999). Entrepreneurial instant exporters in the Scottish arts and crafts sector. *Journal of International Marketing, 7* (4), 67-82.

McDougall, P. P., Oviatt, B. M., & Shrader, R. C. (2003). A comparison of international and domestic new ventures. *Journal of International Entrepreneurship, 1* (1), 59-82.

McKinsey & Co (1993). *Emerging exporters: Australia's high value-added manufacturing exporters.* Melbourne: McKinsey & Co and Australian Manufacturing Council.

Miles, M. B., & Huberman, A. M. (1994). *Qualitative data analysis: an expanded sourcebook.* London: Sage.

Moen, Ø., & Servais, P. (2002). Born global or gradual global? Examining the export behavior of small and medium-sized enterprises. *Journal of International Marketing, 10* (3), 49-72.

Morgan, R. E., & Katsikeas, C. S. (1997). Theories of international trade, foreign direct investment and firm internationalization: a critique. *Management Decision, 35* (1/2), 68-78.

Nieminen, J., Larimo, J. & Springer, R. (2001). Market strategies and performance of Western firms in Eastern Europe: A comparative survey. *Journal of East-West Business, 7* (3), 91-117.

Oviatt, B. M., & McDougall, P. P. (1994). Toward a theory of international new ventures. *Journal of International Business Studies, 25* (1), 45-64.

Oviatt, B. M., & McDougall, P. P. (2005). Defining international entrepreneurship and modeling the speed of internationalization. *Entrepreneurship Theory and Practice, 29* (5), 537-553.

Rasmussen, E. S., & Madsen, T. K. (2002). The born global concept. 28th EIBA Conference. Athens: Athens University of Economics and Business. Retrieved May 9, 2005 from http://www.sam.sdu.dk/~era/EIBA%20Rasmussen%202002%20.pdf

Rennie, M. W. (1993). Born global. *McKinsey Quarterly, 4*, 45-52.

Rialp, A., Rialp, J., & Knight, G. A. (2005). The phenomenon of early internationalizing firms: what do we know after a decade (1993–2003) of scientific inquiry? *International Business Review, 14* (2), 147-166.

Roolaht, T. (2002). Internationalisation of firms from small open transition economies: the intra-firm factors and inward-outward connections. *Journal of East-West Business, 8* (3/4), 123-144.

Simoneti, M., Rojec, M. & Rems, M. (2001). Ownership structure and post-privatisation performance and restructuring of the Slovenian non-financial corporate sector. *Journal of East-West Business, 7* (2), 7-37.

Stuart, I., McCutcheon, D., Handfield, R., McLachlin, R., & Samson, D. (2002). Effective case research in operations management: a process perspective. *Journal of Operations Management, 20* (5), 419-433.

Tsoukas, H. (1989). The validity of idiographic research explanations. *Academy of Management Review, 14* (4), 551-561.

Vahlne, J.-E., & Johanson, J. (2002). New technology, new companies, new business environments and new internationalisation processes? In V. Havila, M. Forsgren & H. Håkansson (Eds.), *Critical perspectives of internationalisation* (pp. 209-227). Amsterdam: Pergamon.

Vissak, T. (2003). *The internationalization of foreign-owned enterprises in Estonia: an extended network perspective.* Doctoral Dissertation No. 8, University of Tartu, Tartu

Voss, C., Tsikriktis, N., & Frohlich, M. (2002). Case Research in operations management. *International Journal of Operations & Production Management, 22* (2), 195-219.

Welch, L. S. & Luostarinen, R. (1988). Internationalization: evolution of a concept. *Journal of General Management, 14* (2), 34-57.

Wiedersheim-Paul, F., Olson, H. C., & Welch, L. S. (1978). Pre-export activity: the first step in internationalization. *Journal of International Business Studies, 9* (1), 47-58.

Wolff, J. A., & Pett, T. L. (2000). Internationalization of small firms: an examination of export competitive patterns, firm size, and export performance. *Journal of Small Business Management, 38* (2), 34-47.

Yin, R. K. (1994). *Case study research design and methods.* London: Sage.

Zahra, S. A., & George, G. (2002). International entrepreneurship: the current status of the field and future research agenda. In M. A. Hitt, R. D. Ireland, S. M. Camp, & D. L. Sexton (Eds.), *Strategic entrepreneurship: creating a new mindset* (pp.255-288). London: Blackwell Publishers.

doi:10.1300/J097v13n01_02

First Mover Advantages
in Central and Eastern Europe:
A Comparative Analysis
of Performance Measures

Kristian Jakobsen

SUMMARY. Businesses entering early into new markets are believed to attain crucial competitive advantages over later entrants. However, this contention receives only mixed support in the empirical literature, in part because performance is measured in different ways. We reexamine the performance difference between early movers and followers entering new geographical markets based on a sample of foreign entrants in Poland, Hungary and Lithuania. We contrast market share with two other measures of firm performance that are based on the managers' perception of their own performance relative to their own prior expectations

Kristian Jakobsen is a doctoral student, Department of International Economics and Management, Copenhagen Business School, Porcelænshaven 24, 2000 Frederiksberg, Denmark (E-mail: kj.int@cbs.dk).

The author thanks the Social Science Foundation for financial support for the project 'Merger and Acquisition Strategies in Eastern Europe, under grant number 24-01-0152.' The author would like to thank Klaus Meyer at the University of Reading for invaluable ongoing support, and the participants at the 8th Vaasa Conference on International Business for helpful comments, and in particular, the commentators for this paper, Jorma Larimo and Zsuzsanna Vincze.

[Haworth co-indexing entry note]: "First Mover Advantages in Central and Eastern Europe: A Comparative Analysis of Performance Measures." Jakobsen, Kristian. Co-published simultaneously in *Journal of East-West Business* (The Haworth Press, Inc.) Vol. 13, No. 1, 2007, pp. 35-61; and: *Market Entry and Operational Decision Making in East-West Business Relationships* (ed: Jorma Larimo) The Haworth Press, Inc., 2007, pp. 35-61. Single or multiple copies of this article are available for a fee from The Haworth Document Delivery Service [1-800-HAWORTH, 9:00 a.m. - 5:00 p.m. (EST). E-mail address: docdelivery@haworthpress.com].

Available online at http://jeb.haworthpress.com
doi:10.1300/J097v13n01_03

and relative to industry standards. We find that market share is strongly related to order of entry, but we did not find a positive relationship between order of entry and perceived performance. We found general support for early mover advantages in Hungary and Poland but a strongly negative relationship for Lithuania, suggesting that early entry is a trade off between risk and return. doi:10.1300/J097v13n01_03 *[Article copies available for a fee from The Haworth Document Delivery Service: 1-800-HAWORTH. E-mail address: <docdelivery@haworthpress.com> Website: <http://www.HaworthPress.com> © 2007 by The Haworth Press, Inc. All rights reserved.]*

KEYWORDS. First mover, early mover, FDI, performance, timing, order of entry, emerging and transition economies

INTRODUCTION

The fairly extensive literature demonstrating the existence of first mover advantages (FMA) (Gal-Or, 1985; Lieberman & Montgomery, 1988) has in recent years been rivaled by a considerable literature on follower or late mover advantages (Rivoli & Salorio, 1996; Lieberman & Montgomery, 1998; Narasimham & Zhang, 2000). Crucial trade-offs have been shown with respect to the costs of waiting or the benefit of accepting more uncertainty by entering early. However, it is as yet unclear whether there is a general advantage to moving first (VanderWerf & Mahon, 1997). In a Meta analysis of 90 empirical studies[1] VanderWerf and Mahon (1997) studied the likelihood of finding first mover advantage. After correcting for the use of market share as a performance measure, a possible self-selection bias and survival bias, they did not find support for a general FMA.

A unique opportunity to investigate FMA has arisen in the transition economies in Eastern Europe and Asia. Over the past two decades they have opened up and embraced foreign direct investment (FDI) as a mean to rebuild their economies (Marinova, Marinov & Yaprak, 2004). This has created new opportunities for multinational enterprises (MNEs) to sell their products in new markets and streamline their global production systems. Thus, the societal quasi-experiment unfolding in transition economies provides an opportunity to investigate change processes in business strategies (Meyer & Peng, 2005). In particular, a fairly large number of firms were simultaneously considering the timing of an entry, which provides a large set of firms on which to investigate a phenomenon that often only can be investigated on specific industries with small numbers of players.

Our empirical analysis is based on a sample of foreign investors in Poland, Hungary and Lithuania. FMA research has primarily been conducted either on product markets in America (Lieberman & Montgomery, 1998) or for transition economies primarily on China. China is still geographically and culturally very distant for Western firms which may suggest a selection bias, furthermore most entry timing research has been conducted on Japanese firms (Delios & Makino, 2003) which may have different entry strategies than western firms (Chang, 1995). We believe the use of a Central and Eastern European (CEE) sample complements the timing literature by testing the first mover advantage in a different economic, institutional and developmental setting. Unlike China, where the process of opening up for FDI has been slow and incremental, the process proceeded very rapidly in CEE. The rapid opening to FDI and the close proximity to Western markets ensured a large number of potential entrants. Freedom in the choice of entry mode was also available from relatively early on. Consequently, we can proceed under the assumption that the entry decision has largely been strategic and competitive. It is therefore our view that the sample offers the best opportunity to date to study competitive entry timing decisions.

This paper contributes to the literature on timing and performance in four ways. First, we employ two unique measures for perceived performance and find that the choice of performance measure crucially influences, if first mover advantages are identified empirically. Secondly, our paper contributes to the growing body of literature on entry timing and performance in emerging and transition economies (Rivoli & Salorio, 1996; Luo & Peng, 1998; Pan, Li & Tse, 1999; Isobe, Makino & Montgomery, 2000; Delios & Makino, 2003; Sui & Lui, 2005). Thirdly, based on two unique performance measures, we identify the influence of endogenous firm specific advantages. Finally, we broaden the scope of the timing literature by studying the performance implications of early mover advantages in new markets.

CONCEPTUAL FRAMEWORK AND HYPOTHESES

A core argument in first mover literature is that first movers are able to preempt late movers by taking control of scarce assets (Lieberman & Montgomery, 1988 & 1998). Typical examples of local resources that can offer an advantage to first movers are the acquisition of a local distribution network, local brands and natural resources. In some industries the acquisition of production facilities can also be a source of FMA, Rockwool–a Danish producer of isolation material–primarily enter new foreign markets through acquisitions, because of the high costs of establishing new production facilities.

In the late 70's and early 80's many studies adopted a game theoretical approach to the role of entry timing and performance. Entry deterrence played a preeminent role in the first mover advantage literature. There is a long held belief dating back to Stackelberg (1934) that the first mover can capture the lion share of a market through his output decision provided that the decision is irreversible. This is generally the case if output is directly linked to investments in capacity and if these investments are sunk (Judd, 1985). Spence (1979) and Fudenberg and Tirole (1983) suggest that through their investment decision first movers can prevent followers from growing. Investments in capacity may even be so large that they effectively make any subsequent entry unprofitable (Spence, 1977; Dixit, 1980; Gilbert & Harris, 1981; Eaton & Ware, 1987). However, there is little empirical evidence that first movers have actually been successful at preempting entry by rivals (Johnson & Parkman, 1983; Glazer, 1985). Later studies have increasingly adopted a resource based perspective on FMA (Lieberman & Montgomery, 1998).

Spatial preemption in geographic or product space has also been suggested as a source of FMA (Schmalensee, 1978). Robinson and Fornell (1985) found that pioneers typically have broader product range than followers.

Other sources of first mover advantages have been suggested, for instance, in the marketing literature. Schmalensee (1982) suggests that the rational consumer, having ascertained the merits of the first mover's product, will be hesitant to switch to a different and as yet untried brand. One study even found FMA derived from the consumers desire to link the pioneering brand image to their individual self-image (Alpert & Kamins, 1995). Brand names may even become synonymous with a specific type of product, for instance in Bulgaria instant coffee is referred to as Nescafé. Moreover, consumers may experience switching cost between products from different suppliers (Lieberman & Montgomery, 1998). This will typically be the case when the customers must spend resources to learn how to use a product. There may even be network effects that prevent customers from switching to another supplier (Katz & Shapiro, 1994). An example of this is the compatibility problems between Microsoft Word and competing products, which has largely insulated Microsoft from competition.

Recently, the relationship between timing and performance in international market entries has received increasing attention. A number of articles have focused specifically on the relationship between FMA and environmental conditions specific to emerging and transition economies. Doh (2000) suggests that strong FMA could be derived from participating in the privatization process. Nakata and Sivakumar (1997) compiled a list of factors that could potentially moderate the role of FMA in emerging markets both positively and negatively. In recent years many studies have been conducted using Chinese data. Isobe, Makino and Montgomery (2000) found a positive link between early entry, technology leadership and performance in China. A study by Li, Lam, Karakowsky and Qian (2003) showed no significant FMA for international entry into China in the telecommunication equipments industry. In fact they found considerable first mover disadvantages for overseas Chinese investing in China. Delios and Makino (2003) found that early entrants in China had larger sales but also a smaller survival rate. Luo (1998) found that early entrants tend to have higher sales, but later entrants have lower risk and greater accounting profit from the first years.

> H1a: The order of firms' entry into new markets is positively associated with market share.

Concerns have been raised both in theoretical and empirical studies about firms' ability to exploit FMA. First, some critics assert that if FMA exist, then competition to enter first would erode all associated profits from early entry (Gilbert & Harris, 1984; Mills, 1988; Glazer, 1985). In a two stage, two player model Hirokawa and Sasaki (2001) find that a Stackelberg (1934) outcome is possible even with two initially homogeneous players if one player commit to a sticky output and in return takes on a prediction risk. Empirically in their meta analysis VanderWerf and Mahon (1997) found no support that early movers enjoy better performance, other than higher market share, over later entrants. In a recent study Boulding and Christen (2003) found support for a lasting market share advantage to the first mover, but also a long term cost disadvantage.

Based on three assumptions, that rivals are alert, homogenous and that uncertainty is resolved gradually over time, we propose a simple relationship between FMA, general business risk and performance in emerging/transition economies. The general business risk in CEE was characterized by high degree of macro economic and demand uncertainty in the first years. These uncertainties have then gradually been resolved over time so it is reasonable to infer that the risk function would be hyperbolic in nature $r = \dfrac{a}{s(t)}$. The discount factor for NPV would be $I = r + b$ where b is the risk free rate. Emerging markets are generally associated with high growth potential which makes it reasonable to assume that the total market dividends D increases at, for simplicity, a steady rate of G. Further, we can include a basic assumption that the first mover gains an advantage over the second mover which we model as X, the share of the total attributable to the first mover through the order of entry effect. We get that the PV of entry at any given time for the second mover would be:

$$PV = \left[\frac{(1-X)*D}{I-G} \right] / (1+I)^{t}$$

The model has some simple reasonable predictions, that the higher the initial risk (a) the later the second mover would choose to enter. Similarly, the faster the rate of uncertainty resolution s(t), the sooner would the second mover enter. In a two-player game the second mover does not face further competition on entry; consequently he will choose the (t) that maximizes PV independently of the first mover's entry decision! However, for the first mover the equilibrium entry time t will be associated with a PV equal to the expected present value for the second mover. Figure 1 graphically illustrates that at any t greater than T_f but lower than T_1 the present value for the first mover is higher than the present value of the optimal for the second mover in T_1. This will automatically induce one of the entrants to enter at T_f. Consequently, with alert rivals we get the proposition that the first mover gain a larger share of the revenues (market share), but have to enter earlier and take on more risk in return.

> H1b: The order of firms' entry into new markets is not associated with better perceived performance.

A common property for all first mover advantages is that they contain an element of exclusivity, the action of the first player dictate or constrain the followers' strategic opportunities. We adapt a rather stringent

FIGURE 1. Entry Timing and Payoff in a Two Player Game

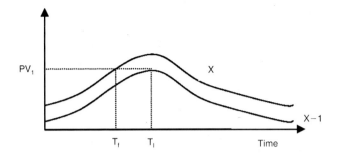

definition of FMA. In essence a first mover advantage is either acquired or created at the moment of the investment. However, this may not always be the case. Some advantages associated with early entry are unrelated to order of entry but instead are related to how long the firm has been in the market. Firms may experience learning effects that build up over time. Many emerging and transition economies offered various forms of concessions on among other taxes to induce early entry. Political goodwill, association with the local business community, financial institutions etc are not linked to order of entry, but to how long the firm has been in the local market. The same may hold true for some location advantages and the availability of skilled local workforce. The order of entry within a given industry is unable to affect the market for either, but the accumulated entry over time of a larger body of foreign firms will affect the relative scarcity of these resources. We shall refer to this type of advantages as early mover advantages rather than first mover advantages. These factors may be particularly important in emerging and transition economies where markets tend to be inefficient and personal relationships more important.

H1c: The age of the affiliate is positively associated with performance.

An endogeneity issue has also been raised. Our assumption is that the independent variable 'entry timing' explains the dependent variable 'performance.' But it is quite possible that the causality go both ways. Lieberman and Montgomery (1988-98) suggest that first movers may be first because they are inherently stronger. Consequently performance differentials between first movers and late mover may be attributed to skill rather than entry timing. Narasimham and Zhang (2000) on the other hand suggest that first movers are weaker firms that attempt to avoid late mover disadvantages. Rivoli and Salorio (1996) suggest that firm with strong ownership advantages will seek to defer entry when uncertainty is high. Delios and Makino (2003) suggest that the fungibility of entrants' resources determine whether they will enter early or late. Boulding and Christen (2003) found strong support that order of entry should be treated as endogenous.

Market size. In a case study of the Wal-Mart chain, Ghemawat (1986) showed that Wal-Mart deliberately targeted smaller southern towns that Wal-Mart's competitors found uninteresting. Wal-Mart would then enter with such a scale and product scope that effectively insulated Wal-Mart from competition. It is thus possible that first movers may derive superior performance not from gaining an early foothold in large and profitable geographical or product markets, but rather from secondary markets where preemption through scale is more likely (Robinson & Fornell, 1985; Ghemawat, 1986). Small markets will be associated with larger MES; consequently, a first mover is more likely to preempt entry in a small market.

> H2: The effect of first mover advantages will be stronger in small markets than in large markets.

Interaction effects. In recent years authors have adapted a contingent approach that includes interactions between entry timing and moderating variables (Cui & Lui, 2005). The choice of entry mode may be motivated by different preferences for risk, the industry structure or even government regulations. Previous literature has primarily focused on the difference between non-equity entry modes/equity based entry modes and timing/performance (Luo, 1998; Li, Lam, Karakowsky & Qian, 2003; Pan, Li & Tse, 1999). We examine the performance implications of different equity based entry modes. A partial acquisition may be a mean to acquire an option on important strategic assets early, while maintaining limited financial commitment. The choice of entry by a greenfield operation may result from the lack of sufficient quality takeover targets. This could mean that early mover advantages are more limited for firms or industries where greenfield operations are the predominant entry mode.

VanderWerf and Mahon (1997) suggested that research on FMA might suffer from a selection bias; ergo we cannot necessarily expect early mover advantages to be consistent across industries. Further, a part of the theoretical argument for FMA relies on preemption, which again is dependent on entry and exit barriers in the market. Since entry and exit barriers tend to differ from industry to industry it is therefore also likely that the advantage to early movers will differ. Finally, firms from different countries are likely to have different entry strategies (Chang, 1995), cultural influence (Li, Lam, Karakowsky & Qian, 2003) or even political good will (Chen & Pereira, 1999). Each of these factors may affect the firm's ability to capitalize on early mover advantages.

H3: The effect of timing varies across firms depending on the choice of entry mode, the industry and home country of the entrant.

THE SURVEY

The testing of early mover advantages requires a context in which new markets with distinct sub-market emerged roughly simultaneously, such that a fairly large number of firms would (potentially) enter this market–thus enabling the creation of a large dataset of early and late movers. Our analysis is based on such data, collected with a questionnaire survey of foreign owned firms in three CEE countries, Poland, Hungary and Lithuania.

The survey was conducted as a joint project in cooperation with a team of researchers in each of the three countries. The survey was administered by the local research teams in 2003. Where appropriate the survey was translated into local languages. The base population was derived from multiple sources and surveys were sent to the chief executive of firms where contact information was available. In most cases, this was followed up by phone contact and personal interviews to achieve a desired rate of response. Relative to the base population of all foreign investors, the sample includes approximately 10 percent for Poland and a higher proportion for Hungary and Lithuania.

The firms included were primarily established during the period 1990-2000 and had at least 10 employees and a foreign ownership participation of no less than 10%. This criterion was selected to eliminate administrative or representation offices and ensure that only fully operating firms are in the sample. The majority, 62 percent of the firms had reported that they had less than 100 employees in 2001, 31 percent reported between 100 and 1000 and the remaining 7 percent reported that they had more than 1000 employees. Our sample is broadly representative for both smaller and larger firms, which may have been a problem for previous studies based on the PIMS database (Szymanski, Troy & Bharadwaj, 1995).

We had 528 firms respond to the questionnaire. Of these 170 reported that their main activity is manufacturing, 49 financial services, 129 trade and distribution, 160 other services, 1 mining & extraction and 13 utilities. Segmented on host country, the sample includes 224 firms from Hungary, 200 firms from Poland and 104 firms from Lithuania. Of the firms in the sample 141 reported that the home country of the primary foreign investor was Germany, 80 from the Nordic countries, 60 from North America, 25 came from Central and Eastern European countries, 176 from other Western European countries, 22 from Asia and other countries, and 24 did not report the home country of the primary foreign investor.

The survey is cross-sectional and by nature contains only data on firms that were operating at the time of the survey. It is, therefore, not possible to control for survival bias, however in their Meta analysis VanderWerf and Mahon (1997) did not find that controlling for survival bias would change the likelihood of finding FMA. Others, however, retain the expectation that survival plays an important role for entry timing, Lieberman and Montgomery (1998) and Delios and Makino (2003) did find that being first increased the likelihood of exit. Consequently survival bias remains a limitation on our findings. With multiple countries in the sample, we can test for or rule out any country specific relationship between entry timing and performance, thus allowing a larger degree of generalization than most studies in the field.

Dependent Variables

Marketshare. As our dependent variable we will use the market share for 2001 for our first model. The market share measure is a percent measure where the range of observations is between $0 < Y \leq 100$. The market share is reported by the respondents[2] which means we do see a tendency towards approximations, e.g., 50% so there is some loss of accuracy.

However, for cross-sectional data with many industries/products it is most practical to rely on respondent supplied information. The average market shares (Table 1) are considerably larger than what Pan, Li and Tse (1999) and other China based studies report, which would be largely due to their decision to use the aggregated market share for all of

TABLE 1. Average Market Share Distributed on Host Country

Country	Average market share
Hungary	31,01
Poland	24,81
Lithuania	55,90
All Countries	31,50

China rather than the market share for the regions that the firms actually operate in.

Industry performance. The industry performance measure is a unique construct based on five different performance indicators of how the firm compares to its rivals. The scale for each of the performance indicators is a 5-point scale, where one indicates that the firm is among the weakest 20% in the industry and five that it is among the strongest. We use the average of the five items (Table 2) as our dependent variable. The construct has a Cronbach's Alfa of 0.9, suggesting the aggregation is reasonable. The advantage of the construct is that it will automatically weed out the part of performance that is attributable to differences across industries. We are then able to measure whether timing is related to perceived successful firms without the need for an excessive number of industry dummies. A potential problem is that there may not be at least five firms in the industry and therefore the respondents have some discretion in the choice of category. Another possible problem is that there may be a tendency to overrate own performance relative to rivals[3]; however, if this occurs consistently then it should only affect the level not the direction of a relationship.

Performance satisfaction. The last performance measure we will employ is a measure of the firms satisfaction with their performance compared to their original objectives. The variable is constructed from the average of three 7-point Likert scale items (Table 3), satisfaction with respectively productivity, profitability and revenue growth. A Cronbach's Alfa of 0.83 suggests that it is reasonable to aggregate the three items. Like the industry performance measure this measure is also comparable across industries and it has the added advantage that it should control for the relative inherent strength of the entrants. Stronger firms will have higher expectations and firms that are inherently weaker will adjust their expectations accordingly. Ideally this measure captures what is important to managers, the fulfillment of objectives.

TABLE 2. Variables Included in Industry Performance

Variable	N	Mean
After tax return on total assets	420	3,41
After tax return on total sales	421	3,41
Firm total sales growth	428	3,62
Productivity	410	3,76
Overall performance	426	3,70

TABLE 3. Variables Included in Performance Satisfaction

Variable	N	Mean
Productivity	479	5,15
Profitability	497	4,87
Revenue growth	493	5,11

Independent Variables

Timing. We use an order of entry construct to determine whether first movers have an advantage over followers. It is a sensible measure to capture the exclusive opportunities that the first movers possess. By his choice the first mover denies a choice to the follower regardless of how soon or late the follower moves. The surveyed firms were asked to state how many competitors were present in the market at the time of entry. The measure is a 5 point-scale where one is no competitors (first movers) and five is more than 10 competitors (late movers). The measure is cognitive neutral unlike PIMS based studies (Gaba, Pan & Ungson, 2002) consequently we find a much smaller ratio of first movers. We capture the order of entry effect by including dummies for category one to four leaving five as the base.

To test for early mover advantage we used the year of entry reported by the respondent, converted it by subtracting it from 2004 so we get the affiliates age. As a result a positive sign imply the existence of early mover advantages.

Small market. To test H2 that small markets should be more favorable for early movers, we use a country dummy for Lithuanian as a proxy for small markets. Our expectations are that early movers are more likely to preempt entry by rivals due to the limited market size. To capture this effect we include an interaction link between market time and the Lithuanian dummy.

Interaction effects. To test our hypothesis on the consistency of first mover advantages across groups, we use interaction links between the affiliate's age and the set of dummies for entry mode, industry and the investor's home country.

Controls. In addition, we include a number of control variables that are summarized in Table 4.

THE MODEL

We use an OLS regression analysis to estimate the relationship between the dependent variable and the independent variables. We then ran regressions for each of the dependent variables a number of times to systematically exclude insignificant control variables and get the best model fit. This was necessary to reduce the number of observations lost due to missing values in insignificant control variables. We found a best fit for each of the three dependent variables and for contrast we ran each of the three models with the three dependent variables. The base model for market share, industry performance and performance satisfaction are as follows:

$Y = \beta$ intercept $+ \beta$ order of entry $+ \beta$ age $+ \beta$ Lithuania*age $+ \beta$ first affiliate $+ \beta$ host market knowledge $+ \beta$ market knowledge Eastern Europe $+ \beta$ entry mode dummies $+ \beta$ low cost labor $+ \beta$ skilled labor $+ \beta$ tech $+ \beta$ human resources $+ \beta$ manufacturing*export intensity[4] $+ \beta$ local resources $+ \beta$ local industry $+ \beta$ no local industry $+ \beta$ host country dummies $+ \beta$ industry dummies $+ \beta$ home country dummies $+ \beta$ CEO $+ \varepsilon$.

Our sample contains both firms that mainly supply the local market, but also a reasonably large number of firms that focus mainly or even entirely on export markets. Since local market share is an irrelevant performance measure for these firms we have decided to exclude them from the analysis for market share. We have also excluded them from the analysis for industry performance because of uncertainties in terms of which industry they compare themselves to. Pan, Li and Tse (1999) corrected for the problem by excluding 22 export oriented industries. We have retained all firms which reported that they exported less than 90 percent of their total sales.[5] For the model for performance satisfaction we found that the variance tended to be larger for smaller firms and decreasing with firm size. To correct for this we ran the model as a WLS

TABLE 4. Control Variables

Group	Variable name	Description
Investment motives	Low cost labor Skilled labor Natural resources Strategic assets	How important access to the before mentioned was for the investment decision. The variables are 5 point Likert scales where 1 is not at all and 5 is very important.
Resources	Human resources Tech	Factor outputs, based on a number of 7 point Likert scale response variables. Human resources capture efforts expended on training and upgrading personnel in the host country. Tech is the availability of technological resources from the parent firm.
Entry Mode	Greenfield, Acquisition, Partial acquisition, Joint Venture	Dummies for the entry mode.
Export intensity	Manuf*export	Export in percent of total sales for the first year of operation for the manufacturing sector.
Advertising and technology	Advertising Technology	7 point scales on the foreign parents expenditure on Advertising and R & D. 1 is 0-0.5%. 7 is over 15%
International Scope and Scale	Worldwide employment (ln) Number of affiliates worldwide (ln)	Worldwide employment is the natural log of the parent company's worldwide employment. Number of affiliates worldwide is the natural log of the number of countries the parent has affiliates in.
Competitive Environment	Local industry Dumnolocal	The strength of the local industry at the time of entry compared to the respondent. Dumnolocal is a dummy for no local competitors
Home country dummies	Germany, Nordic, Other W. European, North American, CEEC, Asia	Dummies for the parent company's home country.
Respondent dummies	CEO, Expatriate, Employed with the parent company before current assignment.	To control for a possible bias derived from the status of the respondent we use three dummies. Whether the respondent is the CEO of the subsidiary. Whether the respondent is an expatriate and whether the respondent was employed by the parent company before his current position.
Standardized products	Standardized products	7 point Likert scale where 1 is not at all and 7 is to a large extent.
Source of Critical resources	Local resources	A 0-100 % scale for to what extent the 3 most critical resources for the firm were obtained from a local partner.
Industry dummies	Financial Services, Other services, Manufacturing, Utilities, Mining & Extraction, Trade	Dummies for the industry type.

with the natural log of the number of employees as the weight. The results are reported in Table 6.

Interaction effects. We introduce one set of interaction links into the three basic models at a time. We do this so we are able to report the impact on the explanatory power, adjusted R square, of the model when controlling for cross group differences. Furthermore this procedure limits a possible problem with multi-collinearity where too many variables attempt to explain the same thing, thus creating computational problems. The model design is,

Dependent variable$(Y1,Y2,Y3) = \beta$ intercept + base model $(x1,x2,x3) + \beta$ dum(1)*age $+ \beta$ dum(2)*age$\ldots \beta$ dum(n)*age $+ \varepsilon$

The results are reported separately in (Table 6) with three regressions for each dependent variable for a total of 9 regressions. The results from the interaction links in model I, II and III indicate the extent to which the relationship between affiliate age and a given group departs from the base group.

Missing values. We do experience a problem with missing values particularly for market share. In order to test whether there was an underlying response bias, we limited the samples for the other performance measures to the firms that actually reported market share. For the limited sample the results were not materially different from the full sample. The models joint explanatory power (adjusted R square) did not change materially nor did the direction and significance level of the independent variables. Consequently we decided to report the results for the full sample.

RESULTS[6]

Timing. In Table 5 we report the results of the three basic models. We find that Order of entry is positively and significantly associated with market share (Table 5). First movers enjoy approximately 31 percent point higher market share than late movers, whereas early followers could expect 26 percent point higher market share. These effects are considerably stronger than what especially the China based studies report. This difference is likely to be attributable to a tendency towards international market segmentation. Aggregating sales on all regions fail to account for the option that later entrants are in fact first movers in other regional markets. Order of entry does not appear to be strongly related

TABLE 5. Regression Analysis for the Three Models

	Modelmarketshare			Modelindustry			Modelperformance		
	Marketshare	Industry	Performance	Marketshare	Industry	Performance	Marketshare	Industry	Performance
(Constant)	-4,053	3,373***	4,488***	-5,876	3,276***	3,774	-32,003***	3,091***	3,156
	(10,627)	(0,306)	(0,420)	(14,563)	(0,350)	(0,507)	(12,150)	(0,323)	(0,416)
Order1	31,313***	0,249	-0,142	24,680***	0,151	-0,544**	23,284***	0,418***	0,095
	(6,322)	(0,180)	(0,242)	(7,250)	(0,169)	(0,244)	(6,176)	(0,158)	(0,196)
Order2	26,116***	0,056	0,183	24,764***	-0,013	-0,006	23,593***	0,141	0,230
	(5,648)	(0,159)	(0,221)	(5,822)	(0,141)	(0,207)	(5,725)	(0,143)	(0,189)
Order3	19,844***	0,267*	0,394*	15,768***	0,111	0,207	11,015**	0,160	0,473***
	(5,131)	(0,150)	(0,208)	(5,333)	(0,131)	(0,195)	(5,275)	(0,138)	(0,182)
Order4	13,785**	0,012	0,075	9,721	-0,191	-0,077	7,514	-0,019	0,014
	(5,891)	(0,168)	(0,227)	(6,273)	(0,147)	(0,212)	(6,370)	(0,152)	(0,205)
Age	-0,506	0,035*	0,056	-0,400	0,006	0,067***	0,585	0,032*	0,072***
	(0,675)	(0,020)	(0,026)	(0,752)	(0,018)	(0,025)	(0,6441)	(0,017)	(0,022)
lithuaniaLinkage	0,919	-0,120**	-0,167**	2,169	-0,088**	-0,126*	2,450	-0,095**	-0,153***
	(2,057)	(0,048)	(0,067)	(2,260)	(0,044)	(0,065)	(2,072)	(0,044)	(0,059)
Firstaffiliate	21,584***	0,201	0,075	21,072***	0,029	-0,096	23,937***	0,002	0,116
	(4,938)	(0,140)	(0,199)	(5,091)	(0,128)	(0,187)	(5,021)	(0,129)	(0,167)
Hostmarket—knowledge	9,672**	0,046	0,092	11,199**	-0,044	-0,050	16,367***	-0,120	0,051
	(4,467)	(0,130)	(0,180)	(4,731)	(0,119)	(0,171)	(4,572)	(0,120)	(0,152)
Marketknow—ledgeEE	-1,355	0,031	0,072	-2,350	-0,068	-0,010	-1,424	-0,033	0,007
	(3,614)	(0,103)	(0,144)	(3,998)	(0,095)	(0,140)	(3,712)	(0,094)	(0,125)
Acquisition	11,955**	0,008	-0,108	8,616	0,098	-0,163	6,632	-0,189	-0,230
	(5,249)	(0,141)	(0,199)	(5,499)	(0,124)	(0,184)	(4,824)	(0,121)	(0,161)
JV	6,519	-0,134	0,316	3,583	-0,014	0,340*	9,392*	-0,157	0,210
	(5,105)	(0,145)	(0,203)	(5,190)	(0,127)	(0,187)	(5,167)	(0,130)	(0,173)

	(1)	(2)	(3)	(4)	(5)	(6)	(7)	(8)	(9)
Part_Acq	8,357	−0,082	−0,472**	0,744	0,099	−0,341	9,843*	−0,008	−0,160
	(5,912)	(0,175)	(0,240)	(6,483)	(0,156)	(0,225)	(5,659)	(0,148)	(0,190)
Lowcostlabor	14,029***	−0,071	−0,164						
	(4,146)	(0,116)	(0,163)						
skilled labor							3,618*	0,023	0,187**
							(2,164)	(0,056)	(0,073)
Tech				0,739	0,086***	0,112***	5,053	0,309***	0,593***
				(1,214)	(0,029)	(0,041)	(4,106)	(0,110)	(0,141)
Humanresources				1,844	0,109**	0,139**	3,040	0,237***	0,183***
				(1,763)	(0,040)	(0,057)	(2,194)	(0,055)	(0,070)
Manuflinkexport	−0,288**	0,000	0,003						
	(0,096)	(0,003)	(0,004)						
Localresources	−0,138***	−0,001	−0,001						
	(0,046)	(0,001)	(0,002)						
Localindustry				−1,420	−0,103***	−0,039			
				(1,009)	(0,025)	(0,037)			
dumNolocal				−4,441	−0,735***	0,211			
				(9,456)	(0,234)	(0,320)			
Lithuania	29,317*	0,498	0,870	19,614	0,293	0,592	13,550	0,527	0,886*
	(15,278)	(0,368)	(0,507)	(16,633)	(0,341)	(0,493)	(16,590)	(0,347)	(0,460)
Hungary	8,690**	0,017	0,206	5,664	0,165	0,038	0,826	0,128	0,249*
	(4,199)	(0,125)	(0,173)	(4,791)	(0,117)	(0,171)	(4,357)	(0,113)	(0,150)
industrydummies*									
Homecountrydummies*									
Respondent dummy*									
N	219	282	314	215	281	313	235	302	343
F test of joint sig.	4,833***	1,600**	1,799***	3,182***	3,827***	3,330***	4,340***	3,453***	4,907***
Adjusted R Square	0,330	0,056	0,067	0,234	0,232	0,183	0,293	0,191	0,249

TABLE 6. Regressions Including Interaction Links

	Performance			Industry performance			Market share		
	I	II	III	I	II	III	I	II	III
Acq.	−0,506			0,070			16,968		
	(0,434)			(0,333)			(13,752)		
JV	0,660			−0,303			−1,210		
	(0,606)			(0,426)			(17,517)		
Part_Acq.	−1,132**			−0,070			4,246		
	(0,488)			(0,420)			(16,727)		
Utilities		−0,416			−1,876**			−24,633	
		(0,997)			(0,775)			(33,059)	
Fin serv.		0,815			1,113***			−35,020*	
		(0,505)			(0,412)			(17,765)	
Trade		0,410			−0,432			−3,852	
		(0,555)			(0,424)			(16,006)	
Other serv.		−0,647			−0,259			−6,185	
		(0,474)			(0,354)			(15,883)	
Nordic			0,109			0,237			−1,424
			(0,557)			(0,442)			(18,619)
Other W. Europe			0,669			1,179***			4,358
			(0,453)			(0,377)			(14,515)
CEEC			−0,657			0,093			21,634
			(0,886)			(0,661)			(26,595)
North A			0,036			0,685			11,792
			(0,698)			(0,511)			(21,801)
Asia and Other			1,311			0,726			39,904
			(0,905)			(0,713)			(24,394)
Age	0,042	0,060*	0,104***	−0,003	0,001	0,090***	−0,539	−0,543	−0,061
	(0,037)	(0,032)	(0,038)	(0,027)	(0,029)	(0,033)	(1,097)	(1,136)	(1,176)
Lithuania*age	−0,165***	−0,159***	−0,153**	−0,088**	−0,096**	−0,115**	1,057	0,441	1,617
	(0,059)	(0,059)	(0,065)	(0,044)	(0,044)	(0,050)	(2,081)	(2,195)	(2,361)

	(1)	(2)	(3)	(4)	(5)	(6)	(7)	(8)	(9)
JV*age	−0,049 (0,068)			0,034 (0,048)			0,910 (1,961)		
Acq*age	0,033 (0,050)			0,003 (0,038)			−0,555 (1,506)		
Part_acq*age	0,121** (0,056)			0,022 (0,051)			0,541 (1,936)		
Utilities*age		−0,014 (0,121)			0,189* (0,100)			1,496 (3,873)	
Finserv*age		−0,024 (0,056)			−0,117** (0,049)			1,671 (1,899)	
Trade*age		−0,028 (0,062)			0,051 (0,048)			−0,699 (1,747)	
Otherserv*age		0,094* (0,053)			0,031 (0,040)			−0,442 (1,724)	
AsiaAO*age			−0,193* (0,104)			−0,134 (0,082)			−4,390 (2,773)
CEEC*age			0,089 (0,120)			−0,041 (0,098)			−3,450 (3,809)
Nordic*age			−0,047 (0,066)			−0,058 (0,052)			−0,296 (2,191)
OtherWE*age			−0,067 (0,051)			−0,141*** (0,043)			0,242 (1,614)
NorthA*age			0,046 (0,073)			−0,087 (0,054)			−1,467 (2,279)
N	342	343	343	281	281	281	219	219	219
F test of joint sig.	4,737***	4,477***	4,437***	3,465***	4,014***	3,709***	4,332***	4,239***	4,197***
Adjusted R square	0.260	0.251	0.255	0.225	0.268	0.253	0.321	0.322	0.326

***p < 0.01. **p < 0.05. *p < 0.1.
Base greenfield, manufacturing, Germany

to performance, only one of the three models suggests that first movers experience statistically significantly superior performance. When we use performance satisfaction as dependent variable the relationship actually appears to be closer to an inverted U shape. Thus we can support both hypotheses 1a and 1b. We found no support that affiliate age should influence market share, the results were also very weak for industry performance in two of the models and insignificant in the primary model. However there was a positive and statistically significant relationship between affiliate age and performance satisfaction. Hypothesis 1c is thus partially supported.

Our results suggest that order of entry is important for acquiring market share, but order of entry as such is unrelated to profitability, productivity and revenue growth. When corrected for entrant quality we found some evidence of early mover advantages. This may suggest the existence of early mover advantages. Our findings suggest that early movers on average are more satisfied with their results, but they do not feel they do relatively better than other firms in their respective industries. This may suggest that early movers in CEE have been inherently weaker. Narasimham and Zhang (2000) suggested that weaker firms would tend to move early to overcome "laggard" disadvantages. Rivoli and Salorio (1996) also suggested that firms with strong firm specific resources, when faced with uncertainty, would tend to wait for uncertainty to be resolved. Here we would like to stress the geographical influence of our results though. It is possible that such a relationship is specific to CEE rather than a general rule. The OLI paradigm suggests that only firms with strong ownership advantages will internationalize in the first place. It is possible that the opening of CEE to FDI have encouraged a host of resource weaker firms that have had little previous international experience to enter. The opening of CEE has propelled firms with little internationalization experience to re-evaluate their "lack" of international commitment. In CEE, European companies in particular, have seen an opportunity to expand in less congested market that are still geographically and culturally close and, in no small part due to these countries' close association with the European Union, within an acceptable risk range. It is possible that the greater geographical and cultural distance that Western firms face when investing in Asia would naturally weed out resource-weak firms.

Small market effect. Our small market test between the Lithuanian dummy and market time was statistically insignificant though positive for market share. However, the interaction link was negative and significant for both industry performance and performance satisfaction in all the regressions indicating that the effect of timing is different for firms in Lithuania, though the direction was not as predicted. We can thus reject hypothesis two that timing related advantages are stronger in smaller markets. Our results may suggest that firms investing early in Lithuania are likely to have suffered comparatively more during the Russian crisis in the late 90's than early movers in Hungary and Poland. Liu (2005) suggest that FMA exist only when realized demand is close to expected demand.

Interaction effect. To test the contingent approach on early mover advantage we ran a number of regressions including interaction links between affiliate age and entry mode, industry group and home country (Table 7). For market share we found no statistically significant differences between any of the groups. Consequently there appears to be neither a general nor a conditional effect of affiliate age for market share.

For industry performance we found a considerable change in the explanatory power of the model when we included links between home countries and age, and especially for the links between industry group and age. Most markedly for the utility industry early entry appears to be positively associated with industry performance. This relationship does not persist when we use the corrected performance measure. This suggests that the observed relationship is primarily related to the relative quality of early entrants in the utility industry. Rivoli and Salorio (1996) suggested that well endowed firms would give up the option to wait when the country specific early mover advantages are high. Since utilities tend to be associated with natural or legal limitations on entry and the potential number of firms in the industry, this may explain the observed relationship. In a study of the international expansion of the telecom industry Sakar, Cavusgil and Aulakh (1999) found strong evidence that firms engage in a pursuit to preempt markets.

Early movers among financial service firms on the other hand seem to be associated with lower performance compared to the industry. Again when corrected for entrant quality the relationship does not persist. This may be explained by great difficulties in estimating credit worthiness, considerable amounts of bad debt to state owned and former state owned firms and possibly an unwillingness by the host countries to relinquish the option to interfere in strategically important industries. Consequently, uncertainty was high and preemption tends to be difficult for the financial service industry, suggesting that firms with strong ownership advantages would choose to postpone entry until uncertainties have been resolved. Conclusively, the advantage to enter

TABLE 7. Pearson Correlation Matrix

	X1	X2	X3	X4	X5	X6	X7	X8	X9	X10	X11	X12	X13	X14	X15	X16	X17	X18	X19	X20
X1 Orderofentry	1																			
X2 Age	-.063	1																		
X3 Firstaffiliate	-.089*	.123**	1																	
X4 Hostmarketknowledge	.083	-.047	-.451**	1																
X5 MarketknowledgeEE	.081	-.112*	-.099*	.050	1															
X6 GreenField	.011	-.014	.119**	-.054	008	1														
X7 Acquisition	-.019	-.051	-.165**	.074	-.011	-.487**	1													
X8 JV	-.047	.093*	.052	-.100*	-.042	-.456**	-.287**	1												
X9 Part. Acq	.062	-.030	.039	.107*	.056	-.321**	-.202**	.189**	1											
X10 Lowcostlabor	-.168**	-.053	.059	-.006	-.092*	-.017	.033	.071	-.113*	1										
X11 Skilledlabor	-.049	-.005	.050	.016	.023	-.037	.029	.031	-.022	.317**	1									
X12 Tech	-.041	.010	.043	.060	.079	.132**	.009	.079	-.112*	-.028	.047	1								
X13 Humanresource	-.038	.084	-.001	.101*	.148**	.070	.017	-.046	-.071	-.063	.087	.370**	1							
X14 % exp_fy	-.196**	-.121**	.056	-.026	-.140*	.025	.067	-.030	-.101*	.414**	.128**	.012	-.097	1						
X15 Localindustry	.254**	-.043	-.134**	.099*	.101*	-.117**	.093*	.024	.027	-.094*	-.078	-.160**	.104*	-.086	1					
x16 dumnoLocal	-.197**	-.013	.093*	-.045	-.152**	.050	-.049	.001	-.018	.078	.038	.108*	.027	.145**	-.748**	1				
X17 Localresources	.066	-.012	-.114*	.063	.069	-.430**	.268**	.130**	.155**	.010	.075	.017	.023	-.074	.067	-.012	1			
X18 Poland	.012	.083	-.043	.081	.022	.032	-.070	-.018	.071	-.103*	-.175**	.173**	.188**	-.151**	.022	-.093*	-.022	1		
X19 Lithuania	-.051	.256**	-.059	-.206**	.131**	-.040	.064	-.012	-.003	.030	.162**	.112*	-.240**	.105*	-.005	-.099*	-.019	-.387**	1	
X20 Hungary	.029	.124**	.090*	.087*	-.127**	.001	.017	.028	-.067	.076	.040	-.080	.007	.061	-.018	.170**	.037	-.670**	.425**	1

56

early may be fairly general, but the quality of early entrants will vary considerably depending on the particularities of the industry.

We tested whether entry mode was associated with performance, but our results where not conclusive. We found a tendency for greenfield operations to have lower market share, but the relationship was statistically weak across the models. Finally, we found some indication that the interaction between affiliate age and entry mode is associated with performance satisfaction.

Our results indicate that early movers amongst joint ventures tended to under perform compared to late movers. A likely explanation is that the use of the joint venture entry mode in the early 90's was motivated primarily by political or regulatory considerations. Consequently, these early movers are likely to have experienced considerable control problems due to incompatible partners. The joint ventures established later in the period are more likely to be motivated by resource/competency complementarities and the entry mode may then have a value adding property.

In the other end of the scale we have acquisitions and in particular partial acquisitions for which moving early is more strongly positively associated with performance. So we do observe a pattern between entry mode, affiliate age and performance. Entry modes that are associated with the acquisition/preemption of local assets are more sensitive to entry timing than other entry modes.

DISCUSSION AND CONCLUSION

In line with previous research we find a positive relationship between order of entry and market share (VanderWerf & Mahon 1997). However, we did not find a positive relationship between order of entry and performance. The results suggest that order of entry is likely to be a tradeoff between greater market share and risk or costs. In the most recent comparative study of performance measures, Cui and Lui (2005) found similar results based on a sample of Chinese firms. Consequently there is growing evidence that these results can be generalized. We did find a positive relationship between the affiliate's age and performance satisfaction. Our findings suggest the existence of early mover advantages. Early movers in emerging/transitional economies may benefit from incomplete markets for factor inputs such as, labor, location, assets, etc., and consequently gain Ricardian rent. However early movers are punished when faced with adverse economic conditions. This suggests that entry timing remains largely a tradeoff between risk and return. We also found that entry mode had a considerable moderating effect on the likelihood of finding an early mover advantage.

Overall our results suggest that the factors that explain performance vary considerably depending on how we measure performance. Order of entry, previous market knowledge and market size are all useful for explaining market share, but they are not very useful for explaining other measures for performance. Rather we found that the length of time the firm has been in the market, the firm's human resource activities and transfer of technology were determinants of firm performance.

Our findings suggest that more empirical studies on timing and performance is warranted, but with other performance measures than market share. Previous literature and the empirical results in this article suggest that endogeneity has a significant impact on the extent to which we observe timing related advantages. It is therefore clear that any attempt to control for the inherent strength of the entrants would also be a fruitful addition to FMA literature. It is possible that more studies that take account of survival would be a valuable addition to the field. However, exit is not necessarily failure and the magnitude of failure associated with exit is not always the same. The challenge will be to find a way to measure failure that takes account of these factors. There has only been a single attempt to study FMA and multiple international market entry (Mascarenhas, 1992), this is clearly an important aspect for the MNE and worthy of more studies. Finally, a key factor in empirical research is often to find an environment that is conducive to studying a specific relationship. We believe the environment and development of CEE are particularly conducive for FMA studies. We would like to urge others to take advantage of this opportunity, ideally by using a contingency approach that can tell us more about the link between firm strategy and FMA.

The managerial implication of our study is that managers should not rush to market in the hope of achieving advantages that may not materialize. Management should carefully consider whether the potential advantages are enduring. Evidence of superior market share for first movers is very strong, which suggest that firms that can leverage a high market share to improved performance may do well to pursue a first mover strategy. If this is not the case, it may often be better to adapt a wait and see or an early follower strategy. Results from recent studies may also be good news for firms that have not yet entered and are afraid they have forfeited their chance. The opportunities are still there!

NOTES

1. From 22 different articles.
2. The question asked was "Market share of the foreign investment in its main domestic market, in percent."
3. The average is higher than the expected 3, which might suggest systematic overestimation. It is quite possible that the exclusion of locally owned firms can account for the upward bias. (Sinani, 2004)
4. As export intensity is highest amongst manufacturing firms we include it as an interaction link.
5. At this level we feel the answers should be acceptable, the remaining part of the export bias is eliminated by including a control.
6. Table of Pearson Correlation is included in Table 7.

REFERENCES

Alpert, F. H., & Kamins, M. A. (1995). An empirical investigation of consumer memory, attitude, and perceptions toward pioneer and follower brands, *Journal of Marketing*, 59(4), 34-45.

Boulding, W., & Christen, M. (2003). Sustainable Pioneering advantage? Profit implications of market entry order, *Marketing Science*, 22(3), 371-392.

Chang, S. J. (1995). International expansion strategy of Japanese firms: Capability building through sequential entry, *Academy of Management Journal*, 38(2), 383-407.

Chen, HC., & Pereira, A. (1999). Product entry in international markets: the effect of country-of-origin on first mover advantage, *Journal of Product & Brand Management*, 8(3), 218-231.

Cui, G., & Lui, H. K. (2005). Order of entry and performance of multinational corporations in an emerging market: A contingent resource perspective, *Journal of International Marketing*, 13(4), 28-56.

Delios, A., & Makino, S. (2003). Timing of entry and the foreign Subsidiary performance of Japanese firms, *Journal of International Marketing,* 11(3), 83-105.

Dixit, A. (1979). The role of investment in entry deterrence, *Economic Journal,* 90(357), 95-106.

Doh, J. P. (2000). Entrepreneurial privatization strategies: Order of entry and local partner collaboration as sources of competitive advantage, *Academy of Management Review*, 25(3), 551-571.

Eaton, B. C., & Ware, R. (1987). A theory of market structure with sequential entry, *Rand Journal of Economics*, 18(1), 1-16.

Fudenberg, D., & Tirole, J. (1983). Capital as a commitment: Strategic investment to deter mobility, *Journal of Economic Theory*, 31(2), 227-250.

Gaba, V., Pan, Y., & Ungson, G. R. (2002). Timing of entry in international market: An empirical study of U.S. Fortune 500 firms in China, *Journal of International Business Studies*, 33(1), 39-55.

Gal-Or, E. (1985). First mover and second mover advantages, *International Economic Review*, 26(3), 649-653.

Ghemawat, P. (1986). Wal-Mart Stores, discount operations, Working paper Case No. 0-387-018, Harvard Business School.

Gilbert, R. J., & Harris, R. G. (1984). Competition with lumpy investment, *Rand Journal of Economics*, 15(2), 197-212.

Glazer, A. (1985). The advantage of being first, *American Economic review*, 75(3), 473-480.

Hirokawa, M., & Sasaki, D. (2001). Strategic choice of quantity stickiness and Stackelberg leadership, *Bulletin of Economic Research*, 53(1), 19-32.

Isobe, T., Makino, S., & Montgomery, D. B. (2000). Resource commitment, entry timing, and market performance of foreign direct investments in emerging economies: The case of Japanese international joint ventures in China, *Academy of Management Journal*, 43(3), 468-484.

Johnson, R. N., & Parkman, A. (1983). Spatial monopoly, non-zero profits and entry deterrence: The case of cement, *Review of Economics and Statistics*, 65(3), 431-438.

Judd, K. L. (1985). Credible spatial preemption, *Rand Journal of Economics*, 16(2), 153-166

Katz, M., & Shapiro, C. (1994). System competition and network effects, *Journal of Economic Perspectives*, 8(2), 93-115.

Li, J., Lam, K. C. K., Karakowsky, L., & Qian, G. (2003). Firm resources and first mover advantages: A case of foreign direct investment (FDI) in China, *International Business Review*, 12(5), 625-645.

Lieberman, M. B., & Montgomery, D. B. (1988). First-Mover advantages, *Strategic Management Journal*, 9, 41-58.

Lieberman, M. B., & Montgomery, D. B. (1998). First-Mover (dis)advantages: Retrospective and link with the Resource-Based View, *Strategic Management Journal*, 19(2), 1111-1125.

Liu, Z. (2005). Stackelberg leadership with demand uncertainty, *Managerial & Decision Economics*, 26(5), 345-350.

Luo, Y., & Peng, M. W. (1998). First mover advantages in investing in transitional economies, *Thunderbird International Business Review*, 40(2), 141-163.

Luo Y. (1998). Timing of investment and international expansion performance in China, *Journal of International Business Studies*, 29(2), 391-408.

Marinova, S. T., Marinov, M. A., & Yaprak, A. (2004). Market seeking motives and market related promises and actions in foreign direct investment privatization in Central and Eastern Europe, *Journal of East-West Business*, 10(1), 7-41.

Meyer, K. E., & Peng, M. W. (2005). Probing theoretically into Central and Eastern Europe: Transactions, Resources, and institutions, *Journal of International Business Studies*, 36(6), 600-621.

Mills, D. E. (1988). Preemptive investment timing, Rand Journal of Economics, 19(1), 114-122.

Nakata, C., & Sivakumar, K. (1997). Emerging market conditions and their impact on first mover advantages, *International Marketing Review*, 14(6), 461-485.

Narasimham, C., & Zhang, Z. J. (2000). Market entry strategy under firm heterogeneity and asymmetric payoffs, *Marketing Science*, 19(4), 313-327.

Pan, Y., Li, S., & Tse, D. K. (1999). The impact of order and mode of market entry on profitability and market share, *Journal of International Business Studies*, 30(1), 81-104.

Rivoli, P., & Salorio, E. (1996). Foreign direct investment under uncertainty, *Journal of International Business Studies*, 27(2), 335-357.

Robinson, W. T., & Fornell, C. (1985). Sources of market pioneer advantages in consumer goods industries, *Journal of Marketing research*, 22(3), 297-304.

Sakar, MB., Cavusgil, S. T., & Aulakh, P. S. (1999). International expansion of telecommunication carriers: The influence of market structure, network characteristics, and entry imperfections, *Journal of International Business Studies*, 30(2), 361-381.

Schmalensee, R. (1978). Entry deterrence in the ready to eat cereal industry, *Bell Journal of Economics*, 9(2), 305-327.

Schmalensee, R. (1982). Product differentiation advantages of pioneering brands, *American Economic Review*, 72(3), 349-365.

Sinani, E. (2004). The impact of foreign direct investment on efficiency, productivity growth, and trade: An empirical investigation, Copenhagen Business School, PhD Series 21.

Spence, M. (1977). Entry, capacity, investment and oligopolistic pricing, *Bell Journal of Economics*, 8(2), 534-544.

Stackelberg, v H. (1934). Marktform und Gleichgewicht. Wien/Berlin.

Szymanski, D., Troy, L., & Bharadwaj, S. (1995). Order of entry and business performance: An empirical synthesis and reexamination, *Journal of Marketing*, 59(4), 17-33.

VanderWerf, P. A., & Mahon, J. F. (1997). Meta-analysis of the impact of research methods on findings of first-mover advantage, *Management Science*, 43(11), 1510-1519.

doi:10.1300/J097v13n01_03

Internationalization
of the Biggest Finnish and Swedish Retailers
in the Baltic States and Russia

Jorma Larimo
Ari Huuhka

SUMMARY. The political changes, together with the economic growth, have made the Eastern European emerging markets increasingly attractive for international retailers. This article analyzes why, where, when and how the eastward expansion of the biggest Finnish and Swedish retailers has taken place. This article focuses on the international behavior of five case companies from both the food and non-food sectors. The article shows that the case companies have expanded first, from their small and saturated domestic markets, to culturally and geographically close target markets. Furthermore, their internationalization has developed from less intensive operation modes towards more intensive modes. The case companies display a great variation in the market and operation strategies used to enter the four target markets. There are also great differences in the present and planned future operations in the Baltic States and Russia. The article proposes managerial and research implications based on the key findings. doi:10.1300/J097v13n01_00 *[Article copies available for a fee from The Haworth Document Delivery Service: 1-800-HAWORTH. E-mail address:*

Jorma Larimo is Professor of International Marketing, University of Vaasa, Department of Marketing, P.O. Box 700, FIN-65101 Vaasa, Finland (E-mail: jorma.larimo@uwasa.fi). Ari Huuhka is Senior Researcher, University of Vaasa, Department of Marketing, P.O. Box 700, FIN-65101 Vaasa, Finland (E-mail: ari.huuhka@uwasa.fi).

[Haworth co-indexing entry note]: "Internationalization of the Biggest Finnish and Swedish Retailers in the Baltic States and Russia." Larimo, Jorma, and Ari Huuhka. Co-published simultaneously in *Journal of East-West Business* (The Haworth Press, Inc.) Vol. 13, No. 1, 2007, pp. 63-91; and: *Market Entry and Operational Decision Making in East-West Business Relationships* (ed: Jorma Larimo) The Haworth Press, Inc., 2007, pp. 63-91. Single or multiple copies of this article are available for a fee from The Haworth Document Delivery Service [1-800-HAWORTH, 9:00 a.m. - 5:00 p.m. (EST). E-mail address: docdelivery@haworthpress.com].

<docdelivery@haworthpress.com> Website: <http://www.HaworthPress.com>
© *2007 by The Haworth Press, Inc. All rights reserved.]*

KEYWORDS. Retailing, internationalization, market strategy, operation strategy, the Baltic states, Russia, Finnish and Swedish retailers

INTRODUCTION

The amount and the variety of forms of international retail operations have increased during the past decades when global retailers from the US and Europe have expanded their network of stores to new international markets (e.g., Dawson, 1994, 2001; Dawson & Lee, 2004; Deloitte, 2006). Recently, there is also an increasing number of smaller retailers have taken part in international retail alliances and international sourcing. So far the main focus of the retailers' international activities has been on the OECD countries. Nevertheless, in last ten years the Asian and Eastern European countries have become more attractive as target markets. The political and economic changes in the 1990s, especially the expansion of the European Union eastwards, have increased the attractiveness of the Central Eastern European and Eastern European markets to the international retailers (e.g., Nagy, 2002; Esbjerg, 2002; Robinson, 1997). Particularly, Russia's attractiveness as a target market has increased significantly the past ten years.

The present article examines the international behavior of the biggest Finnish and Swedish retailers in the Baltic and Russian markets. In more detail, the goal of this article is to analyze what has motivated them to expand to these markets, and what market and operation strategies they have used in their market entries and in their later development. The foreign direct investments and other international activities of manufacturing firms have been subject of academic research for decades. Recently scholars are increasingly interested in analyzing the different aspects of retail internationalization such as the location attractiveness (Ghauri, Elg & Sinkovics, 2004) and retailers' market orientation (Rogers, Ghauri & George, 2005). Moreover, there is a growing number of studies examining the retailing and the retail internationalization in Central Eastern European and Eastern European markets (e.g., Drtina, 1995; Ghauri & Holstius, 1996; Myers & Alexander, 1997; Burt, Dawson & Sparks, 2004; Rogers, Ghauri & Langaard, 2005; Roberts, 2005). However, besides Roberts (2005), analyzing the performance of the French retailer Auchan in the Russian market, there is no other comprehensive scholarly research on the international behavior of big western retailers in the Baltic States and Russia. Thus far, only some research has dealt with the internationalization of Nordic retailers (e.g. Johannson, 2003; Lindblom & Rimstedt, 2004). Nevertheless, none of the studies has analyzed the Finnish and Swedish retailers' activities in the Baltic and Russian markets.

The structure of the rest of the article is as follows. The second section reviews studies on the motives for retail internationalization, and the market and operation strategies. The third section provides an overview of retailing in the Baltic States and Russia. The fourth section focuses on analyzing the market and operation strategies used by the case companies in their eastward expansion. The final section summarizes the key findings, presents managerial implications and offers suggestions for further research.

RETAIL INTERNATIONALIZATION

Most of the literature on retail internationalization has focused on three issues: (1) why retailers internationalize their operations (why), (2) the choice of target country (where), and (3) the methods of entry (how). These questions–applied to the Baltic and Russian context–are also the main issues in this article.

Motives for Retail Internationalization

There are several types of stimuli and/or motives for retail internationalization and they can be classified in many different ways. An often used classification not only in the international retailing literature, but also more generally in the international business literature, divides these motives into push and pull factors (e.g., Treadgold, 1990; Alexander, 1990, 1995; McGoldrick & Fryer, 1993; McGoldrick, 1995; Dawson, 1994, 2001; Moore & Fernie, 2005). The push factors are motives which encourage the firm to internationalize its operations or even make it imperative, as a result of environmental or company-specific conditions in the domestic market (for example small size, saturation, low or declining economic growth). The pull factors are motives which concern foreign markets as attracting retailers to internationalize their operations. These factors include for example the size of the market, the speed of the market growth, the underdeveloped retail structure, and the low prices for land and labor.

In 2004, among the 250 biggest retailers in the world, 148 companies (60 %) had international operations. The retailers operating only in domestic markets were mainly originating from countries with a big domestic market (USA and Japan) (Deloitte, 2006).

Typically of both Finland and Sweden is that they are Nordic countries with highly developed markets. Besides, they both have a rather small population, a low population growth and a high standard of living. The two countries became members of the European Union in 1995. The domestic retail markets are in many ways similar in Finland and Sweden. In both countries, especially food retailing is concentrated and dominated by large retail groups (Table 1). The leading companies have remained the same since the late 1990s. The relatively small and stable domestic markets offer only limited growth opportunities for the leading companies.

Considering the abovementioned motives for retail internationalization, the behavior of the companies can be reactive or proactive. The reactive behavior is based on negative factors caused by the lack of or limited opportunities in the domestic market (for instance small size or saturation). The common view is that retailers seek to satisfy first the demand in the familiar domestic market before they start to consider the expanding possibilities in unfamiliar foreign markets. In the case of proactive behavior, companies actively seek for foreign opportunities, for example before the saturation of domestic markets. Typically, the retailers' foreign operations are not motivated by a single factor but a

TABLE 1. Characteristics of the Finnish and Swedish Food Retailers' Domestic Markets

Finland		Sweden	
Population (millions) 2005	5,2	Population (millions) 2005	9,0
Company/market share (%) in food retailing (2004)		Company/market share (%) in food retailing (2002)	
K Group	35,3	ICA	43,9
S Group	34,3	COOP	22,4
Tradeka	10,0	Axfood	22,7
Spar	6,8	Bergendahls	2,9
Other	13,6	Other	8,1

Compiled by Kauppalehti Extra, 2005; Daunfeldt, Orth & Rudholm, 2005.

combination of several factors, including both pull and push type of motives (e.g., Robinson, Foot & Clarke-Hill, 2000).

According to the OLI-paradigm (e.g., Dunning, 1980, 1993), the company has to have ownership specific advantages to compensate the liability of foreignness. These may be asset-based advantages or transaction-based advantages. In retailing, the asset-based advantages may result from, for instance, innovatory products, retail formats (and based on them, a strong retail brand). Transaction-based advantages may come about because of the way things are done (for example the economies of scale in production, marketing and/or the distribution or the efficiencies due to centralized chain management) (e.g., Sternquist, 1997).

Market Strategy

According to the OLI-paradigm (Dunning, 1980, 1993) the target country/ies should have some location advantages (i.e. pull factors). These include elements like (Dunning, 1980, 1993; Sternquist, 1997): (1) cultural distance/proximity, (2) geographic distance/proximity, (3) market size, (4) market growth, (5) low cost of land and labor, and (6) level of competition/competitors' moves.

The closer the potential target country is culturally, the more similar the values, tastes and the consumer behavior in general are to be expected. Also, the more similar the cultures are, the easier the management of the workforce, subcontractor networks etc., may be. Similarly, the shorter the geographic distance, the lower the transportation costs, the easier contacts to the foreign units, etc. According to the Uppsala model, companies start their foreign operations from culturally and/or geographically close countries and expand gradually to more distant markets (e.g., Johanson & Vahlne, 1977, 1990). In the manufacturing sector however, there are companies that do not necessary follow this stepwise development related to the market and operation strategies. Most of these companies have operated in the high tech sector. Although there is some evidence on this kind of international behavior (e.g., Rialp, Rialp & Knight, 2005), most of the empirical research support the Uppsala model. Also studies on the internationalization of retailing seem to indicate that retailers have often followed the type of market strategy proposed by the abovementioned model (e.g., Evans, Treadgold & Mavondo, 2000; Robinson, Foot & Clarke-Hill, 2000). Nevertheless, there are however examples showing that all retailers do not necessarily locate first to geographically and culturally close countries. For instance, the British fashion retailer Paul Smith entered first into the Japanese market, before its successful operations in UK and elsewhere in Europe (Moore & Fernie, 2005).

Among the 250 world biggest retailers in 2004, a total of 53 were operating in the Central Eastern European market; eight of them in the Baltic States and twelve of them in Russia. Nearly 70 % of the companies operating in these markets were from France, Germany, and the UK (Deloitte, 2006). Only two of the companies in these markets were non-European retailers. Among them, 17 operated in one, 18 in two or three, and other 18 in four or more (three even in at least 10) Central Eastern European and/or Eastern European countries (Deloitte, 2006). For instance, for German retailers the most common target countries have been Hungary, Poland and Czech Republic, that are culturally and geographically close to Germany (Robinson, Foot & Clarke-Hill, 2000).

From the viewpoint of both cultural and geographic closeness, the Baltic States and Russia have several major advantages as target markets for the Finnish and Swedish retailers (Table 2). Based on the dimensions of culture by Hofstede (1980, 2001) and the formula developed by Kogut and Singh (1988), the cultural distance between Finland and Estonia is very short (0,08) and between Finland and Russia moderate (2,59). In the case of Sweden the respective distances are somewhat longer (0,89 and 4,75). The Finnish and Swedish retailers benefit also from the geographic closeness of the Baltic States and the St. Petersburg and Moscow areas in Russia.

In addition to the cultural similarities, the market size and the market growth are also highly important in the retailing. The greater the market size, for example the total population, the size of some segment of the population, and/or the higher the growth rate of population, the buying power, or some segment of the population, the more attractive the target country becomes. Russia's population is the biggest at European level, and there are in the St. Petersburg and Moscow areas more people than in whole Finland (in the Moscow area also more than in Sweden). In general the economic level in Russia is not as high as in Finland and Sweden, but there is higher number of very wealthy people (millionaires) in the St. Petersburg area than in Finland. Besides, the size of the middle class is increasing all the time. The economic growth rate in the Baltic States and Russia has been higher than the European Union's average and this trend is expected to continue (e.g., EBRD, 2005).

Retailers can also have location advantages based on low costs of land and labor. The lower these costs are, the more attractive the country is as a target market. However, the foreign company has to evaluate the possibilities to use the land, the labor productivity/effectiveness, and

TABLE 2. The Baltic States and Russia as Target Countries to Finnish and Swedish Retailers

	Estonia	Latvia	Lithuania	Russia
Cultural distance				
Finland	very short	short	short	moderate
Sweden	short	moderate	moderate	great
Geographic distance				
Finland	very short	moderate	moderate	short[a] to moderate[b]
Sweden	short	short	short	moderate[b]
Population (millions) 2004[c]	1,4	2,3	3,4	144,9
GDP per capita (USD)[c]				
1998	4 036	2 757	3 137	1 802
2004 (estimate)	8 314	5 827	6 454	4 012
Growth in real GDP (%)[c]				
1998	4,4	4,7	7,3	−5,3
2004 (estimate)	7,8	8,5	6,7	7,1
Land and labor cost	moderate	low	low	low to high[b]
Level of competition	moderate	low	moderate	low to moderate[b]
Year of EU membership	2004	2004	2004	-

Note: [a]St. Petersburg; [b]Moscow. [c]Compiled by EBRD, 2005.

the image, networks, and contracts of the local units. Except for Moscow, the cost of land is lower than in the Western European countries. The labor costs are also lower, but there is a greater need to train the local employees that do not have prior experience in modern retail formats.

In general, the lower the level of competition by domestic and foreign competitors, the more attractive the market is. In the Baltic States and Russia the competition has been at a low to moderate level during the past ten years, but the competition is increasing. There has been a lot of discussion on the first-mover vs. late-mover advantages and disadvantages (e.g., Lieberman & Montgomery, 1988; Denstadli, Lines & Grønhaug, 2005; Jakobssen, 2006). The first-mover advantages can concern for example potential joint venture partners and retail spaces. Thus especially for operations demanding bigger spaces, the first-mover advantages may be significant, because there may not be so many prime retail sites available for later entrants. However, for operations demanding only smaller retail spaces the first-mover advantages and the problems for being a late-mover are not necessarily so significant (Sternquist, 1997).

Operation Strategy

There are several different possibilities for the companies to realize their internationalization (e.g., Dawson, 1994; McGoldrick, 1995). The main modes include (1) a general cooperation type of operation (e.g., cooperation in buying), (2) non-controlling interest, (3) franchising, (4) joint venture, (5) acquisition (including merger or takeover), and (6) self-start entry (internal expansion). The resources needed for the realization, the costs, the risks, and the possibilities for control vary according to these modes. Traditional exports, general cooperation and non-controlling modes do not demand so many managerial and financial resources, and the risks and costs are relatively low, but they do not provide any intensive operations in the target country or a tighter control of the operations. Both self-start entries and acquisitions require more resources and the risks and the costs are higher, but these modes provide a more intensive market entry and a tighter control of the operations, as well as a better market information.

According to the Uppsala model, the internationalization of companies develops from less intensive operation modes towards more intensive ones. The model assumes that the development follows the less intensive to the more intensive chain also at the target country level. There may be exceptions when: (1) the target markets are very homogenous, (2) there are restrictions for the step-wise progress/limitations for the use of some modes (e.g., very high import barriers/tariffs), and (3) the company has already gained a lot of international experience and has a lot of management and financial resources (e.g., Johanson & Vahlne, 1990). Depending on the target markets, the companies may use more than one type of the foreign operation as they developed the scale of the internationalization. For instance, the British retailer Marks & Spencer has used several entry modes in its international expansion in Europe, North America and Asia (Dawson, 1994).

Besides the target country specific factors, there are also some other aspects that may influence the choice of a certain operation strategy (e.g., Dawson, 1994, 2001). First, many of the non-food formats are small and require limited capital and managerial cost for their establishment. Therefore the entry and also the exit are relatively easy. Furthermore, non-food formats are often well suited to franchising. Additionally, the choice of the operation mode can also be affected by the market position of the retail brand and the retail format. A strong premium brand might lead to a global approach through internal expansion or tightly controlled franchising. Additionally, a retailer operating on large-scale formats can be expected to use a multinational approach with joint ventures and possibly a takeover form of foreign operations.

All the main modes are possible in the Central Eastern European and Eastern European markets. There are examples showing that the international retailers have entered into these markets by the means of the aforementioned modes (e.g., Myers & Alexander, 1997; Perkins, 2001; Higgins, 2001; Dawson, 2001; Planer, 2005; Rogers, Ghauri & George, 2005). In general, the food retailers have used mainly self-start entries, acquisitions and joint ventures when opening their hypermarkets in these markets, whereas franchising has been used by companies operating in the non-food sectors, especially in clothing retailing. For instance, Tesco's (British retailer) entries into Hungary, Poland, the Slovak and Czech Republic has taken place with acquisitions (Rogers, Ghauri & George, 2005).

OVERVIEW OF RETAILING IN THE BALTIC STATES AND RUSSIA

In the 1990s many political and economic changes have been transforming the formerly state-owned centrally planned Baltic and Russian economies. As a part of these processes, in the Baltic States the liberalization caused an increase in the number of retail businesses, to increase when individuals established small one-shop retail enterprises. Since mid 1990s the total number of retail outlets has declined (Kielyte, 2002a, 2002b; Semionoviene, 2003). In the much larger Russian market both the penetration of modern formats and the level of competition are still at a relatively lower level than in the Baltic States. Although retailing in the Baltic States and Russia has became more competitive and international, due to the introduction of efficient modern formats by international and domestic retailers, the majority of goods are still distributed through traditional forms of retailing such as marketplaces, kiosks and other small-scale retail outlets (e.g., Kielyte, 2002a; Esbjerg, 2002; IGD, 2004).

Still, in the mid 1990s the European food retailers considered Russia as highly unfavorable target market for their expansion (Myers & Alexander, 1997). In ten years (1995-2005) the situation has totally changed and Russia has become one of the most attractive emerging markets. This can be seen in the ranking done by A.T. Kearney (Table 3) which is based on the economic and political risks, the level of retail saturation, and the differences between GDP growth and retail growth. In the aforementioned ranking, Latvia came sixth and Lithuania seventeenth. Only Estonia was not among the top 30 emerging markets.

However, the retail concentration in Estonia is the highest among the Eastern European countries. In 2003 Estonia, with its duopoly retail markets, belonged to the highest concentration category together with Lithuania, Slovenia, and Hungary (Juhász & Stauder, 2005). Since the mid 1990s the Estonian markets have become increasingly competitive (e.g., Kielyte, 2002a): there are more international retailers and they have a stronger position than in the other Baltic countries. International companies like VP Market, Rimi (Rimi Baltic) and S Group compete with the domestic retailers such as Selver and Kaupamaja (e.g., Deloitte, 2006). The competition is likely to intensify since the German Schwarz Group (Lidl chain) has announced its plans to open stores at least in the capital city.

The retail markets in Latvia have developed in a very short time from non-concentrated markets (in 1998) towards an asymmetric oligopoly (in 2003) (Juhász & Stauder, 2005). Among the Eastern European countries, Latvia belongs to the middle concentration category together with Croatia, and Czech Republic. The market leader in food retailing is the Lithuanian company VP Market that entered Latvia in 2001 (Semionoviene, 2003). Other main retailers include Rimi (Rimi Baltic) and the domestic retailers Mego and Nelda (e.g., USDA, 2003; WARC, 2004; Semionoviene, 2003).

In Lithuania, the retail concentration is the highest in the Baltic countries (in 2003) (e.g., Juhász & Stauder, 2005). This is due to the dominant market position of the domestic multiformat retailer VP Market.

TABLE 3. Top Emerging Markets in A.T. Kearney's Global Retail Development Index

Country	2005 rank	2004 rank	2003 rank	1995 rank
India	1	2	5	16
Russia	2	1	1	19
Ukraine	3	11	20	-
China	4	3	3	14
Slovenia	5	4	14	27
Latvia	6	6	19	-
. . .	. . .	. . .	. . .	. . .
Lithuania	17	17	-	-

Source: Adapted from A.T.Kearney, 2003, 2004, 2005.

The company started its activity in 1992 and has since then expanded also to other Baltic markets and gained the leading position there (e.g., Semionoviene, 2003; WARC, 2004). Other domestic retailers include Palink, Norfos Mazmena (Norfa) and Aibe (PWC, 2004; WARC, 2004). However, there are still fewer international retailers in Lithuania than in the other Baltic markets. The main international retailer in the food retail sector is Rimi (Rimi Baltic).

Several studies (e.g., IGD, 2004; A.T. Kearney, 2005) indicate that there is a window of opportunity for the international retailers in Russia due to a low competitive environment with low store densities, low consolidation levels, low levels of non-food sales, and low grocery expenditures per capita. The Russian retail markets are highly heterogeneous and fragmented due to regional differences. For instance the Moscow area alone accounts for nearly one third of the total national retail sales (PWC, 2005a).

It is estimated that in Russia, there are about 330000 food retailers and 90000 non-food retailers (IGD, 2004). Russia's grocery market is the fifth largest in Europe (worth nearly 112 billion USD) (ibid.); but by the year 2020 it is expected to become the largest in Europe (worth nearly 450 billion USD) (Szaleniec, 2005). According to some estimations, the food retail sector is growing 15 % per year and the combined food and non-food sector up to 8 % per year (e.g., Roberts, 2005). Food retailing is dominated by traditional forms of retail businesses such as open markets, kiosks and pavilions. In 2003 in the food retailing sector only 0,5 % of food stores were modern formats (IGD, 2004); thus the share of modern formats is clearly lower in Russia than in general in the Central Eastern European markets.

Large international retailers began to enter into Russia in the 1990s. One of the earliest entrants was the Turkish retailer Mikros Turk (Ramstore) with its hypermarket and supermarket formats. It is one of the few international retailers who survived the Russian economic recession in the late 1990s (e.g., IGD, 2004). After the economic crisis the number of modern formats has increased since Russia's domestic retailers have also began to operate the modern chain type of retail businesses. The leading domestic companies like Pyaterochka, Perekriostok and Sedmoy Continent are modern multiformat retailers (Table 4). International competition has increased in Russia since 2001 after the entries of large European retailers, such as Spar, Metro, and Auchan.

TABLE 4. Major Domestic and International Food Retailers in Russia

Company	Stores 2002	Stores[a] 2004	Sales[b] 2002	Sales[a,b] 2004	Formats
Domestic					
Pyaterochka (Agrotorg)	135	370	540	830	discount, hypermarket
Magnit (Tander)	250	330	230	400	discount
Perekriostok	46	80	340	700	hypermarket, supermarket, discount, cvs
Kopeika (Felma)	27	75	200	400	discount, supermarket
Sedmoy Continent	31	71	301	650	supermarket
Petrovsky	32	53	120	200	supermarket
Paterson	16	46	85	300	supermarket, shopping centre
Lenta	3	8	60	200	hypermarket
Dorinda	2	5	80	150	hypermarket
International/year of entry					
Mikros Turk (Ramenka) (T)/1997	15	35	273	650	hypermarket, supermarket
Spar (NL)/2001	9	26	30	95	supermarket
Metro (G)/2001	3	16	287	950	cash & carry
Auchan (FR)/2002	2	6	237	750	hypermarket
Edeka (Ava) (G)/2003	-	2	-	110	hypermarket
Rewe (G)/2004	-	14	-	n/a	supermarket

Note: [a]estimates; [b]million USD. [c]includes Spar Middle Volga.
Compiled by IGD, 2004; Rewe, 2006; Roberts, 2005; PWC, 2004, 2005a, 2005b

THE CASES OF FINNISH AND SWEDISH RETAILERS' INTERNATIONAL ACTIVITIES IN THE BALTIC AND RUSSIAN MARKETS

The selection of the cases was primarily based on the list of the 250 biggest global retailers ranked by their group sales in USD in 2004 (Deloitte, 2006). There were two Finnish–K Group/Kesko (95) and S Group (101)–and five Swedish companies–IKEA (44), Coop Norden (54), ICA (70), Hennes&Mauritz (93), and Axfood (180)–in the list (their rank order in brackets). Only four of the aforementioned companies operated in 2004-2005 in the Baltic States and/or Russia: K Group, S Group, IKEA, and ICA. In addition to these companies, also the Finnish retailer Stockmann was selected, due to its pioneering role in the Russian markets. Also other major Finnish and Swedish retailers' international activities were examined, but these retailers either had no or very limited activities in the Baltic States and Russia. Data used in the case descriptions is based on the annual reports and web sites of the companies and other information that has been published in the business magazines during 1995-2005.

The Finnish Retailers

Stockmann

Stockmann (established in 1862) is Finland's leading department store retailer. In Finland, it also operates in the book and clothing retailing and in the mail order business. In 2002 the company's sales were nearly 1880 million USD and in 2004 over 2060 million USD (Stockmann, 2006).

Stockmann is the pioneer both in international retailing and in trade with Russia. Its internationalization has taken place gradually. Starting from the 1950s the company had exports to the Soviet Union where the main target groups were the western diplomats and businessmen and their families. Later in 1989 the company opened its first specialty grocery store in Moscow (Table 5). Soon it had a total of five specialty stores in Russia (Seristö, 2003). The financial performance of these stores was, however, rather weak, and in the mid 1990's the company registered severe losses (ibid.). The end of the 1990's was an especially difficult period for the company, as well as to other international retailers, because of Russia's economic crisis which began in August 1998. Most of the international retailers left the Russian market, but Stockmann opted to stay because of the heavy investments in the opening of its first full-size department store in Moscow in 1998 (ibid.).

In the early 2006 Stockmann had seven department stores in Finland. The company's flagship store in Helsinki is the sixth largest department store in Europe on the basis of its annual sales (Taloussanomat, 2004). The company's decision to enter into Russia with its department store format proved out to be the right one. Although the company has faced problems in its operations (mainly bureaucracy, and the difficulties and surprises in the operating environment), it has become during the years the leader in the department store sector (e.g., Taloussanomat, 2004). Stockmann has three department stores in Russia, all of them in Moscow. They are targeted to the middle class and lower upper class consumer segments. The company is one of the pioneers in adopting customer loyalty programs in Russia. Already about 150000 customers have joined the programs. These customers account for half of the com-

TABLE 5. Stockmann's Internationalization in the Baltic States and Russia

Country/chain	Year	Entry mode	Sector	Stores
Estonia				
Hobby Hall	1992	self-start	mail order	1[a]
Stockmann department store	1996	self-start	dep. store	1[a]
Seppälä	1999	self-start	clothing	14[a]
Latvia				
Stockmann department store	1996	self-start	dep. store	1[a]
Hobby Hall	2001	self-start	mail order	-
Seppälä	2003	self-start	clothing	8[a]
Lithuania				
Hobby Hall[c]	2002	self-start	mail order	-
Seppälä	2005	self-start	clothing	3[a]
Russia				
Specialty grocery store	1989	self-start	food	2[a]
Stockmann department store	1998	self-start	dep. store	3[a]
Zara	2003	franchising	clothing	7[b]
Seppälä	2004	self-start	clothing	6[a]
Bestseller	2004/2005	franchising	clothing	6[a]
Outlet	2005	self-start	non-food	1[a]

Note: [a]in 2006; [b]in 2005. [c]divested in 2005.
Compiled by Kehittyvä Kauppa, 2005; Seristö, 2003; Stockmann, 2005; Taloussanomat, 2005b.

pany's department store sales (Taloussanomat, 2006). In St. Petersburg the company operates two smaller Stockmann stores. The company has also one department store in Estonia and one in Latvia. The entry into these markets with the department store format took place in 1996.

As a part of its multiformat business, Stockmann's Hobby Hall is Finland's largest mail order retailer. Stockmann's internationalization in the Baltics started in 1992 in Estonia with the Hobby Hall mail order concept. In 2001 the company expanded these operations to Latvia, and in 2002 to Lithuania (however, divested in 2005).

Stockmann has international operations also in the clothing sector (Table 5). These operations started in Eastern Europe with the opening of the Seppälä clothing store in Estonia in 1999. Since then, the company has expanded its Seppälä chain into Latvia, Lithuania and Russia, and two other clothing chains, Zara and Bestseller into Russia. In the case of Zara and Bestseller stores, the franchising has been used both as an entry mode and as an effective expansion strategy. Stockmann operated Zara stores (of the Spanish company Inditex) as a franchise based first in Finland, and starting in Russia in 2003. In late 2005, there were already seven profitably operating Zara stores in premium locations in Russia. The Zara chain has been successful in Russia since the brand is highly valued among wealthy, fashion conscious consumers. The agreement with Inditex gave Stockmann exclusive rights to run Zara stores in Russia until 2010. In January 2006 however, Stockmann had to give up the Zara operations in Russia. Inditex wanted to anull the franchising agreement, and to control directly its successful chain. In 2004 Stockmann signed a cooperation agreement with the Danish company Bestseller that owns several fashion brands: Vero Moda, Only, and Jack & Jones. The first Bestseller store was opened in Moscow in 2005 (Stockmann, 2006).

In addition to these, in Russia Stockmann is cooperating with the Swedish IKEA. In Moscow they are both located in the same shopping centre premises that are owned by IKEA. In the future also other IKEA's Mega Malls that have been planned to be built in other major Russian cities could provide good locations for Stockmann department stores (e.g., Taloussanomat, 2005b).

The key success factor for Stockmann's expansion primarily in Russia but also in the Baltic States is that the company has gained, during the years, a good understanding of both the risks and the opportunities of the target markets. Furthermore, the company has adopted a straightforward management style that is needed to carry out its operation strategies in these highly dynamic markets, especially in Russia.

Moreover, Stockmann is greatly benefiting from the cooperation with IKEA: it is more flexible to work with the Swedish company than with local partners. Stockmann plans to get the majority of its future growth in the Russian and Baltic markets. The strategic objective is to get one third of the total sales from these markets by the end of 2008 (Stockmann, 2006). To reach this goal, a new department store and shopping centre complex in St. Petersburg is scheduled to be opened in 2008.

The S Group

The Finnish retailer S Group consists of cooperative societies and the SOK Corporation (established in 1904) with numerous subsidiaries. The company operates in several business sectors including food retailing, specialty goods, hotels and restaurants, hardware and agriculture, automobiles, and service stations (S Group, 2005). In 2002 its retail sales were over 5250 million USD and in 2004 nearly 6900 million USD (Deloitte, 2004, 2006).

The S Group (SOK Corporation) started to internationalize cautiously via purchasing alliances in the early 1970s (Robinson & Clarke-Hill, 1995). Today the company belongs to for example International Cooperative Alliance and to the Brussels based Eurocoop. The S Group has focused its international operations only on Estonia. Its more intensive internationalization started in 1994 with the opening of the Sokos department store in Estonia. The market entry took place in the form of a joint venture (Tenco Group), in which S Group's partner was a German department store group Kaufhof (e.g., Emap Retail, 2001). At the time of the entry, the Sokos department stores was the S Group's main department store concept in Finland. In Estonia, however, this store concept was not successful and the joint venture was later divested.

In 1998 the S Group and a retail cooperative from Schleswig-Holstein in Germany started a joint venture, Foodbaltic Oy, in order to introduce the S Group's Prisma hypermarket in Estonia. The first Prisma hypermarket was opened in Tallinn two years later. Presently, the S Group has six Prisma hypermarkets in Estonia. In 2004 their sales were over 142 million USD. Despite the hard local competition these hypermarkets have performed well. S Group has been very cautious in its internationalization. One reason for that may be the cooperative background. However, it has announced its plans to expand the Prisma chain also to the Latvian markets and to open more outlets in Estonia (e.g., Cuthbertson, 2005). It appears that it will try to differentiate itself from other retailers by attracting more local customers with its customer loyalty and membership programs. In addition to its food retail operations, the S Group has in the Baltic States subsidiaries in the restaurant and hotel sectors, and in the agricultural trade. Its significant role in Estonia is mostly based on its skills in transferring retail technology to the market.

The K Group

The Finnish retailer K Group (Kesko Corporation) (established in 1940) is a hybrid organization, with multiple business divisions: food retailing, building and interior decoration, agricultural and machinery, home and specialty goods, international technical trade, branded products trade, cars and spare parts (K Group, 2005). In 2002 its retail sales were over 4900 million USD and in 2004 over 7150 million USD (Deloitte, 2004, 2006). In Finland the company and its many subsidiaries operate chains both in food and specialty retailing, in the department store sector, and in the mail order/e-commerce sectors.

K Group's international operations started already in the 1970s, when the company (Kesko) entered into a strategic alliance with the Swedish ICA. Since then the companies have small equity stakes in one another (Lindblom & Rimstedt, 2004). Like the S Group also the K Group has been active in purchasing cooperation with European food retailers. Today the K Group has international retail operations mainly in food and hardware sectors. Through its subsidiaries it also operates in agricultural and machinery trade in all Baltic countries (K Group, 2005). Additionally, in Estonia it operates in the mail order business sector (via its NetAnttila concept) (Emap Retail, 2001).

In the hardware sector the K Group expanded its K-Rauta chain first into Sweden in the late 1990s. In 2000 it acquired a majority share of the Estonian company AS Fanaali, the owner of the Ehitusmaailm chain (Table 6). In late 2005, the K Group had an approximate 20 % market share in Estonia. The Ehitusmaailm chain was used to enter into the Latvian market in 2000. In Latvia the first store of the K-Rauta chain was opened in 2002. Besides these, the K Group's subsidiary, Rautakesko, has a wholesale network in Latvia. The K Group has experienced substantial delays in the opening of its hardware stores in Latvia as it had some bureaucratic problems (the building permissions pended for three years) (e.g., Taloussanomat, 2005a). Moreover, the operations have not yet been profitable (e.g., Kauppalehti, 2005). In 2005 the K Group (Rautakesko) entered into the Lithuanian market through a joint venture with a Lithuanian company, Senukai. The company is the market's leader in the Lithuanian building supplies trade with over 25 % market share (e.g., Senukai, 2005). The cooperation with Senukai has made Lithuania K Group's foothold in its expansion to Belarus (Kauppalehti, 2005). In 2005 the K Group made two other big acquisitions in the hardware sector; the Stroymaster chain in Russia (five stores in St. Petersburg) and the Byggmakker chain (of Norgros AS) in Norway. Thus the K Group has used acquisition as an entry mode in Russia, although there are several problems related to the valuation of the Russian companies. These problems have limited the use of acquisition as an entry mode in Russia (e.g., Roberts, 2005). In addition to its retail operations in Russia, mainly in St. Petersburg, K Group (Rautakesko) has also wholesale operations (a warehouse in Moscow).

The K Group started to operate in the food retail sector in Estonia in 1999 with its hypermarket chain Citymarket (Semionoviene, 2003) (Table 6). In Estonia the K Group has small-scale discount formats:

TABLE 6. The K Group's Internationalization in the Baltic States and Russia

Country/chain	Year	Entry mode	Sector	Stores
Estonia				
Citymarket	1999	self-start	food	6[a]
SuperNetto	2000	self-start	food	1[d]
K-Rautakesko/Ehitusmaailm	2000	acquisition	hardware	5[a]
Säästumarket	2001	acquisition	food	47[a]
Rimi (Rimi Baltic)[c]	2005	joint venture	food	62[b]
Latvia				
SuperNetto	2000	self-start	food	25[a]
K-Rautakesko/Ehitusmaailm	2000	acquisition[e]	hardware	1[a]
Citymarket	2001	self-start	food	5[a]
K-Rauta	2002	self-start	hardware	4[b]
Rimi (Rimi Baltic)[c]	2005	joint venture	food	78[b]
Lithuania				
Senukai	2005	joint venture	hardware	13[b]
Rimi (Rimi Baltic)[c]	2005	joint venture	food	32[b]
Russia				
Stroymaster	2005	acquisition	hardware	5[b]

Note: [a]in 2004; [b]in 2005; [c]includes Supernetto, Säästumarket, Rimi Supermarket and Rimi Hypermarket stores; [d]in 2000; [e]entry through Ehitusmaailm.
Compiled by K Group, 2005; Rimi, 2005; Senukai, 2005.

SuperNetto and Säästumarket chains. In 2005 the company further intensified its operations in the Baltic States. The K Group's subsidiary Kesko Food and the ICA's (Swedish retailer) subsidiary ICA Baltic started a joint venture, Rimi Baltic. Through this joint venture the K Group will have a large network of both hypermarkets and discount stores in all the Baltic countries. The K Group's success in the Baltic States and Russia is, for the most part, due to its know-how to establish a network of both small-scale and large-scale retail formats, and to build the distribution system to support these stores.

The Swedish Retailers

ICA

The Swedish retailer ICA (established in 1907) is a voluntary wholesale and retail organization that consists of numerous small retailers. ICA's business concept is based on strategic alliances in the form of franchising agreements with independently owned retailers. In 2004 ICA's retail sales were nearly 9800 million USD (Deloitte, 2006).

ICA has had cooperated with the Finnish K Group since the 1970s. In 1999 ICA strengthened its position in the Nordic retail markets when it acquired a share of the Norwegian Hakon Group. ICA made a self-start entry into the Baltic markets in 1996 when it began to operate its Rimi chain in Latvia (Table 7). Three years later, in 1999 ICA expanded its operations to Lithuania. The market entry took place in the form of a joint venture with the Lithuanian retailer Ekovalda. ICA's hold in the Lithuanian food retail market increased in 2000 when the new joint venture acquired the Lithuanian Vikonda chain.

The main event in ICA's history occurred in 2000 when the large Netherlands based retailer Ahold acquired a part of ICA. The new company ICA-Ahold had better resources to continue the intensive expansion through acquisitions. In 2000 the company acquired ISO Supermarked in Denmark, and later in the same year the Latvian retail chain Interprego (e.g., Lindblom & Rimstedt, 2004). In 2005 ICA-Ahold started a joint venture (Rimi Baltic) with the Finnish K Group. The objective of the new joint venture is to achieve market leadership in the Baltic countries: the aim is to have a 25 % market share within three years. The strategy is to operate stores under the Rimi banner. This involves extensive remodeling of the ICA's and K Group's existing hypermarket and discount store concepts in all the Baltic countries (ICA, 2005; Rimi, 2005; K Group, 2005). ICA is greatly benefiting from Ahold's international ex-

TABLE 7. ICA's Internationalization in the Baltic States

Country/chain	Year	Entry mode	Company/acquirer/partner
Estonia			
Rimi	1999/2000	self-start	ICA
Rimi (Rimi Baltic)	2005	joint venture	partners: ICA-Ahold & K Group
Latvia			
Rimi	1996/1997	self-start	ICA
Interprego	2000	acquisition	acquirer: ICA-Ahold
Rimi (Rimi Baltic)	2005	joint venture	partners: ICA-Ahold & K Group
Lithuania			
Ekovalda	1999	joint venture	partners: ICA & Ekovalda
Vikonda	2000	acquisition	acquirer: ICA/Ekovalda
Rimi (Rimi Baltic)	2005	joint venture	partners: ICA-Ahold & K Group

Compiled by Ahold, 2005; ICA, 2005; Lindblom & Rimstedt; 2004; Rimi, 2005.

perience in operating multiple formats in several Central Eastern European markets (for example in Poland). Ahold was expected to enter into Russia years ago (e.g., Higgins, 2001), but by the end of 2005 it was not yet made that move. It has also been suggested that Ahold might enter first in Finland through acquisitions and after that expand to Russia.

IKEA

The Swedish IKEA (established in 1943) is the world's leader in the furniture and home furnishing. The company has a long experience in business operations, including sourcing, manufacturing and retailing, which cover 44 countries. IKEA has over 200 stores in over 30 countries (IKEA, 2005). Nearly 90 % of the stores are owned and run by the company, while the rest of the stores are operated on a franchise basis. In 2002 IKEA's retail sales were over 10000 million USD and in 2004 over 14500 million USD (Deloitte, 2004, 2006).

IKEA started its international operations in the 1960s by entering first into Norway and Denmark and soon into Switzerland and Germany. During the 1970s the company used franchising to internationalize into markets outside Europe (Mårtenson, 1981). In the mid 1970s the company began its activities in Russia by cooperating with a Russian wood processing company (Table 8). During the 1990s IKEA continued to invest in its own production in Russia. Before opening its first store in Russia in 2000 IKEA had already become a global retailer. In the 1990s it had also expanded to Central Eastern European markets: first to Hungary and then later to Poland, Czech Republic, and Slovakia. In 2005 IKEA had two stores based on its shopping center (Mega Mall) concept in Moscow, one in St. Petersburg, and one in Kazan.

Since the 1970s IKEA has made big investments in Russia. In 2003 the company was ranked as the fourth largest European investor in Russia with projects worth nearly 800 million USD (Rogacheva & Mikerova, 2003). Furthermore, IKEA aims to invest in its own production and to make Russia the major supplier of IKEA goods worldwide (e.g., ICSC, 2005). In 2005 the company already had 50 % share of Russia's furniture exports. Although IKEA is popular and it sells well in Russia, it is excepted to take years for the operations to become profitable. One reason for this is Russia's 25 % tariff on imported furniture. In 2004 only 13 % of the IKEA furnitures sold in Russia were locally made. In order to obtain profit, IKEA must continue to increase local production and thus raise the percentage of the locally made merchandise to 30% (ICSC, 2005; Filippov et al., 2005).

TABLE 8. IKEA's Internationalization in Russia

Year	
1976	Starts cooperation with a Russian wood processing company in Leningrad area.
in the 1990s	Invests 24 million UDS in production facilities (in furniture and textile industry).
2000	Has a network of 50 factories and 25 % share of Russia's furniture exports.
2000	First store opened (in Moscow).
2001	Second store opened (in Moscow).
2003	Distribution center opened in Moscow.
2003	Third store opened (in St. Petersburg).
2004	Fourth store opened (in Kazan).
2005	Has 50 % share of Russia's furniture exports.

Compiled by Filippov et al. 2005; ICSC, 2005; IKEA, 2005.

In the future IKEA is planning to open over 20 stores (based on the Mega Mall concept) and to expand its operations to cover all major Russian cities with population over one million. In the development of its shopping centers IKEA is cooperating with other retailers like the Finnish Stockmann and the French Auchan (e.g., Deloitte, 2004). IKEA has faced a number of problems as well as delays in the building of its shopping centers. These have included delays in getting visas, difficulties in coping with the local planning regulations, and widespread corruption (e.g., ICSC, 2005).

CONCLUSIONS AND IMPLICATIONS

During the last ten years there have been many changes in the Central Eastern European and Eastern European retail markets due to the economic and political transformations and the international retailers' intensified activities. This article has focused on analyzing the international behavior of the biggest Finnish and Swedish retailers in the Baltic and Russian markets. The eastward expansion of the five case companies analyzed in the present article–Stockmann, S Group, K Group, ICA and IKEA–has been motivated by several factors related to both their domestic markets (push factors: small size, low and limited growth) and the attractiveness of their target markets (pull factors: high market growth, low to moderate levels of competition). Additionally, the cultural and geographic closeness of the Baltic States and especially the St. Petersburg and Moscow areas in Russia has given the Finnish and Swedish retailers substantial location advantages.

The internationalization of the case companies has followed the stepwise development conceptualized by the Uppsala model. All five companies started their internationalization from culturally and geographically close countries and then gradually moved to more distant markets. Furthermore, all companies started with less intensive modes (such as foreign purchasing cooperation, exports, and mail order sales) and have gradually evolved to more intensive modes (Table 9). IKEA was the only retailer which had several different types of operations in various foreign markets, including the Central Eastern European markets, before making the more intensive entry into Russia with store openings. In the other four cases, either Estonia or Russia were the first markets for the retailers' major foreign operations.

The case companies display a great variation in the market and operation strategies used to enter the four target markets (Table 9). Among them, Stockmann from Finland and IKEA from Sweden were the first retailers in their home countries which internationalized their operations. Both companies were also the first retailers in their fields to enter the Russian markets (Stockmann was also the first in Estonia). IKEA is the only case company that has worldwide operations and a strong brand. Besides that, it is one of the biggest foreign investors and the leading furniture retailer in Russia.

The K Group, ICA (ICA-Ahold), and the S Group are the main foreign food retailers in the Baltic markets. The K Group and ICA have joined their forces in food retailing and are aspiring to become the leaders in the Baltic countries with their Rimi concept. Except for the S Group all the case companies have also informed about big future expansion plans. All the Finnish and Swedish retailers have a significant role in their fields in the Baltic States. This situation might change in food retailing if the world's top international food retailers would enter these markets. Until now Ahold (ICA-Ahold), and Schwarz Group (Lidl chain) are the only European world class food retailers that have been interested in the Baltic markets, which are relatively smaller and thus less attractive than the much bigger Central Eastern European or Russian markets. It is probable that in the near future the Swedish Hennes & Mauritz and KappAhl, or other big western clothing retailers will enter the Baltic and/or Russian markets. Under such circumstances, Stockmann's Seppälä chain would be in clear danger to loose its current market position in these markets.

The article showed that those international retailers that entered into the Baltic States and especially into Russia with modern formats have enjoyed significant first-mover advantages especially because of the

TABLE 9. Summary of Case Companies' International Behavior in the Baltic States and Russia

	Stockmann	The S Group	The K Group	ICA	IKEA
International experience/markets prior the entry into the Baltic States and Russia	No	No	Limited: Sweden 1998.	ICA: Limited: Norway 1999, Denmark 2000. ICA-Ahold: significant.	Significant: Global presence. Stores in Europe, Asia, North America and CEE countries.
Target markets/year or entry	USSR since 1950s, Russia 1989, Estonia 1996, Latvia 1996, Lithuania 2005.	Estonia 1994/1998.	Estonia 1999, Latvia 2000, Lithuania 2005, Russia 2005.	Latvia 1996/1997, Estonia 1999/2000, Lithuania 1999.	Russia 1976/2000.
Entry modes in the target markets	First export sales. Primarily self-start. Franchising in clothing sector.	Joint venture.	Primarily self-start and joint venture (e.g. Rimi Baltic). Acquisitions in hardware sector.	Self-start, acquisitions and joint ventures (e.g. Rimi Baltic).	Cooperation, mainly self-start.
Formats	Dep. stores and clothing stores.	Hypermarkets. Earlier dep. store divested.	Hypermarkets, supermarkets and hardware stores.	Hypermarkets and supermarkets.	Large-scale furniture stores (in its own shopping centers (Mega Malls).
Main sectors	Dep. store, clothing, food, mail order in the Baltics and Russia.	Food. Subsidiaries also in hotel and restaurant business and business and agricultural trade.	Food in the Baltics. Hardware in Russia. Small-scale mail order business in the Baltics.	Food.	Furniture and home furnishing.
Position/role in the target markets	Significant in Russia (in dep. store sector).	Significant in Estonia.	Significant in the Baltic States.	Significant in the Baltic States.	Significant in Russia (market leader; 50 % share of Russia's furniture exports.
Possible future moves/plans	Penetration especially in Russia.	Limited expansion first to Latvia, and later also to Lithuania.	Penetration/leadership in the Baltics in food retailing. Penetration in Russia, and expansion to Belarus in the hardware sector.	Aims to become first the market leader in the Baltics. Later expansion to Russia and Ukraine with the help of Ahold.	Significant expansion inside Russia. Aims to open stores in all major million-cities.

low to moderate levels of competition and the good availability of premium locations. The traditional forms of retailing, such as open markets and kiosks still dominate food retailing in Russia. The retail structure is expected to sensibly change in the future due to the continuing penetration of the modern formats operated by both domestic and international retailers. The competition between the biggest retailers will increase. In the mid 1990s large international retailers showed very low levels of interest in entering into Russia. However, in ten years Russia's attractiveness has increased significantly. That trend will certainly continue, since it has been estimated that by the year 2020 Russia will become Europe's biggest food retail market, worth nearly 450 billion USD.

The findings of this article point out to several managerial implications. The cases show that in order to succeed in the highly dynamic Russian markets, international retailers have to be prepared to take substantial risks and to face several potential problems, caused by factors like the country's uncertain legal system and the high level of bureaucracy. Moreover, difficulties may arise because of the local tax systems or the processes of obtaining building permissions for large-scale retail outlets. Furthermore, the experiences of the case companies demonstrate that it is crucial to set up cooperation and distribution networks with the right partners, since it can often be hard to find good local suppliers. Even if retailers were able to cope with the multitude of problems, to win market shares, and to enjoy high annual sales growth, there were no quick profits. Evidence shows that the time needed for profitable operations seems to be longer than in the Western European countries. So far, retailers entering into Russia with gradual and long-term expansion strategies seem to have been the most likely to succeed in this highly evolving market. However, since the markets are changing fast and the competition increases all the time, the stepwise/gradual progress is becoming more difficult.

This article has drawn a general overview of the international behavior of the selected case companies in the Eastern European markets. A more in-depth analysis should be used in the future research on the subject. Furthermore, the findings suggest several directions for further research. First, there is a need for studies that are based on a more holistic view (an eclectic model) on retail internationalization. Previous research (e.g., Roberts, 2005) supports the findings of this article in that retailers have to take many interdependent decisions related to the selection of target markets, the entry modes and penetration strategies, and the timing of their operations. Second, more detailed analysis should assess the role of networking and cooperation in distribution in the Eastern European context. Especially in Russia the distribution appears to be one of the key problems faced by international entrants. Third, future research should also focus on the valuation process of retail companies, especially in Russia but also in the Baltic States, because there are different local corporate governance procedures. This can provide with a better overview of the possibilities and alternatives for acquisitions in these markets. Finally, so far very little is known about the role of company specific (for example, parent ownership structures, management styles) and target market specific factors in the investment and networking behavior of international retailers in the Eastern European markets. More research is definitely needed also on these issues.

REFERENCES

Alexander, N. (1990). Retailers and international markets: Motives for expansion. *International Marketing Review*, *7* (4), 75-85.

Alexander, N. (1995). Internationalisation: Interpreting the motives. In P. J. McGoldrick & G. Davies (Eds.), *International Retailing. Trends and Strategies* (pp. 77-98). London: Pitman Publishing.

A.T.Kearney (2003). *Emerging Market Priorities for Food Retailers. 2003 Global Retail Development Index*. Chicago: A.T. Kearney, Inc.

A.T.Kearney (2004). *Emerging Market Priorities for Global Retailers. The 2004 Global Retail Development Index*. Chicago: A.T. Kearney, Inc.

A.T.Kearney (2005). *Emerging Market Priorities for Global Retailers. The 2005 Global Retail Development Index*. Chicago: A.T. Kearney, Inc.

Burt, S., Dawson, J., & Sparks, L. (2004). The international divestment activities of European grocery retailers. *European Management Journal*, *22* (5), 483-492.

Cuthbertson, R. (2005). The value of customer-owners: An Interview with Kari Neilimo, CEO, S-Group. *European Retail Digest*, *45*, (Spring 2005).

Daunfeldt, S.-O., Orth, M., & Rudholm, N. (2005). Entry into local retail food markets in Sweden: A real-options approach. Göteborg University, Department of Economics, *Working Papers in Economics 170*, 17 May 2005.

Dawson, J. A. (1994). Internationalization of retailing operations. *Journal of Marketing Management*, *10* (4), 267-282.

Dawson, J. A. (2001). Strategy and opportunism in European retail internationalization. *British Journal of Management*, *12*, 253-266.

Dawson, J., & Lee, J.-H. (2004). Introduction: International retailing in Asia. *Journal of Global Marketing*, 18 (1/2), 1-4.

Deloitte (2004). 2004 Global Powers of Retailing. Stores, January 2004. Section 2.

Deloitte (2006). 2006 Global Powers of Retailing. Stores, January 2006. Section 2.

Denstadli, J. M., Lines, R., & Grønhaug, K. (2005). First mover advantages in the discount grocery industry. *European Journal of Marketing*, *39* (7/8), 872-884.

Drtina, T. (1995). The Internationalisation of retailing in the Czech and Slovak Republics. *The Services Industries Journal, 15* (4), 191-203.

Dunning, J. (1980). Toward an eclectic theory of international production: some empirical tests. *Journal of International Business Studies, 11* (1), 9-31.

Dunning, J. (1993). *Multinational Enterprises and the Global Economy.* Wokingham, England: Addison-Wesley Publishing.

EBRD (2005). *Transition Report 2005. Infrastructure.* London: European Bank for Reconstruction and Development.

Emap Retail (2001). *European retail markets: Finland. Retailing trends and analysis on 16 key countries.* London: Emap Retail.

Esbjerg, L. (2002). Food retailing in Central Europe and the Baltic Republics: Structure and buying behaviour. *European Retail Digest,* Issue 33 (March), 49-51.

Evans, J., Treadgold, A., & Mavondo, F. T. (2000). Psychic distance and the performance of international retailers. A suggested theoretical framework. *International Marketing Review, 17* (4/5), 373-391.

Filippov, P., Boltramovich S., Dudarev, G., Smirnyagin, D., Sutyrin, D., & Hernesniemi, H. (Ed.) (2005). Investoinnit ja investointiedellytykset Venäjälle. Elinkeinoelämän Tutkimuslaitos. Sarja B 215. Helsinki: Edita Publishing Oy.

Ghauri, P. N., & Holstius, K. (1996). The role of matching in the foreign market entry process in the Baltic States. *European Journal of Marketing, 30* (2), 75-88.

Ghauri, P. N., Elg, U., & Sinkovics, R. R. (2004). Foreign direct investment–Location attractiveness for retailing firms in the European Union. In L. Oxelheim & P. N. Ghauri (Eds.), *European Union and the Race for Foreign Direct Investment in Europe* (pp. 407-428). Amsterdam: Elsevier.

Higgins, K. (2001). Global food retailing. *British Food Journal, 103* (10), 749-754.

Hofstede, G. (1980). *Culture's Consequences. International differences in work-related values.* Beverly Hills, CA: Sage Publications.

Hofstede, G. (2001). *Culture's Consequences. Comparing Values, Behaviors, Institutions, and Organizations Across Nations* (2nd ed.). Thousand Oaks: Sage Publications.

IGD (2004). *Central Europe & Russia. Assessing the Opportunities.* February 2004. Watford: Institute of Grocery Distribution.

Jakobssen, K. (2006). First-mover advantages in Central and Eastern Europe. A comparative analysis of performance measures. *Journal of East-West Business,* (in this same issue).

Johanson, J., & Vahlne, J.-E. (1977). The internationalisation process of the firm–A model of knowledge development and increasing market commitment. *Journal of International Business Studies, 8* (2), 23-32.

Johanson, J., & Vahlne, J.-E. (1990). The mechanism of internationalisation. *International Marketing Review, 7* (4), 11-24.

Johannson, U. (2003). Internationalisation through strategic alliances: The Swedish food retailer ICA. In P. Freathy (Ed.), *The Retailing Book: Principles and Applications* (pp. 287-293). Harlow: Pearson Education Limited.

Juhász, A., & Stauder, M. (2005). Hungarian food retailing: Concentration, polarisation and a new entrant. Paper presented at the IAMO Forum 2005 "How effective is the invisible hand? Agricultural and food markets in Central and Eastern Europe?" 16-18 June 2005, Halle (Saale), Germany.

Kauppalehti (2005). Kesko rynnii Valko-Venäjän rautakauppaan Senukain avulla. *Kauppalehti*, 12.7.2005, 9.

Kauppalehti Extra (2005). Halpakaupat eivät vedä Suomessa. *Kauppalehti Extra*, 5.9.2005, 18.

Kehittyvä Kauppa (2005). Ylös, alas, ulos. *Kehittyvä Kauppa*, 5/2005, 10-14.

Kielyte, J. (2002a). Food retailing in transition: An overview of the Baltic countries. *European Retail Digest*, Issue 33 (March), 52-54.

Kielyte, J. (2002b). Lithuanian retailing and wholesaling undergo substantial modernisation. *European Retail Digest*, Issue 35 (September).

Kogut, B., & Singh, H. (1988). The effect of national culture on the choice of entry mode. *Journal of International Business Studies, 19* (3), 411-432.

Lieberman, M. B., & Montgomery, D. B. (1988). First-mover advantages. *Strategic Management Journal, 9*, 41-58.

Lindblom, T., & Rimstedt, A. (2004). Retail integration strategies in the EU: Scandinavian grocery retailing. *International Review of Retail, Distribution and Consumer Research, 14* (2), 171-197.

McGoldrick, P. J. (1995). Introduction to international retailing. In P. J. McGoldrick & G. Davies (Eds.), *International Retailing. Trends and Strategies* (pp. 1-14). London: Pitman Publishing.

McGoldrick, P. J., & Fryer, E. (1993). Organisational culture and the internationalization of retailers. 7th International Conference on Research in the Distributive Trades. Institute of Retail Studies, University of Stirling, 6-8 September 1993.

Moore, C. M., & Fernie, J. (2005). Retailing within an international context. In M. Bruce, C. M. Moore & G. Birtwistle (Eds.), *International Retail Marketing. A Case Study Approach* (pp. 3-38). Oxford: Elsevier Butterworth-Heinemann.

Mårtenson, R. (1981). *Innovations in Multinational Retailing. IKEA on the Swedish, Swiss, German, and Austrian Furniture Markets*. Gothenburg: University of Gothenburg.

Myers, H., & Alexander, N. (1997). Food retailing opportunities in Eastern Europe. *European Business Review, 97* (3), 124-133.

Nagy, E. (2002). Fragmentation and centralisation: Transition of the retail sector in East Central Europe. *European Retail Digest*, Issue 33 (March), 41-44.

Perkins, B. (2001). The European retail grocery market overview. *British Food Journal, 103* (10), 744-748.

Planer, B. (2005). Top 30 grocery retailers in Europe. *European Retail Digest*, Issue 46 (Summer), 66-71.

PWC (2004). *2003/2004 Russia and Central & Eastern European Retail & Consumer Study. Lithuania Country Report*. PriceWaterhouseCoopers.

PWC (2005a). *2004/2005 Global Retail & Consumer Study from Beijing to Budapest*. PriceWaterhouseCoopers.

PWC (2005b). *From Beijing to Budapest: New Retail & Consumer Growth Patterns in Transitional Economies. Executive Summary 2004/2005*. 3rd edition. PriceWaterhouseCoopers.

Rialp, A., Rialp, J., & Knight, G. A. (2005). The phenomenon of early internationalizing firms: what do we know after a decade (1993-2003) of scientific inquiry? *International Business Review, 14* (2), 147-166.

Roberts, G. H. (2005). Auchan's entry into Russia: Prospects and research implications. *International Journal of Retail & Distribution Management, 33* (1), 49-68.

Robinson, T. (1997). Retailing in Eastern Siberia and the Russian far east: A tale of two cities. *International Journal of Retail & Distribution Management, 25* (9), 301-308.

Robinson, T., & Clarke-Hill, C. M. (1995). International alliances in European retailing. In P. J. McGoldrick & G. Davies (Eds.), *International Retailing. Trends and Strategies* (pp. 133-150). London: Pitman Publishing.

Robinson, T., Foot, R., & Clarke-Hill, C. M. (2000). German retailing expansion–a decade of change? *European Business Review, 12* (4), 216-225.

Rogacheva, E., & Mikerova, J. (2003). *European FDI in Russia: Corporate strategy and the effectiveness of government promotion and facilitation.* Belfast: OCO Consulting Ltd.

Rogers, H., Ghauri, P. N., & George, K. L. (2005). The impact of market orientation on the internationalization of retailing firms: Tesco in Eastern Europe. *International Review of Retail, Distribution and Consumer Research, 15* (1), 53-74.

Rogers, H., Ghauri, P. N., & Langaard, H. (2005). An investigation into factors influencing foreign market entry in Eastern Europe. In T. Morrow, S. Loane, J. Bell, & C. Wheeler (Eds.), *International Business in an Enlarging Europe* (pp. 81-95). Houndsmills: Palgrave Macmillan.

Semionoviene, A. (2003). Emerging markets of the Baltic: Getting bigger, quicker. *European Retail Digest,* Issue 33 (Winter), 41-42.

Seristö, H. (2003). A western style department store goes east. Case Stockmann. In P. Mannio, E. Vaara & P. Ylä-Anttila (Eds.), *Our Path Abroad. Exploring Post-war Internationalization of Finnish Corporations* (pp. 134-147). Helsinki: Taloustieto Oy.

Sternquist, B. (1997). International expansion of US retailers. *International Journal of Retail and Distribution Management, 25* (8), 262-268.

Szaleniec, M. (2005). Eastern Europe–the 'promised land' for retailers. *Emerging Europe Retail Update,* Issue 16, 23-24.

Taloussanomat (2004). Hienosen verran itäkauppaa. *Taloussanomat,* 20.3.2004, 11-12.

Taloussanomat (2005a). Rautakesko tilkkii Baltiaa suurmyymälöillä. *Taloussanomat,* 14.6.2005, 10-11.

Taloussanomat (2005b). Stockmann oppi villin lännen. *Taloussanomat,* 26.11.2005, 16-17.

Taloussanomat (2006). Jussi Kuutsa opettaa venäläisiä tavaratalojen tavoille. *Taloussanomat,* 17.2.2006, 12-13.

Treadgold, A. (1990). The developing internationalisation of retailing. *International Journal of Retail and Distribution Management, 18* (2) (March/April), 4-11.

USDA (2003). *Latvia. Retail Food Sector.* Report 2002. Foreign Agricultural Service: GAIN Report #LG3001. 2/4/2003. Stockholm: U.S. Embassy.

WARC (2004). *The European Marketing Pocket Book.* Oxon: World Advertising Research Center Ltd.

www.ahold.com (Ahold, 2005).

www.ica.se (ICA, 2005).

www.icsc.org (ICSC, 2005).

www.ikea.com (IKEA, 2005).

www.kesko.fi (K Group, 2005).
www.rewe-group.com (Rewe, 2006).
www.rimi.lv (Rimi, 2005).
www.senukai.lt (Senukai, 2005).
www.sok.fi (S Group, 2005).
www.stockmann.fi (Stockmann, 2006).

doi:10.1300/J097v13n01_04

Trade and Market Liberalisation in Eastern Europe: The Effects on the FDI Location Decisions of Italian Firms

Antonio Majocchi
Roger Strange

SUMMARY. The question of why multinational companies (MNCs) choose to locate in one region rather than another has been an important topic in IB research for many years, but has recently received even more attention. This paper presents the results of an econometric investigation of the locational determinants of Italian firms in Central and Eastern Europe. Italian firms have been very active investors in the CEE countries. Our results broadly confirm the findings of previous studies, but we also find that both trade liberalisation and market liberalisation are important influences upon the location decision. If the CEE governments wish to attract further

---

Antonio Majocchi is affiliated wth the University of Pavia, Dipartimento di richerche aziendali, Facolta di Economia, via S. Felice, 5, I 27100 Pavia, Italy (E-mail: antonio. majocchi@unipv.it). Roger Strange is affiliated with King's College London, Department of Management, King's College London, 150 Stamford Street, London SE1 9NH, United Kingdom (E-mail: roger.strange@kcl.ac.uk).

[Haworth co-indexing entry note]: "Trade and Market Liberalisation in Eastern Europe: The Effects on the FDI Location Decisions of Italian Firms." Majocchi, Antonio, and Roger Strange. Co-published simultaneously in *Journal of East-West Business* (The Haworth Press, Inc.) Vol. 13, No. 2/3, 2007, pp. 93-114; and: *Market Entry and Operational Decision Making in East-West Business Relationships* (ed: Jorma Larimo) The Haworth Press, Inc., 2007, pp. 93-114. Single or multiple copies of this article are available for a fee from The Haworth Document Delivery Service [1-800-HAWORTH, 9:00 a.m. - 5:00 p.m. (EST). E-mail address: docdelivery@haworthpress.com].

Available online at http://jeb.haworthpress.com
doi:10.1300/J097v13n02_01

(Italian) foreign investment, then further liberalisation of their domestic economies should be a policy priority. doi:10.1300/J097v13n02_01 *[Article copies available for a fee from The Haworth Document Delivery Service: 1-800-HAWORTH. E-mail address: <docdelivery@haworthpress.com> Website: <http://www.HaworthPress.com> © 2007 by The Haworth Press, Inc. All rights reserved.]*

KEYWORDS. Foreign direct investment, Central and Eastern Europe, firms' location decisions

INTRODUCTION

The question of why multinational companies (MNCs) choose to locate in one region rather than another has been an important topic in IB research for many years, but has recently received even more attention. Such increased attention is well-merited as firms' location decisions may well influence their modes of entry, their choice of foreign partner in joint ventures, and the subsequent performance of their foreign affiliates. Much of this work has focused on the FDI location decision within the United States, the European Union (EU) or China. In contrast, there have been few econometric studies of the determinants of the location of FDI in the emerging markets of the Central and Eastern Europe countries (CEECs), in large part due to the fact that these countries have only been recipients of Western FDI since the 1990s. Furthermore, even these studies do not cover the entire period of transition from the 1990s to the early 21st Century, from just after the fall of Communism to the eve of integration with the European Union (EU).

This paper is an attempt to fill these gaps in the literature. We focus on Italian investments in seven Eastern European countries (i.e. Poland, Hungary, Slovenia, the Czech Republic, the Slovak Republic, Romania and Bulgaria) which differ markedly in terms of size, level of development, EU links, degree of liberalisation etc., but which have shared a common objective to integrate with the European Union in the shortest time possible. We estimate a conditional logit model of 272 Italian firms. There are clear differences in the FDI location patterns of Italian, German, French etc. firms, and a multi-country sample of firms would be preferable but there are substantial practical difficulties in assembling such a dataset and this task will have to await future work. However, there are compensatory advantages in that both the home country corporate governance system and the cultural values may be assumed to be similar across all the firms, so permitting a focus on the location-specific attributes of each of the seven alternative locations (Disdier and Meyer, 2004; Hunya and Stankovsky, 2002). Our focus on Italian firms thus means that we do not need to take into account possible country-of-origin effects (Grosse and Trevino, 1996; Chadee et al., 2003). Notwithstanding the various studies on FDI location within China, this paper also provides a contribution by being one of the first to examine the FDI location choice between alternative transition economies. We find *inter alia* that the relative degrees of trade and market liberalisation have very significant effects upon the location choice: a conclusion that has clear policy implications for these emerging economies.

The structure of the paper is as follows. In the first section, we present some background information on the seven selected Eastern European countries and on the growth of inward investment, and some descriptive statistics on the growth and main characteristics of Italian FDI flows. We provide a brief review of the literature on FDI location decisions in the following section to establish the control variables for the model, and also summarise the literature on FDI in Eastern Europe. The model and our hypotheses regarding the expected impacts of the various explanatory variables are then outlined. The next section describes the sample of 272 firms, presents details of the explanatory variables and provides a brief explanation of conditional logit analysis. The penultimate section contains the empirical results and a discussion of their interpretation. The final section considers the policy and managerial implications, highlights the limitations of the analysis, and outlines the ways in which we propose to pursue this line of research.

BACKGROUND

Since the fall of the Berlin Wall, the CEE countries have attracted considerable attention as potential investment destinations from many MNCs but, given their proximity, from EU MNCs in particular. The annual flow of FDI to these countries rose steadily from the early 1990s onwards, and reached US\$168.4bn in 2003, or roughly 25% of total new investment in these countries (UNCTAD, 2004). According to the official data, Italy has been an important investor in all seven of the CEE countries under consideration–see Figure 1–though it still lags behind Germany and, to a lesser extent, Holland. In some countries (e.g., Ro-

FIGURE 1. The Main Investors in the Seven CEE Countries

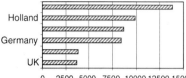

FDI Stock in Poland
millions of US $

Holland
Germany
UK

0   2500 5000 7500 10000 12500 15000
Source: Polish Information and FIA

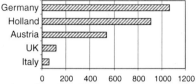

FDI Stock in Slovak Rep.
Millions of US $

Germany
Holland
Austria
UK
Italy

0   200   400   600   800 1000 1200
Source: Slovak Central Republic

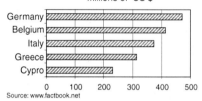

FDI Stock in Bulgaria
millions of US $

Germany
Belgium
Italy
Greece
Cypro

0   100   200   300   400   500
Source: www.factbook.net

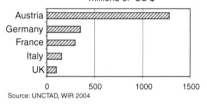

FDI stock in Slovenia
millions of US $

Austria
Germany
France
Italy
UK

0   500   1000   1500
Source: UNCTAD, WIR 2004

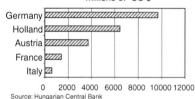

FDI stock in Hungary
millions of US $

Germany
Holland
Austria
France
Italy

0   2000 4000 6000 8000 10000 12000
Source: Hungarian Central Bank

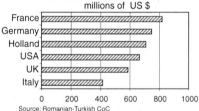

FDI stock in Romania
millions of US $

France
Germany
Holland
USA
UK
Italy

0   200   400   600   800   1000
Source: Romanian-Turkish CoC

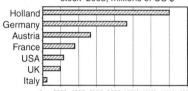

FDI stock in Czech Rep
stock 2003, millions of US $

Holland
Germany
Austria
France
USA
UK
Italy

0 2000 4000 6000 8000 10000 12000 14000 16000
Source: Czech Central Bank

mania), Italy is particularly important in terms of the number of investments, even if less so in terms of the total value. This is a result of the nature of the Italian industrial structure, with its dominance by small and medium-sized enterprises (Mutinelli and Piscitello, 1998).

The interest of MNCs in the region has been particularly significant since the European Union set out its conditions for the accession of the CEE countries in 1993–the so-called Copenhagen criteria (Clausing and Dorobantu, 2005). The prospects of a more favourable environment attracted many new firms (Kalotay, 2004), and FDI has played an important role in the restructuring process of many CEE economies, with foreign-owned firms accounting for substantial proportions of GDP (Konings, 2000; Lizal and Svejnar, 2001). At the beginning, most of the investments in the region were driven by the privatisation of existing public enterprises but, more recently, the surge of greenfield projects is testimony to the attractiveness of the area as an investment location. Some of the CEE countries have also developed specific policy measures to attract inward FDI: one notable example is the Slovak Republic that is now one of the most important production hubs in the European automobile industry (UNCTAD, 2005), after receiving investments by large MNCs such as Volkswagen, PSA and Hyundai.

REVIEW OF THE LITERATURE AND FORMULATION OF THE MODEL

There have been many studies of the determinants of the FDI location decision, but most of these focus on the location decision within the United States, the European Union or China.[1] In contrast, there have been relatively few econometric studies of FDI location in the CEECs, notwithstanding a considerable literature reporting aggregate data, or using case study and survey methods (e.g., Lankes and Venables, 1996; Meyer, 1998). All of the econometric studies (see, for example, Resmini, 2000; Campos and Kinoshita, 2003; Bevan et al., 2004; Bevan and Estrin, 2004) have used aggregate FDI flows or stocks in selected CEEC countries as the dependent variable. Notwithstanding differences in measures, the general consensus is that the FDI flows are positively related to market size (Resmini, 2000; Campos and Kinoshita, 2003; Bevan et al., 2004) and market growth in the host economy (Bevan and Estrin, 2004), the availability of labour (Resmini, 2000), the quality of infrastructure (Campos and Kinoshita, 2003), and agglomeration economies (Resmini, 2000; Campos and Kinoshita, 2003), and negatively related to labour costs (Resmini, 2000; Campos and Kinoshita, 2003; Bevan et al., 2004; Bevan and Estrin, 2004). In addition, both Campos and Kinoshita (2003) and Bevan et al. (2004) find support for bilateral FDI flows being influenced by a range of institutional variables. And all four studies, citing gravity model arguments, find that the geographical proximity of the home and host countries has a significant impact upon FDI flows.

The present study takes a different approach to modelling the FDI location decision, by focusing on the individual FDI projects rather than the aggregate inter-country FDI flows. This approach is preferable for four main reasons. First and foremost, FDI is undertaken by firms not countries, and so it makes sense to focus on the *ex ante* determinants of the individual strategic decisions about location rather than analysing the *ex post* flows of FDI. One corollary of this is that some variables, which may have an impact upon aggregate FDI flows, are likely to be irrelevant at the micro level.[2] For example, GDP in the home country (Bevan et al., 2004) is likely to be correlated with aggregate FDI flows from the home country to all host countries, but it is not clear why it should affect the choice of FDI location. Second, it is widely acknowledged that FDI data do not correspond closely to new investment in overseas affiliates, notably because the figures exclude capital raised in the host economy and are expressed net of any disinvestments. Third, as Bevan et al. (2004: 52) note, FDI flows are 'lumpy' in nature, and investment projects typically have a life span of more than one year. But whereas Bevan et al. (2004) cite this as a reason for using average FDI flows over a five-year period, we would conclude *a fortiori* that FDI data are not particularly useful, and that it is more appropriate to focus on the FDI decisions. Fourth, the lagged value of the FDI stock is traditionally used in the literature as the measure of agglomeration economies but, as pointed out by Campos and Kinoshita (2003: 13), OLS estimation of models with lagged values of the dependent variable as explanatory variables typically generate inconsistent estimates.

To capture the effects of market size and potential, we initially included three variables in the model. The first is population (POP); the second is GDP per capita (PCGDP); and the third is GDP growth (GROW). The first two measures have been widely used (e.g., Resmini, 2000), whilst the third measure has only been used in a few location studies (e.g., Hennart & Park, 1994). However, given the widespread belief (Lankes and Venables, 1996) that many Western European firms have located in the CEECs in order to establish a bridgehead in promising markets, we consider growth potential to be an important variable and past growth to be a reasonable proxy. We would expect foreign investors to be attracted to larger markets with more affluent consumers, and where the market is growing. Hence we would expect the coefficients of all three variables to have positive signs.

All firms are expected *ceteris paribus* to prefer lower wage locations, although lower wages are only attractive insofar as they are not offset by lower productivity. We include a variable (WAGE) which measures relative wages in a common currency, and expect this to have a negative effect upon FDI location. As regards the availability of labour, we include two variables. The first (Basile, Castellani & Zanfei, 2003) is the rate of unemployment (UNEM), with the expectation that a high rate should attract FDI not just because more labour is available but also because of the depressing effect of the excess labour supply on wages. The second (Mariotti & Piscitello, 1995) is a human capital variable (EDUC), measured by government expenditure on health and education as a percentage of GDP. It is assumed that greater government expenditure on employee welfare leads to improvements in both the quality and quantity of human capital, and that this should have a positive impact upon all foreign investment but, in particular, upon strategic-asset seeking investment.

There is plenty of anecdotal evidence that the quality of the infrastructure is an important determinant of the FDI location decision. Unfortunately, it is also a variable that is notoriously difficult to operationalise. Many studies (Chang and Park, 2005; Mariotti and Piscitello, 1995) use the extent of the transportation network in a country as a proxy variable. However, the required data were not available for some countries in the early 1990s so, following Campos and Kinoshita (2003), we use the number of telephone lines (fixed and mobile) per 100 inhabitants (TEL). Given the increasing importance of telecommunications in modern economies, we use this measure as a proxy of the general state of physical infrastructure in a country and expect this variable to have a positive impact upon FDI location.

Agglomeration economies have been shown in numerous studies (Kalotay, 2004) to have a positive impact upon FDI. The theoretical argument is simple: more FDI begets more FDI. More FDI generally leads to better infrastructure, better trained workers, a finer division of labour, the provision of more specialised support services and, in general, lower production costs. We use the natural logarithm of the cumulative FDI stock (LFDI) in each country to proxy agglomeration economies.

In addition, the Eastern European context of this study allows us to test whether or not the process of liberalisation which began in the

1990s has also had an effect on FDI location. As noted in the previous section, all seven countries have undergone massive structural and institutional changes, though the extent of these changes has not been uniform. We hypothesise that the relative speed of these changes will have had an impact upon the distribution of FDI between the seven countries, and include three variables to capture these effects. The first two relate to the extent of market liberalisation. One is the percentage of prices that are administratively controlled (ADM), rather than being set by market forces Bevan et al., 2004). We would expect foreign investors to shy away from countries wherein prices are administratively controlled, and therefore expect this variable to have a negative coefficient. The other is government expenditure as a percentage of GDP (GCON), and again we would expect a negative coefficient as foreign firms might be expected to favour countries where State intervention is lower. The third variable is a proxy for trade liberalisation (Resmini, 2000), and measures the openness of the economy to foreign trade (OTRA). It is likely that a substantial part of Italian FDI in Eastern Europe is for the purposes of production (possibly with imported materials) and re-export to the European Union and elsewhere. We would therefore expect investors to favour countries which are already substantially engaged with in trade with the rest of the world, as not only does this suggest a certain intent by the government but should also be associated with more efficient import/export channels. Furthermore, it has been shown that countries that are more open to trade are likely to have better property rights protection (Ayyagari et al., 2005), and are thus likely to be more attractive to foreign investors. Oxley (1999) and Smarzynska (2002) too report than weak property rights inhibit FDI inflows.

Table 1 summarises the explanatory variables initially included in the model, and their expected impacts upon the choice of location. Each variable is entered into the regression model with a lag of one year to capture the delay between the site selection process and the realization of the investment project. Thus, for example, the locations of affiliates established in 2000 are assumed to depend upon the relative attributes of the seven countries in 1999.

DATA AND METHODOLOGY

In this section, we explain how the dataset of 272 Eastern European affiliates was constructed, provide a brief statistical description of the

TABLE 1. The Explanatory Variables and Their Expected Impacts

Variable	Definition	Expected impact
POP	Population (m)	+
PCGDP	GDP per capita at current prices (US$'000)	+
GROW	Annual GDP growth rate at constant prices (%)	+
WAGE	Average annual wage rate (US$'000)	−
UNEM	Unemployment rate (%)	+
EDUC	Government expenditure on health and education as a percentage of GDP (%)	+
TEL	Number of telephone lines (fixed and mobile) per 100 inhabitants	+
LFDI	The natural logarithm of the cumulative stock of inward FDI (US$m)	+
ADM	The percentage of prices administratively controlled (%)	−
GCON	Government expenditure as a percentage of GDP (%)	−
OTRA	Total exports and imports as a percentage of GDP (%)	+

Compiled by FDI stock: UNCTAD, *World Investment Report* (various years)
All other variables: EBRD, *Transition Report* (various years)

explanatory variables in the seven alternative country locations, and outline the main features of the conditional logit model.

Data Sources

The dataset of 272 firms have been constructed specifically for this study, and is a subset of a larger database that has been assembled as part of project jointly carried out by two Italian universities.[3] This larger database contains data on 969[4] Italian firms with investments in at least one of the seven CEECs, with the information being gathered from several different sources: the Amadeus database, local branches of the Italian Institute for the Promotion of External Trade (ICE), and the seven Italian-CEEC Chambers of Commerce. The 969 firms were then contacted by e-mail and/or telephone to elicit further information, but replies were only received from 288 firms (29.5% response rate).[5] Fourteen of these firms had undertaken their investments before 1990 and two had some missing data, so the final sample consisted of 272 firms which had made investments between 1990 and 2003. Each firm was responsible for just one of the investment projects in the sample, so there were also 272 FDI projects.

Only twenty seven of the 272 firms in the sample were publicly listed, either in Italy or in the host economy. The sample thus consists primarily of small and medium-sized firms,[6] though this is not untypical of the Italian economy. Almost two-thirds of the firms in the sample (172) were classified as manufacturing, whilst the remaining 100 were active in the service sector. Forty eight firms (17,6%) were involved in food, textiles, clothing and footwear manufacture (NACE 15-19), and a further sixty firms (22,1%) operate in the mechanical sectors (NACE 26-31). This industry distribution corresponds to the typical distribution of Italian international firms (Mariotti & Mulinelli, 2005), which is mainly concentrated in these two sectors where Italian firms still have some competitive advantage in the international arena. The geographical distribution of these investments is shown in Table 2. Over half are located in Poland, and a further quarter in Slovenia and Bulgaria combined. These figures on the *numbers* of investments may be compared with the data on the total value of the Italian FDI stock: it appears as though Poland may be over-represented, and Hungary and the Czech Republic are under-represented, in the sample though we are not comparing like with like. Further efforts are needed to ascertain the representativeness of the sample but, in the meantime, the results should be interpreted with caution.

The Characteristics of the Alternative Locations

Table 3 provides some basic descriptive statistics for the explanatory variables in each of the seven countries. More specifically the table re-

TABLE 2. The Sample Distribution of Firms in the Seven Countries

Country	Number of firms in sample	Percentage of total number of firms in sample	Average Italian FDI stock, 1990-2003	Percentage of total Italian FDI stock
		%	US$bn	%
Slovenia	36	13	1997.0	3.6
Czech Republic	13	5	13356.2	23.9
Bulgaria	29	11	1398.9	2.5
Slovak Republic	26	9	2444.6	4.4
Hungary	16	6	15478.3	27.7
Romania	8	3	3375.4	6.0
Poland	144	53	17754.7	31.8
Total	272	100	55805.4	100.0

Compiled by UNCTAD, *World Investment Report*, (various years)

TABLE 3. Descriptive Statistics for the Explanatory Variables, 1990 and 2002

Country	Year	POP	PCGDP	GROW	UNEM	EDUC	TEL	LFDI	ADM	GCON	OTRA
Bulgaria	1990	9.0	950	−9.1	1.50	10.8%	24.2	2.05	70.0%	64.30	91%
	2002	8.0	1984	4.9	17.80	7.0%	37.5	3.56	21.3%	37.20	113%
Poland	1990	38.2	2100	−11.6	6.10	10.0%	8.6	2.13	11.0%	32.70	49%
	2002	38.6	4924	1.4	17.76	1.0%	29.5	4.68	1.0%	44.10	63%
Czech Rep	1990	10.3	2700	−0.4	0.80	10.1%	15.8	3.13	28.0%	60.10	25%
	2002	10.2	6742	1.5	8.80	10.3%	37.8	4.58	12.4%	46.60	125%
Slovak Rep	1990	5.3	2280	−0.4	1.50	9.6%	13.5	1.94	22.0%	60.10	103%
	2002	5.4	4403	4.6	18.53	9.8%	26.1	3.89	21.1%	48.40	151%
Romania	1990	23.2	1300	−5	3.00	6.0%	10.5	0.60	85.0%	39.00	39%
	2002	22.4	2091	5	9.97	4.0%	18.4	3.95	20.4%	32.70	77%
Slovenia	1990	2.0	6400	−4.7	4.70	13.0%	22.0	2.79	24.0%	49.60	116%
	2002	2.0	11026	3.3	11.26	13.5%	40.7	3.61	14.0%	42.60	114%
Hungary	1990	10.4	3300	−3.5	2.50	12.2%	9.6	2.81	16.0%	57.00	63%
	2002	9.9	6581	3.5	5.80	8.5%	36.1	4.55	18.9%	44.00	130%

Note: See Table 1 for details of units.
Compiled: See Table 1

ports the values of the explanatory variables in the years 1990 and 2002. The data show quite clearly the paths undertaken by the seven countries in the process of transition. All the countries, with different degrees of speed and success, have gone from very low levels of growth and *per capita* income in the years immediately after the fall of their Communist regimes towards good levels of economic growth in recent years. Moreover, all the countries have pursued processes of trade and market liberalisation that have led to decreases of the roles of their governments in their domestic economies and higher levels of integration into the world economy.

The correlation matrix, together with average values and standard deviations, for the explanatory variables are provided in Table 4. One figure in particular stands out: the very high correlation (0.9434) between average wages (WAGE) and per capita GDP (PCGDP). This is not surprising, but it does lead to problems when both variables are included in the regressions. The long-term solution is to derive and use a productivity-adjusted measure of wages but, in the short-term, we have simply omitted the wage variable from the analysis.

The Conditional Logit Model

The model assumes that each Italian investor is faced with a choice of $J = 7$ alternative locations in Eastern Europe, and will choose to locate its affiliate i in country j so as to maximise the expected future profits from its investment. More formally, affiliate i will be located in country j if and only if:

$$R_{ij} \quad > \quad R_{ik} \text{ for all } k \neq j. \qquad (k = 1,2, \ldots,J)$$

where R_{ij} = expected profit earned by affiliate i if it is located in country j.

Let Y_i be a random variable that indicates the location chosen for affiliate i, then the probability of choosing a specific country j depends upon the attributes of that country relative to the attributes of the other seven countries in the choice set. If X_j is a vector of location-specific attributes for country j and β is a vector of parameters to be estimated then, following McFadden (1974), the probability of locating in country j (assuming that the disturbance terms are independently distributed) is:

$$\text{Prob}(Y_i = j) \quad = \quad \frac{\exp[\beta X_j]}{\sum_{k=1}^{7} \exp[\beta X_k]}.$$

Estimates of β may be obtained through maximum likelihood estimation. If the explanatory variables have been entered linearly, then a small change Δx in variable x leads to a change in the probability P that a firm will choose a particular location of $\Delta P = \beta_x.P.(1 - P).\Delta x$, where β_x is the coefficient associated with variable x. The effect of Δx thus depends upon the initial probability of choosing location j, which in turn depends upon each attribute set (Greene 2000: 863). The coefficient β_x is thus not the marginal effect, though it will have the same sign. The overall significance of the estimated equations may be assessed by a likelihood ratio test: the test statistic λ follows a *chi*-squared distribution with degrees of freedom equal to the number of restrictions imposed by the null hypothesis.

$$\lambda = 2\,[\,L(m) - L(0)]$$

where $L(m)$ is the log-likelihood of the chosen model, and $L(0)$ is the log-likelihood of a constrained model where all the slope coefficients are set equal to zero. Model fit may be assessed by calculating the pseudo-R^2 as follows:

$$\text{pseudo-}R^2 = 1 - \frac{L(m)}{L(0)}$$

It should be noted that the pseudo-R^2 is not analogous to the R^2 in linear regression though there is an empirical relationship between the two, and a pseudo-R^2 of 0.2 represents an R^2 of approximately 0.4 (Hensher et al., 2005: 338).

EMPIRICAL RESULTS

In this section, we provide the empirical results from the estimation of the conditional logit model. First, we estimate the model using the full sample of 272 firms, and with all ten variables which have been hypothesised to have an impact upon FDI location. We then derive the

TABLE 4. The Correlation Matrix of the Explanatory Variables

Variable	Mean	Standard deviation	POP	GROW	PCGDP	UNEM	WAGE	GCON	TEL	ADM	EDUC	OTRA	LFDI
POP	13.95	11.67	1.0000										
GROW	− 0.774	0.610	0.0173	1.0000									
PCGDP	3499	2286	− 0.3898	0.3641	1.0000								
UNEM	0.0938	0.0486	0.0226	0.2204	0.1407	1.0000							
WAGE	0.13	0.091	− 0.3086	0.2498	0.9434	0.1543	1.0000						
GCON	0.4572	0.873	− 0.4500	− 0.1382	0.0534	− 0.3201	0.0430	1.0000					
TEL	21.91	9.01	− 0.4904	0.4042	0.5293	0.3494	0.4073	− 0.0999	1.0000				
ADM	0.2119	0.1512	− 0.1552	− 0.1954	− 0.2714	− 0.3510	− 0.2411	0.1371	− 0.0791	1.0000			
EDUC	10.09	2.55	− 0.3884	0.0374	0.5750	− 0.0262	0.5769	0.4175	0.0991	− 0.1892	1.0000		
OTRA	0.8537	0.3253	− 0.6841	0.2677	0.4403	0.2562	0.3553	0.0736	0.7017	− 0.0872	0.2547	1.0000	
LFDI	7.16	1.93	0.0557	0.4507	0.4217	0.3225	0.2915	− 0.0558	0.4769	− 0.6649	0.1316	0.2117	1.0000

'base' model, which only includes those variables that were found to be statistically significant. Second, we estimate this 'base' model for the two sub-samples of 172 manufacturing firms and 100 service firms.

Estimation of the Base Model

The results from the estimation of the conditional logit model are show in Table 5. We present the results of three different models, all of which are highly significant. As noted in the previous section, the coefficients do not measure the marginal effects, but they do have the same sign, and we will limit our discussion to them.

The first model (1) reports the coefficient estimates when all the explanatory variables are included. All of the variables have the expected signs, except that for GDP per capita (PCGDP) which is negative though insignificant. This result contrasts strongly with that obtained from most of the other studies of FDI location. The explanation, as discussed above, may be that some foreign investors are motivated by local consumers' purchasing power whilst others look for low labour costs. Yet these two variables are highly correlated, which makes it difficult statistically to separate out the two opposing effects. And when one is omitted, as here, the other picks up the net effect and is then close to zero. The coefficients of the human capital variable (EDUC) and the market liberalisation measure (GCON) have the expected signs, but are statistically insignificant. We therefore excluded these three variables in the subsequent models.

Thus model (2) was estimated with just the remaining seven variables. All seven coefficients had the expected signs, and are statistically significant although two were only so at the 10% level. The model as a whole is very statistically significant (as evidenced by a likelihood ratio test), and the pseudo-R^2 is 0.22 which is reasonable for this type of cross-sectional analysis. Market size (POP), market growth (GROW), the quality of infrastructure (TEL), and agglomeration economies (LFDI) all have significant positive effects upon FDI location, confirming the results of the previous studies. The rate of unemployment (UNEM) too has a significant positive effect, as expected. As regards the two 'liberalisation' variables, we find that openness to foreign trade (OTRA) has a very significant effect upon FDI location, reflecting the importance of both engagement with the rest of the world and strong property rights protection. This finding contrasts with the insignificant effect reported by Resmini (2000: 667), who focused on bilateral trade with the European Union. Finally, Italian investors appear to prefer

TABLE 5. The Conditional Logit Model: Coefficient Estimates

Variable	Model (1)	Model (2)	Model (3)
POP	0.0742** (0.0120)	0.0785** (0.0102)	0.0584** (0.0074)
PCGDP	−0.0134 (0.0521)		
GROW	0.0454** (0.0240)	0.0467** (0.0229)	0.0437** (0.0221)
UNEM	0.120** (0.027)	0.118** (0.027)	0.131** (0.027)
EDUC	0.0105 (0.0481)		
TEL	0.0448** (0.0203)	0.0466** (0.0190)	0.0512** (0.0170)
LFDI	0.162* (0.098)	0.125* (0.076)	0.159** (0.062)
ADM	−0.0109 (0.0085)	−0.0125* (0.0077)	
GCON	−0.0085 (0.0120)		
OTRA	1.415** (0.492)	1.467** (0.474)	
log-likelihood	−410.62	−410.88	−419.55
chi-squared	237.34**	236.82**	219.47**
pseudo-R^2	0.2242	0.2237	0.2073

Notes: (1) The sample size is 272; number of possible locations = 7. (2) Standard errors are in brackets. The symbol * denotes that the coefficient is significant at the 10% level, and ** that it is significant at the 5% level.

countries with freer markets, as confirmed by the significant negative coefficient for the percentage of prices that are administratively controlled (ADM). Our results thus differ from those of Bevan et al. (2004), who found no evidence that the liberalization of domestic prices had a positive effect on FDI inflow. If the two 'liberalisation' variables are removed, as in model (3), there is a very significant loss of explanatory power ($\lambda = 34.7$, $p < 0.01$) though the significance of the infrastructure and agglomeration variables both increase substantially.

The model thus suggests that Italian investors make their location decisions in Eastern Europe taking into account local market size and potential growth, the availability of labour (not necessarily skilled), the quality of the infrastructure, the openness of the economy to foreign trade, the liberalisation of domestic prices, and the decisions of previous investors.

Comparison of Manufacturing and Service Firms

The full sample consisted of 172 manufacturing and 100 service firms. It seemed reasonable to assume that there might be differences between the two sub-samples in the importance of some of the explanatory variables thus we ran two further regressions using the 'base' model: one for the manufacturing firms and one for the service firms–see Table 6. There were two striking results.

The first was that all the coefficient estimates for both the manufacturing and service firms had the expected signs. Some of the coefficients lost statistical significance, but this is unsurprising given the smaller sizes of the sub-samples. But the market size (POP) and labour availability (UNEM) were still significant in both sub-samples, whilst communications infrastructure (TEL) was significant in the services sample but not in the manufacturing sample, and trade liberalisation (OTRA) was significant in the manufacturing sample but not in the services sample. The second striking result was the similarity between the corresponding coefficients in the two sub-samples. We had expected the coefficient for infrastructure (TEL) to be larger for services than for manufacturing, and that for trade liberalisation (OTRA) to be smaller. These expectations were met, though the differences were not statistically significant. This lack of significance does not of course prove that there are no differences, but it is nevertheless interesting that the two sets of coefficients were so similar given the different natures of the two sub-samples.

CONCLUSIONS AND IMPLICATIONS

This paper presents the results of the first econometric investigation of the locational determinants of Italian firms in Eastern Europe. Italian firms have been very active investors in the CEE countries, and their investments have had substantial impacts upon the domestic economies. Our results broadly confirm the findings of previous studies, in that we find that local market size and market growth, labour availability, the quality of infrastructure and agglomeration economies are all important determinants. But the Eastern European setting has also enabled us to break new theoretical ground in testing for the effects of various types

TABLE 6. The Conditional Logit Model: Comparison of Manufacturing and Service Firms

Variable	Manufacturing	Service
POP	0.0758** (0.0132)	0.0862** (0.0169)
GROW	0.0493 (0.0278)	0.0470 (0.0417)
UNEM	0.0980** (0.0321)	0.1683** (0.0489)
TEL	0.0250 (0.0236)	0.0875** (0.0335)
LFDI	0.112 (0.095)	0.156 (0.128)
ADM	−0.0124 (0.0102)	−0.0115 (0.0120)
OTRA	1.856** (0.609)	0.905 (0.773)
Sample size	172	100
log-likelihood	−267.31	−140.23
chi-squared	134.78**	109.73**
pseudo-R^2	0.2013	0.2794

Notes: (1) The number of alternative locations is 7. (2) Standard errors are in brackets. The symbol * denotes that the coefficient is significant at the 10% level, and ** that the coefficient is significant at the 5% level

of liberalisation. We find that both trade liberalisation (as evidenced by the significance of the OTRA variable) and market liberalisation (as evidenced by the significance of the ADM variable) are both important influences upon the location decision. If, and it is a question of 'if' because there are disadvantages as well as advantages from increased inward investment flows, the CEEC governments wish to attract further (Italian) foreign investment, then further liberalisation of the domestic economies should be a policy priority.

From a managerial perspective, it has been alleged (De Chiara & Minguzzi, 2002; Meyer & Skak, 2002) that Italian small and medium-sized firms often pursue international expansion strategies that rely heavily on chance. Yet our results clearly show that, on average, such firms–which make up the bulk of our sample–take into account a range of relevant factors, and act in a rational economic manner, when choosing country locations for the FDI projects. These firms were not lured simply by the promise of low labour costs or by the most populous markets but were aware of, and responded to, a variety of location-specific factors.

As with all econometric studies, there is scope for further refinement and extension of the model. First, alternative proxies should be tried to capture the effects of differing wage rates. Second, the sample should be extended to include more investments in those countries that appear to be under-represented. Third, other potential determinants could be included: tax rates, industry dummies (Barba Navaretti et al., 2001), financial liberalisation variables and a variety of firm-specific variables such as size, experience, and ownership (Lankes & Venables, 1996). Fourth, the issue of EU accession has not been fully explored. Five of the seven countries formally acceded to the European Union in May 2004, but negotiations had begun much earlier and it had been evident for some time that these countries would be among the first wave of successful entrants. It is thus likely that any 'EU accession' effect would have been felt long before 2004. Romania and Bulgaria were never expected to be part of this first wave, and this omission may well have had a negative impact on location in these two economies.

NOTES

1. See, for example, Bartik (1985), Coughlin et al. (1991), Friedman et al. (1992), Friedman et al. (1996), Glickman and Woodward (1988), Head et al. (1995, 1999), Luger and Shetty (1985), Woodward (1992), Shaver (1998) and Shaver and Flyer (2000) on FDI in the United States; Crozet et al (2004), Ford and Strange (1999), Yamawaki (1991), Scaperlanda and Balough (1983) on FDI in the European Union; and Belderbos and Carree (2002), Chang and Park (2005), Cheng and Kwan (2000), Chadee et al. (2003), He (2003) and Head and Ries (1996) on FDI in China. This is a not an exhaustive list, and there are also some interesting studies of FDI location in other regions: see, for example, Woodward and Rolfe (1992) on FDI in the Caribbean Basin.

2. Other 'country' variables, such as the geographical distance between the home and host countries, are also omitted.

3. Insubria University, Varese and the University of Pavia.

4. A detailed questionnaire was sent to 1552 Italian firms which were believed to have investment in the CEEC countries. 583 were returned undelivered, so only the remaining 969 were considered active.

5. This response rate compares well with the 6-16% rates typically obtained in international surveys (Harzing, 1997)

6. Unfortunately we do not have reliable data on the size (e.g., numbers of employees) of the sample of 272 firms.

REFERENCES

Ayyagari, M., Maksimovic, V., & Demirguc-kunt, A. (2005). How well do institutional theories explain firms' perceptions of property rights? Paper presented at the AIB Annual Conference, Quebec City, July.

Barba Navaretti, G., Falzoni, A.M., & Turrini, A. (2001). The decision to invest in a low-wage country: evidence from Italian textiles and clothing multinationals. *Journal of International Trade & Economic Development*, 10(4), 451-470.

Bartik, T.J. (1985). Business location decisions in the United States: estimates of the effects of unionization, taxes and other characteristics of states. *Journal of Business and Economic Statistics*, 3, 14-22.

Basile, R., Castellani, D., & Zanfei, A. (2003). Location choices of multinational firms in Europe: the role of national boundaries and EU policy. *University of Urbino, Faculty of Economics Working Paper* no.23.

Bevan, A., Estrin, S. & Meyer, K. (2004). Foreign investment location and institutional development in transition economies. *International Business Review*, 13(1), 43-64.

Bevan, A. & Estrin, S. (2004). The determinants of foreign direct investment into European transition economies. *Journal of Comparative Economics*, 32(4), 775-787.

Belderbos, R.A. & Carree, M. (2002). The location of Japanese investments in China: agglomeration effects, keiretsu, and firm heterogeneity. *Journal of the Japanese and International Economies*, 16(2), 194-211.

Campos, N.F. & Kinoshita, Y. (2003). Why does FDI go where it goes? New evidence from the transition economies. *IMF Working Paper* WP/03/228.

Chadee, D., Qiu, F., & Rose, E.L. (2003). FDI location at the subnational level: a study of EJVs in China. *Journal of Business Research*, 56, 835-845.

Chang, S-J. & Park, S. (2005). Types of firms generating network externalities and MNCs co-location decisions. *Strategic Management Journal*, 26, 595-615.

Cheng, L.K. & Kwan, Y.K. (2000). What are the determinants of the location of foreign direct investment? The Chinese experience. *Journal of International Economics*, 51: 379-400.

Clausing, K.A. & Dorobantu, C.L. (2005). Re-entering Europe: does European Union candidacy boost foreign direct investment? *The Economics of Transition*, 13(1), 77-103.

Coughlin, C.C., Terza, J.V., & Arromdee, V. (1991). State characteristics and the location of foreign direct investment within the United States. *Review of Economics and Statistics*, 73(4), 675-683.

Crozet, M., Mayer, T., & Mucchielli, J.L. (2004). How do firms agglomerate? A study of FDI in France. *Regional Science and Urban Economics*, 34(1), 27-54.

De Chiara, A. & Minguzzi, A. (2002). Success factors in SMEs' internationalization processes: an Italian investigation. *Journal of Small Business Management*, 40(2), 144–153.

Disdier, A-C. & Mayer, T. (2004) How different is Eastern Europe? Structure and determinants of location choices by French firms in Eastern and Western Europe. *Journal of Comparative Economics*, 32(2), 280-296.

EU Commission. (2004). *Labour costs in Europe 1996-2002*. Luxembourg: Eurostat.

Ford, S. & Strange, R. (1999). Where do Japanese manufacturing firms invest within Europe, and why? *Transnational Corporations*, 8(1), 117-142.

Friedman, J., Gerlowski, D., & Silberman, J. (1992). What attracts foreign multinational corporations? Evidence from branch plant location in the United States. *Journal of Regional Science*, 32(4), 403-418.

Friedman, J., Fung, H-G., Gerlowski, D.A., & Silberman, J. (1996). A note on State characteristics and the location of foreign direct investment within the United States. *The Review of Economics and Statistics*, 78(2), 367-368.

Glickman, N.J. & Woodward, D.P. (1988). The location of foreign direct investment in the United States: patterns and determinants. *International Regional Science Review*, 11(2), 137-154.

Greene, W.H. (2000). *Econometric analysis* (4th ed). New Jersey: Prentice Hall.

Grosse, R. & Trevino, L.J. (1996). Foreign direct investment in the United States: an analysis by country of origin. *Journal of International Business Studies*, 27(1), 139-155.

Harzing A.W. (1997). Response rates in international mail surveys: results of a 22-country study. *International Business Review*, 6(6): 641-665.

He, C. (2003). Location of foreign manufacturers in China: agglomeration economies and country of origin effects. *Papers in Regional Studies*, 82, 351-372.

Head, K. & Ries, J. (1996). Inter-city competition for foreign investment: static and dynamic effects of China's incentive areas. *Journal of Urban Economics*, 40(1), 38-60.

Head, K, Ries, J., & Swenson, D. (1995). Agglomeration benefits and location choice: evidence from Japanese manufacturing investments in the United States. *Journal of International Economics*, 38(3-4), 223-247.

Head, K., Ries, J., & Swenson, D. (1999). Attracting foreign manufacturing: investment promotion and agglomeration. *Regional Science and Urban Studies*, 29(2), 197-216.

Hennart, J.F. & Park, Y.R. (1994). Location, governance, and strategic determinants of Japanese manufacturing investments in the United States. *Strategic Management Journal*, 15(6), 419-436.

Hensher, D.A., Rose, J.M., & Greene, W.H. (2005). *Applied choice analysis: a primer.* Cambridge: Cambridge University Press.

Hunya, G. & Stankovsky, J. (2002). *Foreign direct investment in Central and East European countries and the former Soviet Union with special attention to Austrian FDI activities.* Vienna: Wiener Institut für Internationale Wirtschaftsvergleiche and Österreichisches Institute für Wirtschaftsforschung.

Kalotay, K. (2004). The European flying geese: new FDI patterns for the old continent? *Research in International Business and Finance*, 18(1), 27-49.

Konings, J. (2000). Effects of direct foreign investment on domestic firms: evidence from firm-level panel data in emerging economies. *William Davidson Institute Working Paper* no.344.

Krugman, P. (1991). Increasing returns and economic geography. *Journal of Political Economy*, 99, 483–499.

Lankes, H.P. & Venables, A.J. (1996). Foreign direct investment in economic transition: the changing pattern of investments. *The Economics of Transition*, 4, 331-347.

Lizal, L. & Svejnar, J. (2001). Investment, credit rationing, and the soft budget constraint: evidence from Czech panel data. *William Davidson Institute Working Paper* no. 364.

Luger, M.I. & Shetty, S. (1985). Determinants of foreign plant start-ups in the United States: lessons for policymakers in the South-east. *Vanderbilt Journal of Transnational Law*, 18(2), 223-245.

Mariotti, S. & Piscitello, L. (1995). Information costs and location of FDIs within the host country: empirical evidence from Italy, *Journal of International Business Studies*, 26(4), 815-841.

Mariotti, S. & Mulinelli, M. (2005). *Italia multinazionale 2004. Le partecipazioni italiane all'estero e estere in Italia.* Rubbettino Editore, Soveria Mannelli.

McFadden, D. (1974). Conditional logit analysis of qualitative choice behaviour. In P. Zarembka (ed), *Frontiers in econometrics* (pp.105-142). New York: Academic Press.

Meyer, K.E. (1998). *Direct investments in economies in transition.* Cheltenham: Edward Elgar.

Meyer, K. & Skak, A. (2002). Networks, serendipity and SME entry into Eastern Europe. *European Management Journal*, 20(2), 179-188.

Mutinelli, M. & Piscitello, L. (1998). The influence of firm's size and international experience on the ownership structure of Italian FDI in manufacturing. *Small Business Economics*, 11(1), 43-56.

Oxley, J.E. (1999). Institutional environment and the mechanisms of governance: the impact of intellectual property protection on the structure of inter-firm alliances. *Journal of Economic Behavior and Organization*, 38(3), 283-310.

Resmini, L. (2000). The determinants of foreign direct investment in the CEECs: new evidence from sectoral patterns. *The Economics of Transition*, 8(3), 665-690.

Scaperlanda, A.E. & Balough, R.S. (1983). Determinants of US direct investment in the EEC: revisited. *European Economic Review*, 21(3), 381-390.

Shaver, J.M. (1998). Do foreign-owned and US-owned establishments exhibit the same location pattern in US manufacturing industries? *Journal of International Business Studies*, 29(3), 469-491.

Shaver, J & Flyer, F. (2000). Agglomeration economics, firm heterogeneity, and foreign direct investment in the United States. *Strategic Management Journal*, 21(12), 1175–1193.

Smarzynska, B.K. (2002). Composition of foreign direct investment and protection of intellectual property rights: evidence from transition economies. *World Bank Policy Research Working Paper* no.1786.

UNCTAD (2004). *World Investment Report.* New York and Geneva: United Nations.

Woodward, D.P. (1992). Locational determinants of Japanese manufacturing start-ups in the United States. *Southern Economic Journal*, 58(3), 690-708.

Woodward, D. & Rolfe, R. (1992). The location of export-oriented foreign direct investment in the Caribbean Basin. *Journal of International Business Studies*, 24(1), 121-144.

Yamawaki, H. (1991). Location decisions of Japanese multinational firms in European manufacturing industries. In K.S. Hughes (ed.) *European competitiveness* (pp.11-28). Cambridge: Cambridge University Press.

doi:10.1300/J097v13n02_01

In-Store Shopping Behavior:
A Cross-Cultural Comparison
in Italy, France and Poland

Donata Vianelli
Christian Dianoux
Tomasz Domanski
Jean Luc Herrmann

SUMMARY. The analysis of consumer shopping behavior is one of the most critical aspects which has to be taken into consideration in a context of retailing internationalization, where managers need to define the degree to which international firms can standardize or adapt their strategies in foreign markets. The aim of this research is to analyze and point out the main cross-cultural differences regarding in-store behavior comparing three countries: Italy, France and Poland. The study presents the results of an empirical research carried out on the household goods retail sector, which shows on a global level a positive growth trend that is pre-

Donata Vianelli is Associate Professor of International Marketing, University of Trieste, Trieste, Italy (E-mail: donata.vianelli@econ.units.it). Christian Dianoux is Senior Lecturer of Marketing, University of Paul Verlaine, Metz (France) and member of the CEREMO-GREFIGE team research (E-mail: Christian.dianoux@univ-metz.fr). Tomasz Domanski is Professor of Marketing, University of Lodz, Lodz, Poland (E-mail: tomdom@uni.lodz.pl). Jean Luc Herrmann is Senior Lecturer of Marketing, University of Paul Verlaine, Metz (France) and member of the CEREMO-GREFIGE team research (E-mail: Herrman2@univ-metz.fr).

[Haworth co-indexing entry note]: "In-Store Shopping Behavior: A Cross-Cultural Comparison in Italy, France and Poland." Vianelli, Donata et al. Co-published simultaneously in *Journal of East-West Business* (The Haworth Press, Inc.) Vol. 13, No. 2/3, 2007, pp. 115-142; and: *Market Entry and Operational Decision Making in East-West Business Relationships* (ed: Jorma Larimo) The Haworth Press, Inc., 2007, pp. 115-142. Single or multiple copies of this article are available for a fee from The Haworth Document Delivery Service [1-800-HAWORTH, 9:00 a.m. - 5:00 p.m. (EST). E-mail address: docdelivery@haworthpress.com].

115

dicted to continue in the next years especially through the internationalization of the retailing chains. doi:10.1300/J097v13n02_02 *[Article copies available for a fee from The Haworth Document Delivery Service: 1-800-HAWORTH. E-mail address: <docdelivery@haworthpress.com> Website: <http://www.HaworthPress.com> © 2007 by The Haworth Press, Inc. All rights reserved.]*

KEYWORDS. International retailing, standardization, adaptation, consumer shopping behavior, Italy, Poland, France, Western and Eastern Europe

INTRODUCTION

The analysis of in-store consumer shopping behavior is one of the most critical aspects to be taken into consideration regarding decisions related to the development of a standardized distribution format versus an adapted one. This analysis must be carried out carefully. The retailers need to both match their profit targets with their clients' needs and, clients need to maximize their shopping activity outcome (Putrevu and Lord, 2001; Lugli and Pellegrini, 2002).

The goal of this research is to analyze in-store shopping behavior by comparing three countries: Italy, France and Poland. These countries were once considered representative of Western and of Eastern Europe respectively. Their citizens showed significantly different consumer behavior patterns. Today we wonder if such differences are now less significant. Are we moving toward homogenization in the buying process? Is local adaptation of marketing strategies required to guarantee successful sales in each area?

This paper is divided into two parts. The first is theoretical and provides a review of literature of in-store shopping behavior. As it will be pointed out, quite a lot of research is concentrated on the analysis of different aspects of in-store behavior, but there is a lack of analysis of cross-cultural differences for in-store consumer shopping behavior. The second part presents the results of an empirical research carried out on the household goods market, a product category that can be considered quite complex and could be affected by the local culture. Results have been discussed in relation to the different characteristics of the distribution system for household goods in the three countries considered in the research.

CONSUMER IN-STORE SHOPPING BEHAVIOR: A LITERATURE REVIEW

Internationally conducted research studies regarding different sectors and distribution environments have pointed out that in-store shopping behavior is not a clear process and that it needs to be analyzed from more than one point of view. Shopping visits are for many consumers a spare time spending habit and it does not necessarily involve a buying decision (Wakefield and Baker 1998; Bellenger and Korgaonkar 1980; Ohanian and Tashchian 1992). Depending on the brand and the shopping involvement of the consumer, the experience is perceived differently. Shopping activity itself is not obvious. The store is the place where the consumer enters with information, looks around, thinks about the product, evaluates what to do and subsequently makes a decision to buy (Murthi and Srinivasan 1999; Putrevu and Lord 2001). The shopping activity continues until back at home where the consumer actually uses the product and/or decides to keep it (Granzin, Painter and Valentin 1997). A cross-cultural study in Italy, France and Poland would have to take into account the cultural environments (Cleveland et al. 2003; de Mooij and Hofstede 2002) and different distribution systems (Sternquist 1998). It is, more precisely, the development stage of the distribution system that can determine the expertise and the characteristics of consumer shopping and purchasing behavior: Hofstede's perspective (Hofstede 2001) of national culture applied by Sternquist (1998) to the analysis of international retailing management has presented significant differences. There are other two relevant variables, consumption and media behavior, which are both relevant for international retailing.

Regarding the cross-cultural differences in consumer shopping behavior, Popkowski and Timmermans (2001) argued that consumers shop in a different way relating to certain variables. Characteristics like planning the buying decision, expected benefits, the degree of involvement, the ability to evaluate differences between alternative brands, money, time, and the sensitivity towards prices are all important components. As these parameters vary, it is necessary to identify the behaviors corresponding to each stage of the whole process.

Putrevu and Lord's (2001) research developed a segmentation based on the approach to shopping behavior by identifying different consumer categories relating to the choice and the evaluation of the product/brand while inside the store. They evaluate:

- whether consumers compare the price of a single product and the price-listed products in different formats,
- if they compare different brands,
- if they are interested in using coupons and special offers,
- if they visit more than one outlet for daily or weekly expenses and
- if their purchases are based on parents' or friends' advice or on information collected by reading newspapers and magazines.

Three of the segments have been identified on the basis of this information. The high-search segment is characterized by the fact that the consumer devotes a long time to the research and comparison of different products and brands, as highlighted by Bloch et al. (1986) when talking about "continuous research." Such consumers are usually rewarded by comparing different products and brands, without necessarily buying them. The selective search segment is indeed more selective in a way that it uses only some of the above-mentioned instruments and tends to reduce the time dedicated to comparing different brands. The low search segment is the least involved in the choosing behavior.

These segments are very similar to those identified by previous research studies (Furse et al. 1984). Consumers are identified by analyzing the behavior preceding the evaluation of the product and the purchase itself. "Selective consumers" proposed by Putrevu and Lord (2001) might be further divided into those who mainly rely on in-store collected information, whom we might call *store based*, and those who rely on other sources like parents' and friends' advice, media opinion and so on, whom we might call *non-store based*. The managerial implications for a business company are remarkably evident. If involved consumers are attracted to in-store and out-of-the-store communication, the selective ones require particular attention to the kind of information on which they base their choices. The store-based consumers might be significantly influenced by, for instance, the atmosphere of the store, both according to its physical and social dimensions (de Luca and Vianelli 2001; Lee and Geistfeld 1995), the outlet image (Zimmer and Golden, 1988), in-store indications, special offers shown inside the shop and so on. Those who collect information primarily outside the store will be more sensitive to radio and/or television advertising, outdoor and printed advertising, and word of mouth.

In-store consumer behavior can be influenced by another dimension of analysis, linked to consumer logistics, which involves the consumer himself before and after the in-store shopping activity. Consumer logistics refer to the mode and timing of store visits, and to the transportation and storage of products at home. The primary aspects to consider (Granzin et al. 1997) are: the degree of independence in transportation; the variety of one's shopping activity in terms of variety of stores a consumer decides to visit; the savings factor or what is considered the "more convenient shop"; the mode of transportation and the storage at home.

The analysis of shopping behavior in an international context can be strongly related to other consumer characteristics. More precisely, the demographic (Underhill 1999) and the socio-economic variables may play a vital role in influencing shopping behavior. Low-income individuals tend to be less involved as consumers (Lockshin, Spawton and Macintosh 1997). They usually devote more time to searching for the product, are more saving-oriented (Putrevu and Lord 2001) and are more autonomous with logistics, in order to further reduce expenses (Granzin, Painter and Valentin 1997). Those with higher incomes pay little attention to saving money and go shopping regardless.

The consumer approach towards the marketing mix is another important descriptive aspect. The in-store atmosphere (Volle 2000; Lemoine 2003), the availability of products, the in-store advertising (Harp, Hlavaty and Horridge 2000), price and quality may all vary when linked to the consumer psychographic characteristics (Martinez and Montaner 2006). More precisely, there are many psychographic variables that distinguish consumers from one another and may influence their shopping activity. There are three categories (Table 1):

- personality variables;
- buying process perception variables;
- shopping activity perception variables.

Regarding the time factor, individuals perceive it and evaluate it in different ways (Chettamrongchai and Davies 2000; Marzocchi 1999). It is assumed that consumers, who do not spend much time choosing a product or a brand, are actually those who attach more importance to time. Price and quality variables may also influence shopping activity (Swait and Sweeney 2000; Bucklin, Gupta and Siddarth 1998). Consumers from different countries may differ due to various levels of awareness. The consumer shopping behavior may be influenced by the consumer attitude in enacting explorative behaviors (Baumgartner and Steenkamp, 1996). As it has often been highlighted (Ailawadi, Neslin and Gedenk 2001), the explorative behavior may help the client in be-

TABLE 1. Psychographic Variables and Shopping Behaviour

Personality	Buying process perception	Shopping perception
• Time perception	• Consumer involvement	• Attitude towards shopping
• Price sensitivity	• Risks of products' changing	• Attitude towards store personnel
• Quality sensitivity	• Research and evaluation costs	• Attitude towards the store/store loyalty
• Explorative behaviour	• Purchased goods storage costs	• Importance of in-store atmosphere

having spontaneously as well as in searching for innovation and variety, which in this case may concern both the product and the store typology.

Risk and cost perception associated to the different steps of the buying process constitutes another group of psychographic variables that may be taken into account. To talk about risks and costs means to refer to the various risk typologies identified by Berman and Evans (1989) rather than to financial risks. Would a product or store change involve functional, physical, financial, social, psychological or temporal risks? What would be the cost or time spent searching and evaluating a product/brand? These aspects are strongly related to consumer involvement, which has been thoroughly analyzed in the literature both from a psychology and marketing point of view. Amongst numerous research studies, the most interesting are by Kassarjian and Robertson (1981), Laurent and Kapferer (1985 and 1986), Slama and Tashchian (1985). In particular, Zaichowsky and Sood (1989) put in evidence how such involvement varies significantly from country to country.

Few studies have investigated the in-store shopping behavior in relation to consumer involvement (Slama and Tashchian 1985; Steenkamp and Wedel 1991; Lockshin et al. 1997; O'Cass 2000). The analysis is meaningful not only because it strongly bounds the objectives to the motivations that make up the consumer shopping behavior (Dawson, Bloch and Ridgway 1990) but because it affects the behaviors before entering the shop, the research and purchase evaluation steps, and the post-purchase behaviors. The analysis of the in-store consumer involvement takes into account three different levels: the product, which is the objective of the purchase, the brand, and the shopping involvement. As indicated by O'Cass (2000), the involvement relating to the use of the product may be analyzed as well. Even though this involvement might be assumed to happen following the shopping behavior, it might nevertheless affect the process quite significantly as it is able to influence the behaviors preceding the utilization of the product itself. The degree of involvement in a product identifies the perception of the role played by it relating to the field of activities, behaviors and habits of the consumer from his own point of view (Mittal and Lee 1989; Laurent and Kapferer 1986). The knowledge of the degree of involvement relating to the brand (Kapferer and Laurent 1992) represents, instead, the interest of the consumer in having a shuffle brand choice rather than a sought after and careful one. As to the buying stage, that is, the topic moment of the shopping behavior, the degree of involvement means to evaluate the consumer behavior towards the buying decision.

A last group of variables that may be taken into account is strictly linked to the shopping activity itself. Bellenger and Korgaonkar (1980) and Ohanian and Tashchian (1992) have distinguished recreational shoppers from purchasing-involved shoppers. The first looks at the buying activity as a recreational activity associated to spare time. The second group represents consumers for whom the shopping activity is a means to purchase a previously identified product. The choice is led by the evaluation of what the best product is rather than by the search for amusement during the shopping activity. Starting from Stone (1954), distribution system research has highlighted a great variety of attitudes towards the shopping activity (Reid and Brown 1996) that help us in drafting each segment's consumer profile. Of particular importance is the approach towards the store loyalty, which needs to be taken into account as it may influence the consumers' shopping behavior especially both when choosing more than one store and planning shopping logistics as well.

Lastly, it is important to take into consideration the perception of the store atmosphere. From the retailer's point of view, store atmosphere management is, as a rule, one of the main strategic and operative leverages (Castaldo 2001; Turley and Chebat 2002; Filser, Plichon and Antéblian 2003; Sabbadin 1997), especially in the store environments where the hedonistic and recreational shopping attitudes (Dauce and Rieunier 2002; Arnold and Reynolds 2003) have turned to satisfying particular needs. The ambiance and the atmosphere in their multi-sensorial and experiential dimensions (Bonnin 2000; Pine and Gilmore 1999; Schmitt 1999) can be of diverse importance to final consumers, especially when different shopping habits are considered (de Luca and Vianelli 2004). The attitude towards the store personnel can also be associated with the social dimension of atmosphere, taking into account different ways of perceiving the presence of the personnel inside the store, who may represent a constant presence throughout the whole shopping process.

THE DISTRIBUTION SYSTEM FOR HOUSEHOLD GOODS IN ITALY, FRANCE AND POLAND

The width and the heterogeneity of the household goods product category can include core products used in the kitchen as well as household textiles, furniture, floor coverings, lighting equipment and other accessories. Consumer attention during the research has been primarily focused on the household goods retailing format, which can be very different in terms of length and width of the assortment. In each country the multiplicity of stores where household goods can be bought has been pointed out. In fact, differences in the distribution system could explain some differences regarding in-store shopping behavior.

Before analyzing the peculiarity of the countries considered in the research, it is interesting to point out some global industry trends. The home furnishing retail sector as defined by Datamonitor (2005) (which includes furniture, floor coverings and household textiles), reveals in 2004 a year-on-year growth of 5,7%, a positive trend that is predicted to continue through 2009. For this sector, the European market remains the most important, generating revenues of 230,4 billion euros, which is equivalent to 49,3% of the global sector's value. Ikea is the leading retailer and accounts for 3,40% of the sector's overall value, followed by Bed Bath & Beyond Inc. (1,00%). Their market shares put into evidence an extremely fragmented offer.

Considering the range of countries analyzed in the research, some specific characteristics can be identified. According to Mauri (2004), in Italy the specialized independent retailers represent the most diffused household goods store format, which has revealed on average a constant yearly decrease of 2,5%. But, within this category the sub-segment of specialized franchising stores is characterized by a positive trend. These franchising stores present at least in the Italian context, an increased sensibility toward the topics of shopping and store atmosphere. Regarding Italian retail, franchising stores increased by 6.9% just last year, with a turnover of 18 billion euros (Assofranchising 2005), and "house decoration" and furnishing accessories" constitute together almost 6% of the market share, with turnovers of 581 million euros (3.2%) and 474 million euros (2,6%) respectively. Their importance in the market is highlighted by the number of store brands (85 in all, making up to 11.8%) and of franchisees (3300, equal to 7,3% of the total network). Extremely interesting is the information related to the internationalization of the household goods franchising stores, which is still extremely limited: only 120 stores have been opened in foreign markets, an extremely low number if compared to the franchising distribution of other product categories.

Household goods can be sold also through the modern distribution retailing format: department stores, supermarkets, hypermarkets and large specialized retailers. In Italy department stores (like La Rinascente and Coin) show, after a steady period, an annual growth rate of 1.9%. Supermarkets and hypermarkets' annual growth rates were higher, 7.8% for the former and 11.7% for the latter. Finally, the most interesting case in the field of large specialized stores is Ikea, which is present in the Italian market with 11 stores. To fully complete the outline of the household goods retailing in Italy, domestic appliances and electronics stores, as well as peddlers, street markets, factory outlets and reunion sales should be included. Nevertheless these forms of sales are scarcely relevant to the management of the store atmosphere.

From the point of view of distribution, the French market is, especially compared to the Italian and Polish, more accurate in terms of store atmosphere, and therefore in terms of sensibility toward managerial decisions related to the themes of shopping behavior. Some Authors even highlight how accuracy in the store atmosphere produced, for the French store brands, a positive impact on performance (Dupuis and Savreux 2004). As Lemoine (2004) suggests, in the management of the store, experiential marketing strategies are generally used, such as style and design of the store, music, perfumes, internal signs up to the management of the goods, price, and sales methods. These are strategies which create experience effects like surprise, curiously, theatricality, etc.

When referring to household goods retailing, the distribution system in France is organized around two major categories: the specialty stores and the non-specialized outlets. The latter can be categorized into two major sectors: department stores are mainly represented by store brands like Printemps or Galeries Lafayette. They are not specialized and are extremely important in the French distribution market (Cliquet 2000). Second, a significant category is the hypermarkets, which are increasing and represent the biggest market share (more or less 50% according to the product category). The principal specialty stores are represented by the traditional system with an old-fashioned image, whose number is decreasing. There are also some specialty superstores like Ikea, which are engaged in house furniture and other house-ware. Of importance are also the direct retail stores created by companies like Christofle or Villeroy and Boc. Finally it strongly emerges also the presence of some relevant franchised retail stores like Casa or Geneviève Lethu.

In France, 9.8% of the total franchised retail stores are house-ware stores (Fédération française de la franchise 2006) amounting to 91 names, coming after personal care stores only. In terms of affiliated members, in the category of household goods France reaches up to 3674 units, 9.3% of the franchisees in the whole country. What really differentiates France from the other countries is the degree of internationalization of the networks in franchising, which is relevant to the themes of standardization or adaptation of the store atmosphere. France has the highest export rate of franchised retail stores both on the world level (14%) and on a European level (24%). Such a trend applies to the house-ware category, with 28 names present abroad, which constitutes 33.3% of the names on the French market.

The Polish distribution system has changed dramatically during the last decade 1995-2005. These changes were due to a massive foreign investment in the field of general and specialized retailing. Poland has become a favorite place for new strategies of the biggest European retailers. There has been a rapid development of international retail chains, mostly of French, German and British origin. Similar to other numerous Eastern European countries, Poland is characterized by a strong development of franchising (Picot-Coupey and Cliquet 2004). These changes were possible, mainly thanks to very liberal Polish regulations and rather weak presence of national competitors. This massive investment turned Poland into one of the most competitive and modern innovative retail markets in Europe. Nevertheless the Polish distribution system is very heterogeneous, changing rapidly and showing important differences in the main cities. This explains why the size of the city may have a great influence on consumer behavior. The arrival of new forms of distribution has had a great impact on the behavior of Polish consumers, also in the sector of household goods. This behavior corresponds to a new attitude of the Polish consumer, one of discovering new forms of distribution and trying to make their own judgment on their evolution and quality, particularly in the big cities, where the choice is greater.

The Polish distribution system of household goods results from a very large supply of this product category by international hypermarkets such as French Carrefour, Casino, Leclerc, Auchan, German Real or British Tesco. They extend their usual offers of this product category, mostly due to the relative underdevelopment of specialized retailers in this sector in Poland at the moment of arrival. This product category is available in the large international retail chains, specialized in home and garden equipment and in do-it-yourself assortment, such as: Castorama

(30 stores), Leroy Merlin (16 stores), Praktiker (17 stores in 14 cities), Obi (25 stores) and Nomi (31 supermarkets). There is also a strong and visible presence of the global specialized retailers such as the Swedish Ikea which runs 7 big retail centers in Poland. At the same time, household goods are available in a very large number of medium/small, international/Polish specialized shops, with modern household equipment. We can quote at least 150 well-known Polish and foreign producers of furniture and house accessories. This product category is offered by a very large number of craftsmen and their associations in their own shops or in outlets run by independent retailers.

RESEARCH METHODOLOGY

Consumer shopping behavior variables that can be analyzed in a cross-cultural context are numerous and are the most useful parameters in comparing the three different countries. Should any differences arise, they might deeply influence the marketing strategies to be enforced, particularly those concerning in-store promotion and advertising. The previous analysis of existing literature has led us to define an exploratory research, aiming at studying the phenomenon and at going deep into the existing relationships between the highlighted variables with reference to Italian, French and Polish consumers.

The research has been conducted with the objective of highlighting the existing differences between consumers in different countries regarding the in-store behavior and consumer logistic, putting in to evidence socio-cultural outcomes, consumer involvement and the perception of the store atmosphere. Some detailed interviews helped us identify the household goods market (interior decoration, accessories and so on) as an ideal category developing a research project as it shows both low and high degrees of product, brand and shopping involvement as well as different buying behaviors and logistics management (Quester and Lim 2003).

An on-field research aiming at inquiring the complexity of shopping behavior in the house-related goods sector in the three different geographic areas has been organized subsequently. The empirical and qualitative research was run between March 2004 and May 2005 by means of direct interviews out of a sample of 201 units for France, 332 units for Italy, and 212 units for Poland, composed of women of various ages, mainly involved in house-keeping activities. The data elaboration applied descriptive statistics and processing data with factor analysis and cluster analysis, with the use of SPSS 12.0 software.

The questionnaire submitted to the interviewees was composed of five sections aiming at investigating the different involvement, behavior and consumer logistics dimensions. As a last stage, some personal characteristics such as time perception, store and brand loyalty and the main socio-demographic features was registered. The questionnaire set up was based on the use, with convenient adaptations, of variables and scales of measurement already applied and tested during previous theoretical analysis and privileging retailing related ones. The answers concerning involvement, behavior, logistics and personal variables were obtained by asking the interviewees the degree of agreement with the proposed options by using a Likert scale from 1 (I do not absolutely agree) to 5 (I definitely agree). With the same scale, questions related to atmosphere were designed to find the degree of importance in the different attributes.

FINDINGS

The analysis of the cross-cultural differences in the evaluation of in-store shopping behavior were conducted from different perspectives, attempting to describe the most critical aspects of French, Italian and Polish consumers. Hence, the analysis was divided into the following phases:

- an outline of the demographic, socio-economic and psychographic characteristics of the three samples was provided;
- the means of answers on the different aspects analyzed for consumers of the three countries were compared and commented;
- a factor analysis was processed in order to apply a cluster analysis finalized to the identification of horizontal segments within which the weight of consumers of the three countries was evaluated.

Characteristics of the French, Italian and Polish Samples

The explorative analysis was based on a non probabilistic sample. Before analyzing the most significant differences between French, Italian and Polish consumers for in-store shopping behavior, it was important to provide a synthetic outline of the characteristics of the three samples analyzed. That is, there was an investigation of the differences and the similarities that could influence the results of the empirical research.

Considering the socio-demographic characteristics, the Italian and Polish samples are represented by women aged 30 to 60, while the French sample is mainly constituted (70%) by women aged 40 and 49. In terms of educational structure, the homogeneity of the sample is weak: 47.7% of the French, 42.6% of the Italian and 41.7% of the Polish consumers have a diploma. A university degree is prevalent in the Polish sample with 54%, followed by the French consumers with 38.6% and only 16.3% of the Italians. A high degree of homogeneity can be found in occupation where, apart from housewives (20.2% in France, 26.0% in Italy and 14.8% in Poland), the majority are employed: 47.7% of the French women, 42.6% of the Italians and 25.1% of the Polish sample. Coherently with the higher degree, there is 10.6% of middle-ranking managers in the French sample, while a significant percentage of the Polish women interviewed are retailers (11.8%) and teachers (12.3%). Income is generally perceived to be on the average level for all the three nationalities, even if almost 20% of the Polish consumers did not want to declare it. French consumers of the sample mainly visit hypermarkets (56%), followed by specialist stores (35.5%) and home department of big stores (7.5%). Italian consumers mainly buy in specialist stores (52.7%) and in home departments (33.2%) and only 13.7% buy in hypermarkets. Similar to Italians, Polish women prefer to buy in specialist stores (45.8%), followed by home departments (31.1%) and hypermarkets (23.1%).

Cross-Cultural Differences in In-Store Shopping Behavior

In general, regarding shopping behavior, consumer logistic and evaluation of store atmosphere, a good level of homogeneity emerges with some significant differences.

In terms of the psychographic aspects (Table 2), time pressure (B9), brand (B10) and store loyalty (B11), while France and Italy appear to be quite homogeneous, Polish consumers seem to feel less time-pressured and, in their behavior, they are less loyal to brands and stores. A low brand loyalty is not accompanied by a low brand involvement: Polish consumers reveal a higher brand involvement (I9 and I10) compared to the other nationalities. They prefer to buy branded household goods, to feel to have made the right choice. And they are rarely tempted to buy household goods if they do not need them immediately (B5). These differences indicated in Polish consumers can be related to the fact that

TABLE 2. Consumer Involvement (I) and In-Store Consumer Behavior (B): A Comparison Between French, Italian and Polish Clients

	Total sample *(mean)*	French consumers *(mean)*	Italian consumers *(mean)*	Polish consumers *(mean)*
I like to buy household goods (I1)	4.18	4.33	4.07	4.20
Having the right pieces of furniture and household accessories is really important for me (I2)	4.09	4.34	3.98	4.05
I like spending a lot of time choosing household goods (I3)	3.19	3.14	3.14	3.32
Household goods I buy give an idea of my personality (I4)	3.95	3.76	4.19	3.76
I like buying household goods as a present for friends and relatives (I5)	3.17	2.85	3.24	3.36
When I enter a house I always look at how it is furnished and how different household accessories have been matched (I6)	3.61	3.95	3.42	3.59
I like spending a lot of money on household goods (I7)	2.63	2.54	2.57	2.80
I prefer to give up other expenses, if I can only buy household goods that I like (I8)	2.31	2.40	2.13	2.51
When I buy something for my house, I look for branded products, because I am sure it is the right choice (I9)	2.89	2.76	2.71	3.32
I like reading magazines about house furniture and goods in order to get some information on different brand proposals (I10)	2.85	2.83	2.45	3.48
I like shopping (I11)	3.69	4.05	3.40	3.80
I try to spend a lot of time shopping (I12)	2.51	2.92	2.28	2.49
I like visiting household goods stores, even just for curiosity (I13)	3.50	3.42	3.53	3.54
Most of the time, before entering a household goods store, I already know what I want to buy (B1)	3.63	3.70	3.86	3.21
I never let myself be tempted to buy products that attract me but that I have not planned to buy (B2)	2.85	2.55	3.16	2.65
Before buying household goods, I spend a lot of time comparing the peculiarities of different brands and products sold in the store (B3)	3.21	3.20	3.22	3.18
I am always able to compare and evaluate the quality, price and other important attributes of household goods I want to buy (B4)	3.37	3.48	3.24	3.44
If I see some products on special offer, I am always tempted to buy them even if I don't need them immediately (B5)	2.41	2.46	2.60	2.08
When I buy household goods, I am really influenced by the information I can find reading a magazine, an advertisement, etc. (B6)	2.49	2.57	2.06	3.08
When I buy, I am really influenced by the advice of my friends and relatives (B7)	2.66	3.03	2.26	2.94

When I buy household goods, I usually base my choice on the information I get inside the store (point-of-sale advertisement, shop-assistant's advice, etc.) (B8)	2.74	2.80	2.41	3.20
According to my lifestyle, I always manage not to waste a minute of my time (B9)	2.95	3.37	3.02	2.43
When I like a brand (for example a brand of cooking utensils), I almost never decide to change (B10)	2.82	2.99	2.92	2.49
If I like a store, I almost never decide to visit other ones, just to see if I can find different products or better prices (B11)	2.66	2.71	2.83	2.35

Polish consumers need more time before making the final decision. They want to be sure they have made the right choice, according to the offer available on the market. Having less money at their disposal, they tend to be more rational. They collect all the necessary information to make their own judgment, before the final decision is made. They seem to be less loyal to brands and stores, because they are just discovering new retailers and new brands arriving largely on the Polish market at the same time. Polish consumers, though, make decisions in a more unstable and changing retail environment in comparison to France or Italy.

Higher brand involvement reflects the search for good quality products and for extra guaranties offered by the brands they may trust. Foreign retail chains try to become a synonym for good quality offers. This is particularly true for Ikea, which has a higher positioning in Poland than in West European countries.

Another interesting dimension, is the source of information influencing in-store behavior. French consumers considered seem to be significantly influenced by the advice of friends and relatives. The same relevance cannot be recognized for the Italian sample, for which the role of the different information sources seems to be weak. Word-of-mouth is important for Polish consumers. They seem to rely not only on information provided by different *media* (B6) but especially on point-of-sale advertising (B8). The importance of information provided on the point-of-sale has a very special meaning for the Polish consumers. They need time to discover new forms of retailing and brands in a new environment. They need to be reassured by the salesperson before making the final decision. This is also the reason why the same international retail chains employ more salespeople in Poland than in France or Italy. These salesclerks play the role of real consumer consultants and advisers, helping make the final decision.

The evaluation of consumer logistic variables (Table 3) appears to be quite similar within the three groups, with the only exception that Polish consumers seem to be more concerned about transportation (L1 and L2), which can be related to the lower rate of car ownership especially by women.

It is the role of store atmosphere to point out the main unexpected result of this research (Table 4). Contrary to what could have been expected, atmosphere plays an important role in the French and Polish sample of consumers, while in the Italian sample it is significantly below the average, especially when sensorial variables like smell, music, etc., are taken into consideration. Only those elements whose role is to simplify consumer shopping within the store (such as indications, etc.) are taken into consideration by the Italian sample.

The great importance of the store atmosphere in the case of the Polish sample may be explained by the high degree of innovation in this sphere, due to a significant role of foreign investment in this field. Most of the stores in this category have been opened only recently and the investors very often pay a lot of attention to the sophisticated atmosphere of the shop. After the "dark time" of the former economic system, Polish consumers seem to be more sensitive to the store atmosphere, espe-

TABLE 3. Consumer Logistic (L): A Comparison Between French, Italian and Polish Clients

	Total sample (mean)	French consumers (mean)	Italian consumers (mean)	Polish consumers (mean)
I always ask myself if I can manage to bring it home (L1)	3.04	2.99	2.95	3.24
I always take into consideration if I am doing shopping alone or, vice versa, with someone that will help me to bring my products home (L2)	2.90	2.78	2.66	3.42
I never ask myself if I have enough space to fit it in at home. If I like it, I will buy it and then. . . I will figure out how to! (L3)	2.15	2.06	2.10	2.31
I always visit different stores in order to compare the characteristics of different brands and products (L4)	3.18	3.44	2.92	3.34
I always visit different stores in order to find the best price (L5)	3.38	3.38	3.33	3.45
To make sure I am buying at the cheapest price, not only do I visit shops that are close to my house, but I am always ready to visit farther stores (L6)	2.64	2.33	2.81	2.65

TABLE 4. The Role of Atmosphere (A) in the Shopping and Buying Process: A Comparison Between French, Italian and Polish Consumers

	Total sample (mean)	French consumers (mean)	Italian consumers (mean)	Polish consumers (mean)
A nice atmosphere (A1)	3.92	4.38	3.55	4.09
A nice furnishing (A2)	3.56	4.00	3.04	3.96
A nice and particular style and design (A3)	3.33	4.29	2.46	3.79
A good lighting of the shop (A4)	3.92	4.38	3.57	4.04
An agreeable smell and perfume in the store (A5)	3.30	3.62	2.69	3.98
A large shop, where I can easily move around (A6)	3.66	4.43	2.98	4.00
Little noise and confusion (A7)	3.87	3.74	3.70	4.26
Background music (A8)	2.99	3.95	2.37	3.05
Some indications that can help me to easily find those products and departments I am looking for (A9)	4.43	4.66	4.18	4.59
When I buy household goods, the kindness and politeness of the personnel are a must (A10)	4.20	4.41	3.94	4.40
When I buy household goods, it is essential for me to perceive that clients in the store are quite similar to me (in lifestyle, etc.) (A11)	2.51	2.55	2.56	2.41

cially when referring to good lighting, an agreeable smell and little noise. Shopping is seen by the consumer as a very special moment, in a very special environment protected from the outside world. The social dimension of atmosphere for the Polish consumers not only attach great importance to the advice of personnel, but they appreciate kindness, which reflects the prevalent lack of satisfaction during the former communist system. The Italian sample seems to be more traditionalist, linked to the characteristics of a distribution system that still has some difficulty in evolving with reference to the experiential attributes of a store. Recent researchers (Borghini 2004) have pointed out the increasing significance of household goods for Italian consumers, that can be reflected in the search for emotions also during the shopping activities. Consumer shopping behavior still remains more functional and rational and the store experience is only partially appreciated. Polish consumers are impressed by the most innovative stores. In Italy, with the exception of some franchising networks, the old stores are changing, but this process is slow and with less impact for the final consumer.

In order to investigate the comparison of the different variables, a factor analysis has been processed for each of the three groups of consumers. Since the factors identified appear to be quite similar within the nationalities, a final factor analysis has been developed for the total sample, in order to have the possibility of comparing the three groups on the same basis (Table 5).

As emerges in Table 5, factors identified during the analysis of the total sample can be labeled as follows: Factor 1–"emotional atmosphere"; Factor 2–"product involvement"; Factor 3–"explorative behavior"; Factor 4–"information sources"; Factor 5–"shopping involvement"; Factor 6–"planning"; Factor 7–"consumer logistic"; Factor 8–"functional atmosphere"; Factor 9–"impulse behavior"; Factor 10–"gift."

The identification of the above factors, allows us to process a cluster analysis in order to identify the horizontal segments which characterize the multicultural group of French, Italian and Polish consumers considered in the research.

In-Store Shopping Segmentation of Italian, French and Polish Consumers

To simplify and increase the reliability of the cluster analysis, only the first seven factors (emotional atmosphere, product involvement, explorative behavior, information sources, shopping involvement, planning and consumer logistic) have been considered in the analysis, since they thoroughly describe the different dimensions of in-store shopping behavior. The results of the cluster analysis (K-Means method; Anova test) processed on the total sample and a description of the characteristics of the segments can be read in Table 6.

Consumers of the three clusters have been described also in terms of weight taken by the French, Italian and Polish clusters within the horizontal segments previously defined. As emerges in Table 7, considering the values related to the percentage within the country, the French consumers belong to the "Influenceables" and the "Shopping lovers" clusters, even if a good part of them can be also defined as "Explorers." Almost half of the Polish women consumers can be described as "Influenceables" while a significant percentage of the sample is represented by the "Explorers" and only a 12.7% are "Shopping lovers." The high presence of the Polish sample in the cluster of the "Influenceables" may be explained by their open attitude towards new forms of marketing communication. To justify their choice, they rely on the different types of information that can be received in a store, including the atmo-

TABLE 5. Factor Analysis on Consumer Shopping Behavior by French, Italian and Polish Consumers–Rotated Component Matrix

	F1	F2	F3	F4	F5	F6	F7	F8	F9	F10
A nice and particular style and design (A3)	0.813									
A nice furnishing (A2)	0.793									
A good lighting of the shop (A4)	0.734									
A large shop, where I can easily move around (A6)	0.701									
An agreeable smell and perfume in the store (A5)	0.661									
A nice atmosphere (A1)	0.659									
Background music (A8)	0.538									
Having the right pieces of furniture and household accessories is really important for me (I2)		0.740								
I like to buy household goods (I1)		0.707								
I like spending a lot of time choosing household goods (I3)		0.699								
I like spending a lot of money on household goods (I7)		0.683								
I prefer to give up other expenses, if I can only buy household goods that I like (I8)		0.621								
Household goods I buy give an idea of my personality (I4)		0.477								
I like reading magazines. . . in order to get some information on different brand proposals (I10)		0.471								
When I enter a house I always look at how it is furnished. . . (I6)		0.449								
I like visiting household goods stores, even just for curiosity (I13)		0.431								
I always visit different stores in order to find the best price (L5)			0.862							
I always visit different stores in order to compare. . . different brands and products (L4)			0.809							
To make sure I am buying at the cheapest price, . . . I am always ready to visit farther stores (L6)			0.726							
Before buying household goods, I spend a lot of time comparing different brands and products sold in the store (B3)			0.610							
When I buy household goods, I am really influenced by the information I can find reading a magazine, an adv. etc. (B6)				0.682						
When I buy, I am really influenced by the advice of my friends and relatives (B7)				0.674						

TABLE 5 (continued)

	F1	F2	F3	F4	F5	F6	F7	F8	F9	F10
When I buy household goods, I usually base my choice on the information I get inside the store (point-of-sale advertisement, shop-assistant's advice, etc.) (B8)				0.541						
When I buy something for my house, I look for branded products... (I9)				0.480						
I like shopping (I11)					0.714					
I try to spend a lot of time shopping (I12)					0.680					
Most of the time, before entering a (...) store, I already know what I want to buy (B1)						0.763				
I never let me tempt to buy products that attract me but that I did not plan to buy (B2)						0.724				
I always ask myself if I can manage to bring it home (L1)							0.858			
I always take into consideration if I am doing shopping alone or, vice versa, with someone that will help me to bring my products home (L2)							0.835			
Some indications (...) to easily find those products and departments I am looking for (A9)								0.719		
Little noise and confusion (A7)								0.479		
When I buy household goods, the kindness and politeness of the personnel are a must (A10)								0.431		
I never ask myself if I have enough space to fit it in at home. If I like it, I will buy it... (L3)									0.639	
If I see some products on special offer, I am always tempted to buy... (B5)									0.573	
When I buy h.g., it is essential for me to perceive that clients in the store are quite similar to me (in lifestyle, etc) (A11)									0.567	
I like buying household goods as a present for my friends and relatives (I5)										0.647
I am always able to compare and evaluate the quality, the price... (B4)										-.367

Extraction method: Principal component analysis; Rotation method: Varimax with Kaiser Normalisation. Rotation converged in 4 iterations. Variance explained at 57.8%.

TABLE 6. Cluster Analysis and Clusters Profiles in the Evaluation of Store Atmosphere

Total sample (n = 745)	Cluster 1 (n = 179; 24.0%)	Cluster 2 (n = 185; 24.8%)	Cluster 3 (n = 160; 21.5%)	Cluster 4 (n = 221; 29.7%)	Sig. (Anova)
Factor 1-emotional atmosphere	0.261	0.473	−1.439	0.434	.000
Factor 2-product involvement	−0.251	0.133	0.135	0.217	.000
Factor 3-explorative behavior	0.782	−0.107	−0.154	−0.433	.000
Factor 4-information sources	−0.171	−0.647	−0.254	0.864	.000
Factor 5-shopping involvement	−0.648	0.804	0.046	−0.182	.000
Factor 6-planning	−0.586	0.320	0.121	0.119	.000
Factor 7-consumer logistic	−0.170	0.275	−0.166	0.028	.000

Cluster 1: The Explorers	−A low importance is ascribed to factors 5 and 6 (shopping involvement and planning) −A high importance is ascribed to factor 3 (explorative behaviour) From an emotional perspective, shopping is not their passion and they do not worry if they cannot devote time to that. Nevertheless, they are the kind of consumers that, when entering an household goods store, they do not really know what they want to buy. As a consequence, they tend to have an highly explorative behaviour visiting various stores in order to compare different prices, brands and products: in this way, they try to be sure to do the most convenient choice in terms of the quality/price ratio. Low income consumers mainly fall in this segment.
Cluster 2: The Shopping Lovers	−A low importance is ascribed to factor 4 (information sources) −A modest importance is ascribed to factor 1 and 6 (emotional atmosphere and planning) −A high importance is ascribed to factor 5 (shopping involvement) Among the different segments, they are the most involved in the shopping activity that is appreciated from an emotional as well as from a rational point of view. In fact, they rather attach importance to store atmosphere but they also do shopping basically to find what they have already planned to buy. They are very independent in their choices and they do not like to be influenced either by friends or relatives, nor by external communication or in-store advertising.
Cluster 3: The Indifferents	−A very low importance is ascribed to factor 1 (emotional atmosphere) Their shopping behaviour can be defined as "on the average level," but what really does not play any role in their life is the store atmosphere, especially in its emotional ad sensitive attributes. They are mainly over 40, and when they buy household goods, they prefer speciality stores to hypermarkets.
Cluster 4 The Influentiables	−A high importance is ascribed to factor 4 (information sources) −A good importance is ascribed to factor 1 (emotional atmosphere) −A low importance is ascribed to factor 3 (explorative behaviour) When they buy household goods, they like to visit stores where atmosphere plays an important role and it is very coherent in all its emotional elements. But their main characteristic is that, in their choice, they do not like to spend time comparing products, brands and prices. On the contrary, they strongly rely on the advice they receive from their friends and relatives, on the information provided by the magazines and advertising, as well as on all the information they can gather within the store. High income consumers are mainly represented by this segment.

TABLE 7. Horizontal Clusters and Consumer Nationality in the Perception of Store Atmosphere

Total sample (n = 745)		France	Italy	Poland	% of total segment
Explorers	% within the cluster % within the country	23,4 **20,9**	36,9 **19,9**	39,7 **33,5**	100
Shopping lovers	% within the cluster % within the country	41,1 **37,8**	44,3 **24,7**	14,6 **12,7**	100
Indifferents	% within the cluster % within the country	3,1 **2,5**	90,0 **43,4**	6,9 **5,2**	100
Influenceables	% within the cluster % within the country	35,3 **38,8**	18,1 **12,0**	46,6 **48,6**	100
% of total country		100	100	100	

sphere. The role of the "Explorers" in the Polish sample is due to the difficult economic situation in a large number of Polish households. Consumers must be more rational in their behavior, because of their lower income. Their shopping decisions are usually better prepared and planned in advance, and also accompanied by personal quality/price ratio research. Most of the Italians (43.4%) can be defined as "Indifferents," even if it is possible to identify a discrete number of "Shopping lovers" and "Explorers." Though the unequal numerousness of the three samples, it is possible to underline how the "Explorers" and the "Influenceables" are mainly represented by the Polish women, the "Shopping lovers" by the French ones and the "Indifferents" by the Italians.

CONCLUSIONS AND MANAGERIAL IMPLICATIONS

From the analysis of in-store consumer behavior for the French, Italian and Polish consumers considered in the research, it clearly emerges that ignoring cross-cultural differences can lead retailing companies to centralize and homogenize operations and marketing, resulting in declining profitability instead of increasing efficiency. Hence the alternative: standardization versus adaptation has to be deeply evaluated with its costs and benefits (Vianelli 2001), also referring to the retailing context (Kaufmann and Eroglu 1998; Evans and Bridson 2005). Cost minimization is one of the main motives for standardization, that is a homogeneous approach to the development of research, purchasing and marketing activities, from which scale economies and easier implementation of management programs and monitoring systems derive. The second important driver of standardization is the global image that a uniform retailing format is able to convey. Standard unique elements of the store, together with an homogeneous communication strategy, allow the development of a distinct and clearly positioned perceived retail image. A number of factors which can favor adaptation can be evaluated. Market differences can be so significant as to inhibit standardization, if not in the core elements of the retailing format, at least in the peripheral ones. Decisions on the standardization/adaptation dilemma strongly depend on the development stage of the distribution system, which determine the expertise and the characteristics of consumer shopping and purchase behavior. Evaluating the results obtained in the present analysis, a significant number of aspects should be pointed out in relation to the standardization/adaptation decision.

The importance given to store atmosphere by French and Polish consumers requires more attention in relation to the definition of atmosphere design. It is not so relevant for the Italian consumers considered in the analysis.

The fact that Polish consumers reveal high brand involvement and a high sensitivity to external and internal sources of information (external and in-store advertising, seller's advice, etc), has to convince retailers about the importance, in particular to this country, of developing marketing actions that can reinforce brand value and can influence consumer behavior providing a continuous stream of information both outside and inside the store. Special attention should be paid to different forms of marketing communication related both to the retail chain as a whole and to the different affiliates of the network. Retailers should concentrate on informing, motivating and advising the consumer in the store. Special recruitment is recommended for sales personnel, orienting their training towards playing more the role of consumer's advisors and internal consultants.

The exploratory behavior that characterizes the Polish sample requires particular attention to the price/quality ratio. The strategy of retailers should be clear and precise, also for price positioning. The retailers should learn how to deal with the "Explorers," who may need more time to make the final decision, and who should be invited to come back to the store after making their own "market research." Retailers are encouraged to give the consumer the guarantee of the lowest price on the local market for a given product category.

The French consumers are similar to the Polish in how they are influenced, but the French are strongly involved in the doing of shopping itself. The customer may not systematically be looking for experiential stimulation, as confirmed by the regularly market share of hard discount (Filser 2004). However a retailer can facilitate, improve and emotionally enrich the shopping experience. The retail manager has to adopt a wide atmosphere approach, taking into account the multiple physical and social dimensions and interactions of the store environment (Lemoine 2004).

In the Italian context, "Shopping lovers" is consistent with the strong presence of a high number of consumers not recognizing the role of store atmosphere. It is not important to emphasize this aspect especially in its emotional perspective, but vice versa try to improve the characteristics of the store mainly with functional solutions that can simplify the shopping activity.

It is not possible to say that consumers of the three countries can be considered homogeneous in all their characteristics, even if it is interesting to point out that French and Polish women seem to be more similar. This finding can be mainly interpreted as the result of the dynamics that have characterized the Polish market in the last years, especially due to the entrance of new successful international retailing companies. The distribution system is changing also in Italy in terms of store experience and atmosphere. We can observe the evolution of the previous structures towards a more modern approach, and this process perhaps requires more time then entering directly with new and modern stores as it happens in Poland.

The primary limit of this research can be recognized in its exploratory approach, mainly related to the numerousness of the three samples and to their non probabilistic structure. This is particularly true in relation to the characteristics of the geographical territories analyzed, that can significantly influence the structure of the retailing context and the shopping habits. Nevertheless, in spite of these limits, the findings can be generally helpful from a managerial point of view especially because they can make retailing managers aware of the problem of standardization/adaptation of their managerial solutions in terms of marketing, services and sales strategies. Future research should be focused on a specific retailer operating with the same store format in all the countries considered in the research. This would guarantee that homogeneity, which represents the base for international and cross-cultural comparisons and can be particularly interesting in terms of managerial implications in a context of retailing internationalization.

REFERENCES

Ailawadi, K.L., Neslin, S.A., & Gedenk, K. (2001). Pursuing the value–conscious consumer: store brands versus national brand promotions. *Journal of Marketing, 65* (1), 71-89.

Andrews, J.C., Durvasula, S., & Akhter, S.H. (1990). A framework for conceptualizing and measuring the involvement construct in advertising research. *Journal of Advertising, 19* (4), 27-40.

Arnold, M.J., & Reynolds, K.E. (2003). Hedonic shopping motivations. *Journal of Retailing, 79,* 77-95.

Assofranchising (2005). *Il franchising in Italia: proiezioni 2005–Quadrante Srl.* Retrieved January 26, 2006, from http://www.assofranchising.it/statistiche/DatiAssofrProvvisori2005.swf

Baumgartner, H., & Steenkamp, J.E.M. (1996). Exploratory consumer buying behavior: conceptualization and measurement. *International Journal of Research in Marketing, 13,* 121-137.

Bellenger, D.N., & Korgaonkar, P.K. (1980). Profiling the recreational shopper. *Journal of Retailing, 56* (3), 77-92.

Berman, B., & Evans., J.R. (1989). *Retail management: a strategic approach,* New York: MacMilllan Publishing Company.

Bloch, P.H., Sherrell, D.L., & Ridgway, N.M. (1986). Consumer search: an extended framework. *Journal of Consumer Research, 13* (1), 119-126.

Bonnin, G. (2000). *L'expérience de magasinage. Conceptualisation et exploration des rôles du comportement physique et de l'aménagement de l'espace.* Dijon, Université de Bourgogne: Thèse de Sciences de Gestion.

Borghini, S. (2004). La donna, la casa e i prodotti per la casa. In C. Mauri (a cura di), *Innovazione nel retailing nei prodotti per la casa* (pp.68-90). Milano: Franco Angeli.

Bucklin, R.E., Gupta, S., & Siddarth, S. (1998). Determining segmentation in sales response across consumer purchase behaviors. *Journal of Marketing Research, 35* (2), 189-197.

Castaldo, S. (2001). *Retailing & Innovazione. L'evoluzione del marketing nella distribuzione.* Milano: Egea.

Chetthamrongchai, P. & Davies, G. (2000). Segmenting the market for food shoppers using attitudes to shopping and to time. *British Food Journal, 102* (2). Retrieved on July 18, 2005, from Proquest data base.

Cleveland, M., Babin, B.J., Laroche, M., Ward, P., Bergeron, J. (2003). Information search patterns for gift purchases: a cross-national examination of gender differences. *Journal of Consumer Behaviour, 3 (1),* 20-47.

Cliquet, G. (2000). Large format retailers: a French tradition despite reactions. *Journal of Retailing and Consumer Services, 87,* 183-195.

Collesei, U., (2000). *Marketing.* Padova: Cedam.

Datamonitor (2005). *Global Home Furnishing Retail.* Retrieved December 14, 2005, from http://dbic.datamonitor.com.ucfproxy.fcla.edu/industries/

Dauce, B. & Rieunier, S. (2002). Le marketing sensoriel du point de vente. *Recherche et Application en Marketing, 17* (4), 45-65.

Dawson, S., Bloch, P.H., & Ridgway N.M. (1990). Shopping motives, emotional states and retail outcomes. *Journal of Retailing, 66* (4), 408-427.

de Luca, P., & Vianelli, D. (2001). *Il marketing nel punto vendita. Strumenti di gestione della densità e dell'affollamento.* Milano: Franco Angeli.

de Luca, P., & Vianelli, D. (2004). Coinvolgimento del consumatore e valutazione dell'atmosfera del punto vendita. *Micro & Macro Marketing, 3,* 581-594.

De Mooij, M., & Hofstede, G. (2002). Convergence and divergence in consumer behavior: implications for international retailing. *Journal of Retailing, 78,* 61-69.

Domanski, T. (2001), *Marketingowe strategie duzych sieci handlowych,* Warszawa: PWN.

Domanski, T. (2005), *Strategie rozwoju handlu,* Warszawa: PWE.

Dupuis, M., & Savreux, D. (2003). Marketing expérientiel et performances des enseignes de distribution. *Revue Française du Marketing, 194 (3/5),* 89-106.

Evans, J., & Bridson, K. (2005). Explaining retail offer adaptation through psychic distance. *International Journal of Retail and Distribution Management, 33* (1) 69-78.

Fédération française de la franchise (2006). *Les chiffres de la franchise en 2005.* Retrieved February 8, 2006, from http://www.franchise-fff.com/index.php

Filser, M. (2004). La stratégie de la distribution: des interrogations managériales aux contributions académiques. Revue Française du Marketing, 198 (3/5), 7-16.

Filser, M., Plichon, V., & Antéblian, B. (2003). La valorisation de l'expérience en magasin: analyse de l'adaptabilité d'une échelle de mesure de la valeur perçue. In *Actes du 6ème Colloque Etienne Thil,* Université de La Rochelle.

Furse, D.H, Punj, G.N., & Stewart, D.W. (1984). A typology of individual search strategies among purchasers of new automobiles. *Journal of Consumer Research, 10* (4), 417-431.

Gonzalez-Benito, O., Greatorex, M., & Munoz Gallego, P.A. (2000), Assessment of potential retail segmentation variables. An approach based on a subjective MCI resource allocation model. *Journal of Retailing and Consumer Services, 7,* 171-179.

Granzin, K.L., Painter, J.J., & Valentin, E.K. (1997). Consumer logistics as a basis for segmenting retail markets: an exploratory inquiry. *Journal of Retailing and Consumer Services, 4* (2), 99-107.

Harp, S.S., Hlavaty, V., & Horridge, P.E. (2000). South Korean female apparel market segments based on store attributes. *Journal of Retailing and Consumer Services, 7,* 161-170.

Hofstede, G. (2001). *Culture's consequences* (2nd ed.), Thousand Oaks, CA: Sage.

Kapferer, J., & Laurent, G. (1992). *La sensibilité aux marques.* Paris: Les Editions d'Organisation.

Kassarjian, H., & Robertson, T. (1981), *Perspectives in Consumer Behavior,* Chicago: Scott Foresman.

Kaufmann, P.J., & Eroglu, S. (1998). Standardization and adaptation in business format franchising. *Journal of Business Venturing, 14* (1), 69-85.

Laurent, G., & Kapferer J.N. (1985). Measuring consumer involvement profiles. *Journal of Marketing Research, 22* (1), 41-53.

Laurent, G., & Kapferer J.N. (1986). Les profils d'implication. *Recherche et Application en Marketing, 1* (1), 41-57.

Lee, J.K., & Geistfeld, L.V. (1995). A hierarchy of store characteristics: a conceptual advancement. *8th International Conference on Research in the Distributive Trades,* Milano: Cescom.

Lee, W., (1991). *Consumer In-Store Exploratory Behavior: The Effects of Perceived Retail Crowding and Cognitive Control.* U.S.A.: The Pennsylvania State University, UMI.

Lemoine, J-F. (2003). Vers une approche globale de l'atmosphère du point de vente. *Revue Française du Marketing, 194 (4)*, 83-101.

Lemoine, J-F. (2004). Magasins d'atmosphère: quelles évolutions et quelles perspectives d'avenir ? *Revue Française du Marketing, 198* (3/5), 107-116.

Lesser, J.A., & Hughes, M.A. (1986). The generalizability of psychographic market segments across geographic locations. *Journal of Marketing, 50* (1), 18-27.

Lockshin, L.S., Spawton, A.L., & Macintosh, G. (1997). Using product, brand and purchasing involvement for retail segmentation. *Journal of Retailing and Consumer Services, 4* (3), 171-183.

Lugli, G., & Pellegrini, L. (2002). *Marketing distributivo.* Torino: Utet.

Martinez, E., & Montaner, T. (2006). The effect of consumer's psychographic variables upon deal-proneness. *Journal of Retailing and Consumer Services, 13*, 157-168.

Marzocchi, G.L. (1999). *Tempo, impresa e consumatore–Il waiting management nelle imprese di servizi*, Roma: Carocci.

Mauri, C. (a cura di) (2004). *Innovazione nel retailing nei prodotti per la casa.* Milano: Franco Angeli.

Mehrabian, A., & Russell, J.A. (1974). *An approach to Environmental Psychology*, Cambridge, MA.: MIT Press.

Mentzer, J.T., Flint, D.J., & Hult, G.T.M. (2001). Logistic service quality as a segment–customized process. *Journal of Marketing, 65* (4), 82-104.

Mittal, B., & Lee, M.S. (1989). A causal model of consumer involvement. *Journal of Economic Psychology, 10*, 363-389.

Moye, L.N., & Kincade, D.H. (2002). Influence of usage situations and consumer shopping orientations on the importance of retail store environment. *International Review of Retail, Distribution and Consumer Research, 12* (1), 59-79.

Murthi, B.P.S., & Srinivasan, K. (1999). Consumers' extent of evaluation in brand choice. *Journal of Business, 72* (2), 229-256.

O'Cass, A. (2000). An assessment of consumers product, purchase decision, advertising and consumption involvement in fashion clothing. *Journal of Economic Psychology, 21* (5), 545-576.

Ohanian, R., & Tashchian A. (1992). Consumers' shopping effort and evaluation of store image attributes: the roles of purchasing involvement and recreational shopping interest. *Journal of Applied Business Research, 8* (4), 40-49.

Picot-Coupey, K., & Cliquet, G. (2004). Internationalisation des distributeurs dans les pays en transition d'Europe de l'Est: quelles perspectives pour le choix de la franchise comme mode d'entrée? *Revue Française du Marketing, 198* (3/5), 19-35.

Pine, B.II, & Gilmore, J.H. (1999). *The Experience Economy. Work Is Theatre & Every Business A Stage.* Boston: Harvard Business School Press.

Popkowski, P., & Timmermans, H. (2001). Experimental choice analysis of shopping strategies. *Journal of Retailing, 77* (4), 493-509.

Putrevu, S., & Lord, K.R. (2001). Search dimensions, patterns and segment profiles of grocery shoppers. *Journal of Retailing and Consumer Services, 8* (3), 127-137.

Putrevu, S., & Ratchford, B.T. (1997). A model of search behavior with an application to grocery shopping. *Journal of Retailing, 73* (4), 463-486.

Quester, P., & Lim, A.L. (2003). Product involvement/brand loyalty: is there a link? *Journal of Product & Brand Management, 12* (1), 22-38.

Reid, R., & Brown, S. (1996). I hate shopping! An introspective perspective. *International Journal of Retail & Distribution Management, 24* (4), 4-16.

Sabbadin, E. (1997). *Marketing della distribuzione e marketing integrato.* Milano: Egea.

Samli, A. (edited by) (1989). *Heterogeneity of markets and segmentation in retailing.* New York: Retailing Marketing Strategy Quorum.

Schmitt, B.H. (1999). *Experiential Marketing.* New York: The Free Press.

Sciarelli, S., & Vona, R. (2000). *L'impresa commerciale.* Milano: McGraw-Hill.

Severin, V., Louviere, J.J., & Finn A. (2001), The stability of retail shopping choices over time and across countries. *Journal of Retailing, 77* (2), 185-202.

Slama, M.E., & Tashchian, A. (1985). Selected socioeconomic and demographic characteristics associated with purchasing involvement. *Journal of Marketing, 49* (1), 72-82.

Smith, M.F., Carsky, M.L. (1996). Grocery shopping behavior: a comparison of involved and uninvolved consumers, in *"Journal of Retailing and Consumer Services,"* Vol.3, no 2, 1996. 73-80.

Steenkamp, J., & Wedel, M. (1991). Segmenting retail markets on store image using a consumer-based methodology. *Journal of Retailing, 67* (3), 300-320.

Sternquist, B. (1998). *International retailing,* New York: Fairchild Publications.

Stone, G.P. (1954). City shoppers and urban identification: observation of the social psychology of city life. *American Journal of Sociology, 60* (1), 36-45.

Swait, J., & Sweeney, J.C. (2000). Perceived value and its impact on choice behavior in a retail setting. *Journal of Retailing and Consumer Services, 7,* 77-88.

Turley, L.W., & Chebat J. (2002). Linking retail strategy, atmospheric design and shopping behaviour. *Journal of Marketing Management, 18* (1/2), 125-144.

Underhill, P. (1999). *Why we buy: the science of shopping.* London: Orion Business Books.

Vianelli, D. (2001). *Il posizionamento del prodotto nei mercati internazionali.* Milano: Franco Angeli.

Volle, P. (coordonné par) (2000). *Etudes et Recherches sur la Distribution.* Paris: Economica.

Wakefield, K.L., & Baker, J. (1998). Excitement at the mall: determinants and effect on shopping response. *Journal of Retailing, 74* (4), 515-539.

Zaichkowsky, J.L. (1985). Measuring the involvement construct. *Journal of Consumer Research, 12* (3), 341-352.

Zaichkowsky, J.L., & Sood, J.H. (1989). A Global Look at Consumer Involvement and Use of Products. *International Marketing Review, 6* (1), 20-34.

Zimmer, M.R., & Golden, L.L. (1988). Impressions of Retail Stores: A Content Analysis of Consumer Images. *Journal of Retailing, 64* (3), 265-293.

doi:10.1300/J097v13n02_02

Regionalization
in Central and Eastern Europe:
Searching for Regiocentric Orientations
in MNC Strategies

Arnold Schuh

SUMMARY. Regional players among the MNCs operating in Central and Eastern Europe have to decide if they should regard their businesses as a collection of individual markets or as a homogeneous region. The purpose of this paper is to examine if and how regionalization concepts have actually been implemented by foreign MNCs in CEE. The analysis focuses on the preconditions for the emergence of a regional strategy, on the identification of the main areas of regional integration, and the relationship between strategy and organizational structure. By using a longitudinal case study approach a better insight is gained on how regional strategies have emerged during the internationalization process of the firm and, if they have emerged, in which way they have manifested themselves in business decisions. The findings raise new questions about the regionalization construct with regard to the

Dr. Arnold Schuh is Assistant Professor, Department of Marketing Management, Vienna University of Economics and Business Administration (WU Wien), Augasse 2-6, 1090 Vienna, Austria (E-mail: arnold.schuh@wu-wien.ac).

The author gratefully acknowledges research assistance from Barbara Dittrich and Daniela Kirtcheva.

[Haworth co-indexing entry note]: "Regionalization in Central and Eastern Europe: Searching for Regiocentric Orientations in MNC Strategies." Schuh, Arnold. Co-published simultaneously in *Journal of East-West Business* (The Haworth Press, Inc.) Vol. 13, No. 2/3, 2007, pp. 143-166; and: *Market Entry and Operational Decision Making in East-West Business Relationships* (ed: Jorma Larimo) The Haworth Press, Inc., 2007, pp. 143-166. Single or multiple copies of this article are available for a fee from The Haworth Document Delivery Service [1-800-HAWORTH, 9:00 a.m. - 5:00 p.m. (EST). E-mail address: docdelivery@haworthpress.com].

143

operationalization of regionalization, the relationship between strategy and structure, and its applicability to services. doi:10.1300/J097v13n02_03 *[Article copies available for a fee from The Haworth Document Delivery Service: 1-800-HAWORTH. E-mail address: <docdelivery@haworthpress.com> Website: <http://www.HaworthPress.com> © 2007 by The Haworth Press, Inc. All rights reserved.]*

KEYWORDS. Regionalization, regional strategy, Central and Eastern Europe

INTRODUCTION

Since the political and economic opening of Central and Eastern Europe (CEE) foreign MNCs have entered the markets of the region aggressively and have invested heavily to build up a presence–today, they play a major role in the business landscape of this region. Their entry has been accompanied by a massive inflow of capital, technology, global business standards, and management techniques, which has greatly contributed to the restructuring of local companies, markets, and industries (Lewis, 2005). They typically started their expansion with the entry of the markets in Central Europe, which were more advanced economically and also in the transition process, and the largest market in the region, namely Russia, and later on expanded further to the South-East (Shama, 1995; UNCTAD, 2005). However, during this expansion and market penetration process the strategic priorities have undergone a change. While at the beginning management was mainly preoccupied with finding the right entry and marketing strategy for each individual market, the constellation has changed somewhat in the past years. We now register the rise of regional players, mostly Western MNCs, which have built a remarkable presence in many countries of the region (Kozminski & Yip, 2000). They are faced with the question if they should regard their business in CEE as a collection of individual markets or as a (homogeneous) region. The special merits of the first approach are the high attention given to individual market situations and, as a result, the higher responsiveness to consumer needs and competitive situations that is mirrored in localized marketing strategies and a relatively high autonomy of the local management. This strategic approach is crucial for business success when national environments and market conditions in the region differ strongly from each other.

However, there are integrating forces at work that change the business landscape of CEE (Schuh, 2000): Trade agreements such as CEFTA, the accession of eight Central European countries to the European Union, the adoption of technical standards imposed by the EU, and the emergence of a middle class with increasingly West European consumption patterns are developments that are offering the opportunity to think in regional dimensions–at least from a business point of view. In addition, rising costs, intensified competition, and highly price-sensitive consumers are forcing the management of MNCs to exploit economies of scale and synergies across country operations to stay competitive. The concept of regionalization, which can be viewed as a middle course between localization and globalization could offer a promising strategic option for MNCs operating in the region.

The purpose of this paper is to examine if and how regionalization concepts have been actually implemented by Western MNCs in CEE. The purpose of this study is to provide insight into the following questions: (a) What are the preconditions for the emergence of regional strategies or regionalization concepts? (b) What are the main areas of regional integration? (c) How is a regional approach integrated into the organizational structure of an MNC? (d) Does the product type–tangible goods vs. services–affect the implementation of regional strategies? While the presented research questions have been the subject of other studies in this field, the research design is innovative. By using a longitudinal case study approach better insights are expected on how regional strategies have emerged during the internationalization process of the firm and, if they have emerged, in which way they have manifested themselves in business decisions.

THE CONCEPT OF REGIONALIZATION

Organizational vs. Strategic Perspective

Regionalization is a commonly used term in international management, especially in the context of finding the best fitting corporate structure for an MNC. Regionalization is generally understood as the grouping of countries along regional lines (Jain, 1990). Many multinational corporations organize their worldwide operations into regions, such as Western Europe, Middle East and Africa, or Asia Pacific. Geographic proximity makes it easier to manage countries which are grouped together due to easier communication and shorter travel time. Fortunately, countries in the same geographic region often share several common traits. These common traits can be found in a shared history, culture, similarities in language and membership in the same trade bloc. As foreign trade takes place to a high extent between neighboring countries, a more or less de-facto economic integration exists which favors business relations within a regional group. Corporate management is well aware that considering similarities between markets in the formation of regional groups helps to create a workable structure. However, in reality the existing regional structures often deviate from "logical groupings" reflecting the influence of historical development of the corporate group or differences in the kind of presence and importance of individual markets. As such organizational decisions also affect the delineation of areas of responsibility, performance comparisons, status of managers in the organization, and personal careers, micro-politics have a strong influence on organizational structuring (Prahalad & Doz, 1987).

Approaching the question of regionalization from a strategic perspective, the homogeneity of the grouped country markets and the assessment of the associated advantages of this higher degree of transnational integration and coordination are starting points for the analysis. Following Mintzberg's (Mintzberg 1988; Miller & Friesen, 1984) view of strategy as emergent patterns of decision, regionalization can be seen as a distinct type of strategy that appears within an MNC as a response to internal (e.g., cost savings, achieving critical mass) and external challenges (e.g., removal of trade barriers, emergence of regional channels). The underlying construct holds that dominant, logical, consistent, and–as far as time is concerned–relatively stable patterns of decisions, namely strategies or "configurations," can be identified. The characteristics of a regionalization strategy are outlined by the research school grouped around the EP(R)G-framework. Perlmutter (1969) originally distinguished three different archetypes (or configurations) of strategic orientation of an MNC, the ethnocentric, the polycentric and the geocentric orientation. Starting point for this differentiation is the strategic orientation of management (or "states of mind"), namely the way executives think about doing business around the world. The strategic orientation of management is reflected by the way key product, functional, and geographic decisions are made. This basic international orientation is conceived as a strategic predisposition which shapes the mission, governance structure, strategy, organizational structure and culture of the MNC. Heenan and Perlmutter (1979) and Chakravarthy and Perlmutter (1985) later added the regiocentric orientation as a separate step in the corporate development process. The authors argue that the regiocentric stage represents a transitional phase from the polycentric to the geocentric types. Regiocentrism is together with geocentrism a relatively new profile among MNCs. Regiocentrism is a predisposition that tries to blend the interests of the parent company with that of the subsidiaries at least on a limited regional basis.

The regiocentric predisposition of a firm is described by the following main characteristics (Chakravarthy & Perlmutter, 1985; Schmid & Machulik, 2005; Wind et al., 1973):

- A regiocentric MNC tries to balance viability and legitimacy at the regional level.
- Goals are mutually negotiated between regional management and its subsidiaries.
- Regions allocate resources under guidelines from corporate headquarters.
- Strategies are regional integrative and national responsive at the same time.
- Product and regional organizations are tied through a matrix.
- The culture is regional.
- The focus is on the development of integrated product and marketing programs for the whole region.
- People from the region are chosen for the key positions of the regiocentric MNC.
- Profits and cash flow are redistributed within the region in order to support the overall market position in the region and in order to seize the most promising opportunities.

Regional strategies are conceptually similar to global strategies in that they are only applied to a smaller set of countries. Under both orientations (as well as under the ethnocentric perspective) management aims at realizing economies of scale and scope through the integration and coordination of activities across country operations. Global integration or "transnational integration," as it is more aptly called, refers to the centralized management of geographically dispersed activities on an ongoing basis (Prahalad & Doz, 1987; Birkinshaw et al., 1995). The need for integration arises in response to pressures to reduce costs and optimize investments. MNCs integrate across borders through the standardization of products, the rationalization of production and the centralization of R & D when the benefits of transnational integration exceed the costs of a limited recognition of national social and political differences (Kobrin, 1991). Strategic coordination refers to the central management of resource commitments across national boundaries in the pursuit of a strategy (Prahalad & Doz, 1987). For instance, it encompasses determining R&D priorities across several units, coordinating pricing to global accounts, and synchronizing launching dates of a new product within the group. The associated advantages and disadvantages of regionalization are summed up in Table 1.

In addition to the strategic profile of regiocentrism, which relates to strategy content and highlights the differences in key decisions of a MNC vis-à-vis other strategic predispositions, the point of time when regiocentrism emerges in the corporate development of the MNC is an important theoretical issue. Theory holds that regiocentrism occurs in a later stage of the internationalization process (Perlmutter & Heenan, 1979; Wind et al., 1973). According to this stage perspective regiocentrism is regarded as a transitional phase in corporate evolution in the move from the polycentric to the geocentric type. The argument is that it is more realistic to assume that internationally expanding firms don't move directly to geocentrism but use regiocentrism as an intermediate step (Morrison & Roth, 1992). Rugman even discounts globalization and global strategy as a myth and based on his research suggests that most business activity by large global firms takes place within regional blocks, the Triade regions (Rugman, 2000; Rugman & Verbeke, 2004).

Regionalization in CEE

The success of regionalization hinges on a sufficient degree of similarity between the countries included. Although the considerable cultural diversity among the countries in CEE and the necessity for foreign MNCs to act in a cultural sensitive way are emphasized by IB researchers (Luthans et al., 1995; Lascu et al., 1996; Marinov et al., 2001), there are some strong arguments that justify viewing the countries of the region as one region, at least from a business perspective (Schuh, 2000). The fall of the Iron Curtain in 1989 prompted an economic and political reform process in the countries of Central and Eastern Europe. Never before has a whole bloc of countries started such a far reaching transition process from a centrally planned economy to a market economy. In this case it is not the creation of a free trade area that ignited the idea of a homogeneous country cluster but the similarity in recent and current developments, the shared history, as well as commonalities in culture, consumption patterns and market structures among the countries in the

TABLE 1. Advantages and Disadvantages of Regionalization

Advantages/Opportunities	Disadvantages/Risks
• There is likely to be greater awareness of environmental and market conditions specific for a region. • Better allocation of resources through optimization on a regional level helps to gain synergies among operations and improves overall efficiency. • Standardization of products and marketing campaigns across the region allow exploiting economies of scale and a faster transfer of successful campaigns. • Pooling of resources reduces product development costs and increases the variety of products available. • Through a reduced span of control it is easier to monitor and control foreign subsidiaries on a regional basis than centrally from corporate headquarters.	• A regional structure adds an additional layer of management and communications between national subsidiaries and head office. This can complicate communications within the group, incurs additional costs which have to be justified, and may hinder the efficient implementation of global (product) strategies. • When the principle of homogeneity is ignored in the forming of the region, integrative decisions such as the standardization of products, brands, and communications campaigns that affect directly the appeal of the offered products and services in a market may have a detrimental effect, namely less effectiveness and additional costs. • Overidentification with the region may threaten overall effectiveness of the corporate group and may lead to corporate suboptimization when decisions for which a global or local approach would be more appropriate are "regionalized." • Regional management must be truly regional in character and staffing and should not be the extension of one nationality over others in the region.

Compiled by Daniels, 1987; Ferencikova & Schuh, 2003; Heenan & Perlmutter 1979; Morrison & Roth, 1992; Schmid & Machulik, 2005; Wind et al., 1973.

region (Bakacsi et al., 2002). Possibly, it is not so much the past that leads to the emergence of commonalities but its rejection and the future-oriented efforts and aspirations of governments, businesses and consumers in CEE. Thus, despite the huge diversity found between the countries of CEE a number of important factors integrate the region from a business point of view (Kozminski & Yip, 2000):

- Geographic proximity: given the geographic proximity of the countries the management of an MNC has to expect market interdependencies that make an autonomous management more problematic. So you may find positive interdependencies that help to pool resources and to save costs in product development due to homogeneous tastes, preferences and attitudes towards products.
- Transition process from a centrally planned to a market-based economy: all reforming countries are trying to get rid of their systemic heritage, namely state socialism and the model of a centrally planned economy. By undergoing this transition, they all are faced with the same challenges (EBRD, 1999 and 2005).

- Stage of market development and standard of living: a similar standard of living and stage of economic development can be addressed with product concepts that are adapted to the existing (lower) purchasing power levels in the region (Schuh & Holzmüller, 2003). The appreciation of Western brands and the Western consumption model by the emerging middle class allows the transfer of international brands, sales methods, and promotional campaigns. At the level of marketing infrastructure different country clusters with regard to the development of the distribution and promotion infrastructure can be distinguished (Manrai et al., 2001).

The existence of a regional headquarters for CEE in Vienna, Warsaw, Prague, and Budapest shows that numerous MNCs use a regional organization to deal with this particular market situation in the reforming countries of CEE (Ferencikova & Schuh, 2003; BCG, 2005).

RESEARCH DESIGN

Basic Framework for the Analysis of Regionalization in CEE

The purpose of this study is to detect regionalization as a strategic orientation in MNCs operating in CEE. While in the extant literature regionalization is mostly approached from an organizational perspective, namely by studying the types and roles of regional headquarters (Enright, 2005a; Lasserre, 1996; Schütte, 1997; Yeung et al., 2001), the strategic dimension of regionalization has so far been rather under-represented in international business research (Ghemawat, 2005; Rugman & Verbeke, 2004). It seems to be a worthwhile endeavor to uncover the triggers leading to a regional strategy in order to identify the main areas of regionalization and how the regional approach is integrated into the organizational structure. These three aspects, namely the favorable external constellation, the existence of a regional strategy, and the organizational implementation, were viewed as constituent determinants of the regionalization construct. While the driving and restraining forces of regionalization are well known, a better understanding of their specific interaction triggering the move towards regionalization could offer some new insights. In a further step, the study then focuses on the appearance of regionalization in the decision making process: Which areas are primarily the targets of regionalization? How does regional integration compare with other forms of integration such as the vertical integration between parent company and national subsidiaries? In the context of organizational integration, causality seems to be an important issue that needs greater scrutiny: was the regional strategy developed before a regional management unit was established or is the organizational step the precondition for a regional strategy? While there is some proof in the literature for regionalization in the sector of tangible goods, few examples are known so far for services (Enright, 2005b; Li, 2005). While tangible goods can be produced centrally and then be exported, services are always produced locally, to a certain extent. Therefore, a special emphasis was put on services, namely insurance and banking services, in this sample.

According to the findings of the EPRG school the emergence of regionalization as a strategic concept requires, first, a certain fit between the external and internal constellations and, second, experience in international business in general and with the individual regional markets in particular, as regionalization typically occurs in a later phase of the internationalization process. With regard to external aspects a sufficient degree of similarity between the markets (purchasing power, consumer attitudes and preferences, product usage, distribution channels, competitive situation etc.) has to be given as well as the absence of major trade barriers hindering or limiting the transport or transfer of products, services, capital, brands, people, and promotional campaigns within the region (free trade zone, regional common market etc.). When at the same time the management of MNCs operating in this region is looking for ways to reduce costs incurred by the (unnecessary) duplication of value-added activities of local subsidiaries and to concentrate resources to achieve a better impact (brand budgets, product development etc.), regionalization could be seen as a solution. Regionalization has to be adopted by the top management as the dominant strategic orientation towards internationalization and, as a consequence, has to be reflected in the key decisions of the MNC affecting the activities and configuration of operations in the defined region (Chakravarthy & Perlmutter, 1985). Central to the regional strategy concept is the notion of optimization on a regional level through regional integration (e.g., centralization of production sites), coordination (e.g., price structure, key account management) and standardization (e.g., products, brands, promotion campaigns). In order to enable an efficient implementation of the regional strategy a distinct regional management structure has to be established. Regional headquarters or management centers are mostly mentioned as the adequate structural match for a regional strategy (Ghemawat, 2005; Schütte, 1997).

Ideally, the optimal fit between the external and internal elements, will result in a superior performance. In Figure 1 the conceptual framework for the analysis of regionalization is depicted. The focal areas of this study–the firm-related preconditions and the regionalization concept–are highlighted. This model is rooted in the tradition of the contingency theory and configuration theory in organizational and strategy research (Bartlett & Ghoshal, 1989; Doz & Prahalad, 1993; Miller & Friesen, 1984). According to these research perspectives the "fit concept," namely to attain a "double fit" between environment and strategy and strategy and structure, is central for the explanation of business success. From this perspective under certain conditions a regional strategy produces a superior performance compared to alternate strategic orientations or modes of transnational integration.

In contrast to other studies on regionalization (Enright, 2005; Lassere, 1996; Schütte, 1997; Yeung et al., 2001), which typically use the organizational unit, i.e. the regional headquarters, that is in charge of a region within an MNC as a starting point for their analysis, we tracked the expansion of selected firms into CEE and analyzed their "going east" chronology. Approaching the issue through following the internationalization process into the region matches the underlying evolutionary character of the phenomenon–regionalization as a stage in the internationalization process–and might generate new insights that are overlooked when starting after a regional management unit had already been established. Thus this approach offers the additional advantage that one is able to capture the alternatives to regionalization, especially with respect to other models of transnational integration.

Sampling and Data Collection

The character of this study is explorative. Data for this study was collected in a two-step process. In a first step, the six chosen cases were drawn from a pool of case studies that describe in detail the "going east" of Western firms, i.e., the expansion into the region of CEE in the past years. Each case study covers the motives for expansion into the region, the date and method of country market entry as well as the sequence of market entries, also the evolution of presence over the years, employed marketing strategies, and the organization of the CEE activities. Data sources were publicly available secondary data (annual reports, company histories, published articles in the business press) and interviews with managers in charge of the CEE business. Then, a second project focused especially on the identification of regionalization in the interna-

FIGURE 1. Conceptual Framework for the Analysis of Regionalization in CEE

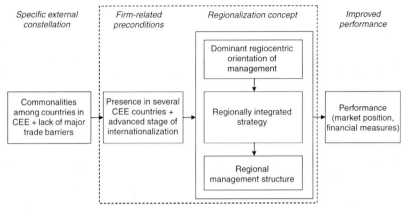

Focal areas of study

tionalization strategy in this group of companies. Building on the existing data set interviews were conducted aiming at identifying the strategic shift towards a regional strategy. This research project was done independently of the first round. Six companies were selected based on the following criteria and in accordance with the basic research questions and the conceptual framework: by duration and scope of regional presence (a minimum of 5 years of presence in at least 3 countries of the region as a precondition for the emergence of regionalization), by industry (insurance, banking, consumer goods), and by type of control over CEE activities (corporate vs. regional headquarters). In each industry examples of both organizational models are included. The final sample compromises two banks, Bank Austria Creditanstalt and Erste Bank, two insurance companies, Generali Vienna Holding and UNIQA, and two consumer goods producers, Henkel CEE and Agrana. Interviews were conducted personally with senior managers in charge of the CEE business in the corporate or regional headquarters in late 2003. Interviews followed a specified guideline mirroring the research questions, were open-ended, and centered around the presented research questions.

FINDINGS

In order to obtain a quick overview and to highlight the differences and similarities between the firms studied, the main facts and findings are presented in a comparative form in Tables 2 and 3. The matrix contains the major influencing factors according to the research model as well as the main results with regard to the realization of a regionalization strategy. To begin with, it is quite a surprise that only one out of the 6 MNCs studied, namely the consumer goods producer Henkel CEE, has pursued a regionalization strategy that fits the theoretical conception. Henkel CEE formulates comprehensive strategies for the whole region and coordinates and controls the business in 29 countries as 100% owner of the local subsidiaries in CEE and CIS. The regional scope of the mandate had been constantly extended in the past years due to the success and accumulated competence of Henkel CEE. Corporate goals and strategic thrust for the region are mutually negotiated between corporate and regional headquarters.

In Central Europe Henkel CEE has been following a regional concept right from the beginning. Regional strategies can be found in production, product policy (product formulas, packaging, product name), communications and sales. Global and local brands are sold parallel with regional brands in the individual markets. Regionalization is not a dogma, the company tries to blend all three perspectives in its brand and product policy ("portfolio-concept"). In communications sub-regional clusters such as "core markets" and "emerging markets" are used to cope with the heterogeneity in market situations. A price corridor allowing a 10% variation between country markets for the same brands is designed to prevent parallel imports. A centralized key account management deals with the regional key accounts in the retail sector. The European origin of Henkel and the self-characterization as "European player" facilitates the thinking in regional categories. As a European company they are rather willing to adapt to differences in local markets and to respect them. The regionalization concept helps them to be somewhat closer and responsive to local market conditions and to save costs. Considerable cost savings and a successful tradition of regionalization as a management model were mentioned at Henkel CEE as the main drivers for the use of a regional strategy in CEE.

In no other company of the sample could we find such a high degree of regional integration. This is astonishing insofar as Bank Austria Creditanstalt and Generali Holding Vienna have a regional headquarters status in their corporate groups. In both firms integration is largely confined to the vertical relationship between the regional headquarters and the individual national subsidiary. Integration primarily happens in the areas of standards and processes ("process standardization") which are more or less imposed on the subsidiary organization. Core product

TABLE 2. Overview of Selected Findings of the Study (1)

	Insurance		Banking		Consumer Goods	
	UNIQA Group	Generali Vienna Holding	Bank Austria Creditanstalt	Erste Bank	Henkel CEE	Agrana Group
Nationality of MNC	Austrian	Italian	German	Austria	German	Austrian
Product categories	All insurance sectors (life/non-life)	All insurance sectors (life/non-life)	Corporate & retail banking	Commercial & retail banking	Detergents, adhesives, personal care & cosmetics	Sugar, starch, fruit juice concentrates & preparations
Presence in CEE (in 2003)	5–CZ, H, HR, PL, SK	7–CZ, H, HR, PL, RO, SK, SLO	10–BG, BIH, CZ, H, HR, PL, RO, SCG, SLO, SK	4–CZ, H, HR, SK	29–CEE, SEE, CIS	4–CZ, H, RO, SK
First entry into CEE	1991	1989	1990	1997	1987	1990
Mode of entry	Mainly green-field but also acquisitions	Via joint ventures & greenfield	Acquisitions & greenfield	Acquisitions (100% or majority stake)	Via joint ventures & greenfield	Acquisitions (majority stake)
Status of HQ (Established)	Corporate HQ	Regional HQ (2000)	Regional HQ (2000)	Corporate HQ	Regional HQ (1998)	Corporate HQ
Alternate forms of organizational integration	CEE dept. in matrix structure at CorpHQ			Regional coordination office at CorpHQ		Country managers at CorpHQ
Organizational model	International	International	International	Multidomestic/International	Regional/Global	International
Degree of int'l I&C	Low-medium	Low-medium	Low-medium	Low-medium	High	Low-medium

155

TABLE 3. Overview of Selected Findings of the Study (2)

	Insurance		Banking		Consumer Goods	
	UNIQA Group	Generali Vienna Holding	Bank Austria Creditanstalt	Erste Bank	Henkel CEE	Agrana Group
Areas of int'l I&C	• Core product & channel concepts • Uniform brand, CI & sales strategy • Common standards & IT processes • Central services	• Core product concepts • Uniform brand & CI strategy • Common standards & processes (IT)	• Integrated services to regional accts. • Core product concepts • Uniform CI strategy • Standardized procedures & IT processes • Common standards (risk mgt.)	• Few standardized core products • Uniform CI & sales strategy • Common standards (risk mgt.) • Training of personnel	• Production network with specialized plants • Global, regional & local brands • Identical products, formulas, packaging • Price corridor • Key acct. mgt. for int'l retail groups	• Uniform brand & CI in all markets except Romania • IT system integration • Common standards in production processes
Active regionalization	No	No	No	No	Yes	No
Main drivers of regionalization					• Regiocentric orientation • Cost savings	
Main hindrances to regionalization	• Legal framework • Market development stage	• Legal framework • Degree of de-monopolization of insurance market	• Legal framework • Market development stage	• Legal framework • Market development stage	• Market development stage	• Local character of sugar • Price sensitive consumers

concepts are still developed centrally in Vienna and then offered to the subsidiaries whose management has to decide if the market is ripe for the product and has to adapt them to their specific market needs and legal regulations.

However, recent discussions at Bank Austria Creditanstalt about moving certain business processes from the center to subsidiaries in CEE (e.g., back office tasks such as document management, credit card processing) indicate that regional integration may be in the offing. Both company examples offer further evidence that it is necessary to distinguish between regionalization as a strategy concept and as a principle for organizational structuring. In the case of Bank Austria Creditanstalt the misfit between concept and reality is even enhanced by the fact that a "contract of regions" exists in which the HVB Group, the parent company, lays down the policy to run its banking business following a regional concept.

As main barrier to regionalization differences in the stage of market development between Austria and the Central European markets or among the CEE countries themselves were mentioned. In the financial services businesses dissimilarities in the legal and institutional framework are a major reason for the lack of regional integration. This finding should not create the impression that no kind of integration happens in the MNCs studied—we found ample evidence for it. Transnational integration occurs right from the moment the MNC establishes a subsidiary in a country. However, it is not the "horizontal type" of integration originating outside the headquarters, tapping ideas and competencies of subsidiaries and spreading them across the regional operations but the vertical, unidirectional center-subsidiary type of integration. In all cases we found examples for this "vertical integration" happening between parent and subsidiary, probably reflecting the special East-West constellation after the fall of the Iron Curtain. Due to the large gap in management expertise, technology, and market development in the 1990s, local subsidiaries in CEE were highly dependent on the parent company for the transfer of capital, new products, efficient business processes, and managerial know-how.

The assignment of executives and specialists from the headquarters, intensive training of subsidiary staff at the parent company and locally, the transfer of planning methods, operational procedures, software programs, product concepts and manuals not only produced a corporate integration in an administrative and cultural sense but the corporate group as a whole benefited by capitalizing on potential synergies. While product standardization in the banking and insurance business was often impossible and therefore restricted to a concept level, the firms focused on process standardization and the introduction of (minimum) standards (e.g., in risk management). Some product categories, such as life insurance, did not even exist before 1990, as there was no need for it in a socialist society in which the state took care of everything in its citizens' lives. In banking, less than 30% of households in Central Europe had a checking account. So it is quite understandable to find a high level of assistance and transfer of modern technology coupled with a high level of control and integration in this early phase of presence.

The analytic challenge arises when you look for regional integration in this totality of integration and coordination measures. All the integrative measures taken between the corporate headquarters and each individual subsidiary finally will end up in a certain degree of regional homogeneity. However, even the interview partners (except those at Henkel CEE) did not describe their integration activities as regionalization. The integration pattern of these other five MNCs resembles more the "ethnocentric orientation" of Chakravarthy and Perlmutter (1985) and the "international organizational model" of Bartlett and Ghoshal (1989). In firms like Agrana, Uniqa and Erste Bank that are still in the early stage of the internationalization process this integration pattern can be expected. A different explanation is probably necessary for the Generali Group and Bank Austria Creditanstalt, which are internationally more exposed and experienced. Here the pronounced local character of the banking and insurance business in combination with the massive need for capital and expertise from the headquarters could be a plausible explanation.

Looking at regionalization from an evolutionary perspective makes it hard to locate the point that marks the shift to regionalization. First, at Henkel CEE regionalization existed as a concept right from the beginning, it did not emerge later. Here the sequence that starts with a regiocentric orientation among top management which is transformed into a regional strategy and then executed by a regional management center corresponds with the extant literature and the model in Figure 1. In the other MNCs studied numerous integration and coordination measures could be found. To judge them as regional or attributing them to a regiocentric orientation is often difficult. The introduction of corporate design guidelines of the parent company in the newly acquired local branch network in order to signal the affiliation to the banking is a corporate process as long as it is not only region specific. The same is true of the substantial efforts leading to the unification of processes and standards. As long as there is no specific reference to regional peculiarities or a regional strategy the attribution to regionalization is not justified.

An interesting case is given when the CEE countries along with the Austrian home market constitute the so called "extended home market" (e.g., Erste Bank)–then the notion of "region" collapses with the overall geographical presence of a MNC. Does this mean that the original home market of the MNC will gradually be absorbed in a regional conception? Is the overall strategy of the MNC then a regional one (see for instance the positioning as a "regional player")? Second, we learned that the existence of a dedicated organizational unit, such as a regional headquarters, is not necessarily an indicator of a regional strategy. In the case of Henkel CEE the presumed connection between strategy and structure is given, but in the cases of Bank Austria Creditanstalt and Generali Holding Vienna despite the existence of regional headquarters no regional strategy was found. This underlines the necessity to differentiate between regionalization as a pure organizational design principle and a more comprehensive strategic orientation in the analysis. Third, the observed vertical and uni-directional center-subsidiary relationships on a country-by-country basis may also end up in common processes, standards, and product offerings throughout the region although the underlying orientation driving this process is an ethnocentric one.

Given the constellation in many markets in CEE in the 1990s and even now, the ethnocentric/international organization model may have been the most effective one. All important competences and resources came from the center, the local management could not contribute much except local expertise in the early years of presence. With the increase of managerial expertise over the following years, strong growth of revenues and profitability, and, as a consequence, enhanced self-confidence, the local management has improved incrementally its bargaining and resource position vis-à-vis the head office. Today, searching for regional business optimization under this new resource and power constellation can lead to various solutions. As we learned during the interviews it is not considered a sacrilege anymore to discuss organizational models that give the local management a greater say in regional decisions and would include the moving of value added activities, which have been carried out until now at the center to subsidiaries in CEE. This shift would take place if it is economically justified (e.g., lower production costs, access to a greater pool of expertise) and the managerial competence is available at the location. Such developments might be early signals for more real regional solutions in the future.

CONCLUSION AND DISCUSSION

The findings of this study provide support for the fact that regionalization is a meaningful strategy construct, namely as a sub-form of global integration, and that it can play a role in the advanced stage of the internationalization process of a firm. That is at least the view of the involved international management researcher. It was interesting to learn that for most of the interviewed practitioners regionalization is not a very familiar concept. They first of all associate an organizational structuring principle with it. The additional advantages of a homogeneous country group are understood but often immediately questioned when applied to their industry and businesses. Differences in environmental and market conditions between the countries served as well as in their market positions and in the stage of business development often hamper the realization of regional strategies.

The case studies showed that transnational integration is a major consideration in the management and that it is omnipresent in an MNC. The distinctive feature of regionalization, namely the exclusive application of a measure for a defined group of neighboring countries based on commonalities between these markets and driven by integration and co-ordination advantages ("optimization on a regional basis"), is often difficult to discern as a guiding principle of an integration measure. So a prevailing regiocentric orientation–as it is nicely demonstrated in the case of Henkel CEE–is crucial for the identification of a regional strategy. Integration measures imposed by the center on individual subsidiaries in a successive way can also lead to homogeneity of systems, processes, product offerings and appearance in the markets of the region. However, this mode of management is rather characteristic for the ethnocentric orientation or international organizational model. A more pronounced de-centralized management approach that is characterized by a greater involvement of the subsidiaries in the decision making process and implementation of the regional strategy would be expected–understand this as a call for striving for a clearer definition of regionalization.

Regionalization is sometimes on the minds of managers right from the beginning of the expansion into CEE as a vision but its implementation is by definition only possible in a later stage of the internationalization of a firm when a certain presence in terms of scope has been built in the region. The antecedent conditions for the emergence of a regionalization concept relate to the number and geographic distribution of foreign markets in which the MNC is present and the extent of similarities within the defined region. To name a minimum number of foreign markets as a threshold value for regionalization is difficult as this decision is interrelated with other aspects (e.g., length and kind of presence, size of local business).

With regard to the geographic distribution, when the foreign markets are clustered around the home market of the MNC, transnational integration is normally effected centrally through corporate headquarters (Enright, 2005b). Regionalization becomes more likely when the country cluster is far away from the center. With increasing geographic and cultural distance as well as dissimilarities in market conditions the center might rather be willing to delegate decision making to a regional headquarters located in the region. Interestingly, the three regional headquarters located in Vienna, Austria, in our study were geographically in proximity to the corporate headquarters (Triest, Italy; Duesseldorf and Munich, Germany). So the reason for this move can rather be attributed to the specific competences of the Austrian management team and the often mentioned "hub-function" of Vienna to the markets in CEE (BCG, 2005).

The findings also challenge some basic assumptions about the emergence and existence of regionalization concepts and therefore provide fruitful ideas for future research:

Relationship regional strategy–regional structure: A major insight of this study is that the existence of a regional management center does not imply the presence of a regionalization strategy. This corresponds with the results of other studies (Ghemawat, 2005; Schütte, 1997). However, there is some evidence for the inverse relationship, namely that MNCs following a regionalization strategy need a regional headquarters or regional management center for implementation. Here a more focused inquiry could provide better insights in the interaction of strategy and structure:

Character of strategy shift: The shift to regionalization is described by the EPRG school as an evolutionary one. In an advanced stage of internationalization regionalization is conceived as an intermediate stage to globalization. Our findings point at a different direction: regionalization is related to the assignment of a regional management mandate by the corporate headquarters to an organizational unit of the MNC. This was the case at Henkel CEE and also the other two regional headquarters in our sample were constituted by such an act. The transfer of decision making authority to the regional management unit is a precondition for the formulation of a regional strategy. The organizational decision is leading the actual formulation of an integrated regional strategy but it does not guarantee it.

Regionalization vs. alternate management models: Regionalization is not an exclusive concept when striving for transnational integration and coordination advantages. The final choice is still depending on its comparative advantage over alternate strategy and management concepts. Regionalization represents just one out of several strategic options to achieve integration advantages and as the findings of this study show it is not the most likely, even when the preconditions are given. There exist alternate concepts that are also capable of delivering the desired integration gains:

- Continue with the successful transnational integration model: corporate headquarters plan, coordinate, and control integration activities across country operations and provide supporting services for local implementation (e.g., functional expertise, IT resources, central purchasing). As long as the number of foreign subsidiaries is still manageable and the centrally devised strategy is successful in the CEE markets, the transfer of product and management technology will continue to be unidirectional from the center to the subsidiaries.
- Country clustering by stage of market development: the grouping by the stage of market development in which advanced markets are distinguished from less developed markets is quite popular in international management (Economist Corporate Network, 2004). This segmentation helps in designing standardized product and communications strategies that often better match the actual consumption and usage situation in these markets. The grouping by market development stage is often found in combination with regional groups as a sub-cluster in a region.
- Stable vs. flexible structures: given the fast and often unpredictable changes of market and environmental conditions, particularly in emerging markets, MNCs nowadays are reluctant to rely too much on formal organizational structures (Hedlund, 1986). Increasingly they use flexible, project-type approaches and virtual management models (Blackwell et al., 1991; Lasserre, 1996). International teams are formed on a temporary basis, the project purpose (e.g., management model for dealing with regional key accounts, launch coordination for a new product in a region) is clearly defined and the involved countries and management groups are chosen on pragmatic grounds. Managers from the headquarters

and the national units assume project specific tasks in addition to their basic functions. The groups are quickly dissolved when the project goal is accomplished. The benefits of regionalization are reaped through flexible project management.

Applicability of regionalization to the service sector: The increasing importance of services in the world economy demands that theories and conceptual frameworks primarily developed with a focus on tangible goods are tested for their validity in the service sector. The lack of significant regionalization in the banking and insurance sector raises the question of whether the basic assumptions of the EPRG framework are also applicable to services. In particular, transnational integration issues including the geographic concentration of production appear to be influenced by the type of the good. What is the additional value that the regional level can provide when considering the application of centrally developed service concepts to local markets? Do back office functions necessarily have to be carried out in the region? Following the line of research of Kobrin (1991) and Birkinshaw et al. (1995) who analyzed the impact of different structural and competitive determinants on integration benefits (economies of scale and scope, technology intensity) a similar approach could be useful in the context of regionalization in the service sector. Knowing the different sources and their relative contributions to the benefits of regionalization would provide a better understanding of the cause-effect-chains and importance of regionalization for MNCs involved in the production and marketing of services.

The limitations of this study should be also acknowledged. The sample of just six firms makes it difficult to draw strong conclusions. By coincidence just in one out of all cases studied could a regiocentric concept be identified. In order to learn more about this critical shift to a regionalization concept we need a larger sample of cases in which this strategic reorientation has taken place. The sample is biased in terms of products and the location of headquarters. While services are overrepresented, other industries such as capital goods manufacturers are missing. All firms in the sample run their operations out of Vienna which has become a gateway to CEE in the past decade. MNCs headquartered outside of Europe have possibly a different approach to the region. The focus on the CEE region may limit the generalization to other regions of the world. Future research shall place more emphasis on the relationship between the interplay of the global, regional and local level. The idea of exclusively followed strategic orientations as described in the EPRG framework does not seem to mirror the management reality in MNCs in our globalized world anymore. Regional strategies of large MNCs are in general embedded in a global strategy concept and often contain regional sub-clusters. The analysis of the interaction with these other strategy and implementation levels will contribute to a more realistic account of regionalization and its relative position vis-à-vis alternate transnational integration measures at the beginning of the 21st century.

REFERENCES

Bakacsi, G., Sandor, T., Karacsonyi, A., & Imrek, V. (2002). Eastern Europe cluster: tradition and transition. *Journal of World Business 37* (1), 69-80

Bartlett, Ch., & Ghoshal, S. (1989). *Managing across borders.* Boston: HBS Press.

BCG–Boston Consulting Group (2005). *Die De-Zentrale als Chance–Die Osteuropazentralen als Kompetenznetzwerke der Zukunft.* Vienna: BCG Austria.

Blackwell, N., Bizet, J., Child, P., & Hensley, D. (1991). Shaping a pan-European organization. *The McKinsey Quarterly, 1991/2,* 94-111.

Birkinshaw, J., Morrison, A., & Hulland, J. (1995). Structural and competitive determinants of a global integration strategy. *Strategic Management Journal, 16,* 637-655.

Chakravarthy, B., & Perlmutter, H. (1985). Strategic planning for a global business. *Columbia Journal of World Business, 20* (2), 3-12.

Daniels, J. (1987). Bridging national and global marketing strategies through regional operations. *International Marketing Review, 4* (3), 29-44.

EBRD (1999). *Transition report.* London: European Bank for Reconstruction and Development.

EBRD (2005). *Transition report.* London: European Bank for Reconstruction and Development.

Economist Corporate Network (2004). *The right fit: Corporate structures in the new Europe.* Vienna: The Economist.

Enright, M. (2005a). Regional Management Centers in the Asia-Pacific. *Management International Review, 45* (1), 59-82.

Enright, M. (2005b). The Roles of Regional Management Centers. *Management International Review, 45* (1), 83-102.

Ferencikova, S., & Schuh, A. (2003). Regionalization in Central and Eastern Europe: A discussion of strategic and organizational aspects of its implementation. *Slovak Journal of Economics, 51* (5), 592-611.

Ghemawat, P. (2005). Regional strategies for global leadership. *Harvard Business Review, 83* (10), 98-108.

Hedlund, G. (1986). The hypermodern MNC: A heterarchy? *Human Resource Management, 25* (1), 9-36.

Heenan, D., & Perlmutter, H. (1979). *Multinational organization development.* Reading: Addison-Wesley.

Jain. S. (1990). *International Marketing Management.* Boston: PWS-Kent.

Kobrin, St. (1991). An empirical analysis of the determinants of global integration. *Strategic Management Journal, 12* (Special Issue), 17-31.

Kozminski, A., & Yip, G. (2000). *Strategies for Central and Eastern Europe*. New York: St. Martin's Press.

Lascu, D., Manrai, L., & Manrai, A. (1996). Value differences between Polish and Romanian consumers: A caution against using a regiocentric marketing orientation in Eastern Europe. *Journal of International Consumer Marketing, 8* (3/4), 145-167.

Lasserre, P. (1996). Regional Headquarters: The Spearhead for Asia Pacific Markets. *Long Range Planning, 29* (1), 30-37.

Lewis, Ch. (2005). *How the East was won–The impact of multinational companies on Eastern Europe and the Former Soviet Union*. New York: Palgrave Macmillan.

Li, Lei (2005). Is regional strategy more effective than global strategies in the US service industries? *Management International Review, 45* (1), 37-57.

Luthans, F., Patrick, R., & Luthans, B. (1995). Doing Business in Central and Eastern Europe: Political, Economic and Cultural Diversity. *Business Horizons, 38* (4), 9-16.

Manrai, L., Manrai, A., & Lascu, D. (2001). A country-cluster analysis of the distribution and promotion infrastructure in Central and Eastern Europe. *International Business Review, 10*, 517-549.

Miller, D., & Friesen, P. (1984). *Organizations: A quantum view*. Englewood Cliffs: Prentice-Hall.

Mintzberg, H. (1988). Opening Up the Definition of Strategy. In J. Quinn, H. Mintzberg & R. James (Eds.), *The Strategy Process–Concepts, Contexts & Cases* (pp. 13-20). Englewood Cliffs: Prentice-Hall International.

Morrison, A., & Roth, K. (1992). The regional solution: an alternative to globalization. *Transnational Corporation, 1* (2), 37-55.

Perlmutter, H. (1969). The tortuous evolution of the multinational corporation. *Columbia Journal of World Business, 4* (1), 9-18.

Prahalad, C.K., & Doz, Y. (1987). *The multinational mission*. New York: The Free Press.

Rugman, A. (2000). *The end of globalization*. London: Random House.

Rugman, A., & Verbeke, A. (2004). A perspective on regional and global strategies of multinational enterprises. *Journal of International Business Studies, 35* (1), 3-18.

Schmid, St., & Machulik, M. (2005). What has Perlmutter really written? A comprehensive analysis of the EPRG-concept. In G. Benito (Ed.), *Landscapes and mindscapes in a globalized world,* 31st EIBA Conference Proceedings, December 2005, Oslo, Norway.

Schuh, A. (2000). Global Standardization as a Success Formula for Marketing in Central and Eastern Europe? *Journal of World Business, 35* (2), 133-148.

Schuh, A., & Holzmüller, H. (2003). Marketing Strategies of Western Consumer Goods Firms in CEE. In H. Stüting, W. Dorow, F. Claasen & S. Blazejewski (Eds.), *Change Management in Transition Economies* (pp. 176-188). New York: Palgrave Macmillan.

Schütte, H. (1997). Strategy and Organisation: Challenges for European MNCs in Asia. *European Management Journal, 15* (4), 436-445.

Shama, A. (1995). Entry Strategies for U.S. firms to the former Soviet Bloc and Eastern Europe. *California Management Review, 37* (3), 90-109.

UNCTAD (2005). *World Investment Report–Transnational Corporations and the Internationalization of R&D*. United Nations Publications: New York

Wind, Y., Douglas, S., & Perlmutter, H. (1973). Guidelines for Developing International Marketing Strategies. *Journal of Marketing, 37* (2), 14-23.

Yeung, H., Poon, J., & Perry, M. (2001). Towards a Regional Strategy: The Role of Regional Headquarters of Foreign Firms in Singapore. *Urban Studies, 38* (1), 157-183.

doi:10.1300/J097v13n02_03

The Interconnections of Regional and Domestic Cluster Development Processes: Using the Example of Estonian Wood and Forest Industries

Tonu Roolaht

SUMMARY. The regional clusters have an important position in the modern world. One of the most prominent clusters in the Nordic area (Scandinavia, Baltic region and Russia) has been formed in the wood and forest industries. The aim of this study is to investigate the dual impact of regional clusters on the development of local clustering and networking ties. In this respect the positive impact in terms of technology transfers, financial support and market access are analysed alongside potentially more detrimental aspects, such as replacing local value-adding processes with roundwood and paperwood exports and limiting the international marketing options of the acquired producers. The results indicate that regional clustering has several positive influences on the development of local/domestic wood and forest clusters in terms of tech-

Tonu Roolaht is Senior Researcher, University of Tartu, Faculty of Economics and Business Administration, Department of International Business, Narva Road 4–A219, 51009 Tartu, Estonia (E-mail: tonu.roolaht@mtk.ut.ee).

This study has been prepared with financial support received from the Estonian Science Foundation (Grants 6493 and 5840) and from the Ministry of Education and Research (Target Financing T0107).

[Haworth co-indexing entry note]: "The Interconnections of Regional and Domestic Cluster Development Processes: Using the Example of Estonian Wood and Forest Industries." Roolaht, Tonu. Co-published simultaneously in *Journal of East-West Business* (The Haworth Press, Inc.) Vol. 13, No. 2/3, 2007, pp. 167-189; and: *Market Entry and Operational Decision Making in East-West Business Relationships* (ed: Jorma Larimo) The Haworth Press, Inc., 2007, pp. 167-189. Single or multiple copies of this article are available for a fee from The Haworth Document Delivery Service [1-800-HAWORTH, 9:00 a.m. - 5:00 p.m. (EST). E-mail address: docdelivery@haworthpress.com].

167

nology transfer and foreign market access, but dominant intra-corporate networks can also lead to centralised operations that set a lower value on local supply chain relationships. doi:10.1300/J097v13n02_04 *[Article copies available for a fee from The Haworth Document Delivery Service: 1-800-HAWORTH. E-mail address: <docdelivery@haworthpress.com> Website: <http://www.HaworthPress.com> © 2007 by The Haworth Press, Inc. All rights reserved.]*

KEYWORDS. Networking, economic clusters, wood and forest industry, Nordic region

INTRODUCTION

The intention of production companies is to profit from providing added value to consumers. Large increases in the efficiency of the value-adding transformation process become visible via innovations and continuous improvements. However, in an era of integrated business processes, the company often becomes embedded within a much broader value-chain, consisting of several companies. These regional clusters of related companies provide cluster members for example with knowledge, technology and support for complementary development. However, so called 'flagship' companies, which are relatively independent in their choices and form a cluster core, can also limit the development possibilities of other companies in the cluster, who have to adapt to a strict role distribution enforced by the cluster core. These possibly adverse influences of clustering and networking deserve further investigation.

Wood and forest industries form one of the leading clusters in Scandinavia and the adjacent region. The activities in that cluster range from round- and paperwood trade to the production of fine paper and wooden furniture. The Nordic cluster initially formed in highly forested countries, Finland and Sweden, but now it is expanding to Baltic countries and to Russia. This enlarged vision has been prompted by the need to find additional sources for roundwood as well as by the lower operating expenses in these regions.

The aim of this study is to analyze the dual influence of regional clustering on the development of local/domestic clusters and networks. Thus, this study will clarify how the existence and dynamics of international network ties within the Nordic cluster impacts the development of local relationships and an integrated value chain.

In terms of research methodology, the study will be based upon short case studies of Estonian wood and forest companies, where interviews with corporate managers serve as primary data, and surveys conducted among these companies as secondary data. Numerous other public resources are used during the desk research process. These triangulation efforts should provide enough alternative sources for making valid conclusions based upon the Estonian cooperative and internationalisation practices. Several illustrative examples should also highlight the dual nature of regional intra-cluster cooperation.

The first section gives an overview of relevant cluster development and networking literature. The discourse concerning the domination of multinational corporations (MNCs) should be incorporated as well. Yet another stream of literature to be used in providing the theoretical rationale behind business practice, deals with strategic choices at the corporate level and autonomy issues. The empirical section offers a multifaceted analysis of international and domestic network relations that characterise Estonian wood and forestry companies based on case studies and survey data.

REGIONAL CLUSTERS AND INNOVATIVE DEVELOPMENT

One of the characteristics of modern business is the formation of clusters. Business clusters have been defined in several ways. In Porter's (1998, p. 199) view a cluster is "a geographically proximate group of interconnected companies and associated institutions in a particular field, linked by commonalities and complementarities." This definition sets considerable importance on complementarities between cluster members. Enright (2000, p. 114) describes regional clustering as "the development of multiple firms in the same or closely related industries in the same location." Although, this is an even more general notion, it still stresses the industry specific and geographically connected nature of clusters. According to de Langen (2002, p. 210) a cluster is "a population of geographically concentrated and mutually related business units, associations and public (private) organisations centred around a distinctive economic specialisation." This definition brings into spotlight the regional, relationship-based and specialised nature of clusters. According to this notion, a cluster is not a unitary formation, but a population of several parties involved.

In general, the cluster definitions introduced in the literature differ in their geographic scope, breadth (horizontal industry scope or involvement of companies/industries from the same level of the value-adding process), depth (vertical industry scope or involvement of companies/industries positioned at the different levels of the value-adding process), activity scope, capacity for innovation, competitive position, industrial organisation and transaction governance (Hallencreutz & Lundequist, 2003). In the author's view, Porter's definition of regional clusters is most suitable for this study and will be followed unless indicated otherwise.

Marshall (1916) introduced three fundamental reasons for special clustering (Birkinshaw, 2000):

1. the existence of a pooled market for specialised workers;
2. the provision of specialised inputs from suppliers and service providers;
3. the relatively rapid flow of business-related knowledge among companies, resulting in technological spillovers.

Although, it is often very difficult to predict *a priori* the actual location, where this kind of spatial agglomeration of companies will lead to the emergence of a cluster, the subsequent growth of the cluster is straightforward. New companies simply have strong economic incentives, related to the following: co-locating with competitors and other related firms (Birkinshaw, 2000).

The study of relationships between the extent to which a company belongs in a cluster and its innovativeness has showed that clustering alone is not conducive to higher innovative performance, although location among a dense population of innovative companies increases the likelihood of being innovative. However, quite strong disadvantages might arise from the presence of non-innovative companies in the clustered sector (Beaudry & Breschi, 2003). Thus, the cluster facilitates innovation when the key companies have innovative mindsets.

Enright (2000) has studied the role of industry clusters in the operations of multinational companies. He argues that instead confronting clusters to multinationals, clusters and multinational companies ought to be viewed as highly interdependent, because the overall strategy of these companies receives a strong impetus from cluster-based subsidiaries.

Maskell and Lorenzen (2004) view regional clusters as suitable spatial configurations of economy for the creation, transfer and use of new knowledge. Thus, clusters can become affordable alternatives to the formation of global networks. In some situations, where barriers make global networks a less feasible solution, regional clusters can be utilised instead. Before we discuss the connections between networks and clusters, the next section will introduce the diverse views about the nature of business networks.

NETWORKS AND CLUSTERS–
WHAT IS THE CONNECTION?

The network approach emerged as a result of the criticism of the sequential approach (see for example Madsen & Servais, 1997; Tyebjee, 1994; Reuber & Fisher, 1997). There are many definitions of networks. Thorelli defines a network "as the one intermediary between the single firm and the market–that is, two or more firms which, due to the intensity of their interaction, constitute a subset of one or several markets" (Thorelli, 1986, p. 38). Zeffane argues that networks are faster, smarter and more flexible than reorganisations or downsizings, thus to be considered as an alternative to vertical integration, or in other words internalisation, for high-growth entrepreneurial firms. Networks help to make bureaucratic organisations more innovative (Zeffane, 1995).

In the modern era, the notion of a market versus an internalised hierarchy inevitably has to be extended to include the network approach as well as cooperative forms of internationalisation in more general terms. There are cases when vertical integration, in terms of mergers with suppliers or retailers, is inappropriate, for example if transactions are only occasional and involve very specific assets (Johanson & Mattson, 1987). Thus, networks as institutional arrangements are somewhat less strict than hierarchical intra-company arrangements, but still offer higher control and formalisation than market relations.

In a more theoretical view, the network approach has three main features: actor bonds, shared resources and integrated actions (Johanson & Mattson, 1988). Actor bonds determine also the actor's network position. Network position has been defined as a semi-autonomous decision centre that in most cases coincides with a firm, a strategic business unit, or a profit centre (Thorelli, 1986). Shared resources indicate that an actor's success in operating depends on other participants' choices. Inside the network, there could be competition for the use of common resources (Thorelli, 1986). Integrated actions imply that networks can be viewed as economic entities, although much more complex than organisations.

In addition to three main dimensions, one aspect mentioned is mutual trust (Bengtsson & Kock, 1999). In many respects, networking is about building and reinforcing trustworthy connections between actors. This aspect of networks is especially important in Asian networks as indicated by several authors (Wong, 1998; Haley & Tan, 1999). Mutual trust is a basis for cooperation between competitors therefore forming links of cooperation (Bengtsson & Kock, 1999). These network aspects discussed clearly indicate the important role of highly developed mutual dependencies within networks, which in the case of clusters might be far less prominent.

The inward-outward connections in business networks depend on the strength and type of actor bonds, while the strength of bonds can increase according to changes in the network environment (Johanson & Mattson, 1987). Given that within networks, bonds between actors are so important, this implies certain institutional efforts towards building and reinforcing them. This conscious approach towards relationship reinforcement is also more characteristic of networks than clusters.

The network also has its own network horizon. When we define a network as a complex set of integrated relationships, then within the horizon there are those connections in the network considered important by the actor. This forms the network context (Johanson & Johanson, 1999). Therefore, although networks are separable, the network boundaries are very hard to define. Cluster boundaries tend to be somewhat more identifiable.

It is argued that the network approach helps to remedy many problems related to, for example, the transaction cost concept (see Johanson & Mattson, 1987), and it is often looked upon as an alternative to internalisation. The author of the current study believes that under certain assumptions those two concepts are not as different as they are often considered to be and therefore an attempt is made to highlight the similarities. In some instances, it is down to terminological differences. For example, Ghoshal and Bartlett differentiate between multinational network and external networks (Ghoshal & Bartlett, 1990). Under multinational or inter-organisational networks, they are referring to "a group of geographically dispersed and goal-disparate organisations that include its headquarters and different national subsidiaries" (Ghoshal & Bartlett, 1990, p. 603). This notion is obviously closer to the internalisation concept than to the classic network approach. Some sources (like Peng & Heath, 1996) treat mergers and acquisitions as strategic choices differentiated from inter-organisational or network relationships. This separation stems from the definition of a network as an external network by

Ghoshal and Bartlett. Mergers and acquisitions are in turn related to internalisation and corporate networks. These definitions also depend somewhat on the extent of managerial control gained in the process, where the network describes a less controlled situation and acquisitions a higher ability to direct actions.

On the other hand, it has been argued that the network approach within a corporate structure could lead to a more specialised, coordinated and integrated structure than, for example, in decentralised organisations that use polycentric strategies (Malnight, 1996). Although this view relies again upon the definitions of Ghoshal and Bartlett, we can see that sometimes the network approach might mean better coordination than internalised but nevertheless quasi-autonomous activities.

Although these concepts use the term network for describing intra-corporate rather than purely relational cooperative arrangements, they still represent a shift from a solely hierarchical subordination to certain partnerships within corporate structures. However, it is true that intra-corporate networks tend to be more formalised than simple relational networks. Still, even inter-corporate networks, much like intra-corporate ones, tend to have clearly set codes of conduct.

In conclusion, while the classic network approach helps avoid the concentration of administrative complexities that are characteristic of highly integrated hierarchies, it retains many elements of control and coordination. Thus, networked operations help to achieve a more effective and more competitive solution at a higher level than intra-firm operations. At the same time specialisation within the network helps to avoid organisational problems and facilitates the changes necessary in the modern business environment.

Although far less location- or industry-bound than clusters, networks can also be divided into multinational, regional and local. This division, however, relies upon a somewhat arbitrary perception of the network boundaries that are often fuzzy. Multinational networks cover several regions or continents, while regional networks are established within a region, for example Northern America. Local networks refer to domestic or even more local networking ties. In this study local and intra-country networks are used as synonyms.

Although, Maskell and Lorenzen (2004) see networks as formations with much stronger bonds between members than clusters (in their view a cluster is in short a loosely integrated social setting (environment)), the differentiation between the two is often not that straightforward. In fact, considerable overlaps are visible. Maskell and Lorenzen (2004) also imply this by denoting networks as institutional arrangements and clusters as institutional environments. Indeed, it is possible that in a regional or domestic cluster, there emerge several different partnership arrangements among companies. Thus, in time, the co-location of companies can become a facilitator of networking.

Moreover, one cluster of companies might occasionally consist of several competing networks, where rivalry between them could even support the innovative spirit within the cluster. From a different viewpoint, this is also the reason why a regional cluster with its networks and a domestic cluster, defined from this point forward as a host country cluster, can have conflicting development interests. These conflicts could be related to the domination of multinational corporations (MNCs) in local industries and to the subsequent reduction of strategic autonomy in its local subsidiaries or allies.

Rondinelli and Black (2000) address the issue of MNCs entering emerging markets in Central and Eastern Europe via acquisitions or alliances with private or state-owned companies. They argue that these relational or even ownership ties can render many competitive advantages to the MNCs in the transition environment. However, because host country interest groups often oppose foreign domination in domestic industries, MNCs should build win-win arrangements that benefit not only their shareholders but also the host country partners and governments. Thus, the domination issue formerly discussed in connection with developing countries (for example in Galloway & Kapoor, 1971) has now found attention also in the transition setting, where local companies alone might be too weak or unwilling to withstand pressure from large multinational corporations. Still, following the suggestion given above, MNCs themselves are often better off by accounting for local interests as well. Despite this, conflicts between interests within the host country's industry and the prospect of the development of MNC are possible and cannot always be avoided. The aspirations of a company towards foreign expansion are in some instances substantially supported or inhibited by its inclusion in a larger intra-corporate network or by its belongingness in a regional business cluster. Then, a local company can fulfil different kinds of management tasks. These tasks determine the subsidiary's role and subsequently it's autonomy within a multinational corporation, which could be strategic or functional.

Strategic decision-making is often seen as the role of corporate headquarters or top management (Raelin, 1989). On the basis of this traditional understanding, strategic autonomy could be defined as a high level of independence in determining corporate mission, goals and future directions. However, several contributions (Hedlund, 1980; Hamel & Prahalad, 1983; Williams, 1998; Andersen, 2004) imply a slightly different definition. Strategic autonomy is the high level decision-making authority of a corporate unit as an integral part of corporate strategy. It is this more elaborate definition of strategic autonomy–autonomy within the strategy–that will be adopted in this research.

Due to an increased need for integration between subsidiaries, brought on by globalisation, or alternatively due to the need for increased local responsiveness (Hamel & Prahalad, 1983), the strategic roles of subsidiaries become increasingly specialised. Some units are assuming the co-ordinating functions of (regional) headquarters, while others constitute at arms-length operations. In terms of domestic industry cluster arms-length units often have lower local responsiveness and favour intra-corporate ties over local partnerships. The theoretical construct is summarised in Figure 1.

The circles in the figure represent clusters. The large circle represents a regional location that covers several neighbouring countries that in turn contain domestic industry clusters (smaller circles). The rectangles are either intra-corporate or relational networks. The overlaps on this figure describe interests on several levels of the regions. MNC, for example, also has operations outside this particular region and in both local clusters. The arrows imply the domination of positive or negative influences from corporate networks on clusters. Similar arrows could be drawn for regional relational networks, but are omitted for better

FIGURE 1. Interplay of Relational Networks, MNC Networks and Clusters on the Regional and Local Level

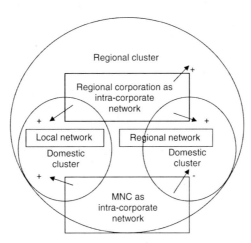

clarity in the figure. The empirical part of this study intends to offer preliminary evidence about these connections; the results will be introduced in the concluding section.

THE METHODS AND DATA USED

Because this empirical analysis deals with managerial processes and perceptions about the positive or negative impacts of clustering, the main research method utilised is case study analysis. This method helps us obtain elaborate insights into the motivations, beliefs and experiences of corporate level managers who have been responsible for the internationalisation process in their companies. In order to generalise from the results of the inter-case analysis, the case data is on some occasions amended using survey data.

The case study method has been scrutinised by Robert Yin. According to him (Yin, 1992), a case study is an empirical inquiry that investigates a contemporary phenomenon within its real-life context, when the boundaries between phenomenon and context are not clearly evident, and in which multiple sources of evidence are used.

In the case of the present study, the phenomenon under investigation is the interplay between regional and local clusters. Therefore, it is a study that attempts to determine the diverse impacts of clustering on local level cooperation. In order to draw upon intra-case as well as inter-case evidence the multiple case study analysis was selected as a sub-method. An intra-case narrative helps us highlight the specific features of the phenomenon in that particular unit of research, while inter-case evidence offers an opportunity to make generalisations based on the common features of all or a majority of the case companies (Yin, 1992).

The selection of the companies was based on theoretical rather than statistical sampling. The main theoretical considerations were related to:

- field of activity (to involve several aspects of the wood and forest industry value chain);
- company size (the representation of large companies and SMEs);
- type of inward connection (companies with foreign ownership or other relationships);
- level of foreign commitment (having companies with considerable exporting activities or other international activities).

Given these criteria, the selection was not completely random, but depended somewhat on the availability of alternative sources of evidence (participation in earlier surveys, level of exposure in the media, availability of corporate homepage, etc.) and on prior contacts. This should be viewed as one important limitation, because there is potentially some selection bias towards the inclusion of well-known companies, which also tend to be leading companies. On the other hand, the author considers this kind of sampling justified because it allows for a more extensive use of scarce public data and secondary evidence, thus increasing the construct validity, while the diversification of the sample should increase the external validity and reliability.

Four companies were included in the sample, two of which are sawmilling companies (with some wood procurement activities), one pulp and sack paper producer and one manufacturer of windows and doors. The interviews with managers were conducted in autumn 2003. The survey data was collected in March 2005 via fax and e-mail. Since follow-up efforts to gain more responses still continue, the final response rate has yet to be determined, but in October 2005 the dataset included 65 Estonian wood and forest companies. This survey was initiated as a complex survey of the entire sector. Thus, this study uses only a small fraction of the information concerning cooperative ties. In the next section, we discuss the first four cases and, thereafter, survey responses.

ESTONIAN COMPANIES IN THE NORDIC WOOD AND FORESTRY CLUSTER

Toftan Sawmill

Toftan is a Nordic-owned manufacturer of sawnwood that started operations in 1995. The company was co-owned by Swedish sawnwood manufacturer Hebeda Trä AB (60%) and Finnish wood procurement company Thomesto OY (40%). Now Hebeda Trä AB owns 100%. In 2003 Toftan employed around 111 people and produces about 118 500 m^3 sawnwood annually (2005). The company specialises in pinewood and exports to Egypt (13% of its turnover), Netherlands (11%), Morocco (9%), Japan (9%) and Ireland (7%). Toftan's turnover in 2005 was about 20 million euros and investments around 3.5 million euros. Although, the Finnish company only had a minority ownership in the sawmill, an important role was and is played by its wood procurement subsidiary Metsäliitto Eesti, which supplies Toftan with roundwood. Thus, Thomesto's wider corporate network and its parent company Metsäliitto, provides Toftan with procurement support. Toftan has also received long-term financing from both former co-owners and cooperates in sales with Hebeda Trä AB. The company can use also Swedish sawmills as a base for training its employees.

According to Kolk (2003), during the start-up period, the management and key employees came from the Swedish parent company, but after ten years of operation the strategic involvement of the foreign owner has been reduced to joint discussions in board meetings about development strategies. During the first five years of operations, the Swedish owner also provided Toftan with expatriate sales personnel. As the domestic sales increased, the need for Swedish salesmen diminished. Now Toftan has gained considerable strategic autonomy in its operations, because the Swedish owner has delegated several management tasks to the local managers.

Since 2001, the company has devoted more attention to serving domestic producers, while earlier the export activities where set as the sole priority. Thus, this Nordic-owned company has started to position itself more consciously as a supplier in the local value-chain of wood-based products. In fact, some of these consumers (producers of wood-based panels) have also located themselves close to Toftan. At the same time, cooperative relationships with Estonian logwood house producers have proved to be more problematic, because of wood type mismatches and payment considerations. The company's contacts with direct competitors are via membership in the professional union, but also via export sales in a very distant market, Egypt, where Toftan uses Stora Enso's distribution channels.

Sylvester–Stora Enso

Initially Estonian-owned, Sylvester Ltd. was established by four Estonians in 1990. In 1991 and 1992 five more employees of the company became co-owners. The company's activities ranged from wood procurement to sawmilling. One especially important step in the history of Sylvester was the successful participation in a Greenfield investment into the Imavere Sawmill established in 1994. This sawmill started regular production in 1995, and is now the largest sawmill in the Baltic countries with a sawing capacity of 400,000 cubic metres per year (see Table 1). It is interesting to note that Enso already acquired a minority share of close to 20 percent in Imavere Sawmill in 1995. Thus, the mar-

TABLE 1. The Key Figures from Stora Enso Wood Processing Companies in the Baltic States (Stora Enso Annual Report, 2004; Homepage of Stora Enso, 2006)

Mill	Location	Sawing Capacity 1000 cubic metres	Further Processing Capacity (1000 cubic metres)	Employees
Imavere	EST	400	120	320
Paikuse	EST	220	80	140
Näpi	EST	150	80	145
Sauga	EST	130	90	140
Launkalne	LAT	215	-	144
Alytus	LIT	180	90	-
Viljandi	EST	-	12	53

ket entry process already started in mid-1990s, although the initial commitment was relatively low.

Sylvester's second-largest sawmill, in Paikuse, was established in 1997 (see Table 1 for capacity). At first the main focus was, as it had also been in Imavere, on increasing the sawing capacity, but now the focus of further investments is on quality improvements (Homepage of Stora Enso, 2006). Although, Näpi Sawmill–the third-largest production company of Sylvester in Estonia–was already established in 1991, it has received several investments into modernised equipment and other technological solutions. The Sauga Sawmill established in 2000 was initially used for processing non-coniferous wood, like black and grey alder or aspen. However, in 2002 sawing of these species was terminated and the sawmill started to process coniferous roundwood (Homepage of Stora Enso, 2006).

Soon Sylvester also started investments into Latvia and Lithuania. Launkalne Sawmill in Northern Latvia was established in 2001 and started regular operations in 2002. The newest sawmill, already finished after acquisition by Stora Enso, is the Alytus Sawmill in Lithuania, starting operations in September 2003 (Ibid.).

In addition to these sawing capacities established in the Baltic market, in 1997 Sylvester acquired Viljandi Component Mill producing door and window components, finger-jointed and multi-layered glued blanks, and other construction materials. By 2002, the Sylvester Group also consisted of several affiliate companies offering vital procurement or support services. The business policy at Sylvester had been to not require whole or even majority ownership in these companies, but to expand its network of activities by minority partnerships and mutual interest.

However, when the owners of Sylvester received an acquisition offer from Stora Enso, the equity of Sylvester was expanded using targeted issue so that the owners of affiliated companies became co-owners of the Sylvester Group. Thus, the circle of owners was increased from 9 to 97 people, who all signed the acquisition agreement with Stora Enso. This consolidation of ownership was needed in order to successfully implement the acquisition process. According to the agreement, Stora Enso acquired 100% of Sylvester's wood procurement operations in the Baltic States and 2/3 or 66% of the ownership of the sawmilling operations. Although, the exact numbers were never disclosed, the price of this deal has been estimated to be close to 127.8 million euros.

Despite the fact that in Baltic sawmilling, Stora Enso acquired only a majority ownership, this step has considerably reformed the geographical distribution of Stora Enso's wood producing capacities. The Baltic States, especially Estonia, now have a very important share in Stora Enso's sawing capacity portfolio. In order to reinforce the potential of the newly acquired production sites, Stora Enso decided to follow through on the investment plans in Lithuania already started by Sylvester by investing around 20 million euros in total into the Alytus Sawmill. A further 30 million euros was invested in Estonia and Latvia in order to facilitate an increase in production capacities and improvements in quality. The intention was also to increase the processing capacity in addition to sawing capacities.

At the moment, Stora Enso's Nordic-owned sawmilling and procurement capabilities tend to dominate the market in Estonia. It has also been pointed out by competitors and local consumers that the management of sawmills and procurement units throughout Estonia has become more centralised. For example, the logistics of sawnwood exports is now governed by Stora Enso's specialised business unit rather than by the managers of the sawmills. All in all, this has led to a certain detachment of the group from the domestic cluster and network because intra-corporate coordination has taken priority over local involvement.

Horizon Pulp & Paper Ltd.

The predecessor of Horizon Pulp & Paper, the new sulphate pulp mill in Kehra was inaugurated on the 25th of August 1938. In the summer of

1940, after Estonia was incorporated into the Soviet Union, sales of pulp were redirected to the East. In the 1950s an integrated paper and sack plant was launched in order to convert the pulp into finished product. From 1989, the economy of the USSR deteriorated fast and the sales as well as the procurement activities became difficult (Homepage of Horizon Pulp & Paper, 2005).

Finally, investors from the Singaporean company Tolaram Group acquired it in 1995. Tolaram has since then invested significantly in achieving new heights in quality, efficiency and environmental protection. The Tolaram Group is an International group with vastly diversified activities that range from its core business of manufacturing textiles, fibres and polymers to trading distribution, pulp and paper and real estate. The group headquarters are in Singapore and it has operations in more than 20 countries in Asia, Africa, Europe and in America. Horizon Pulp & Paper Ltd is now a stable, independent company, which has a lengthy experience and tradition of unbleached pulp and sack paper production. Some key financial figures about the company are shown in Table 2.

According to Botvinkina (2003), the supply base of the company is broad, consisting of several sawmills and procurement companies in the range of 150-160 km from Kehra. The company buys wood chips as well as roundwood, because it has also its own wood barking equipment. However, the acquisition of Sylvester by Stora Enso has also influenced Horizon's procurement possibilities. Although, the company still purchases some chips from the Imavere Sawmill, the prices of roundwood offered by Stora Enso have increased too much. In addition to that, Stora Enso's aggressive procurement policy has also contributed

TABLE 2. The Key Financial Figures from Horizon Pulp & Paper (in thousands euros) (Homepage of Horizon Pulp & Paper, 2005)

	1998	1999	2000	2001	2002	2003	2004
Paper production (t)	42,525	47,698	51,943	53,163	62,054	63,864	65,659
Turnover	19,872	24,225	31,058	32,956	38,478	38,635	36,571
Operating profit	1,132	1,801	5,593	5,545	7,598	6,846	2,327
EBITDA	2,164	2,994	6,746	6,931	9,238	8,936	4,419
Current Ratio	1.68	1.37	1.94	0.91	1.06	1.44	1.40
Long-Term Debt to Equity Ratio (%)	42	48	86	85	52	35	30

*2004 are unaudited figures

to the supply problems that emerged with other suppliers of wood. These suppliers found it difficult to fulfil their contractual obligations because Stora Enso's procurement units had intensively bought the available wood, leaving other companies short. In that sense, the internalisation of Sylvester into Stora Enso had a direct as well as an indirect impact on Horizon's purchasing activities.

Viking Window Ltd.

Viking Window Ltd. was created as a joint venture between a local company and a Danish window producer. In addition to these two companies, about one third of all its shares were owned by the investment fund providing venture capital. The relationship between the partners was successful because the foreign partner provided leading-edge technology, while the local management was instrumental in building up modern production facilities on the new developing market. In addition to improvements in the quality of the internal business processes, the success of cooperation could also be seen from the financial performance. Viking Window Ltd. began to produce quality wooden windows and entrance doors in August 1997. In 1998, the export turnover was about 612 000 euros and the turnover in the Estonian market was about 345 000 euros. The turnover for 1999 was already close to 1.8 million euros. The turnovers for the following years were as follows–2000: 2.3 million euros, 2001: 3.06 million euros, 2002: about 4.4 million euros, 2003: 4.8 million euros from which about 2.4 million euros was export turnover (Homepage of Viking Window, 2005; Viking Window Annual Report, 2003).

The foreign investment fund had already initially planned to withdraw after a period of time, which it also did. At some point, the management of the Danish partner changed and the new management team opted for buying out the shares of the local partner in the joint venture. This was not in accordance with the initial agreement, which did allow the local partner to increase its shares in the company. When the foreign partner made a proposal for the intended full ownership, the Estonians found means to raise enough money in order buy out the foreign owned shares instead. Thus, Viking Window Ltd. is now a 100% Estonian company. However, despite the changed ownership good relations with foreign experts affiliated to the previous management of the foreign company, where retained for an extended period in the form of management contracts. In export markets, the company has representatives in Stockholm, Gothenburg and Oslo. Viking Window Ltd. was designated

ISO 9001 compliant in April 2000. The company cooperates with Toftan and Stora Enso's Imavere Sawmill, as well as with the producer of wooden houses, Kodumaja.

Because company only needs sawnwood of exceptionally good quality for its production process, close cooperation with suppliers is often very important. Sawmills have to make an extra effort to select and stock products suitable for the production of high-quality wooden windows. Agasild (2003) described a situation where Imavere sawmill, which is located close to Viking Window, even pre-selects material, but then Stora Enso's central coordinator directs it to be exported rather than sold locally. In general, Viking Window has found it difficult to agree with local sawmills on the quality requirements, and a considerable share of its raw materials will also be imported.

The Survey of Estonian Wood and Forestry Companies

Here the preliminary results of the survey conducted in March 2005 will be introduced in order to generalise and verify the case evidence described above. Four companies from 65 reported that withdrawal from some foreign markets has been directly related to the strategy of the company's foreign owner. In that respect, the role of foreign parent companies is not dominant, but still exists. In terms of turnover, products are mostly sold to third-party foreign companies or to third-party (not affiliated) Estonian companies. Only one company reported that parent company foreign affiliates represented the main sales channel. Thus, in terms of direction, sales seem mostly non-corporate, at least when highlighting the final recipient. On average about 69% of goods is sold to permanent partners, whereas again third-party companies rather than corporate affiliations dominate. Estonian wood and forest companies make about 80% of their purchases from permanent supply partners, which are again predominantly non-affiliated foreign or domestic suppliers. This result should be interpreted with caution, because at present the sample includes mostly more independent smaller companies and several large companies have not yet responded or would not disclose their views (Survey. . . , 2005).

However, five companies have cooperated with domestic procurement units owned by their foreign parent, and four respondents with the parent's production company or a further processing unit in Estonia. Yet, only one company reported cooperation with the foreign parent's subsidiary in Nordic countries, and one elsewhere. In this sample of companies, cooperative ties with other Estonian, Nordic or simply foreign supply, production, further processing or sales companies are much more common than with the parent's units. For example 40 out of 65 companies reported cooperation with other supply companies in Estonia, 40 with production companies and 34 with other Estonian sales companies. Six companies had cooperation with non-affiliated Nordic suppliers and six companies with Nordic producers. Despite the reported low importance of cooperation within intra-corporate networks, 14 companies out of 65 explicitly found that cooperation with the parent and its other units is rather important or very important, but yet again cooperation with suppliers, clients and even with competitors and other companies in the sector was seen as very important by an even larger number of companies. Cooperation is mostly inhibited by competition (35 companies pointed it out as a rather important or very important obstacle) or by a lack of trust (32 companies said it to be a rather important or very important problem) (Survey..., 2005).

To conclude, unlike in the case of large companies like Stora Enso and Toftan, smaller Estonian wood and forest companies rely much less on intra-corporate Nordic networks and much more on the local relational network, which indicates that the regional cluster influences them more indirectly (competition for forest resources) than the large players, who have direct corporate support and restrictions.

DISCUSSION AND CONCLUDING REMARKS

The case evidence indicated that Nordic companies from Finland, Sweden and Denmark have played a considerable role in the development of the Estonian wood and forestry sector as a domestic cluster. These owner companies have supported technology transfers into Toftan, Viking Window and the former Sylvester. In all of these cases, the ownership ties have also facilitated access to foreign markets. However, after these initial similarities all three companies have found different development paths. Toftan is still foreign owned and vertically related with its former co-owner's wood procurement subsidiary. Despite that, the company is managed in a decentralised fashion and as a result is increasing its role in the domestic cluster of further processing activities. Sylvester, after gaining a dominant position in Estonia already prior to acquisition by Stora Enso, has now become to a great extent merged into the intra-corporate network of the Stora Enso group. Being part of MNC has, according to its local customers (Horizon Pulp & Paper; Viking Window), reshaped its policy towards regional corporate priorities, and has in certain situations complicated Stora Enso's relationships in the local wood-based value chain. In fact, it is first and foremost the market domination of Stora Enso's Estonian units that has created slight conflicts between the interests in the regional cluster (wood procurement in Estonia for own usage and exporting purposes) and the domestic cluster (wood procurement for further processing before exporting). Although, its fair to point out that Toftan's relationship with its procurement partner offers a rivalry between Metsäliitto and Stora Enso for forest resources.

Horizon pulp & paper offers indications of yet another impact of the Nordic cluster. Namely, this company has no Nordic ownership and has to compete for wood chips and other inputs with the exports of Stora Enso into paper mills in Nordic countries. Thus, from the viewpoint of the regional cluster, high-end value adding operations are not facilitated in the Estonian domestic cluster, and can even be hampered by price increases that result from aggressive procurement policies.

However, as preliminary survey evidence indicated, these cases offer only part of the story. On the basis of the sample containing 65 Estonian wood and forest companies, which are less prominent market actors, it was revealed that for several companies networks with non-affiliated foreign and domestic suppliers, producers and distributors are more important than those with parent company units. Since the survey is partially still in progress, one should exercise caution in generalising these results. Still, there is an indication that the detrimental effects of MNC domination concern smaller players more indirectly than focal domestic competitors addressed by the case studies. The findings are summarised in Table 3.

This research has several limitations because the case selection was based on theoretical sampling, and so the possibility of a certain selection bias towards better-known companies does exist. Although, the information collection procedures involved both desk research as well as interviews with managers, a more holistic picture would require further collection of information. The interviews were also conducted earlier than the survey, which further complicates the comparability between the two. The survey evidence presented is also preliminary, and more detailed connections are to be identified in the future. The generalisations based on the four company cases should also be verified using follow-up studies. The rapidly changing business environment in Estonia after EU enlargement might have introduced some important changes in the companies' strategies.

TABLE 3. A Summary of Case Studies and Survey Results

Company/-ies	Ownership:	Regional and domestic cluster connection:
Toftan	Nordic-owned	Regional cooperation supports domestic connections. The company is actively involved in supporting further processing activities in local companies.
Sylvester-Stora Enso	Nordic-owned	Regional links also inhibit domestic cooperation, because company's wood procurement process favours corporate ties over local processing.
Horizon Pulp & Paper	Singapore-owned	Domestic connections that compete with regional links. The company has difficult task to compete with large corporate networks for resources.
Viking Window	Estonian-owned (Formerly Nordic)	Regional connections have had dual impact on domestic developments. The company has got support from its former owner, but it also faces limitations related to procurement possibilities.
Survey respondents (mostly small companies)	Predominantly Estonian-owned	Regional and international connections are less influential than for case companies, but have positive direct impact.

In the light of Figure 1, we can draw the following theoretical implications. Regional clustering in the wood and forest sector can indeed have both positive and negative influences on the development of local/domestic sub-clusters. Although, Maskell and Lorenzen (2004) differentiate between networks as a strong form of cooperation and clusters as a co-existence with weak bonds, this research advances the view that networking within a regional cluster, and also rivalry between networks, can considerably support cluster development, while possibly having some detrimental effects. Thus, international marketing and purchasing activities in a regional cluster are often related to the complex interplay of relational and intra-corporate networks (MNC domination), changes in actors' autonomy and local versus regional development interests. These are the factors that in extreme situations might start to facilitate the dissolution of clusters (tensions between actors starts to reduce regional advantages). Because of these somewhat intrinsic factors, regional clusters should be further deconstructed into smaller units of analysis, thus assisting the capture of both the environmental and the relational logic behind cluster formation.

In terms of managerial implications, this contribution points to the need to find a balance between regional (or global) coordination within the corporate network and local win-win arrangements in the Estonian wood and forest sector in the medium-term, which are important for preserving the cluster's integrity. In that sense, the 'local supplier–global exporter' mix in Swedish-owned Toftan offers a better example of good management practice than Stora Enso's attitude of 'corporate interests first' when leading Nordic wood and forest MNCs. Thus, the Nordic-owned Stora Enso seems to induce market distortions that inhibit domestic cooperation more than any other regional cooperation. Due to logistic considerations, local value adding in wood and forestry is often more beneficial than immediate exporting (value to weight ratio supports further processing). Stora Enso's corporate policy seems to ignore these development opportunities. Management of a forestry company should use stepwise positioning: (1) our position on the global market; (2) our position in key regions; and (3) our position in local clusters. This process could be guided by a detailed plotting of value adding processes and supplier-distributor partnerships.

The future research of regional wood and forest industry clusters and the vertical integration within them, should aim for a closer integration of the location aspect and company features with networking aspects. Intra-cluster competition of not only companies but also sub-hubs (for example countries involved in a cross-border cluster) should be investigated further as well. The notion of a 'flagship' company in a regional cluster is well known. At a more disintegrated level, important local players or 'tug-boats' could be identified and their role in a cluster explained. The relationship between MNCs and regional clusters has found some research attention, but how global interests might harm cluster cooperation on the regional level are yet to be explained in detail.

REFERENCES

Agasild, T. (2003). *Wood and forest sector development*, (CEO of Viking Window Ltd.), *Author's interview*, transcript from 10. November 2003

Andersen, T. J. (2004). Integrating the strategy formation process: An international perspective. *European Management Journal, 22* (3), 263-272.

Beaudry, C., & Breschi, S. (2003). Are firms in clusters really more innovative? *Economics of Innovation & New Technology, 12* (4), 325-342.

Bengtsson, M., & Kock, S. (1999). Cooperation and competition in relationships between competitors in business networks. *Journal of Business & Industrial Marketing, 4* (3), 178-193.

Birkinshaw, J. (2000). Characteristics of foreign subsidiaries in industry clusters. *Journal of International Business Studies, 31* (1), 141-154.

Botvinkina, Z (2003). *Wood and forest sector development*. (CEO of Horizon Pulp & Paper), *Author's interview*, transcript from 30. October 2003.

de Langen, P. W. (2002). Clustering and performance: The case of maritime clustering in the Netherlands. *Maritime Policy & Management, 29* (3), 209-221.

Enright, M. J. (2000). Regional clusters and multinational enterprises. *International Studies of Management & Organization, 30* (2), 114-138.

Galloway, R. J., & Kapoor, A. (1971). Asia: Problems and prospects for the MNC. *Columbia Journal of World Business, 6,* 33-40.

Ghoshal, S., & Bartlett, C. A. (1990). The multinational corporation as an inter-organisational network. *Academy of Management Review, 15* (4), 603-625.

Haley, G. T., & Tan, C.-T. (1999). East vs. west: Strategic marketing management meets the Asian networks. *Journal of Business & Industrial Marketing, 14* (2), 91-101.

Hallencreutz, D., & Lundequist, P. (2003). Spatial clustering and the potential for policy practice: experiences from cluster-building processes in Sweden. *European Planning Studies, 11* (5), 533-547.

Hamel, G., & Prahalad, C. K. (1983). Managing strategic responsibility in the MNC. *Strategic Management Journal, 4* (4), 341-51.

Hedlund, G. (1980). The role of foreign subsidiaries in strategic decision-making in Swedish multinational corporations. *Strategic Management Journal, 1* (1), 23-36.

Homepage of Horizon Pulp & Paper (2005). Retrieved April 19, 2005, from http://www.horizon.ee/?m1=&m2=17&m3 =25

Homepage of Stora Enso (2006). Retrieved January 24, 2006, from http://www.storaenso.com

Homepage of Viking Window (2005). Retrieved April 19, 2005, from http://www.viking.ee

Johanson, J., & Johanson, M. (1999). Developing business in Eastern European networks. In J.-A. Törnroos & J. Nieminen (Eds.), *Business entry in Eastern Europe: A network and learning approach with case studies* (pp. 46-71). Helsinki: Kikimora.

Johanson, J., & Mattson, L.-G. (1987). Inter-organizational relations in industrial Systems: A network approach compared with transaction cost approach. *International Studies of Management and Organization, 17* (1), 34-48.

Johanson, J., & Mattson, L.-G. (1988). Internationalization in industrial systems–A network approach. In N. Hood & J.-E. Vahlne (Eds.), *Strategies in global competition* (pp. 287-314). New York: Croom Helm.

Kolk, T. (2003). *Wood and forest sector development,* (CEO of Toftan Ltd.), *Author's interview,* transcript from 7. October 2003

Madsen T. K., & Servais, P. (1997). The internationalization of born globals: An evolutionary Process? *International Business Review, 6* (6), 561-583.

Malnight, T. W. (1996). The transition from decentralized to network-based MNC structures: An evolutionary process. *Journal of International Business Studies, 27* (1), 43-65.

Maskell, P., & Lorenzen, M. (2004). The cluster as market organisation. *Urban Studies, 41* (5/6), 991-1009.

Peng, M. W., & Heath, P. S. (1996). The growth of the firm in planned economies in transition: Institutions, organisations, and strategic choice. *Academy of Management Review, 21* (2), 492-528.

Porter, M. (1998). *On competition.* Cambridge, MA: Harvard Business School Press.

Raelin, J. A. (1989). An anatomy of autonomy: Managing professionals. *The Academy of Management Executive, 3* (3), 216-228.

Reuber, R. A., & Fisher, E. (1997). The influence of the management team's international experience on the internationalization behaviours of SMEs. *Journal of International Business Studies, 28* (4), 807-825.

Rondinelli, D. A., & Black, S. S. (2000). Multinational strategic alliances and acquisitions in Central and Eastern Europe: Partnerships in privatisation. *Academy of Management Executive, 14* (4), 85-98.

Stora Enso Annual Report (2004) Retrieved January 24, 2006, from http://search. storaenso.com/mini/2004/

Survey of Estonian wood and forestry Companies (2005), data file, University of Tartu, March-July.

Thorelli, H. B. (1986). Networks: between markets and hierarchies. *Strategic Management Journal, 7* (1), 37-51.

Tyebjee, T. J. (1994). Internationalization of high tech Firms: Initial vs. extended involvement. *Journal of Global Marketing, 7* (4), 59-80.

Viking Window Annual Report (2003). Retrieved April 19, 2005, from http://www. economy.ee

Williams, D. (1998). The development of foreign-owned manufacturing subsidiaries: Some empirical evidence. *European Business Review, 98* (5), 282-286.

Yin, R. K. (1992). The case study method as a tool for doing evaluation. *Current Sociology, 40* (1), 121-137.

Zeffane, R. (1995). The widening scope of inter-organisational networking: Economic, sectoral and social dimensions. *Leadership & Organization Development Journal, 16* (4), 26-33.

doi:10.1300/J097v13n02_04

Local Heroes, Regional Champions or Global Mandates? Empirical Evidence on the Dynamics of German MNC Subsidiary Roles in Central Europe

Stefan Eckert
Frank Rossmeissl

SUMMARY. In this paper we analyze the influence of a subsidiary's external environment, of its task and of its mode of ownership and its mode of market entry on the development of its role for the case of German subsidiaries in Central Europe. We define a subsidiary's role as a three-dimensional construct, consisting of a subsidiary's tasks, its value chain activities and its respective geographical scope. Drawing on a sample of 99 subsidiaries from the Czech Republic, Hungary, and Poland, we find that a subsidiary's host country, its tasks and its mode of market entry influence the development of its role. We find no evidence for the influence of subsidiary's mode of ownership. Especially, "geo-

Stefan Eckert is Full Professor, Department for International Management, International Graduate School Zittau, Markt 23, D-02763 Zittau, Germany (E-mail: eckert@ ihi-zittau.de). Frank Rossmeissl is a PhD student and Research Assistant, Department for International Management, International Graduate School Zittau, Markt 23, D-02763 Zittau, Germany (E-mail: rossmeissl@ihi-zittau.de).

[Haworth co-indexing entry note]: "Local Heroes, Regional Champions or Global Mandates? Empirical Evidence on the Dynamics of German MNC Subsidiary Roles in Central Europe." Eckert, Stefan, and Frank Rossmeissl. Co-published simultaneously in *Journal of East-West Business* (The Haworth Press, Inc.) Vol. 13, No. 2/3, 2007, pp. 191-218; and: *Market Entry and Operational Decision Making in East-West Business Relationships* (ed: Jorma Larimo) The Haworth Press, Inc., 2007, pp. 191-218. Single or multiple copies of this article are available for a fee from The Haworth Document Delivery Service [1-800-HAWORTH, 9:00 a.m. - 5:00 p.m. (EST). E-mail address: docdelivery@haworthpress.com].

Available online at http://jeb.haworthpress.com
© 2007 by The Haworth Press, Inc. All rights reserved.
doi:10.1300/J097v13n02_05

graphical market proximity seeking"-subsidiaries seem to follow a different path of development than subsidiaries where this task is of minor importance as they tend to perform a smaller number of value chain activities and tend to expand these value chain activities with regard to their geographical scope more incrementally. doi:10.1300/J097v13n02_05 *[Article copies available for a fee from The Haworth Document Delivery Service: 1-800-HAWORTH. E-mail address: <docdelivery@haworthpress.com> Website: <http://www.HaworthPress.com> © 2007 by The Haworth Press, Inc. All rights reserved.]*

KEYWORDS. Subsidiary role, Central Europe, multinational corporation (MNC), acquisition, greenfield investment, joint venture, wholly owned subsidiary, geographical scope, value chain activities, subsidiary task

INTRODUCTION

The past decades have been extremely challenging for the management of multinational companies (MNCs). Simultaneous trends towards globalization and towards regionalization changed their competitive environment to a remarkable extent. The fall of the iron curtain and the transition of formerly central planned economies to market economies on the one hand offer unique chances for MNCs but on the other hand lead to substantial changes in their task environment which may threaten their very existence. Consequently, how to respond adequately to these new challenges became an important issue of international management research. The notion that headquarters of MNCs could cope with these challenges in a centralistic manner in the meantime got replaced by the concept of the integrated network (Bartlett & Ghoshal, 1989) which enables the MNC to be globally efficient and locally responsive at the same time. Based on this concept of the integrated multinational network a new perspective about the different organizational entities within the MNC became popular in international management. Accordingly, the spectrum of possible roles for MNCs' subsidiaries nowadays ranges from apparatchiks reliant upon the parent company to self-sufficient clones of the parent company to centres of competence with worldwide mandates. But, even though there is a quite well developed body of literature regarding such typologies of subsidiary roles the dynamic aspect of the development of these roles has not found full attention yet.

The aim of this paper is to contribute to this gap. We analyze the development of the roles of German subsidiaries in the Czech Republic, Hungary, and Poland. Subsidiaries in these countries are of special interest due to several reasons. First, as the age of a subsidiary, i.e., the duration it belongs to the multinational network, may affect the development of the subsidiary's role we are able to reduce the effect of this factor as subsidiaries in these the Czech Republic, Hungary, and Poland do vary much less concerning their age than subsidiaries in Western developed countries. Second, subsidiaries in the Czech Republic, Hungary, and Poland have been embedded in a turbulent environment, which is characterized by processes of both transition and integration. Research on the effects of transition and integration on the development of subsidiaries is still insufficient. Our results may therefore also help to shed more light concerning this issue. The rest of this paper is organized as follows: in the next section we set the theoretical background. In section three we present the sample characteristics. Next we present our empirical results. The paper closes with a discussion of the managerial and policy implications of our findings.

THEORETICAL BACKGROUND

The subject of our research is the subsidiary. Following Birkinshaw, Hood ans Jonsson (1998) "a subsidiary is defined as any operational unit controlled by the MNC and situated outside the home country" (p. 261). There are numerous approaches to classify the foreign subsidiaries of multinational companies. See, for example, White and Poynter (1984), D'Cruz (1986); Bartlett and Ghoshal (1986, 1989), Ghoshal and Nohria (1989), Ferdows (1989, 1997), Jarillo and Martinez (1990), Gupta and Govindarajan (1991, 1994), Forsgren and Pedersen (1991, 1997), Birkinshaw and Morrisson (1995), Surlemont (1996), Birkinshaw (1996, 1998), Taggart (1997a, 1997b, 1998), Randøy and Li (1998), Mudambi (1999), Tavares and Pearce (1999), Delany (2000) and Benito, Grøgaard and Narula (2003). For an overview on role typologies see prior works of Martinez and Jarillo (1989), Birkinshaw (1994), Young, Hood and Peters (1994), Schmid, Bäurle and Kutschker (1998), Rank (2000) and Schmid (2004).

Although much has been said about the roles subsidiaries might take in the multinational network and about the characteristics that define these roles, little attention has been paid to the dynamics a subsidiary goes through over the course of time and in particular to *how* the role of the subsidiary changes (White & Poynter, 1984; Jarillo & Martinez, 1990; Papanastassiou & Pearce, 1994; Ferdows, 1997; Birkinshaw & Hood, 1998). One of the few exceptions regarding this is Birkinshaw (1996) who addressed this question in a study on world product mandates.

Although numerous definitions of a subsidiary's role have been developed in the meantime, we introduce a new one because in our opinion, extant concepts do not consider all aspects relevant for the classification of the role of an MNC's subsidiary. The role of a (foreign) subsidiary comprises the whole of expectations concerning its future actions from the perspective of a certain actor or a certain group of stakeholders. From this point of view the *task* a subsidiary is expected to fulfil seems to be crucial for the subsidiary's role. In order to fulfil its task a subsidiary gets equipped with the resources and competences to perform certain value chain activities. Subsidiaries which have been raised in order to gain access to a local market may perform distribution activities; maybe they also are in charge of marketing or product development activities, depending on their specific "role." We assume that the particular *value chain activities* a subsidiary is performing say something about its role. Furthermore, in the multinational context the *geographical scope* of each particular value chain activity seems to be important for the classification of a subsidiary's role. To differentiate in this respect concerning the specific value chain activities seems to be essential, because the geographic scope of a subsidiary's different value chain activities may vary considerably, e.g., a subsidiary may have responsibility for the local market concerning marketing and distribution, but on the other hand it may have global responsibility in terms of production. In sum, our frame of reference to analyze a subsidiary's role comprises three dimensions, applicable to each product or each business the subsidiary is responsible for: (1) the *task* the subsidiary has to fulfil, (2) the *value chain activities* a subsidiary carries out in order to fulfil its task(s), and (3) the *geographical scope* of the respective value chain activities. This definition seems to correspond to an understanding of the concept of a subsidiary's role which is quite present in academic research, e.g., Rank (2000, p. 4) defines the role of an organizational entity as the sum of its functions, tasks and areas of responsibilities.

Overall, many variables may influence the development of a foreign subsidiary's role. These factors can be categorized into different subgroups: Factors related to the parent company, those related to the parent company's environment, the ones related to the foreign subsidiary, those related to the foreign subsidiary's environment, and finally those related to other entities of the multinational network. In this contribution, we want to focus on factors related to the foreign subsidiary and its environment. Specifically we want to analyze the effect of the following variables on the development of a foreign subsidiary's role: Foreign subsidiary's home country, task, ownership structure, and mode of market entry. In the following we will lay out the hypothetical relationships between these potential determinants and the development of a foreign subsidiary's role.

Foreign subsidiaries may have different tasks. Whereas some subsidiaries may have been installed in order to gain access to foreign markets, others may have been raised in order to reduce labour costs, and other subsidiaries may have been raised to save taxes. A foreign subsidiary's task is an important dimension defining its role. Nevertheless, its current task (being a part of its role characteristics) may also influence its potential with regard to the future development of its role. In an in-depth case study of the development of the mandates of Canadian subsidiaries Birkinshaw (1996) differentiates between subsidiaries with regard to their specific task, thus indicating the importance of this factor for the development of a subsidiary's role.

For companies operating in Central Europe in order to explore the local markets a liberalization of foreign trade and a convergence towards Western Europe in terms of consumer attitudes and purchasing power which is taking place seems especially relevant. We assume, that for these companies there is an increasing potential to operate in Central European markets in a standardized way. In some industries these processes of convergence may already have gone so far that a pan-European strategy is possible. As a result we expect that market orientated foreign subsidiaries develop concerning their geographical scope from national to regional responsibility (the particular definition of the region depending on industry specifics)–at least concerning market-orientated value chain activities such as marketing and sales. On the other hand subsidiaries operating in Eastern Europe in order to realize efficiency gains do primarily depend on location advantages compared to other locations of the multinational network. Due to the advantageous location factors for production in Central Europe we assume that "efficiency-orientated" subsidiaries in Central Europe have the potential to get geographical competencies concerning production which exceed the regional level.

Decisions concerning the development of the role of a foreign subsidiary in a multinational network are made in response to location specific conditions in the home country of the subsidiary (Ghoshal & Nohria, 1989; Ghoshal & Bartlett, 1991; Rosenzweig & Singh, 1991; Westney, 1994; Davis & Meyer, 2004). If these conditions are favourable from the perspective of the MNE, decision makers from the parent company are more prepared to increase corporate commitment in that country. We may therefore assume that foreign subsidiaries roles in different countries do have different potentials for change depending on the specific location conditions of the host country and that these potentials for change respond to changes in their environment. Egelhoff, Gorman, and McCormick (1998) make obvious how investments in the development of local resources such as infrastructure fostered the development of foreign subsidiaries located in Ireland. Birkinshaw and Hood (1997) demonstrate in an in-depth study of Canadian and Scottish subsidiaries that incentives created by host country governments in the form of tax concessions or direct subsidies can be crucial for the development of subsidiaries. Further studies such as the ones by Doh, Jones, Teegen, and Mudambi (2003), Walsh, Linton, Boylan, and Sylla (2002) and Delany (1998) confirm the relevance of host country conditions for subsidiary development.

In the case of Central European subsidiaries a specific effect on subsidiary development may be attributed to the integration of these countries into the European Union (Eckert & Rossmeissl, 2005). Benito, Grøgaard and Narula have compared the development of European subsidiaries located in European countries belonging to the European Union (Denmark and Finland) to the development of subsidiaries located in European countries outside of the European Union (Norway). They find that the development of subsidiaries is dependent on whether the country has EU membership status (Benito, Grøgaard & Narula, 2003). Although Central European countries do all have EU-membership status these countries now face different economic conditions due to the different transformation strategies which local politicians have chosen. Furthermore, Central European countries differ concerning location advantages such as population size, purchasing power, labour costs etc. Consequently, we assume that the development of subsidiaries located in Central European countries differs according to the country where the subsidiary is located.

The development of a subsidiary should also be influenced by its ownership structure. Wholly owned subsidiaries are entities where the parent company has full control over the resources allocated abroad. On the contrary, in the case of Joint Ventures the risk of conflicts of interest between the joint venture partners is ubiquitous. In the case of a breaking up of the joint venture and a forced exit of the parent company, resources acquired by the joint venture through performing its role may get lost (Mudambi & Navarra, 2004). Therefore, MNCs may be more hesitant to upgrade or enrich the role of a joint venture compared to a wholly owned subsidiary. Unfortunately, the relationship between a subsidiary's ownership structure and the development of its role has not been analyzed sufficiently up to now. One of the few exceptions is Williams (1998) who found that joint ventures tend to perform less value chain activities than wholly owned subsidiaries. In Central European countries, Western MNCs often chose ownership structures where local partners were involved, even after they were no longer bound by law to such arrangements. As we assume the general (hypothetical) relationship between ownership structure and role development to be valid for subsidiaries in these countries, we may as well suppose that if our expectation holds, in Central European countries an extraordinary large portion of foreign subsidiaries may be disadvantaged concerning their potential for development to the detriment of the economic development of these countries.

The development of foreign subsidiaries may also depend upon whether these subsidiaries are greenfield investments or whether they have been acquired. In a survey of UK based subsidiaries Williams finds that greenfield investments tend to have a smaller number of value chain activities compared to acquisitions at the time when they are founded or acquired. However, this difference seems to disappear over time as he notes that at the time his survey was conducted statistically significant differences could no longer be detected (Williams, 1998). In Central Europe, subsidiaries which have been acquired by MNCs nearly exclusively have been state owned enterprises before and have been operating a broad range of value chain activities usually (Nowinski & Rechkemmer, 2004). Through the acquisition and the subsequent integration of formerly state owned enterprises into the multinational network often a specialization is taking place, which implies that certain value chain activities are not performed by the acquired subsidiary any more (Specker, 2002). Therefore, in the case of acquisitions in Central Europe we would expect a reduction in value chain activities. On the contrary, greenfield investments in Central Europe are growing and in the course of transformation processes in these countries we expect these subsidiaries not only to grow in terms of revenues, balance sheet and employees but also in terms of competencies and value chain activities performed.

SAMPLE CHARACTERISTICS AND OPERATIONALIZATION OF VARIABLES

In order to examine our hypotheses and to find out more on the development of subsidiaries' roles in Central European countries we conducted a survey among Central European subsidiaries of German MNCs based on a highly standardized questionnaire. E-mail addresses of these subsidiaries in the Czech Republic, Hungary, and Poland have been obtained from the German chamber of commerce in the respective country. The standardized questionnaires were sent by e-mail to the top-management of the subsidiary in German language as well as in the respective host country language. In order to ensure vocabulary and idiomatic equivalence translation from German to the respective host country language and back translation from the respective host country language to German were conducted independently by two bi-lingual natives.

Birkinshaw (1996) notes that although in general subsidiary managers tend to have relatively few autonomy in determining their role, nevertheless sometimes subsidiaries may adapt certain roles without the parent company knowing about that. Therefore, subsidiary managers seem to be the primary source of information on a subsidiary's role. Nevertheless, the answers obtained may include some bias as subsidiary managers' perceptions on the role of their subsidiary in the multinational network may differ from the judgment of parent company managers. In order to control this bias it is planned to scrutinize the information by asking managers from the respective German parent company about the development of the role of their respective subsidiary in Central Europe, too. As these data are not yet available however, we have to be cautious in interpreting the preliminary results presented here. In Table 1, the response rates for the different host countries are presented.

Table 2 presents an overview over median values of important structural variables of the subsidiaries in our sample for the time the subsidiary was founded or acquired (t_{-1}), for the time of the survey (t_0) and for the mid-term future (t_{+1}). Table 3 provides an overview over the share of wholly owned subsidiaries versus joint ventures and illustrates the sample's distribution with regard to greenfield investments and acquisitions.

We operationalize a subsidiary's role as follows. Concerning the dimension "*value chain activities*" we differentiated between the following activities: "procurement," "production," "marketing," "sales," "customer

TABLE 1. The Response Rates of the Survey Distributed by Countries Where the Subsidiaries Are Located

	Hungary	Poland	Czech Republic
Total number of E-Mail addresses	850	1584	955
Outdated E-Mail addresses	167	48	286
Number of usable questionnaires	25	41	33
Response rate	3.7%	2.7%	4.9%

TABLE 2. Sales, Number of Employees and Balance Sheet Totals of the Investigated Subsidiaries in Poland (PL), Czech Republic (CZ) and Hungary (HU)

	Sales in EUR			Number of employees			Balance sheet totals in EUR		
	PL	CZ	HU	PL	CZ	HU	PL	CZ	HU
t_{-1}	500,000	188,328	132,372	4.5	12	11	722,274	889,362	190,753
t_0	19,000,000	11,534,040	12,500,000	74	90.5	57	15,709,580	10,093,809	5,970,000

Note: Numbers are median values

TABLE 3. Market Entry Mode and Ownership Structure (at t_{-1}) of German Subsidiaries in Hungary, Poland and Czech Republic

	Hungary (n = 25)	Poland (n = 41)	Czech Republic (n = 33)
Greenfield investment	19 (= 76.0%)	28 (= 68.3%)	25 (= 75.8%)
Acquisition	6 (= 24.0%)	11 (= 26.8%)	8 (= 24.2%)
Missing values	0	2 (= 4.9%)	0
Wholly owned subsidiary	14 (= 56.0%)	29 (= 70.7%)	18 (= 54.5%)
Joint Venture (share of German MNC < 100%)	11 (= 44.0%)	9 (= 22.0%)	11 (= 33.4%)
Missing values	0	3 (= 7.3%)	4 (= 12.1%)

service," "research," "development," "IT infrastructure," "finance," "accounting," "controlling," "human resources management," "inbound-und outbound logistics" and "administration" (Porter, 1985). Regarding this (as well as regarding the other dimensions) the management of the subsidiaries was asked whether the respective value chain activity existed at the moment of the subsidiary's foundation/acquisition (t_{-1}), at the time the survey was conducted (t_0) and whether it will be carried out in the mid-term future (t_{+1}), which was put in concrete terms by a three year period.

For examining the "*task*" of the subsidiaries we used the categories Dunning (1993) suggested as motives for FDI: "efficiency-seeking," "market-seeking," "resource-seeking" and "strategic asset-seeking" In the case of subsidiaries established for reasons of *efficiency seeking* the relocation of certain value chain activities to places providing lower input-costs is implied in order to create or maintain a competitive market position. Through this type of FDI "MNEs might assist the internationalisation of CEE economies by moving the production of some of their currently most price-sensitive goods to low-cost parts of the region, with these then being mainly exported back to their established (notably Western European) markets" (Manea & Pearce, 2001, p. 6). Subsidiaries built for reasons of *resource seeking* form a second category. This kind of foreign direct investment is undertaken in order to secure or improve the firm's access to certain resources acquired abroad and is directed to reducing the uncertainty that comes from the geographical spread of the value chain. Another category of foreign subsidiaries is characterized by Dunning as *strategic asset seeking*. In this category subsidiaries, which are undertaken in order ". . . to protect, sustain or advance the *global* competitive position of the investing company *vis-à-vis* its major national and international competitors" (Dunning, 1993, p. 380) are subsumed. Concerning this motive, we distinguished between strategic assets in the form of specific capabilities such as management systems, processes and organizational structures and strategic assets in the form of specific resources such as know-how, technology, patents, or brand names (Hungenberg, 2004).

Market-seeking subsidiaries form a last category. Subsidiaries that fall in this group are established in order to significantly improve foreign market proximity. Regarding this type of subsidiary we differentiated between those foreign subsidiaries established for reasons of geographical market proximity and those foreign subsidiaries, through which the MNC is targeting to reduce psychic market distance, i.e. seeking to achieve psychic market proximity. By geographical market proximity the location of a firm is described in terms of its geographical range to a specific foreign market. This kind of market proximity can be accomplished through establishing a subsidiary in a foreign market. A high degree of geographical market proximity should for example be necessary for foreign market activities, where the costs of transportation amount to a considerable proportion of the total costs of a certain product. Also for certain kinds of services a high degree of geographical market proximity seems to be unavoidable. On the other hand, market seeking foreign subsidiaries may also be built not due to reasons of geographical market proximity, but rather to realize psychic market proximity. With this concept, the ability of a firm to communicate effectively with a certain foreign market is meant. Communicating with foreign markets appears to be difficult, since these markets are shaped by actors that differ concerning their cultural background from the dominant cultural background of decision makers inside the firm. The degree of cultural diversity between the firm and the market has been termed in the literature as "cultural distance." The influence of cultural distance on market entry decisions and market performance has been discussed intensively among international management scholars (e.g., Johanson & Wiedersheim-Paul, 1975; Johanson & Vahlne, 1977; Vahlne & Nordström, 1992; Kutschker, 2002). Actors from foreign markets may interpret symbols that the firm transmits into these markets in a way not intended by the firm, e.g., Meissner quotes the case of Mitsubishi, which was quite unsuccessful when introducing a car named "pajero" in Spain due to the Spanish interpretation of that word (Meissner, 1997, p. 8).

Answers concerning the importance of these different tasks could be given along a five-point Likert-type scale ranging from 1 ("absolutely unimportant") to 5 ("very important"). For every motive we asked the respondents to assess the relevance of the respective task at t_{-1}, at t_0 and for t_{+1} in order to depict the changes over the course of time.

To depict the *geographical responsibility of each function* at the three points of time considered, we distinguished between "national," "regional" and "global" responsibility. Whereas concerning "national responsibility" we differentiated between the host country where the subsidiary was located and any country other than the host country, in the case of "regional responsibility" we made a distinction between carrying responsibilities for Central European countries, Central and East European countries, West European countries, and West European as well as Central and East European Countries. The last classification named "global responsibility" equals worldwide responsibility for a specific value chain activity.

Contrary to other role concepts we do not include product scope as a part of a subsidiary's role. According to our understanding of a subsidiary's role, this concept is tailored to a certain business segment. Hence, a subsidiary operating in different business segments may have different roles with regard to these specific business segments. Consequently, in our questionnaire we asked the participants to respond according to the circumstances of their most important business segment (in case there was more than one).

RESULTS

The Impact of a Subsidiary's Task on the Development of Its Role

Our first hypothesis was that the development of a subsidiary's role depends upon its task(s). In order to analyze this relationship we differentiated our sample concerning the relevance of the particular tasks in two subsamples each time: one where the task was judged with 4 or 5 (we will characterize this subsample in the following by the phrase "important task") on a scale ranging from 1 = absolutely unimportant to 5 = very important and another where the task was rated with a degree of 3 or less (we will characterize this subsample in the following by the phrase "less important task"). When comparing the most frequent value chain activities of subsidiaries which judge different tasks as important or very important, we find that for those subsidiaries which judge "geographical market proximity seeking" or "psychic market proximity-seeking" as an important task (we will characterize these subsidiaries in the following as "geographical market proximity seeking-subsidiaries" and "psychic market proximity seeking-subsidiaries respectively) that they tend to be focussed towards the downstream end of the value chain: Sales, marketing, and customer services are the most frequent value chain activities throughout the whole period of analysis (Table 4). On the contrary, in the case of subsidiaries which judge "efficiency seeking" as an important task (we will characterize these subsidiaries in the following as "efficiency seeking-subsidiaries" or "efficiency seekers") production as a value chain activity seems to be much more important. Regardless of the task-orientation of the subsidiaries analyzed research and development are the least frequent value chain activities throughout the whole period of analysis.

In order to assess the significance of differences concerning the number of value chain activities between subsidiaries pursuing different tasks we employed ANOVA-analysis. For each task we compared the number of value chain activities of those subsidiaries which judged the importance of this task with a 4 or 5 ("important task") on a 5-point scale against those of the rest ("less important task"). Especially noteworthy are the results concerning the tasks "psychic market proximity seeking," and "geographical market proximity seeking." As implied by

TABLE 4. Most Frequent Value Chain Activities for Different Tasks Considered as "Important or Very Important"

Important Task	Value chain activities most frequently pursued (n)		
	t_{-1}	T_0	t_{+1}
Efficiency-seeking	• Production (20) • Marketing, Customer Services, and Administration (each 15)	• Production (22) • Customer Services (20) • Sales and Administration (each 17)	• Customer service (22) • Production (21) • Marketing (19)
Resource-seeking	• Marketing (11) • Production, Customers Services, Sales, and Accounting (each 10)	• Production and Customer Services (14) • Marketing (13)	• Marketing (15) • Customer Services (14) • Production (13)
Market-proximity seeking (geographical proximity)	• Marketing and Sales (each 33) • Customer services (32)	• Customer Service (39) • Marketing and Sales (each 36)	• Customer services (39) • Marketing and Sales (36)
Market-proximity seeking (psychic proximity)	• Marketing (32) • Sales (30) • Customer Services (27)	• Marketing (35) • Customer Services (34) • Sales (32)	• Marketing (35) • Sales (32) • Customer Services (34)
Strategic asset seeking (special resources)	• Marketing, Production, Accounting, and Administration (each 13)	• Marketing, Accounting, and Administration (each 15)	• Marketing (16) • Accounting, Controlling, HRM, and Administration (each 15)
Strategic asset seeking (special capabilities)	• Marketing (10) • Customer Services (9) • Sales, Accounting, and Controlling (8)	• Customer Services (12) • Marketing (11) • Sales, Accounting, and Controlling (9)	• Marketing (12) • Customer Services (11) • Accounting (10)

Note: Numbers in parentheses are absolute frequencies of subsidiaries judging the respective task as important or very important and performing the specific value chain activity

Table 5 the differences are highly statistically significant for the task "geographical market proximity seeking." "Geographical market proximity seeking"-subsidiaries perform a significant smaller number of value chain activities than the rest of the subsidiaries analyzed. And this difference remains highly significant over the entire period of analysis. This does not only imply that the path of development for "geographical market proximity seeking"-subsidiaries is different from the one of other subsidiaries but also that this difference is lasting (at least for the mid-term).

The results for "psychic market proximity seeking"-subsidiaries are similar with regard to the observation that for the whole period of analysis these subsidiaries on average perform a smaller number of value

TABLE 5. Results of ANOVA for the Number of Value Chain Activities Depending on the Degree of Importance for Selected Tasks at T_{-1}

	t_{-1}	t_0	t_{+1}	n
Average number of value chain activities for subsidiaries judging geographical market proximity as less important at t_{-1} (1,2,3)	6.08	8.24	8.63	38
Average number of value chain activities for subsidiaries judging geographical market proximity as important at t_{-1} (4,5)	4.35	5.74	6.09	54
F-Value (significance)	4.546 (.036)	7.386 (.008)	6.673 (.011)	
Average number of value chain activities for subsidiaries judging psychic market proximity as less important at t_{-1} (1,2,3)	5.65	7.80	8.23	40
Average number of value chain activities for subsidiaries judging psychic market proximity as important at t_{-1} (4,5)	4.77	6.15	6.57	47
F-Value (significance)	1.106 (.296)	2.983 (.088)	2.608 (.110)	
Average number of value chain activities for subsidiaries judging resource seeking as less important at t_{-1} (1,2,3)	5.77	7.98	8.25	53
Average number of value chain activities for subsidiaries judging resource seeking as important at t_{-1} (4,5)	5.20	5.95	6.65	20
F-Value (significance)	0.297 (.598)	3.155 (.080)	1.656 (.202)	

chain activities compared to those subsidiaries where "psychic market proximity seeking" is not considered an important task (Table 5). However, at t_{-1} the number of value chain activities of "psychic market proximity seekers" does not differ significantly from the rest of the subsidiaries analyzed. Nevertheless, at t_0 the difference is statistically significant and remains weakly significant for t_{+1}. "Psychic market proximity seeking"-subsidiaries tend to diverge from the other subsidiaries concerning the development of their role.

In the case of "resource seeking"-subsidiaries we find a significant difference in the number of value chain activities at the time our survey was conducted (Table 5). However, for t_{-1} as well as for t_{+1}, no significant differences between resource seekers and the rest can be observed. Moreover, for the "efficiency-seeking"-subsidiaries as well as for the "strategic asset seeking"-subsidiaries (through resources or capabilities) no significant differences with regard to the number of value chain activities performed could be found.

Concerning the geographical spread of the respective value chain activities less than 50 percent of all "efficiency seeking"-subsidiaries performing production were confined to the Central European host country at t_{-1}. This number is declining over the course of time, e.g., at t_0 this applies to 7 out of 22 subsidiaries (31.8%). On the contrary a relatively high number of "efficiency seekers" performing production attain global responsibility concerning this task. For t_{-1} this applies to 4 of those subsidiaries (20%). And their share is increasing over the course of time. At t_0 6 of 22 "efficiency seeking"-subsidiaries (27%) had global responsibility concerning production and for t_{+1} this share is going to rise to 33 percent.

A similar phenomenon can be observed concerning the value chain activities research and development. At t_0 as well as at t_{+1} the number of "efficiency-seeking"-subsidiaries performing research and development with global responsibility is at least as high as the number of those with national responsibility concerning this value chain activity. On the contrary the share of "efficiency-seeking"-subsidiaries with global responsibility concerning marketing and sales is much lower, e.g., only one out of 16 of those subsidiaries had global responsibility concerning marketing at t_0.

In the case of "geographical market proximity"-seeking subsidiaries, we find that a relatively high share of them is restrained concerning marketing, sales, and customer services to the national level of the host country. Nevertheless this percentage tends to decline over time with regard to those value chain activities. For "sales" the percentage is as follows: t_{-1}: 81.8%, t_0: 63.9%, t_{+1}: 47.2%. [For "marketing": t_{-1}: 72.7%, t_0: 75%, t_{+1}: 55.5; for customer services: t_{-1}: 84.4%, t_0: 66.7%, t_{+1}: 41.0]. This reduction of the number of subsidiaries with national responsibility concerning activities at the downstream end of the value chain corresponds to an increase in the number of subsidiaries attaining regional responsibility for Central and East European countries for exactly these activities. The share of subsidiaries having responsibility for this region with regard to marketing develops as follows: 18.2% (t_{-1}), 22.2% (t_0), 27.8% (t_{+1}). [For sales: 12.1% (t_{-1}), 19.4% (t_0), 25.0% (t_{+1}). For customer services 12.5% (t_{-1}), 17.9% (t_0), 25.6% (t_{+1})].

Similar results are found for "psychic market proximity seeking"-subsidiaries. The number of subsidiaries with national responsibility concerning activities at the downstream end of the value chain (marketing, sales, customer services) is relatively high at t_{-1}. Although a substantial share of them remains confined to the national level concerning these activities their percentage declines remarkably. In contrast, the percentage of "psychic market proximity seeking"-subsidiaries attaining regional responsibility for Central and Eastern European countries rises remarkably over the period of analysis.

Regarding activities from the upstream end of the value chain such as procurement, research, development, and production most "strategic resources seeking"-subsidiaries operate on a national level. But the number of those subsidiaries having global responsibility for these value chain activities rises considerably over the period of analysis and is accompanied by a corresponding decline in the number of subsidiaries operating at the national level. However, "strategic resources seekers" hardly operate on a regional level with regard to these activities. In the case of those subsidiaries, which judged "resource seeking" as an important task as well as in the case of those subsidiaries which judged "strategic capabilities seeking" as an important task no remarkable effects could be observed.

THE INFLUENCE OF THE SUBSIDIARY'S HOST COUNTRY

We hypothesized that the development of foreign subsidiaries' roles in Central Europe is affected by the country where these subsidiaries are located. Comparing the value chain activities which subsidiaries perform in these different markets we find that especially Polish subsidiaries tend to be orientated to the downstream end of the value chain, as marketing, sales, and customer services are the most frequent activities throughout the whole period of analysis (Table 6). In contrast, Czech subsidiaries relatively more often perform production activities. In the case of Hungarian subsidiaries supportive activities like administration or controlling seem to be relatively more important than in the other countries.

When testing whether there are differences according to the number of value chain activities between the countries analyzed, we find that at t_{-1} no significant differences occur (Table 7). However, for t_0 as well as for t_{+1} we find weakly significant differences, which seem to be the consequence of the less dynamic development of Czech subsidiaries. Whereas the number of value chain activities for Polish subsidiaries increases from 5.37 (t_{-1}) to 7.27 (t_0) to 7.63 (t_{+1}), in the case of Czech subsidiaries the number grows from 4.12 (t_{-1}) to 5.27 (t_0) to 5.55 (t_{+1}).

With regard to "efficiency seeking" our findings correspond to the results concerning the relative frequency of different value chain activities, where we observed production to be of special relevance in the case

TABLE 6. Most Frequent Value Chain Activities for Subsidiaries Located in Different Countries

	Most frequently pursued value chain activity in **Hungary** (n) [%]	Most frequently pursued value chain activity in **Poland** (n) [%]	Most frequently pursued value chain activity in **Czech Republic** (n) [%]
t_{-1}	• Sales (17) [68] • Administration (15) [60] • Marketing and controlling (each 13) [52]	• Customer Services (25) [61] • Marketing (25) [61] • Sales (24) [58.5]	• Sales (16) [48.5] • Production (15) [45.5] • Customer Services and Accounting (each 13) [39.4]
t_0	• Sales and Customer Services (each 17) [68] • Procurement and Administration (each 16) [64]	• Customer Services (30) [73.2] • Marketing (27) [65.9] • Sales (28) [68.3]	• Sales and Production (each 18) [54.5%] • Marketing (16) [48.5] • Customer Services and Accounting (each 15) [45.5%]
t_{+1}	• Customer services (17) [68] • Procurement, Marketing, and Administration (each 16) [64]	• Customer Services (31) [75.6] • Marketing (28) [68.3] • Sales (28) [68.3]	• Sales (20) [60.6] • Marketing (18) [54.5%] • Production (17) [51.5]

of Czech subsidiaries: the relative number of Czech subsidiaries judging efficiency seeking as an important task is higher than in the case of Hungarian and Polish subsidiaries. At t_0 63.7 percent evaluated efficiency seeking as an important task compared to 52 percent in the case of Hungary and 43.9 percent in the case of Poland. Concerning market seeking, to realize geographical market proximity was judged (relatively) more frequently as an important task by Polish subsidiaries throughout the period of analysis compared to subsidiaries from Hungary and the Czech Republic. With regard to realizing psychic market proximity however, the picture is not so unambiguous. At t_{-1} Polish subsidiaries (relatively) more often judged this as an important task compared to Hungarian and Czech subsidiaries. However, this changed. At t_0 a higher share of Hungarian subsidiaries evaluated this as an important task compared to subsidiaries from Poland and the Czech Republic. And, this is the only host-country-difference regarding the importance of the respective tasks which turned out to be statistically significant (Kruskal-Wallis: significance: 0.065). Concerning "resource seeking" a relatively higher number of subsidiaries from the Czech Republic evaluate this as an important task compared to subsidiaries from Poland and Hungary throughout the period of analysis. Furthermore, a higher share of subsidiaries from Hungary evaluate to achieve strategic assets as an important task compared to subsidiaries from the Czech Re-

TABLE 7. Results of ANOVA for the Number of Value Chain Activities Performed Depending on Subsidiary's Location

	Average number of value chain activities of subsidiaries operating in Hungary	Average number of value chain activities of subsidiaries operating in Poland	Average number of value of chain activities of subsidiaries operating in the Czech Republic	F-Value (Significance)
t_{-1}	5.48	5.37	4.12	1.237 (.295)
t_0	7.24	7.27	5.27	2.240 (.112)
t_{+1}	7.56	7.63	5.55	2.123 (.125)

public and Poland regardless whether these strategic assets appear in the form of special resources or in the form of specific capabilities.

With regard to differences concerning the geographical responsibilities of subsidiaries the most striking difference can be observed concerning the value chain activity sales. Whereas subsidiaries from the Czech Republic in most cases remain restrained to the national level concerning sales, the sales operations of Hungarian subsidiaries in our sample are more often expanded to the Central and Eastern European region. At t_0 29.4 percent of those Hungarian subsidiaries performing sales had mandates for this region. Compared to Hungary and the Czech Republic, Polish subsidiaries still more often realize responsibilities concerning sales which exceed the national level. In our sample at t_0 25 percent of those subsidiaries were mandated to perform the value chain activity sales for the Central and Eastern European region. 14 percent even had global mandates.

Overall, the development of foreign subsidiaries appears not to be independent of the respective environment in which it is embedded. Subsidiaries in different countries develop differently. Especially striking seems to be the stronger market orientation found in the case of Polish subsidiaries which may have to do with the size of the local market. The expansion of regional responsibilities concerning value chain activities from the downstream end of the value chain such as marketing and sales on the one hand corresponds to the market seeking task of these subsidiaries but on the other hand illustrates that market seeking-subsidiaries in larger markets are advantaged concerning their potential for development with regard to the value chain activities from the downstream end of the value chain compared to market seeking subsidiaries in smaller markets.

THE EFFECT OF A SUBSIDIARY'S OWNERSHIP STRUCTURE

Concerning ownership structure we differentiated between subsidiaries wholly owned (100%) at t_{-1} and those where the German parent held less than 100 percent of ownership at t_{-1}. Those subsidiaries where the German parent had less than 100 percent at t_{-1} were classified as "joint ventures" the others as "wholly owned subsidiaries." Regarding the most frequent value chain activities the differences between joint ventures and wholly owned subsidiaries appear to be rather marginal. Notwithstanding, in our sample joint ventures relatively more often perform production as a value chain activity.

No statistical significant differences between the number of value chain activities performed by wholly owned subsidiaries compared to joint ventures could be detected. With regard to the relevance of the specific tasks from the point of view of joint ventures and wholly owned subsidiaries we employed the non-parametrical Kolmogorov-Smirnov-test. Except for one task-time-evaluation mentioned in the following, the differences proved not to be statistically significant In the case of "efficiency-seeking" a growing number of subsidiaries judge this as an important task. This applies to joint ventures as well as to wholly owned subsidiaries. The differences are neglectable. Similar results can be observed regarding "resource seeking," and "strategic resources seeking": the share of subsidiaries which rates this as an important task rises both in the case of joint ventures and wholly owned subsidiaries over the period of analysis. Concerning "geographical market proximity"-seeking, the differences between wholly owned subsidiaries and joint ventures appear to be more profound: whereas at t_{-1} 41.9 percent of all joint ventures judged this as an important task in the case of wholly owned subsidiaries this share amounts to 62.3 percent. This difference is still valid for the time the survey was conducted: 48.4 percent of all joint ventures rated "geographical market proximity"-seeking as an important task, for wholly owned subsidiaries this percentage is as high as 72.1 percent. Employing the Kolmogorov-Smirnov-test we find that this difference is weakly significant ($Z = 1.181$, asymptotic significance: 0.123). For the future, however, this difference seems to decrease (and is no longer statistically significant): 61.3 percent of all joint ventures evaluate "geographical market proximity" seeking as an important task compared to 70.5 percent of wholly owned subsidiaries. With regard to "psychic market proximity-seeking" the results seem to be similar to those reported concerning "geographical market proximity." At t_{-1} 50.8 percent of all wholly owned subsidiaries judge "psychic market proximity-seeking" as an important task. In contrast, the share of joint ventures judging the same task as important only amounts to 38.7 percent. The gap even widens for t_0: 51.6% of the joint ventures judge "psychic market proximity-seeking" as an important task compared to 68.9 percent of all wholly owned subsidiaries. Concerning "strategic capabilities seeking" the differences between joint ventures and wholly owned subsidiaries seem to be more remarkable. At t_{-1} only 14.8 percent of all wholly owned subsidiaries judged "strategic capabilities seeking" as an important task compared to 25.8 percent of all joint ventures. For t_0 this percentage amounts to 31.1 percent for wholly owned subsidiaries and 35.5 percent for joint ventures. However, for t_{+1} this difference seems to increase: for wholly owned subsidiaries the percentage amounts to 39.3 percent compared to 61.3 in the case of joint ventures, thus emphasizing the high importance of strategic capabilities in the case of subsidiaries which were originally configured as joint ventures.

With regard to the geographical responsibility of the respective value chain activities we find that for the activities from the downstream end of the value chain such as marketing, sales, and customer services most wholly owned subsidiaries performing these tasks appear to be confined to the host country level. However, the share of those tends to decline over the period of analysis. This tendency is accompanied by a growing number of wholly owned subsidiaries attaining regional or global responsibility for exactly these value chain activities. In the case of joint ventures–although some of them have regional or even global responsibility concerning these tasks–a clear shift from national to regional or global responsibility can not be observed.

THE INFLUENCE OF MODE OF MARKET ENTRY

Our hypothesis that the entry mode (acquisition or greenfield investment) which the German parent company chose influences the development of the role of the subsidiaries in Hungary, Poland and Czech Republic appears to be in line with what can be found in our data. For the greenfield subsidiaries activities from the downstream end of the value chain are the most frequent throughout our period of analysis. In contrast, in the case of acquisitions production as a value chain activity seems to be much more important (Table 8).

We find significant differences concerning the number of value chain activities performed by greenfield subsidiaries and by acquisitions. At

TABLE 8. Most Frequent Value Chain Activities with Regard to Ownership Structure and Mode of Market Entry

	t_{-1}	t_0	t_{+1}
Joint Ventures (n) [%]	• Sales (20) [64.5%] • Marketing (18) [58.1] • Production (17) [54.8]	• Sales (22) [71.0] • Marketing and Customer Services (each 21) [67.7]	• Marketing (22) [71.0] • Production, Sales, and Customer Services (each 20) [64.5]
Wholly owned subsidiaries (n) [%]	• Sales (35) [57.4] • Customer Services (33) [54.1] • Marketing (30) [49.2]	• Sales (39) [63.9] • Customer Services (40) [65.6] • Marketing (36) [59.0]	• Sales (40) [65.6] • Customer Services (41) [67.2] • Marketing (38) [62.3]
	•	•	•
Greenfield investments (n) [%]	• Sales (42) [58.3] • Customer Services (36) [50.0] • Marketing (35) [48.6]	• Sales (48) [66.7] • Customer Services (44) [61.1] • Marketing (42) [58.3]	• Sales (47) [65.3] • Customer Services (45) [62.5] • Marketing (43) [59.7]
Acquisitions (n) [%]	• Production (19) [76.0] • Administration (15) [60.0] • Accounting and Sales (14) [56.0]	• Production (19) [76.0] • Administration and Customer Services (17) [68.0]	• Production and Marketing (each 18) [72.0]

t_{-1} greenfield subsidiaries on average had 4.5 value chain activities compared to acquisitions (6.48 value chain activities at t_{-1}). At t_0 greenfield subsidiaries had 6.08 value chain activities compared to 8.32 for acquisitions. For t_{+1} the average difference with regard to the number of value chain activities between greenfield subsidiaries and acquisitions is 2.87. All differences are statistically significant (Table 9).

For greenfield subsidiaries we observed that activities from the "downstream" end of the value chain are most frequent during the period of analysis. In contrast, in the case of acquisitions other value chain activities are more frequent. This corresponds to differences concerning the task of these different types of subsidiaries. In the case of greenfield investments the share of subsidiaries which judge market seeking (regarding both physical and psychic market proximity) as an important task is much higher than in the case of acquisitions over the entire course of time. For example, 61.1 percent of all greenfield subsidiaries at t_{-1} assessed physical market proximity as an important task. In contrast of all acquired subsidiaries only 36 percent evaluate physical market proximity as an important task (Table 10). The differences are statistically significant over the entire period of analysis except for psychic market seeking at t_{+1} (Table 10).

TABLE 9. Results of ANOVA for the Number of Value Chain Activities Depending on Mode of Market Entry

	Greenfield	Acquisition	F-Value (significance)
t_{-1}	4.50	6.48	5.015 (.027)
t_0	6.08	8.32	4.817 (.031)
t_{+1}	6.25	9.12	7.153 (.009)
N	72	25	

On the contrary, over the entire period of analysis the task "efficiency seeking" is relatively more often judged as an important task by acquired subsidiaries compared to greenfield subsidiaries. For example, at t_0 of all acquired subsidiaries 64 percent judged efficiency seeking as an important task compared to 48.7 percent of all greenfield subsidiaries. With regard to resource seeking, the share of greenfield subsidiaries which evaluate this task as important is smaller than in the case of acquisitions. The dynamics concerning "strategic resources seeking" seem to be especially remarkable for acquired subsidiaries: Whereas in the case of greenfield subsidiaries the share of companies evaluating "strategic resources seeking" as an important task rises from 26.4 percent at t_{-1} to 34.7 at t_0 to 40.3 for t_{+1}, the increase of the relevance of this task for acquired subsidiaries over time is much higher: from 20 percent at t_{-1} to 48 percent at t_0 to 60 percent for t_{+1}. Similar results apply to the "strategic capabilities seeking"-task. Obviously acquisitions appear to be especially important as vehicles through which strategic assets are supposed to be created.

The percentage of greenfield subsidiaries performing activities from the downstream end of the value chain which are confined concerning their geographic scope to the host country is higher throughout the period of analysis (except for sales at t_{+1}). In contrast, the share of subsidiaries where the geographical scope of these activities is expanded to the global level is much higher in the case of acquisitions. On the other hand, in the case of greenfield subsidiaries the data reveal a more dynamic progress concerning the geographical scope of these value chain activities compared to the case of acquisitions. Over the period of analysis (except for marketing between t_{-1} and t_0) the share of greenfield subsidiaries being restrained to the national level with regard to these activities diminishes considerably. Corresponding to this reduction in national scope we observe a remarkable increase of greenfield subsid-

TABLE 10. Test for Differences with Regard to the Importance of Market Seeking Between Greenfield Subsidiaries and Acquisitions

	Geographical Market Seeking		Psychic Market Seeking	
	Kolmogorov-Smirnov-Z	Asymptotic Significance	Kolmogorov-Smirnov-Z	Asymptotic Significance
t_{-1}	1.825	0.003	1.303	0.067
t_0	1.686	0.007	1.569	0.015
t_{+1}	1.255	0.086	1.163	0.134

iaries who perform these activities attaining regional responsibility for Central European countries or for Central and East European countries, e.g., with regard to marketing 14.3 percent of all greenfield subsidiaries performing this task at t_{-1} attain responsibility for the Central and East European region. At t_0 this percentage amounts to 19.0 percent and at t_{+1} to even 27.9 percent.

CONCLUSION AND IMPLICATIONS

In this paper we presented the results of a survey of 99 German subsidiaries located in the Czech Republic, Hungary, and Poland. Our focus was on the development of the role of these subsidiaries. We analyzed the effect of several factors which might influence the development of a subsidiary's role. In detail the factors analyzed were the importance of specific tasks, the host country, the mode of ownership, and the mode of market entry. In correspondence to the study of Williams (1998) our findings highlight the importance to differentiate between greenfield subsidiaries and acquisitions when analyzing or discussing the development of the role of foreign subsidiaries located in Central Europe. Furthermore, in line with a number of studies mentioned above, we are able to support the influence of a subsidiary's host country as a determinant of the development of its role. Supporting Birkinshaw (1996) we are able to demonstrate the effect of subsidiary's task on its role development.

We found that greenfield subsidiaries in Central Europe tend to be market proximity seekers whereas in the case of acquisition this task often does not seem to be a major task. Furthermore, market proximity seekers (no matter whether it regards geographical or psychic market proximity) tend to operate a smaller number of value chain activities.

Corresponding to the relevance of the market proximity seeking-task these activities focus on the downstream end of the value chain. And, the geographical scope of market proximity seekers is often restrained to the national level, but tends to be incrementally enlarged over time comprising other countries from the same region.

On the contrary, the number of value chain activities which acquired subsidiaries perform is (on average) higher than the number of value chain activities of greenfields. Other tasks such as efficiency seeking and strategic asset seeking seem to be more important regarding this mode of market entry. And for a considerable portion of efficiency seekers as well as for strategic asset seekers activities from the upstream end of the value chain are upgraded to global scale over the course of time.

For Central European countries attracting foreign direct investment our findings imply that the role of foreign subsidiaries in Central Europe corresponds to their environment. Larger countries with a bigger domestic market are in charge of a natural advantage compared to smaller countries concerning the attraction of market proximity-seeking subsidiaries. Moreover, market proximity seeking-subsidiaries in larger markets seem to have a bigger chance of expanding the geographical scope of their most important value chain activities, namely marketing, sales, and customer services. However, pure size may not be satisfying. As our findings show market proximity seeking subsidiaries develop a different role than subsidiaries where other tasks are more important. They tend to operate less value chain activities and at the moment their geographical scope increases only incrementally.

Especially concerning the allocation of activities from the upstream end of the value chain (activities which may be especially important when spill-over effects from MNCs' subsidiaries are expected in order to improve a country's global competitiveness) and concerning the expansion of the geographical scope of these activities efficiency-seeking subsidiaries as well as strategic asset seeking subsidiaries may be superior to market proximity seeking subsidiaries not only at the time of their establishment, but also for the future. The lesson seems to be: do not expect a local market proximity seeking-subsidiary to turn into a global research centre.

The most important implication for the management of MNCs is that there seems to be still potential for expansion or restructuring concerning MNC's activities in Central Europe. As our analysis has shown, Central European subsidiaries often are constrained concerning their value chain activities to the national market of the host country. This means that MNCs either should consider entering other Central or East European markets or if they are already present in other Central or East European countries, it may be reasonable to consider a restructuring of activities in these countries: Value chain activities which have been tailored to the local markets may be redesigned to serve a larger region called Central Europe, Central and Eastern Europe, or even Europe. Reallocation and concentration of resources will be the consequence for Central European subsidiaries.

As a final caveat, we have to point out that our findings must be interpreted with caution. Our response rates are rather low. No test was undertaken to check for a possible response bias due to unsufficient information about the total population of foreign subsidiaries in the Czech Republic, Hungary, and Poland. Moreover, as up to now (February 2006) only subsidiary managers were questioned, our data may be biased by the "subsidiary perspective." The perspective of the parent company may look different in some cases. Combining the subsidiary's perspective with the perspective of the parent is an important topic which we intend to pursue as a sequel of this study. In addition, due to the fact that all our countries in the meantime are members of the EU, we were not able to analyze the effect of EU-membership on the development of a subsidiary's role. This is a direction where future research should be heading.

REFERENCES

Bartlett, C., & Ghoshal, S. (1986). Tap your subsidiaries for global reach. *Harvard Business Review, 64 (6)*, 87-94.

Bartlett, C., & Ghoshal, S. (1989). *Managing across boarders. The transnational solution.* Boston: Harvard Business School Press.

Benito, G.R.G., Grøgaard, B., & Narula, R. (2003). Environmental influences on MNE subsidiary roles: Economic integration and the Nordic countries. *Journal of International Business Studies, 34 (5)*, 443-456.

Birkinshaw, J. (1994). Approaching heterarchy: A review of the literature on multinational strategy and structure. *Advances in Comparative Management, 9*, 111-114.

Birkinshaw, J. (1996). How multinational subsidiary mandates are gained and lost. *Journal of International Business Studies, 27 (3)*, 467-495.

Birkinshaw, J. (1998). Foreign-owned subsidiaries and regional development: The case of Sweden. In J. Birkinshaw & H. Hood (Eds.), *Multinational corporate evolution and subsidiary development* (pp. 268-298). Houndsmill et al.: Macmillan/St Martin's Press.

Birkinshaw, J., & Hood, N. (1997). An empirical study of development processes in foreign-owned subsidiaries in Canada and Scotland. *Management International Review, 37* (4), 339-364.

Birkinshaw, J., & Hood, N. (1998): Multinational subsidiary evolution: Capability and charter change in foreign-owned subsidiary companies. *Academy of Management Review, 23 (4)*, 773-795.

Birkinshaw, J., & Morrison, A.J. (1995). Configurations of strategy and structure in subsidiaries of multinational corporations. *Journal of International Business Studies, 26 (4)*, 729-753.

D'Cruz, J. (1986). Strategic management of subsidiaries. In H. Etemad & L. Dulude (Eds.), *Managing the multinational subsidiary. Response to environmental changes and to host nation R&D policies* (pp. 75-89). London/Sidney: Croom Helm.

Davis, L.N., & Meyer, K.E. (2004). Subsidiary research and development, and the local environment. *International Business Review, 13 (3)*, 359-382.

Delany, E. (1998). Strategic development of multinational subsidiaries in Ireland. In J. Birkinshaw & N. Hood (Eds.), *Multinational corporate evolution and subsidiary development* (pp. 239-267). Houndsmill et al.: Macmillan/St Martin's Press.

Delany, E. (2000). Strategic development of the multinational subsidiary through subsidiary initiative-taking. *Long Range Planning, 33 (2)*, 220-244.

Doh, J., Jones, G., Teegen, H., & Mudambi, R. (2003). Foreign research and development and host country environment: An empirical examination of U.S. international R&D, Paper presented at the *29nd Annual Conference of the European International Business Academy (EIBA), Copenhagen,* December 11-13.

Dunning, J.H. (1993). *Multinational enterprises and the global economy.* Workingham: Addison Wesley.

Eckert, S., & Rossmeissl, F. (2005). Consequences of convergence–Western firms FDI activities in Central and Eastern Europe at the dawning of EU enlargement. *Journal for East European Management Studies, 10 (1)*, 55-74.

Egelhoff, W.G., Gorman, L., & McCormick, S. (1998). Using technology as a path to subsidiary development. In Birkinshaw, J. & N. Hood (Eds.), *Multinational corporate evolution and subsidiary development* (pp. 213-238). New York: St Martin's Press.

Ferdows, K. (1989). Mapping international factory networks. In K. Ferdows (Ed.), *Managing International Manufacturing* (pp. 3-21). Amsterdam: Elsevier.

Ferdows, K. (1997). Making the most of foreign factories. *Harvard Business Review, 75 (2)*, 73-88.

Forsgren, M., & Pedersen, T. (1996). Are there any centres of excellence among foreign-owned firms in Denmark? Paper presented at the *22nd Annual Conference of the European International Business Academy (EIBA), Stockholm,* December 15-17.

Forsgren, M., & Pedersen, T. (1997). Centres of excellence in multinational companies: The case of Denmark, *Working Paper 2/1997,* Institute of International Economics and Management, Copenhagen Business School, Denmark.

Ghoshal, S., & Bartlett, C. (1991). The multinational corporation as an inter-organizational network. *Academy of Management Review, 15 (4)*, 603-625.

Ghoshal, S., & Nohria, N. (1989). Internal differentiation within multinational corporations. *Strategic Management Journal, 10 (4)*, 323-337.

Gupta, A., & Govindarajan, V. (1991). Knowledge flows and the structure of control within multinational corporations. *Academy of Management Review, 16 (4)*, 768-792.

Gupta, A., & Govindarajan, V. (1994). Organizing for knowledge flows within MNCs. *International Business Review, 3 (4)*, 443-457.

Hungenberg, H. (2004). *Strategisches Management in Unternehmen*. Wiesbaden: Gabler.

Jarillo, J.C., & Martinez, J.I. (1990). Different roles for subsidiaries: The case of multinational corporations in Spain. *Strategic Management Journal, 11*, 501-512.

Johanson, J., & Vahlne, J.-E. (1977). The internationalization process of the firm–a model of knowledge development and increasing foreign market commitments. *Journal of International Business Studies, 8 (1)*, 23-32.

Johanson, J., & Wiedersheim-Paul, F. (1975). The internationalization of the firm–four Swedish cases. *Journal of Management Studies, 12 (3)*, 305-322.

Kutschker, M. (2002). Internationalisierung der Unternehmensentwicklung. In K. Macharzina & M.-J. Oesterle, (Eds.), *Handbuch Internationales Management*, 2nd ed. (pp. 45-67) Wiesbaden: Gabler.

Manea, J., & Pearce, R. (2001): Industrial restructuring in European transition economies and MNEs' investment motivations. *Working paper*, University of Reading.

Martinez, J.I., & Jarillo, C. (1989). The evolution of research on coordination mechanisms in multinational corporations. *Journal of International Business Studies, 20 (3)*, 489-514.

Meissner, H.G. (1997). Der Kulturschock in der Betriebswirtschaftslehre. In J. Engelhard (Ed.), *Interkulturelles Management–Theoretische Fundierung und funktionsbereichsspezifische Konzepte* (pp. 1-12). Wiesbaden: Gabler

Mudambi, R. (1999). MNE internal capital markets and subsidiary strategic independence. *International Business Review, 8 (2)*, 197-211.

Mudambi, R., & Navarra, P. (2004). Is knowledge power? Knowledge flows, subsidiary power and rent-seeking within MNCs. *Journal of International Business Studies, 35 (5)*, 385-406.

Nowinski, W., & Rechkemmer, K. (2004). Relative importance of restructuring and integration in cross-border acquisitions of firms in Poland. Static versus dynamic view, Paper presented at the *30th Annual Conference of the European International Business Academy (EIBA), Ljubljana,* December 5.8.

Papanasstasiou, M., & Pearce, R. (1994). Determinants of the markets strategies of US companies. *Journal of the Economics of Business, 2*, 199-217.

Porter, M.E. (1985). *Competitive advantage*. New York: Free Press.

Randøy, T., & Li, J. (1998). Global resource flows and MNE integrations. In J. Birkinshaw & H. Hood (Eds.), *Multinational corporate evolution and subsidiary development* (pp. 76-101). Houndmills et al.: Macmillan/St Martin's Press.

Rank, O. (2000). *Rollentypologien für Tochtergesellschaften. Ansätze und strategische Implikationen für das internationale Management*. Stuttgart: Döbler&Rössler.

Rosenzweig, P., & Singh, J. (1991). Organizational environments and the multinational enterprise. *Academy of Management Review, 16 (2)*, 340-361.

Schmid, S. (2004). The roles of foreign subsidiaries in network MNCs–a critical review of the literature and some directions for future research. In J. Larimo & S. Rumpunen (Eds.), *European research on foreign direct investment and interna-*

tional human resource management, 112 (pp. 237-255). Vaasan Yliopiston Julkaisuja, Vaasa, Finland.

Schmid, S., Bäurle, I., & Kutschker, M. (1998). Tochtergesellschaften in international tätigen Unternehmen–Ein „State of the Art" unterschiedlicher Rollentypologien. *Discussion Paper No. 104*. Catholic University of Eichstaett-Ingolstadt.

Sekaran, U. (1983). Methodological and theoretical issues and advancement in cross-cultural research. *Journal of International Business Studies, 14 (2)*, 61-73.

Specker, T. (2002). *Postmerger-Management in den ost- und mitteleuropäischen Transformationsstaaten*. Wiesbaden: Gabler.

Surlemont, B. (1996). Types of centres within multinational corporations: An empirical investigation. In Institute of International Business (Ed.): Innovation and international business, part 2 of the *Proceedings of the 22nd Annual Conference, EIBA, Stockholm*, December 15-17, 745-765.

Taggart, J.H. (1997a). Autonomy and procedural justice: A framework for evaluating subsidiary strategy. *Journal of International Business Strategies, 28 (1)*, 51-76.

Taggart, J.H. (1997b). An evaluation of the integration-responsiveness framework: MNC manufacturing subsidiaries in the UK. *Management International Review*, 37 (4), 295-318.

Taggart, J.H. (1998). Identification and development of strategy at subsidiary level. In J. Birkinshaw & H. Hood (Eds.), *Multinational corporate evolution and subsidiary development* (pp. 23-49). Houndmills et al.: Macmillan/St Martin's Press.

Tavares, A., & Pearce, R. (1999). The industrial policy implications of the heterogeneity of subsidiaries' roles in a multinational network. *Discussion Paper No. 5*. Institute for Industrial Development Policy.

Vahlne, J.-E., & Nordström K.A. (1992). Is the globe shrinking? Psychic distance and the establishment of Swedish sales subsidiaries during the last 100 years. Paper presented at the *Annual Conference of the International Trade and Finance Association, Laredo*, April 22-25.

Walsh, S., Linton, J., Boylan, R. & Sylla, C. (2002). The evolution of technology management practice in developing economies: Findings from Northern China. *International Journal of Technology Management, 24 (2/3)*, 311-329.

White, R.E., & Poynter, T.A. (1984). Strategies for foreign-owned subsidiaries in Canada. *Business Quarterly, 49, Summer*, 59-69.

Williams, D. (1998). The development of foreign-owned manufacturing subsidiaries: Some empirical evidence. *European Business Review*, 98 (5), 282-286.

Westney, D.E. (1994). Institutionalization theory and the multinational corporation. In S. Ghoshal & D.E. Westney (Eds.), *Organization theory and the multinational corporation* (pp. 53-76). New York: St Martin's Press.

Young, S., Hood, N., & Peters, E. (1994). Multinational enterprises and regional economic development. *Regional Studies*, 28 (7), 657-677.

doi:10.1300/J097v13n02_05

The Impact of the Change
from Partial to Full Foreign Ownership
on the Internationalization
of Foreign Subsidiaries:
Four Estonian Cases

Tiia Vissak

SUMMARY. This paper aims to study how host country firms' internationalization has been impacted by their foreign owners' achievement of full ownership if the companies were not fully foreign-owned at first. It starts with a review of the existing traditional internationalization literature: the Uppsala model, the innovation-related internationalization models and the Finnish model. Then it reviews other research streams: born global, foreign direct investment (FDI) and network literature and the literature on subsidiary roles. A conceptual framework is developed. Then, after a methodology section, four Estonian cases–two from banking and two from the textiles industry–are introduced. After the discussion of the results, some managerial and research implications are drawn. doi:10.1300/J097v13n02_06 *[Article copies available for a fee from The Haworth Document Delivery Service: 1-800-HAWORTH. E-mail address: <docdelivery@haworthpress.com> Website: <http://www.HaworthPress.com> © 2007 by The Haworth Press, Inc. All rights reserved.]*

Tiia Vissak is Senior Researcher, Faculty of Economics and Business Administration, University of Tartu, Narva Road, 4-A211, 51009, Tartu, Estonia (E-mail: tiia.vissak@ut.ee).

[Haworth co-indexing entry note]: "The Impact of the Change from Partial to Full Foreign Ownership on the Internationalization of Foreign Subsidiaries: Four Estonian Cases." Vissak, Tiia. Co-published simultaneously in *Journal of East-West Business* (The Haworth Press, Inc.) Vol. 13, No. 2/3, 2007, pp. 219-242; and: *Market Entry and Operational Decision Making in East-West Business Relationships* (ed: Jorma Larimo) The Haworth Press, Inc., 2007, pp. 219-242. Single or multiple copies of this article are available for a fee from The Haworth Document Delivery Service [1-800-HAWORTH, 9:00 a.m. - 5:00 p.m. (EST). E-mail address: docdelivery@haworthpress.com].

KEYWORDS. Subsidiary roles, internationalization, Estonia, case study

INTRODUCTION

Some authors–for example, Andersson, Furu and Holmström, 1999; Birkinshaw, 1996; Delany, 2000; Ginsberg and Hay, 1994–have claimed that in multinational networks, subsidiaries are reaching more important roles and a higher decision-making freedom, especially if they are innovative, have strong economic results and/or their managers are actively trying to reach higher autonomy in the parent company's network. Some other authors–for instance, Martínez and Quelch, 1996; Morgan et al., 2002–have reached different conclusions: multinationals have reduced their subsidiaries' autonomy. In addition to having no agreement whether, in general, subsidiary roles have expanded or narrowed, different authors have not reached consensus on whether inward foreign direct investments and network relationships quicken or slow down host country firms' internationalization (for the dual impact of FDI, see, for example, Dunning, 1994) and which are the other main factors influencing this process. There is also a considerable lack of evidence on whether some multinationals' aim to achieve full ownership would quicken their subsidiaries' internationalization–after becoming the sole owner, the parent company can develop the firms just like it wishes–or slow it down: the subsidiaries' decision-making freedom may be reduced, that may decrease their innovativeness and through that, international competitiveness. So, this paper tries to contribute in filling to some extent this relatively extensive research gap.

The paper aims to study how Estonian firms' internationalization has been impacted by their foreign owners' achievement of full ownership if the companies were not fully foreign-owned at first. This country was selected because transition economies have clearly received less attention in the international business literature than more advanced countries. Moreover, with a population of 1.35 million, the largest inward FDI stock per capita in Central and Eastern Europe and a high place in several FDI attractiveness indices–like the ones of UNCTAD and Forbes–Estonia is highly dependent on foreign capital. As the country received first foreign investments in 1989 and most after 1996, local subsidiaries' position in multinational networks should be not stable yet, and there are several enterprises where the share of foreign ownership has increased relatively recently. This makes the country a very interesting research object.

The paper starts with a review of the existing literature on internationalization and subsidiary roles and, based on it, brings out ten internationalization paths of foreign-owned enterprises. Then, after a methodology section, four cases–Hansabank Group, SEB Eesti Ühispank, Wendre and Krenholm Group–are introduced, each illustrating a different path. After the discussion of the results, some managerial and research implications are drawn.

LITERATURE REVIEW

The internationalization literature consists of several research streams. The Uppsala (or the U- or the internationalization process) model (Johanson & Vahlne, 1977, 1990; Johanson & Wiedersheim-Paul, 1975; Vahlne & Johanson, 2002) assumes that internationalization is usually a long, slow and incremental process driven by experiential market knowledge: it generates business opportunities, reduces market risk and uncertainty. In a specific country, companies are expected to make stronger commitments to foreign markets and operations incrementally as they gain experience from current activities in the market: in other words, they pass through steps from no regular export activities to export via independent representatives/agents, overseas sales and, finally, production/manufacturing subsidiaries. As the acquisition of knowledge is gradual and possible mainly through personal experience from operations abroad, they first begin exporting to neighboring countries or the comparatively well-known and similar ones, and after that, try to enter farther markets. The U-model states that enterprises can internationalize more easily if they are large or resourceful, have considerable experience in similar markets and if market conditions are stable.

Innovation-related internationalization (I-) models agree that foreign market expansion is incremental and dependent on an enterprise's experiential learning and uncertainty regarding the decision to internationalize (Fina & Rugman, 1996; Morgan & Katsikeas, 1997). Unlike the U-model, they state that besides knowledge, several other internal and external (f)actors, like other firms, government agencies, top managers, the companies' competitive advantages and general economic conditions, impact internationalization (for an overview, see, for example, Bilkey, 1978). Foreign-owned firms' internationalization might differ from locally-owned ones' increasing international involvement because the headquarters might take the initial decision to start exporting and then organize sales through their own global marketing networks (Wiedersheim-Paul, Olson & Welch, 1978).

The authors of the Finnish model agree that at first, firms tend to penetrate closest countries and, as they gain confidence, start seeking more distant markets and change their method of operating (Luostarinen & Welch, 1997; Welch & Luostarinen, 1988). They also imply that inward internationalization–like imports and inward FDI–might precede and influence the development of outward activities and vice versa (Korhonen, 1999) and several firms can speed up their internationalization by leapfrogging some stages (Chetty, 1999). On the other hand, they also pay attention to de- and re-internationalization (Luostarinen, 1994).

The literature on born globals implies that some companies "leapfrog" into internationalization despite being very young and small, having constrained resources, most volatile markets and, by definition, little or no experience in any market (Oviatt & McDougall, 1994). The authors propose that these enterprises may be able to compensate the lack of a broad resource base by using a narrow but critical set of skills. Internationally experienced managers may also allow them to effectively compete in a broader domain (Wolff & Pett, 2000). A new term, born-again global, refers to the enterprises that are well established in their domestic markets having apparently no great motivation to internationalize, but which have suddenly done it. Mostly, this has been caused by a critical incident: for example, takeover by another enterprise, acquisition of a company with international connections or the internationalization of a domestic client (Bell, McNaughton & Young, 2001).

The authors of the network approach have demonstrated that through network relationships, a firm can increase its ability to innovate and develop its technology (Håkansson and Snehota, 2000), acquire brands, skills and local market knowledge (Adarkar et al., 2001) without necessarily going through the same experiences (Eriksson et al., 1998). In addition to learning about the partners' capabilities, needs and strategies, it can obtain knowledge about their business conditions and market networks (Johanson & Johanson, 1999). As a result, a typical internationalization sequence has changed from gradual expansion to expansion in leaps by joining the nets (Hertz, 1996). On the other hand, network relationships can sometimes also inhibit this process, instead of quickening it (Ford, 1998).

Substantial research has been made on the relationships between FDI and host country exports. Several authors have shown that foreign subsidiaries usually export more than locally owned firms. This is caused by several reasons: subsidiaries have better business contacts abroad, higher management and marketing skills, superior technology, greater general know-how and the right to use their parents' brand names; the owners can help them follow industrial norms, safety standards and consumer tastes; deal with product design, packaging, distribution in their own home country and in other markets and shaping a new product image (Blomström, 1990; Dunning, 1994; Lauter & Rehman, 1999; Marinova, Marinov & Yaprak, 2004; Roolaht, 2002; Simoneti, Rojec & Rems, 2001). It has also been found that such firms have higher market shares; they can use multi-plant operations and have higher advertising and R&D to sales ratios and a large share of professional technical workers in their workforce than locally owned enterprises (Anastassopoulos, 2003). On the other hand, many of those positive effects–including a larger export share–happen only after the investor gains full ownership or at least a qualified majority of the firm (Chhibber & Majumdar, 2005; Delios & Beamish, 1999; Schuh & Holzmüller, 2003). Moreover, some of the high exporters are tightly controlled by the headquarters, and their R&D capabilities may be relatively low (Tavares & Young, 2002). Sometimes foreign direct investments may also be harmful for subsidiaries (for an overview, see also Dunning, 1994): for instance, a local firm may be bought to neutralize its (potential) exports to the investor's home market (Marinova, Marinov & Yaprak, 2004).

The literature on subsidiary roles has attracted considerable attention. The authors supporting the idea of increasing subsidiary autonomy state that dramatic changes in the competitive environment have highlighted the need to move toward network-based structures (Malnight, 1996) and lead to the understanding that strategic innovation requires a high level of freedom (Ginsberg & Hay, 1994). Increasingly, multinational corporations let their subsidiaries have multiple connections with the other entities both inside and outside the corporations' formal boundaries (Birkinshaw, 1997) and encourage some of them to develop their own strategy and a greater strategic role (Birkinshaw, 1996; Birkinshaw & Hood, 1998; Delany, 2000). Over time, these subsidiaries should accumulate valuable resources and capabilities, leading to an increased status and thus to an extension of the scope of their activities (Birkinshaw & Hood, 1997; Hedlund, 1986; Prahalad & Doz, 1981).

Some other authors say that for the most part of the 20th century, headquarters granted enough autonomy and sovereignty to subsidiary top managers to design and implement the strategy in "their territory," but not any longer: due to increased competition and more standardized consumer needs, multinationals have retained or even steadily raised the level of integration and interdependence across subsidiaries and national boundaries (Legewie, 2002; Martínez & Quelch, 1996; Morgan et al., 2002; Quelch & Bloom, 1996). They no longer allow the local managers to decide how, when, and even whether their units will implement a particular strategic initiative (Bartlett & Ghoshal, 1992, 2003) even if they themselves have no experience on the local or even other similar markets. Thus, some local subsidiary managers may perceive that their required interactions with the headquarters are more of a hindrance than a help (Quelch & Dinh-Tan, 1998).

Some authors state that if the parent corporation gives its subsidiary more autonomy, both can gain. By occupying a central network position, a unit is likely to access useful knowledge from others (Tsai, 2001), develop value-added strategic activities (Birkinshaw, 1993), pursue innovative and risky projects (Birkinshaw, 1999), strengthen its reputation and further increase its potential bargaining power (Birkinshaw, 1993; Zahra, Dharwadkar & George, 1999). Consequently, it can play a key role in determining the success of its parent corporation (Zahra, Dharwadkar & George, 1999).

Still, there are also some arguments in favor of decreased subsidiary autonomy: it gives operational freedom to the multinational in relation to its global activities, allowing planning and modifying production routinely across plants in different countries (Chhibber & Majumdar, 2005) and attaining a sustainable, competitive cost advantage (Martínez & Quelch, 1996). Thus, the plants producing standardized commodities like car parts and electronic components face increased pressure on productivity and costs and a threat of closing down if the results do not please the owner (Legewie, 2002; Morgan et al., 2002; Quelch & Bloom, 1996). Sometimes, a subsidiary has to give priority to servicing important MNC customers over its local ones, and it can be forced to retaliate against a certain competitor or to specialize on a narrow product range and export it to other subsidiaries even if it does not allow profit maximization (Martínez & Quelch, 1996). In other words, in the era of intense competition around the world, MNCs cannot afford to permit a subsidiary manager to defend parochial interests as "king of the country" (Bartlett & Ghoshal, 2003).

From the above, *some preliminary conclusions* can be made. It can be concluded that some foreign-owned firms may internationalize faster than locally-owned companies–they do not necessarily have to start their foreign operations from closest countries and simplest foreign entry modes–because they can benefit from getting access to the parent company's and its other subsidiaries' market knowledge, networks and other resources. If the owner grants them enough decision-making autonomy, both may gain. Still, this does not always happen: some parent companies prefer to control their subsidiaries very tightly and even force to pull off some profitable market or product segments in order to maximize their own profits. This may sometimes hinder such foreign-owned firms' internationalization.

Figure 1 brings out ten internationalization paths of foreign-owned enterprises. Based on the above discussion, it can be proposed that becoming foreign-owned can both quicken and slow down a firm's internationalization. After the foreign owner obtains 100 percent of the company, the process may be affected again. Some enterprises may internationalize very quickly due to (full) foreign ownership and even develop some characteristics of born globals, while some others may de-internationalize completely. There are naturally several possibilities in between. Two of those–paths IX and X–are also brought out: some companies may not be affected considerably at first at all, but after the foreign owner acquires the rest of their shares, their internationalization may quicken or slow down.

METHODOLOGY

To examine the above-made conclusions, case study methodology was chosen. This method has been an essential form of research in social sciences and management (Chetty, 1996). The need for case study and firm-level data is also increasing in studying multinationals' activities (Gestrin, 2002). By combining previously developed theories with new empirically derived insights (Yin, 1994), it is especially appropriate in new topic areas. This method allows transcending the local boundaries of the investigated cases and capturing new layers of reality. Its use can result in developing novel, testable and empirically valid theoretical and practical insights (Eisenhardt, 1989; Tsoukas, 1989; Voss, Tsikriktis & Frohlich, 2002). The case study method also enables us to conduct research in a country–like Estonia–where the small sample base means that there might not be enough firms to justify using statistical generalization (Chetty, 1996). Moreover, contrary to some other research methods, which aim at statistical correlations with less regard for the underlying explanations, case research is capable of discovering true causal relationships (Hillebrand, Kok & Biemans, 2001): the researcher can go far beyond a cross-sectional snapshot of a process and

FIGURE 1. The Internationalization Paths of Foreign-Owned Firms: A Conceptual Framework

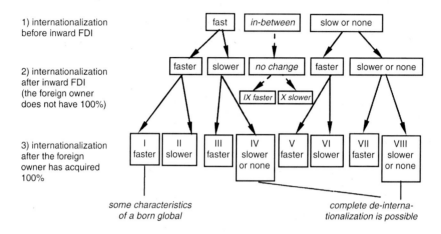

understand how and why things happen as they do (Miles & Huberman, 1994).

In this paper, multiple case study approach was used. This may reduce the depth of study but it can both augment external validity and help guard against observer bias (Voss, Tsikriktis & Frohlich, 2002). There is no ideal number of cases in the multiple-case approach. Still, it is difficult to generate theory with less than four case companies, and with more than ten cases, the data volume is not easy to cope with (Eisenhardt, 1989). In addition, once a pattern emerges, each new field site adds to the research data but at a diminishing rate (Stuart et al., 2002). This paper is based on four cases. The four case companies were active in two sectors: two in services–banking–and the other two in manufacturing–textiles–and they were among the two largest firms in their respective industry. They were all Swedish-owned. This should reduce the possibility that cultural differences impacted their autonomy in their owner's network. The sample was chosen because the data from the companies could be used for replication–producing contrasting results (Yin, 1994) as each case illustrated a different internationalization path–rather than because the enterprises were representative of the whole population (Chetty, 1996).

In the following section, the case descriptions are provided. Each case is at first looked at as a separate entity, enabling unique patterns, which can be generalized across cases, to emerge (Eisenhardt, 1989). The results are discussed in the final part of the paper. To increase the validity and reliability in studying these firms' autonomy and internationalization, several data sources were used. They included newspapers and journals, the firms' homepages, annual reports and two previous personal interviews.

CASE DESCRIPTIONS

Case 1. Hansabank Group's history dates back to July 1991 when Hansabank started operating as a branch of Tartu Commercial Bank. It launched independent operations in January 1992. At first, Hansabank operated locally. In 1995, it opened a representation in Riga and launched Hansa Leasing Latvia. In June 1996, Hansabank also purchased Deutsche-Lettische Bank that soon started operating under the name Hansabank-Latvia–in 1999, the name was changed to Hansabanka–and established Hansa Leasing Lithuania (in 1997, Hansa Leasing also entered Ukraine but there, operations are still relatively minor and Hansabank only employs a couple of people). In 1998, after it merged with Savings Bank (Hoiupank), it became Estonia's largest bank.

Swedish FöreningsSparbanken (Swedbank: a leading Nordic-Baltic banking group with 10.2 million retail customers and approximately 15, 700 employees in 21 countries) obtained 49.98 percent of Hansabank Group in 1998 through a share issue. Swedbank's share soon increased to over 50 percent and stabilized at 59.7 percent until the beginning of 2005. The bank's internationalization continued. In July 1999, its Lithuanian subsidiary Hansabankas was opened and in April 2001, Hansabank purchased 90.7 percent of Lietuvos Taupomasis Bankas that was merged with Hansabankas.

In November 2002, Hansa Capital and the EBRD established Hansa Leasing Russia (Hansabank Group had some previous knowledge of the market: Hansa Capital operated in Russia during the years 1997-1998; moreover, through the merger with Savings Bank, Hansabank Group also acquired FABA Bank in Russia, but it sold the bank in April 1999) to offer asset-based financing to railroads and ports. In March 2005, Hansabank reached an agreement to purchase EBRD's 25-percent share in the enterprise. By the end of 2005, Hansa Leasing Russia became Russia's second largest leasing enterprise with a portfolio of over 200 million USD. In September 2004, Hansabank signed a purchase agreement of the Russian Kvest Bank–a small corporate bank–in order to offer funding to Baltic, Scandinavian and Russian companies for developing their operations in Russia. In 2006, the EBRD is supposed to buy 15 percent of Hansabank's daughter bank in Russia. In the end of 2004, Hansa Capital's subsidiary OOO Hansa Leasing set up a subsidiary for leasing industrial equipment and vehicles in Kaliningrad. Hansabank Group has announced its plan to expand its banking operations to St. Petersburg and Kaliningrad and increase the number of employees in Russia to 190, but it has limited its Russian presence to 10% of its risk-weighted assets.

By the end of the third quarter of 2005, Hansabank Group's number of employees grew to over 6850 (this number should increase in the near future as in January 2006, Hansabank announced of its intention to establish a non-life insurance company which will provide property insurance services to private and business clients), it reached a 1/3 share in the Baltic market and its Internet bank had over 1.5 million customers. In 2004, the firm's market value increased over 80%: to 3.05 billion EUR, its Latvian unit–Hansabanka–became the leading bank in Latvia and its Lithuanian operation also showed clear improvement: net profit increased by 56, loans by 46 and deposits by 26 percent, while for the whole group, net profit grew 40 percent: to 182.8 million EUR. Compared to all other Estonian enterprises, Hansabank had the largest turnover and profit. Between 1996 and 2004, Hansabank produced an average cumulative annual return of 39% for its shareholders. By 2007 it wants to become a benchmark of a modern banking in Europe and its share in Swedbank's total profits should increase to over 50 percent in the near future.

In February 2005 Swedbank announced that they would buy the 40.3% of shares owned by Hansabank's minority shareholders. They succeeded after raising the offer from 11 to 13.5 EUR per share and achieved full ownership in the end of June. Already in April, Mr. Indrek Neivelt, the Chairman of the Board of Hansabank Group since 1999, left as he did not wish to work in a fully foreign-owned subsidiary and he did not feel it was "his" bank any longer.

Swedbank announced that their full ownership would not change Hansabank's business culture, strategies and plans for the future and the management would continue its everyday operations and implementation of the published strategy. Mr. Neivelt agreed that in the near future, probably there will not be a substantial change of business culture, but later, the bank's values might become more similar to Swedbank's. Swedbank also promised to intensify its communication with Hansabank's management. In August 2005, it decided to form a new Group Executive Management. Two members from Hansabank group were included: Erkki Raasuke, the head of Baltic and Russian banking and Ingrida Bluma, the head of Hansabank in Latvia. The employees of Hansabank Group have been invited to discussions of Swedbank's future strategies and they have even led some discussion groups.

Some of Hansabank's previous board members claimed that after Swedbank reached full ownership, it would take larger risks and Hansabank's operations in Russia might increase. This became true: the bank announced in September 2005 that during the following two years, it does not plan to expand its customer base in Russia beyond Swedbank's corporate customers and their employees, but it may overlook its decision after that; so, in the future, its involvement may increase. In addition, in December 2005, Hansabank announced that its investment fund will expand to Latvia, Lithuania and Finland in the near future. Moreover, Hansabank's credit rating improved further as proposed: in November 2005, Moody's Investor Service rating of financial strength grew from C to C +. In the future, the bank may also benefit from joint risk management. The other benefits may be minor: the Swedish and Baltic markets are quite different and the banks' IT platforms also differ. Still, in the future, there might be some opportunities for joint product and IT development and Swedbank may transfer some of its operations to Estonia, Latvia or Lithuania.

Until now, from being foreign-owned, Hansabank has mostly gained: the owner has helped it with internal audit and risk management. In addition, the bank's credit rating has improved. The fact in itself that Hansabank Group has a foreign owner has been a sign of stability and trust and improved the bank's image in Latvia and Lithuania. For instance, in 2001 when it bought a bank in Lithuania, Hansabank defined itself as a Swedish bank. In addition, by sharing knowledge within the Group and with Swedbank, Hansabank was able to exploit synergies and avoid making mistakes in its business judgments. At the same time, the owner has managed them employing a "hands-off" approach. Hansabank, in the majority of cases, has taken the decisions in the areas of pricing, advertising, personnel and R&D. Some distribution and financing decisions have been made jointly with the parent company.

Case 2. SEB Eesti Ühispank. In December 1992, ten small banks decided to merge under the name of Eesti Ühispank (Union Bank of Estonia). In 1996 it was quoted at the Tallinn and Helsinki stock exchanges. At the same year it acquired Põhja-Eesti Pank (North-Estonian Bank) and two years later, Tallinna Pank. In 1998, in co-operation with advisors from Nomura International plc, Eesti Ühispank identified two strategic investors: Scandinavia's second largest bank Skandinaviska Enskilda Banken–or SEB, listed in Stockholm; it has 670 branch offices around Sweden, Germany, the Baltic countries, Poland and Ukraine– and the International Finance Corporation. The new shareholders acquired a 34 percent and nearly 10 percent stake respectively. In October 1999 SEB decided to increase its stake in Eesti Ühispank to 50.51 percent; in 2000, it grew to 96.4%; in 2003, to 100%. Currently it is the second largest bank in Estonia with over 1400 employees.

From April, 2005 the bank's name is SEB Eesti Ühispank. A new name format emphasizes the relationship of the bank with SEB. Together with the new name, also a novel visual identity was applied, similar to that of the parent bank. Currently SEB Eesti Ühispank has the following subsidiaries: SEB Ühisliising (established in 1994, it offers a wide range of leasing and factoring services), SEB Ühispanga Fondid–founded in 1996, it manages investment funds and institutional portfolios–and SEB Ühispanga Elukindlustus: a life insurance company established in 1998. It also fully owns three real estate companies and is a partial owner of five other firms in Estonia. SEB Eesti Ühispank offers leasing services in Russia (in 1998-1999, Eesti Ühispank also owned Saules Banka in Latvia that it had acquired with the merger with Tallinna Pank, but it sold the bank in order to focus on its activities in Estonia) and supports the customers of the SEB Group in investing their assets in Central and Eastern Europe. In 1997, in co-operation with Neva-Rus Ltd it established Venemaa Ühisliising LTD (SEB Russian Leasing) based in St.Petersburg. Being a member of the SEB Group, SEB Eesti Ühispank is more international than the local banks. In the future, it plans to pay more attention to Russia and to those Finnish firms that have operations in Estonia.

Since March 1998, Eesti Ühispank co-operates with SEB Unibanka of Latvia and SEB Vilniaus Bankas–both majority-owned by SEB–in providing cross-border customer service, joint investments and development projects, syndicates and inter-bank funding. Such co-operation has enabled the banks to focus on their fast-growing domestic financial services' markets and targeted projects in neighboring countries. Belonging to the SEB group has been also beneficial for Ühispank in other ways. Top and middle managers continuously take part in the management training of the SEB Group in Europe and America. The bank has grown considerably–between 1999 and 2005, its assets have increased from 1.0 to 2.3 billion EUR–and it has become able to develop new services. Its credit ratings have also improved. The bank has taken over its parent's accounting principles. In May 2005, SEB Eesti Ühispank received a right to offer its services to Deutsche Bank's and Société Générale's business customers in Estonia. Moreover, in the near future, SEB Groups' East-European competence centre will be established in Estonia on basis of the SEB Eesti Ühispank Asset Management. The latter will manage all SEB's Eastern European investment funds worth over 250 million EUR. The gains have been mutual: in 2004, SEB Eesti Ühispank's balance sheet was 1.3% of SEB but they brought 4.4% of SEB's profit.

According to the chairman of the supervisory board Mats Kjaer, there is very little power hierarchy and many actions are team actions in SEB Eesti Ühispank. Mr. Neivelt has commented that compared to Swedbank, SEB has controlled Eesti Ühispank more tightly, especially in everyday decisions. Since 1999, the parent's strategy has not changed considerably–they keep costs under control and all fields profitable–but its management has changed recently: Ain Hanschmidt, the bank's chairman of the supervisory board, left in August 2005. He had managed the bank since 1992 and been the chairman of the management board until February 2005. SEB claimed it did not have any pretensions against him, although a large scandal emerged in Estonia in 2005, when it became public that Mr. Hanschmidt had become one of major shareholders of two Estonian firms–Tallink and Haapsalu HMR to which the bank granted loans in 1996-2001 when they were in a relatively poor financial state and could not get financing from elsewhere–by obtaining for himself their shares for more than a thousand times below the market price.

Case 3. Wendre. The company was founded in 1930s as a flax processing plant. In 1965, it started to produce non-woven fabric products and in 1990, quilts and pillows based on polyester fiber. In 2000, Wendre was given the ISO 9001-2000 certificate. It also has the ACTICARD, ÖKO-TEX and, since 2005, the ISO 14001 certificate. Currently, it is one of the Baltic and Scandinavian countries' largest pillow, mattress, bedspread and home textile producers. In 2004, its turnover was 26.8 million EUR and it had 570 employees.

Peter Hunt, originating from Estonia, but having spent many years in Sweden and having over 20 years of experience in running textile businesses, started to co-operate with Wendre in 1993. He began to deliver fabrics and synthetic fibers and sell the company's products. In 1995, his company Trading House Scandinavia AB (founded in 1991 and registered in Sweden) acquired 25 percent of Wendre. In 1999, his share increased to 67 and in March 2002, to 100 percent. After the takeover,

Wendre began to buy all raw materials from Hunt's three textile companies in Sweden. Due to belonging to the Swedish concern, the enterprise has achieved easier access to foreign markets–Germany, Spain, Switzerland, Denmark, United Arabian Emirates, the UK, Finland, Norway, Latvia, Lithuania, Holland, Russia, Austria, France, Italy and the USA–but its main foreign market is still Sweden. Its main customer is IKEA, buying about a half of Wendre's products. Wendre has built a special warehouse for sending its products to some IKEA's customers directly and it has a three-year contract for increasing its sales to IKEA almost twice. In the future, the company plans to diversify its customer base. In total, Wendre exports about 95 percent of its turnover. In 2005, it launched another plant in Estonia–as a result, its annual turnover dropped to 25.4 million EUR, as the production was re-organized, but in the second half of 2005, the turnover increased considerably–and one in Wux, China. Both plants employ over 200 people. In the future, this number may increase substantially. The Estonian plant is capable of producing 7 million blankets and 10 million pillows a year and it has already signed contracts for the following three years. In China, polyester fiber, feather blankets and pillowcases are also produced. One of their customers is IKEA that has several shops in China. Wendre may soon become the largest blanket producer in Europe. In spring 2006, the company's subsidiary Wenfom may start producing porolone in Estonia together with an Austrian company Eurofoam GmbH and also increase its mattress and garden furniture production. By 2007, Wendre's annual turnover should grow to 64 million EUR. In the near future, it plans to expand even further and enter Europe with its own trademark.

Peter Hunt has actively participated in the management of Wendre. "I cannot remain passive: business is so interesting," he has admitted. When he became a sole owner–he also bought the shares of the company's former managing director Tõnu Laks after which the latter left the firm because Hunt wanted to intervene very often in Wendre's management and Laks refused to buy raw materials from Hunt's firms as their prices were higher and the terms of payment worse than those of the other companies–Hunt started to meet the most important clients and do most of the marketing himself. Wendre began to buy 100 percent of raw materials from Hunt's other companies (he also currently owns Bema Sellen, Bema Quilting and Bema Bedline) in Sweden. In the future, it may also start buying some of them through its Chinese subsidiary. In total, Hunt has invested about 32 million EUR into the firm, about a half of it in 2002-2005.

Case 4. Krenholm Group was established in 1857. It soon became Europe's largest textile producer. It produced cotton thread, fabric and wadding, which were sold to several countries, including Russia and China. After Estonia became independent in 1918, the firm was restructured. It started exporting to Western Europe, but its turnover decreased five times. After World War II, the firm was nationalized and its production reoriented to the Soviet market. Before becoming Estonian state-owned in 1991, Krenholm Group had 11 000 employees. As the Soviet market fell off, the company had to find new buyers. In 1991-1995 it filled unsolicited export orders for intermediate buyers from different countries but had no resources, knowledge or original products to export directly. Krenholm's main advantage was low cost. However, it faced serious financial difficulties. In 1995, after Borås Wäfveri AB bought a 75.5 percent share of the enterprise (since 1999, Krenholm has been fully owned), it started developing and exporting its own products. In 1995, Krenholm opened a fully owned sales subsidiary, Krenholm Scandinavia AB, in Sweden (at that time, its main market was the USA with a 48% share, but later, Sweden became the main market). Two years later, it established a sales office in Germany. In 2001, it acquired a new subsidiary–Aurora Fabrics Ltd–to market the mother company's production in the UK. The firm has also exported to Finland, Latvia, Lithuania, Norway, Belgium, Holland, Italy, Switzerland and other countries.

In 2002, Krenholm Group announced that having a solid foreign owner was one of its main strengths, although it had not gained considerably in terms of technological solutions or finding foreign customers. Borås Wäfveri AB has brought marketing and management know-how (their managers had a very long experience in the textile business), valuable experience in restructuring as well as financial investments in machinery to Krenholm (in 2005, the parent company brought some machinery from Sweden that allows Krenholm to produce wider fabrics: before, the maximum width was 1.5 meters: not enough for many potential customers). The firm received the European Eco-label in 2003. Also, the takeover in a way improved Krenholm Group's image. In 2002, Krenholm announced of its plans to open an office in Holland by taking over a small sales company and invest in its products' sales in Southern Europe, but these plans have not realized. The firm's economic results improved at first, but in 2002, they started to worsen. In 2004, Borås Wäfveri had to invest a considerable sum into the enterprise to keep it from going bankrupt; and the firm had to sell some of its real estate and a mail-order trade department. Krenholm's annual turnover decreased from 74 to 64 million EUR. It owes over 30 million EUR to different creditors.

In January 2003, Meelis Virkebau, the general manager of Krenholm since 1995, resigned. Mats Skogman, the general director of the parent company Borås Wäfveri AB since October 2002, took over. Under Virkebau's management, Krenholm was quite active in increasing its value-added, developing its own brand and renewing its technology. Until 2002, it made all strategic plans and decisions. This changed in 2003, as in 2002, the firm lost about 3 million EUR and the management of Borås Wäfveri AB changed. Virkebau claimed: "It is not right for a CEO abandon his beliefs and become an obedient puppet. An enterprise is successful only if it has a thinking leader." The leader of the trade union has characterized the firm's new general director Matti Haarajoki as a man who follows the orders of the head office: if they tell him to reduce the employees' wages, then he does it. Meelis Virkebau was more popular among the workers and he spoke Russian: the language that is mostly spoken by them. The new management does not speak it.

Despite a change in management, 2003 and 2004 were not more favorable years for Krenholm than 2002: the turnover continued to decrease and the firm did not earn any profit. In 2005, its CEO (since November 2003) Matti Haarajoki even told that the enterprise might move some of its operations from Estonia to Russia in the near future because the labor costs are lower there. In 2004, Krenholm had to lay off 600 and in 2005, 500 employees. By the end of 2005, only 3100 remained. Still, the firm has announced that in 2005, it may earn a small profit (of about 0.03 million EUR), although its turnover for the first half of the year decreased by 14 percent.

DISCUSSION

From the four cases (see also Table 1) it can be concluded that (full) foreign ownership can both inhibit and quicken companies' internationalization. Hansabank has managed to increase its presence in Latvia, Lithuania, Russia and enter Finland and it has also benefited from servicing its parent company's foreign customers in Estonia, SEB Eesti Ühispank has only entered Russia and that happened before becoming foreign-owned; moreover, it sold a bank in Latvia soon after that, but it has also become to service some of its parent company's foreign customers and manage one of its owner's investment funds. Wendre has also mostly benefited from being foreign-owned: due to the owner's

TABLE 1. The Internationalization of the Case Companies and the Role of (Full) Foreign Ownership

Firm name and the number of a path (see Figure 1)	Hansabank Group I	SEB Eesti-Ühispank IX	Wendre V	Krenholm Group VI
The year of establishment/first FDI/full ownership	1991/1998/2005	1992/1998/2003	1930/1995/2002	1857/1995/1999
Internationalization before inward FDI	1995: Latvia, 1996: Lithuania (involvement increased gradually), low involvement in Russia since 1997	1997: leasing services in Russia	Unsolicited export orders first, some more regular exports since 1995	Several periods of de- and re-internationalization; since 1991, unsolicited export orders
Internationalization after inward FDI (but not yet full ownership)	Higher involvement in Latvia and Lithuania, lower involvement in Russia at first and more operations later	Continued involvement in Russia (leasing), sales of banking operations in Latvia	Increasing involvement in exporting, especially to Sweden	Subsidiaries in Sweden and Germany, increasing exports to several countries
Internationalization after inward FDI (after the owner acquired full ownership)	High involvement in Latvia and Lithuania, higher involvement in Russia and small involvement in Finland; the internationalization may quicken in the near future	Growing involvement in Russia (leasing); in Estonia, servicing international customers may increase	Exports to Germany, Spain, Switzerland, Denmark, United Arabian Emirates, the UK, Finland, Norway, Latvia, Lithuania, Holland, Russia, Austria, France, the USA and Italy; a production subsidiary in China	Subsidiary in the UK, exports to Sweden, Latvia, Lithuania, Finland, Norway, Belgium, Holland, Italy, Switzerland, the USA and other countries, decreasing exports to the USA
The level of autonomy before/after full ownership	Relatively high/still quite high even in making some strategic decisions	Not very high/a bit lower, especially in strategic areas	Not very high/very low (the owner controls and manages the firm personally)	Relatively high/at first still quite high, but since 2003, very low
The impact of FDI	Considerable local and international growth, a higher credit rating, improved image, know-how, better access to financing	Considerable local growth, a higher credit rating, better access to financing, know-how and training	Some local and considerable international growth, better access to financing, sales networks, know-how and raw materials	Better access to foreign markets, know-how, financing, technology and raw materials, growth at first, but problems later

personal contacts and investments, the firm has become able to export to a large number of countries and even establish a subsidiary in China. For Krenholm, foreign ownership has not brought as many benefits as it was initially hoped: it has not been able to solve its financial difficulties and its number of employees has decreased considerably. Still, it has managed to establish subsidiaries in Sweden, Germany and the UK and export to many countries, including the USA. While the two banks' internationalization has more or less followed the more classical (the U- and I-models') route, the textile producers have internationalized faster since the 1990s but not like the born global literature would have expected: due to their long history before Estonia regained its independence, they rather have some characteristics of born-again globals.

In addition to getting easier access to foreign markets, the firms have benefited in terms of technology, additional capital, foreign market knowledge, improved image or management know-how (such positive effects are often brought out in the FDI and network literature). Three enterprises have grown considerably, only Krenholm's turnover and a number of employees have decreased in the last years.

Foreign owners' success in obtaining full ownership in their companies has also impacted some case firms' strategies: for instance, their management changed. In Wendre, the former shareholder and managing director left soon after that because he had a different view about the firm's future and he did not agree to buy most of the raw material from the full owner's other subsidiaries. Hansabank's chairman of the board (he was also a minor shareholder) decided to leave at once because he did not feel it was "his" bank any longer, but it is still a bit too early to tell how it would impact the bank's strategy in addition to intensified communication between the bank and the head office and an increase of the bank's operations in Russia. Krenholm's general manager left more than three years after the firm became fully foreign-owned. He complained that in the last year, when the firm' financial results worsened, the owners did not give him enough decision-making autonomy. The new management has considerably reduced the firm's number of employees but they have not improved the results yet. In addition, they have had to face problems with trade unions. Ühispank's general manager left two years after SEB obtained full ownership, but a change in the bank's strategy was probably not the reason as this bank has not been as autonomous in its decision-making in Hansabank.

Mihkel Pärjamäe, the owner of an Estonian consultancy and training company Invicta, has reached a conclusion similar to some of the case study results: in Estonia, the times have changed. Instead of builders, the organizations need leaders who can manage stability. In other words, they must obediently do what the owners say. Agu Vahur from CV-Online, a large Estonian online recruitment company, has stated that compared to 1990s, the board's role has changed. Now they make strategic decisions themselves and often even intervene in everyday management. The top managers' functions have been narrowed. Instead of developing spectacular projects, they have to ensure that everyday routines continue. The case results show that the changes in management and the success in obtaining full ownership have increased some foreign owners' control over their Estonian subsidiaries, but this is not a strict rule. Moreover, in general, the firms have not lost from it in terms of internationalization.

CONCLUSIONS AND FUTURE RESEARCH DIRECTIONS

Some of the current literature indicates that in parent companies' networks, the roles of subsidiaries are expanding and managers should be especially active in order to achieve larger decision-making autonomy from the multinational. Some other authors have shown that the opposite might be true. There is also no consensus on how firms internationalize: some authors have stated that the process is mostly slow and starts from closest markets and simplest entry modes, while some others have pointed out that many enterprises internationalize much faster, enter several farther markets and even make some foreign direct investments soon after their establishment. The case evidence showed that there was no clear pattern in terms of decision-making autonomy in the four case firms after the parent companies achieved full ownership: for instance, Krenholm remained relatively autonomous until its financial results worsened while the new owner started to manage Wendre directly at once although its results were relatively sound. All the four firms have internationalized relatively successfully (only Krenholm has lately faced some difficulties) and two of them–Wendre and Krenholm–have also entered some markets outside Europe. Thus, while from their owners' achievement of full ownership, some firms may lose their autonomy, it does not have to slow down their internationalization but retaining a firm's autonomy does not have to speed up or slow down the process considerably, either.

As the results are mixed and the number of case companies is small, it is hard to offer any strict suggestions to the managers of (fully) foreign-owned companies. It seems that in some corporations, control over subsidiaries' actions has increased and the managers' activities toward achieving higher decision-making autonomy may not be approved. In some others, on the other hand, such activities could be appreciated. It should be also kept in mind that there does not seem to be a clear connection between decision-making autonomy, the share of foreign ownership and the level of a company's internationalization: both strictly and loosely controlled firms may succeed and fail in their internationalization and other activities. So, managerial decisions should be made taking in mind the organization's, its owner's and surrounding environment's specific characteristics.

This paper covered only some issues. Several aspects should be studied further. For example, the evidence from some other transition economies should be collected. Some evidence should also be gathered from subsidiaries that have managed to increase their autonomy but have not succeeded in quickening their internationalization process, or from those that have been forced by their parent companies to pull back from foreign markets completely. It would be also interesting to study if there is a reverse relationship between the level of foreign ownership and a subsidiary's internationalization: if the multinational would try to increase its ownership in internationally successful subsidiaries or not.

A larger sample would also allow using other methods besides case study analysis. In Estonia, the number of such foreign owners that have later achieved full ownership in their subsidiaries is relatively small, but in larger countries, it should be possible to collect more data: for example, by conducting a survey. Then, it should become clearer, how some managers succeed in achieving higher decision-making autonomy, why some parent companies prefer to increase their control while the others do not and what other factors impact foreign subsidiaries' internationalization. In addition, a more longitudinal approach could be taken. This should help to predict whether in the long run, in general, subsidiaries' autonomy increases or decreases and to what extent it impacts their internationalization.

REFERENCES

Adarkar, A., Adil, A., Ernst, D., & Vaish, P. (2001). Emerging market alliances: must they be win-lose. In M. R. Czinkota & I. A. Ronkainen (Eds.), *Best practices in international business* (pp.142-158). Fort Worth: Harcourt College Publishers.

Anastassopoulos, G. (2003). MNE subsidiaries versus domestic enterprises: an analysis of their ownership and location-specific advantages. *Applied Economics, 35* (13), 1505-1514.

Andersson, M., Furu, P., & Holmström, C. (1999). Development, recognition, and integration of competence of subsidiaries in the multinational corporation. *25th Annual EIBA Conference* [CD-Rom]. Manchester: University of Manchester Institute of Science and Technology.

Bartlett, C. A., & Ghoshal, S. (1992). What is a global manager. *Harvard Business Review, 70* (5), 124-132.

Bartlett, C. A., & Ghoshal, S. (2003). What is a global manager? *Harvard Business Review, 81* (8), 101-108.

Bell, J., McNaughton, R., & Young, S. (2001). 'Born-again global' firms. An extension to the 'born global' phenomenon. *Journal of International Management, 7* (3), 173-189.

Bilkey, W. J. (1978). An attempted integration of the literature on the export behavior of firms. *Journal of International Business Studies, 9* (1), 33-46.

Birkinshaw, J. (1993). *Entrepreneurial behaviour in multinational subsidiaries* (Working Paper No. 93-07). London, Ontario: Richard Ivey School of Business.

Birkinshaw, J. (1996). How multinational subsidiary mandates are gained and lost. *Journal of International Business Studies, 27* (3), 467-495.

Birkinshaw, J. (1997). Entrepreneurship in multinational corporations: the characteristics of subsidiary initiatives. *Strategic Management Journal, 18* (3), 207-229.

Birkinshaw, J. (1999). The determinants and consequences of subsidiary initiative in multinational corporations. *Entrepreneurship: Theory & Practice, 24* (1), 9-36.

Birkinshaw, J., & Hood, N. (1997). An empirical study of development processes in foreign owned subsidiaries in Canada and Scotland. *Management International Review, 37* (4), 339-364.

Birkinshaw, J., & Hood, N. (1998). Multinational subsidiary evolution: capability and charter change in foreign-owned subsidiary companies. *The Academy of Management Review, 23* (4), 773-795.

Blomström, M. (1990). *Transnational corporations and manufacturing exports from developing countries.* New York: United Nations.

Chetty, S. (1996). The case study method for research in small- and medium-sized firms. *International Small Business Journal, 15* (1), 73-85.

Chetty, S. (1999). Dimensions of internationalisation of manufacturing firms in the apparel industry. *European Journal of Marketing, 33* (1/2), 121-142.

Chhibber, P. K. & Majumdar, S. K. (2005). Property rights and the control of strategy: foreign ownership rules and domestic firm globalization in Indian industry. *Law & Policy, 27* (1), 52-80.

Delany, E. (2000). Strategic development of the multinational subsidiary through subsidiary initiative-taking. *Long Range Planning, 33* (2), 220-244.

Delios, A., & Beamish, P.W. (1999). Ownership strategy of Japanese firms: transactional, institutional, and experience influences. *Strategic Management Journal, 20* (10), 915-933

Dunning, J. H. (1994). Re-evaluating the benefits of foreign direct investment. *Transnational Corporations, 3* (1), 23-51.

Eisenhardt, K. M. (1989). Building theories from case study research. *Academy of Management Review, 14* (4), 532-550.

Eriksson, K., Johanson, J., Majkgård, A., & Sharma, D. D. (1998). Time and experience in the internationalization process. In A. Majkgård (Ed.), *Experiential knowledge in the internationalization process of service firms* (pp. 185-217). Uppsala: Department of Business Studies.

Fina, E., & Rugman, A. M. (1996). A test of internalization theory and internationalization theory: the Upjohn Company. *Management International Review, 36* (3), 199-213.

Ford, D. (1998). Two decades of interaction, relationships and networks. In P. Naudé & P. Turnbull (Eds.), *Network dynamics in international marketing* (pp. 3-15). Oxford: Elsevier.

Gestrin, M. (2002). *The relationship between trade and foreign direct investment: a survey* (OECD Document No. TD/TC/WP (2002) 14/FINAL), Paris: OECD Working Party of the Trade Committee.

Ginsberg, A., & Hay, M. (1994). Confronting the challenges of corporate entrepreneurship: guidelines for venture managers. *European Management Journal, 12* (4), 382-389.

Håkansson, H., & Snehota, I. (2000). The IMP perspective: assets and liabilities of business relationships. In J. N. Sheth & A. Parvatiyar (Eds.), *Handbook of relationship marketing* (pp. 69-94). London: Sage.

Hedlund, G. (1986). The hypermodern MNC: a heterarchy? *Human Resource Management, 25* (1), 9-35.

Hertz, S. (1996). The dynamics of international strategic alliances. *International Studies of Management & Organization, 26* (2), 104-130.

Hillebrand, B., Kok, R. A. W., & Biemans, W. G. (2001). Theory-testing using case studies: a comment on Johnston, Leach, and Liu. *Industrial Marketing Management, 30* (8), 651-657.

Johanson, J., & Mattson, L.-G. (1988). Internationalization in industrial systems–a network approach. In N. Hood & J.-E. Vahlne (Eds.), *Strategies in global competition* (pp. 287-314). London: Croom Helm.

Johanson, J., & Vahlne, J.-E. (1977). The internationalization process of the firm: a model of knowledge development and increasing foreign market commitments. *Journal of International Business Studies, 8* (1), 23-32.

Johanson, J., & Vahlne, J.-E. (1990). The mechanism of internationalisation. *International Marketing Review, 7* (4), 11-24.

Johanson, J., & Wiedersheim-Paul, F. (1975). The internationalization of the firm: four Swedish cases. *Journal of Management Studies, 12* (3), 305-322.

Korhonen, H. (1999). *Inward-outward internationalization of small and medium enterprises*. Doctoral dissertation No. A-147, Helsinki School of Economics, Helsinki.

Lauter, G. P., & Rehman, S. S. (1999). Central and East European trade orientation and FDI flows: preparation for EU membership. *International Trade Journal, 13* (1), 35-52.

Legewie, J. (2002). Control and co-ordination of Japanese subsidiaries in China: problems of an expatriate-based management system. *International Journal of Human Resource Management, 13* (6), 901-919.

Luostarinen, R., & Welch, L. (1997). *International business operations*. Helsinki: Kyriiri.

Malnight, Y. W. (1996). The transition from decentralized to network-based MNC structures: an evolutionary perspective. *Journal of International Business Studies, 27* (1), 43-65.

Marinova, S. T., Marinov, M. A., & Yaprak, A. (2004). Market-seeking motives and market-related promises and actions in foreign direct investment privatization in Central and Eastern Europe. *Journal of East-West Business, 10* (1), 7-41.

Martínez, J. I., & Quelch, J. A. (1996). Country managers: the next generation. *International Marketing Review, 13* (3), 43-55.

Miles, M. B., & Huberman, A. M. (1994). *Qualitative data analysis: an expanded sourcebook.* London: Sage.

Morgan, G., Sharpe, D. R., Kelly, W., & Whitley, R. (2002). The future of Japanese manufacturing in the UK. *Journal of Management Studies, 39* (8), 1023-1044.

Morgan, R. E., & Katsikeas, C. S. (1997). Theories of international trade, foreign direct investment and firm internationalization: a critique. *Management Decision, 35* (1/2), 68-78.

Oviatt, B. M., & McDougall, P. P. (1994). Toward a theory of international new ventures. *Journal of International Business Studies, 25* (1), 45-64.

Prahalad, C. K., & Doz, Y. L. (1981). An approach to strategic control in MNCs. *Sloan Management Review, 22* (4), 5-13.

Quelch, J. A. & Bloom, H. (1996). The return of the country manager. *McKinsey Quarterly, 2,* 30-43.

Quelch, J. A., & Dinh-Tan, C. M. (1998). Country managers in transitional economies: the case of Vietnam. *Business Horizons, 41* (4), 7-20.

Roolaht, T. (2002). Internationalisation of firms from small open transition economies: the intra-firm factors and inward-outward connections. *Journal of East-West Business, 8* (3/4), 123-144.

Schuh, A., & Holzmüller, H. (2003). Marketing strategies of Western consumer goods firms in Central and Eastern Europe. In H-J. Stüting, W. Dorow, F. Claassen & S. Blazejewski (Eds.), *Change management in transition economies–integrating corporate strategy, structure and culture* (pp. 176-188). London: Palgrave Macmillan.

Simoneti, M., Rojec, M. & Rems, M. (2001). Ownership structure and post-privatisation performance and restructuring of the Slovenian non-financial corporate sector. *Journal of East-West Business, 7* (2), 7-37.

Tavares, A. T., & Young, S. (2002). *Explaining the export intensity of multinational subsidiaries: an EU-based empirical study* (Working Paper No. 2002/02). Glasgow: University of Strathclyde.

Tsai, W. (2001). Knowledge transfer in intraorganizational networks: effects of network position and absorptive capacity on business unit innovation and performance. *Academy of Management Journal, 44* (5), 996-1004.

Tsoukas, H. (1989). The validity of idiographic research explanations. *Academy of Management Review, 14* (4), 551-561.

Vahlne, J.-E., & Johanson, J. (2002). New technology, new companies, new business environments and new internationalisation processes? In V. Havila, M. Forsgren & H. Håkansson (Eds.), *Critical perspectives of internationalisation* (pp. 209-227). Amsterdam: Pergamon.

Voss, C., Tsikriktis, N., & Frohlich, M. (2002). Case Research in operations management. *International Journal of Operations & Production Management, 22* (2), 195-219.

Welch, L. S. & Luostarinen, R. (1988). Internationalization: evolution of a concept. *Journal of General Management, 14* (2), 34-57.

Wiedersheim-Paul, F., Olson, H. C., & Welch, L. S. (1978). Pre-export activity: the first step in internationalization. *Journal of International Business Studies, 9* (1), 47-58.

Wolff, J. A., & Pett, T. L. (2000). Internationalization of small firms: an examination of export competitive patterns, firm size, and export performance. *Journal of Small Business Management, 38* (2), 34-47.

Yin, R. K. (1994). *Case study research design and methods.* London: Sage.

Zahra, S. A., Dharwadkar, R., & George, G. (1999). Entrepreneurship in multinational subsidiaries: the effects of corporate and local environmental contexts (Working Paper No. 27). Atlanta: GT CIBER

doi:10.1300/J097v13n02_06

The Role of Cooperation and Innovation in Reducing the Likelihood of Export Withdrawals: The Case of the Estonian Wood Sector

Ele Reiljan

SUMMARY. This study concentrates on analyzing the role played by innovation and cooperation in the likelihood of Estonian wood industry enterprises' export withdrawals. The data obtained from two different databases show that about 40% of the Estonian wood sector firms have withdrawn from (some of) their foreign markets. The results indicate that export withdrawls are more typical of those firms that have not introduced new products, services or processes. In the case of cooperative activities the data present mixed results, not allowing us to draw explicit conclusions. doi:10.1300/J097v13n02_07 *[Article copies available for a fee from The Haworth Document Delivery Service: 1-800-HAWORTH. E-mail address: <docdelivery@haworthpress.com> Website: <http://www.HaworthPress.com>* © 2007 by The Haworth Press, Inc. All rights reserved.]

KEYWORDS. Internationalization, export withdrawls, innovation, networks, wood sector

Ele Reiljan is Senior Researcher and Head of Marketing Department, Faculty of Economics and Business Administration, University of Tartu, Narva mnt. 4-A214, Tartu 51009 (E-mail: ele.reiljan@mtk.ut.ee).

[Haworth co-indexing entry note]: "The Role of Cooperation and Innovation in Reducing the Likelihood of Export Withdrawals: The Case of the Estonian Wood Sector." Reiljan, Ele. Co-published simultaneously in *Journal of East-West Business* (The Haworth Press, Inc.) Vol. 13, No. 2/3, 2007, pp. 243-261; and: *Market Entry and Operational Decision Making in East-West Business Relationships* (ed: Jorma Larimo) The Haworth Press, Inc., 2007, pp. 243-261. Single or multiple copies of this article are available for a fee from The Haworth Document Delivery Service [1-800-HAWORTH, 9:00 a.m. - 5:00 p.m. (EST). E-mail address: docdelivery@haworthpress.com].

INTRODUCTION

Research in the field of international business has been active for several decades. In the last few years discussions have been initiated about the most important future research topics. Buckley (2002) has expressed an opinion that the field is running out of steam. Peng, on the other hand, is more optimistic, suggesting that the main question that has been the focus of research and still needs attention is "What determines the international success or failure of firms?" (Peng 2004, p. 100).

Globalization of the economy and formation of regional economic blocks leads to removal of trade barriers and promotes increase in international trade and foreign direct investments. In order to survive in an increasingly competitive environment, firms have to focus on innovative and/or cooperative activities (Tödtling 1999). This is especially important for the Central and Eastern European (CEE) transition countries since firms from these countries are losing their low cost-based competitive edge in international markets due to convergence of their cost levels with the European Union's average. Moreover, competitiveness of the CEE economies is decreasing because of the emerging Asian economies that provide new opportunities in the huge local markets and significantly lower cost levels.

By comparison with the beginning of the transformation processes, innovative activities have intensified in the Central and Eastern European countries, but both the level of R & D costs and the intensity of innovative activities are still relatively lower than those of developed economies as the investments into development in these countries are often determined by financial constraints. Besides the lack of resources, foreign owners' policies and either absence or low level of cooperation with other network members play a significant role in financing innovative activities.

Since Estonia regained independence at the beginning of the 1990s, its manufacturing industry has been characterized by rapid developments both in the local and foreign markets. However, the international orientation of different sectors of the manufacturing industry varies significantly. It is believed that the main reason for the rapid rise in the importance of foreign markets in some sectors is the activities of foreign investors who use the production of these industries as an input in their production plants in other countries or guarantee the market for the production through their distribution channels (see Reiljan 2005). For example, in the wood sector, Stora Enso in 2002 acquired majority ownership in the leading Estonian wood manufacturer Sylvester Ltd., after which a rapid increase in foreign activities has taken place both in terms of export and establishment of foreign subsidiaries. A number of other Estonian wood sector firms are also tightly integrated into the Nordic wood cluster through ownership by Finnish or Swedish investors. Despite these relationships, or due to them, several Estonian wood sector firms have withdrawn from foreign markets.

This study attempts to identify the influence of cooperative and innovative activities on reducing the likelihood of withdrawals from the foreign markets in the case of Estonian wood sector enterprises. The analysis is based on the results of "Wood Sector Survey 2005" and "Community Innovation Survey 2001." In addition to the previously mentioned databases, aggregated data of the Estonian manufacturing industry are used for characterizing the developments that have taken place in the Estonian wood sector.

The study is divided into three parts. First, the theoretical foundations of export withdrawals and the influence of innovative and cooperative activities on withdrawals are discussed. Next the main developments in the Estonian wood sector are studied. Finally, the influence of cooperative and innovative activities on Estonian wood sector firms' export withdrawals is analyzed.

THEORETICAL FRAMEWORK

Export withdrawals are defined as a firm's strategic decisions to remove a particular combination of product and market from its international portfolio (Pauwels & Matthyssens 1999). Besides strategic withdrawals (these include also failures) from the foreign market(s), forced export withdrawals caused by the actions of the host country governments are possible. It is important to keep in mind that export withdrawals do not necessarily mean a failure of foreign operations (see Crick 2002 for a more detailed discussion), but there are also several other reasons that may easily influence the decision to close down (some of) the foreign activities. These factors can roughly be divided into three categories: (1) lack of international experience, (2) changes in strategy, and (3) poor performance or increase in production costs (see also Reiljan 2005).

Lack of international experience as a reason for export withdrawal is pointed out in several previous empirical studies. Sometimes firms are not prepared for unwritten social and market customs, power structure and several other aspects characteristic of the particular target market (see for example, Anderson et al. 1998, Crick 2004). According to Welch and Wiedersheim-Paul (1980) there is clear evidence that first export attempts are often experimental in their nature and thus a failure or withdrawal from exporting after having made a start is in many cases inevitable (a position of withdrawal in their framework can be seen in Figure 1). They emphasize that the planning and research of cultural and employment issues should have been more thorough. Cavusgil (1984) has indicated that only a few exporters considered the analysis of foreign markets to be a complex task that requires a high level of analysis. Empirical evidence also suggests that the major reasons for drawbacks are internal and could have been avoided by market research and proper planning before the venture (Luostarinen 1989). These results suggest that in several cases firms either do not perceive the need for in-depth analysis of the target market or do not realize that due to the differences in cultural, economic and political environments there are several other aspects to be considered besides the market potential and demand.

Mistakes deriving from insufficient planning and analysis in selecting a proper degree of commitment to foreign markets may also cause withdrawals from them. Some firms commit too many resources and these unwise investments need liquidation in order to rationalize the use

FIGURE 1. Influences on Initial Export Marketing Behavior

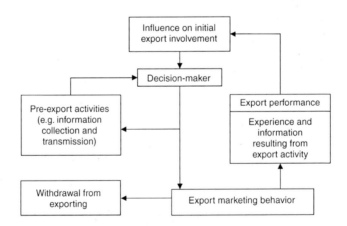

Source: Adapted from Welch & Wiedersheim-Paul 1980.

of resources (Sachdev 1976). On the other hand, small firms are often eager to ensure that they can leave foreign markets with low costs as soon as necessary (Bonaccorsi 1992). Hence, they tend to avoid investments needed for granting success in the target market. As at the beginning of international activities international and market-specific knowledge and experience tend to be poor, mistakes are likely to happen and can lead to withdrawals.

Besides the lack of international experience, change in strategy may also have a significant impact on the decision to close down all or some of the foreign activities. Vahlne and Nordström suggest that in the case of global firms withdrawal is a normal process as it enables better use of scarce resources. Economies of scale, global standardization of products and decreasing transportation costs also favor this kind of backward movement (Vahlne & Nordström 1993). However, there are other opinions too, as several authors claim that foreign market exits are seldom strategic in nature because they are usually not based on long-term planning processes and are mostly the result of environmental changes (Boddewyn 1983). For example, 43% of the failed exporters mentioned external environmental changes as the determining factor in their withdrawals (Welch & Wiedersheim-Paul 1980). Therefore, it is important to keep the company updated about the changes in the target market conditions. In addition to changes in customers' needs, implementation of new rules and policies by the host governments have to be monitored carefully because in several cases new laws favor local enterprises, thereby increasing their competitiveness. In addition to the developments that take place in the international markets, changes in home country are also important to monitor. Home market growth can influence the firm's decision to reduce its commitment to foreign markets significantly (Elango 1998) since the risks that are related to local operations are usually smaller than those related to international ones.

The third group of reasons that can lead to export withdrawals includes poor performance and increase in production costs (see for example, Lindgren & Spångberg 1981; Pauwels & Matthyssens 1999). Poor performance is often the result of either lack of managerial and personnel capabilities for handling foreign operations properly (Luostarinen & Welch 1997), increase in production and/or transportation costs and tariffs, or emergence of new competitors.

The impact of all the three above-mentioned groups of reasons behind export withdrawals can be reduced by developing and maintaining the competitive advantages. The two factors that have aroused particular interest in the discussions about international competitiveness are cooperation with other network members and introduction of innovations.

A number of previous studies in the field of international business point out the influence of cooperative activities on internationalization processes and contribution of other network members. Although the classical Uppsala model emphasized only one source of knowledge–own experience–several additional sources of knowledge acquisition may also be suggested (see Figure 2). Accelerated knowledge gathering or knowledge transfer from outside sources is possible, for example, in the case of change in ownership (a foreign investor may provide knowledge about its home market and/or other target markets). Acquisition of an enterprise or establishment of joint venture or alliance also serve in several cases as sources of gaining access to knowledge about (how to operate in) foreign markets (Forsgren 2002; Hagedoorn 1993; Hennart 2000; Welch & Welch 1996).

Network theory emphasizes the importance of other network members in improving the knowledge base and mediating or even generating impulses for moving abroad. For example, Madsen and Servais (1997) suggested that, by comparison with other firms, the internationalization process of subcontractors may be much faster and different, and they may expand into many markets very fast.

FIGURE 2. Sources of General and Market Knowledge

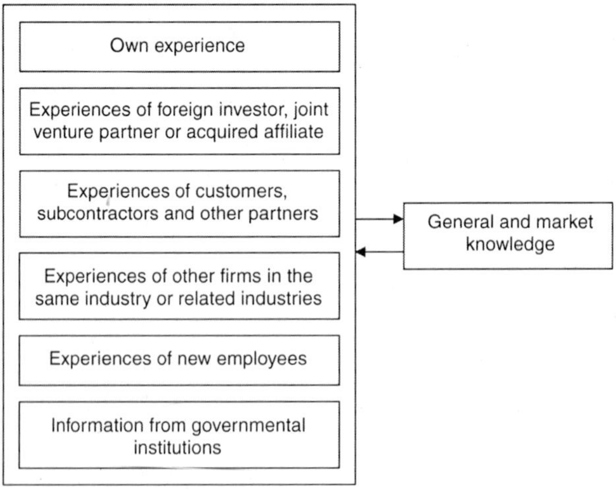

Source: Reiljan 2005.

Rapid changes in market conditions and competitive pressure favor exchange of knowledge with other network members and promote the cooperative activities in order to increase competitiveness both in the local and foreign markets. It can be expected that cooperation with other network members would reduce the uncertainty related to international markets and would therefore shrink the likelihood of export withdrawals. This applies especially to those withdrawals that are caused by lack of experience.

Innovative activities, on the other hand, enable increasing competitiveness through introduction of new products, services, processes, organizational structures, management systems, production systems, or commercial arrangements (Trott 2002). Innovation includes both the development and commercialization of new knowledge (Afuah 2003; Jorde & Teece 1990). Competitive edge that can be obtained through introduction of innovation may help overcome several obstacles in foreign markets. It can be expected that innovative activities reduce the likelihood of export withdrawals, particularly of those related to increase in production costs.

Besides the two strands of literature that analyze the nature and importance of cooperation and innovative activities, there is also a growing body of contributions that discuss the increasing importance of cooperation within networks in enhancing innovative activities (see for example, Tödtling 1999). Cooperation may, for instance, help overcome the disadvantages deriving from the small size of the firm and is therefore likely to contribute to innovative activities. However, in order to make use of the knowledge of other network members, the firm needs knowledge and/or experiences about handling cooperative relationships (Koschatzky 1999).

The role of other network members, motivation and impediments to cooperation depend significantly on the stage of innovation process (Chiesa & Toletti 2004). Moreover, the extent of cooperation tends to vary between firms and industries. The need for cooperation with other enterprises is modest if the firm prefers to follow internally initiated impulses for innovation and does not pay attention to external ones. Therefore, cooperation with other network members and positive influences on innovative activities can be expected if the firm chooses to act in accordance with the simultaneous models of innovation. The traditional serial model neglects this possibility (Jorde & Teece 1990).

The above discussion suggests that there are three different effects that result from innovative and cooperative activities:

- direct effect of cooperative activities is likely to reduce the likelihood of withdrawals from foreign markets,
- direct effect of innovative activities is also likely to reduce the likelihood of withdrawals from foreign markets,
- cooperative activities may have an effect on withdrawals through enhancing or restricting innovative activities.

The following parts of this study will concentrate on analyzing the occurrence of these effects in the case of Estonian wood sector firms. Unfortunately, the available data allow us to study only the first two effects.

MAIN DEVELOPMENTS
IN THE ESTONIAN WOOD SECTOR

In the years of regained independence, the Estonian wood industry has made rapid progress.. This industry started its international activities in the first half of the 1990s by exporting roundwood, but now the focus has shifted towards refining timber and adding higher value to the products. For example, in the last few years the manufacture of sawn timber has doubled and the export of gluewood has increased significantly (Saetööstuse. . . 2004). The wood industry constitutes 16% of the whole manufacturing industry and accounts for 18% of the exports in Estonia (Aggregated Data. . . 2004), therefore influencing the whole economy to a large extent. In the world context the production capacity in Estonia is quite small, but considering the small size of the country, it constitutes a significant share as Estonian sawmills produced 1.86 million m^3 in 2003, which is ca 2.2% of the EU production and 0.5% of the world production of sawnwood (EFIA. . . 2004).

Table 1 summarizes the main developments that have taken place in the Estonian wood sector in 1995-2002. The sector started in 1995 with 54 companies, only 4 of which were foreign-owned. Since that time the number of firms has grown 17.8 times and the share of foreign-owned firms has dropped from the level of 7.4 in 1995 to 5.5 in 2002. At the same time, the average number of employees has significantly decreased in all groups of enterprises. The data in Table 1 suggest that most of the Estonian wood sector enterprises are small. Therefore, their innovative potential can be expected to be rather limited unless they have tight linkages and cooperation with their foreign parent companies and/or other network members.

TABLE 1. Main Indicators of the Estonian Wood Sector

	1995	1996	1997	1998	1999	2000	2001	2002
Number of companies								
All	54	607	639	698	810	735	833	964
Foreign	4	46	37	39	47	42	59	53
Domestic	50	561	602	659	763	693	774	911
Employees per company								
All	100.2	19.3	18.9	18.5	16.5	19.2	17.9	17.8
Foreign	77.0	24.8	40.5	38.8	52.3	63.7	55.0	68.9
Domestic	102.1	18.8	17.5	17.3	14.3	16.5	15.1	14.9
Export sales in net sales (%)								
Domestic	62.4	34.6	53.2	46.7	51.4	55.7	52.5	50.1
Foreign	95.6	38.4	68.9	79.4	77.7	82.3	77.9	79.4
Net sales per employee (EEK, thousands)								
All	267.3	202.8	303.6	353.0	401.3	487.5	539.2	621.4
Foreign	1342.9	238.0	371.6	492.5	495.4	637.8	621.8	678.6
Domestic	202.4	198.9	294.0	334.6	380.1	452.4	516.3	605.9

Source: The author's calculations on the basis of Aggregated Data. . . 2004.

In terms of foreign activities and net sales per employee, there are significant differences between the enterprise groups. While foreign-owned enterprises faced only one year with export share in turnover being less than 2/3, locally owned companies exported about half of their production during the period 1995-2002. Among other explanations for such development, differences in efficiency can be suggested. In terms of net sales per employee foreign-owned companies were producing 6.6 times more than the local ones. However, the difference has decreased over the years but this is not reflected in the propensity to export. One explanation here is that locally owned companies often produce inputs for the foreign-owned ones that have invested heavily in increasing the share of value-adding activities carried out in Estonia. The other explanation that can be offered here is that local companies are inexperienced players in the international markets and can therefore easily be reluctant to export or face export withdrawals more often.

In the wood sector, Stora Enso acquired majority ownership in the leading Estonian wood manufacturer Sylvester Ltd. in 2002 and after that a rapid increase in international activities has taken place both in terms of export and establishment of foreign subsidiaries. Since this one company constitutes a high share of industry–26% of turnover and

7.6% of workforce in 2002–it heavily influences developments in the whole sector.

It is also important to compare the developments that have taken place in the wood sector with other branches of the manufacturing industry in Estonia. Taking into account the developments in international activities, four groups of industries can be distinguished, depending on their levels of internationalization in 1996 and 2002 as compared to the manufacturing industry average (see Table 2). There are six industries in the first group where both in 1996 and 2002 the share of foreign sales was higher than the manufacturing industry average. The export by these sectors constituted 41% in 1996 and 36% in 2002 of all manufacturing export sales. The second group, whose share of export has dropped below the industry's average, exported 11% of manufacturing production in 1996 and 13% in 2002. At the same time, these sectors experienced high growth both in the home market (2.6 times) and export sales (3.3 times) during the period and therefore this slight change does not indicate that they lack competitiveness in foreign markets.

The wood sector belongs to the third group where the share of export in turnover increased above the manufacturing industry average during the years under investigation. The main reason behind this development was mentioned above–the acquisition of Sylvester by Stora Enso. However, Table 2 also indicates significant shifts in efficiency, which may likewise contribute to positive changes in international markets.

The above discussion suggests that the Estonian wood sector has experienced positive developments in international markets and its export share is above the manufacturing industry average. This enables us to expect export withdrawals to be rather rare. On the other hand, since the average size of the enterprises in terms of employees is small, they probably do not have enough resources for innovative activities and this may easily result in a higher rate of withdrawals from foreign markets.

EXPORT WITHDRAWALS, INNOVATIVE AND COOPERATIVE ACTIVITIES IN THE ESTONIAN WOOD INDUSTRY

The following analysis is based on two databases–"Wood Sector Survey 2005" and "Community Innovation Survey 2001." The former was carried out by the Faculty of Economics and Business Administration of the University of Tartu. The sample involved all wood sector firms of Estonia. This database presents information about withdrawals

TABLE 2. Export Share in the Turnover of Different Industries in 1996 and 2002

		2002	
		Above manufacturing industry average	Below manufacturing industry average
1996	Above manufacturing industry average	• Paper and paper products • Chemicals and coke • Furniture, others, recycling • Wearing apparel, dressing • Motor vehicles and transport equipment • Tanning and dressing of leather	• Metals and products • Machinery and equipment n.e.c. • Rubber and plastic
	Below manufacturing industry average	• Wood • Office, electrical , radio and medical equipment • Textiles	• Publishing, printing • Food products, beverages • Other non-metallic minerals

Source: Composed by the author on the basis of Aggregated Data. . . 2004.

from international markets and the main reasons for them. The data allow us to distinguish between the firms that have carried out innovative activities (here product, service, and process innovations are considered) and those that have not focused on innovation yet. Finally, it is possible to determine the level of cooperative activities and analyze the differences in the existence, nature and strength of linkages with suppliers, consumers, educational and governmental institutions between those firms that have withdrawn from the foreign markets as compared to the rest. The data were gathered through a mail survey during the first half of 2005. The database contains 65 responses (the response rate was 8%). Most of the respondents were small and medium-size companies (the average size–53 employees). 31% of the companies only sold locally, while others had operations both in the local and foreign markets.

The above Community Innovation Survey was carried out by the Estonian Statistical Office in 2001 and provides information about innovative and cooperative activities of the Estonian enterprises in the period 1998-2000. In the case of innovative activities only product and process innovations are distinguished between; therefore this dataset is more limited than the one gathered in a wood industry survey. The latter also contains data about the export activities and the share of international sales in turnover. The number of wood sector enterprises that provided all data necessary for the analysis carried out in the present study, is 256 and represents 26.6% of the sector.

Since wood industry developments in the international markets have been rapid over the past years, withdrawals from foreign markets can be expected to be rare. However, Figure 3 presents a rather different picture–40% of the firms indicated in 2005 that they had withdrawn from (some of) their foreign markets and 39% of the firms had faced a decrease in their export volume during the years 1998-2000. Therefore, two different databases suggest that a large share of the firms have experienced backward movements in their internationalization patterns.

Figure 4 presents an overview of the importance of different reasons behind the decision to withdraw from the foreign markets. Three most important reasons represent the motives that are related to changes in strategy. Termination of a cooperation contract with the current partner and the foreign owner's strategy both indicate the significant role of network relationships. At the same time, insufficient knowledge of foreign markets and internationalization processes is considered to be the least important reason behind withdrawal decisions. There are two potential explanations for the low importance of this factor. Firstly, entrepreneurs are often reluctant to admit their lack of knowledge. Secondly, the share of foreign ownership in terms of net and export sales is high in the Estonian wood sector and most of the international activities are coordinated by the experienced parent company.

Figure 5 provides information about innovative activities in the Estonian wood sector. The share of those companies that have not introduced new solutions is in most cases significantly higher than the share of innovative companies. The only exception here is new product development. Low commitment to innovative activities may easily be the result of lack of resources determined by the small size of companies. Moreover, since quite a significant number of enterprises carry out the

FIGURE 3. Share of Firms That Have Withdrawn Some of Their Foreign Activities

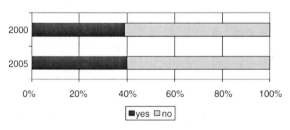

Source: Author's calculations on the basis of Wood. . . 2005 and Community. . . 2001.

FIGURE 4. Reasons for Withdrawals from Foreign Markets in the Estonian Wood Industry (1-Completely Unimportant. . . 4-Very Important)

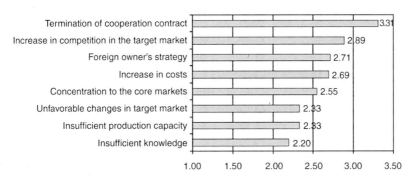

Source: Author's calculations on the basis of Wood. . . 2005.

FIGURE 5. Introduction of Innovations in the Estonian Wood Industry (%)

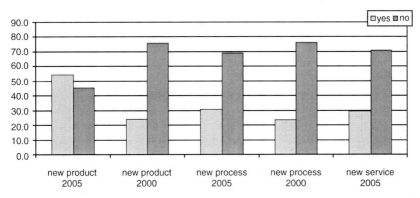

Source: Author's calculations on the basis of Wood. . . 2005 and Community. . . 2001.

operations that are situated at the lower end of the value chain, it is likely that they fail to realize what vital role is played by innovative activities in sustaining competitive edge in the longer run.

Figure 6 presents enterprises' perceptions about the importance of cooperation with other network members. As can be seen, higher importance is assigned to the cooperative activities with customers, suppliers, competitors and other enterprises belonging to the same branch, and other subsidiaries of the firm. Therefore, the close relationships

FIGURE 6. Importance of Cooperation with Other Network Members in the Estonian Wood Industry

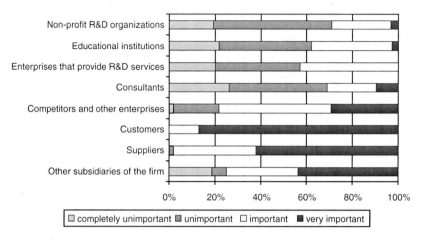

Source: Author's calculations on the basis of Wood. . . 2005.

with (foreign) parents and other members of the value chain as suggested in the discussion in the previous part of this study are acknowledged by the companies. On the other hand, cooperation with those network members who can also contribute heavily to enhancement and support of innovative activities, is in many cases perceived to be unimportant.

Figure 7 gives information about the share of export withdrawals among innovating companies and those that have not introduced innovative solutions during the period under consideration. As expected, innovative firms have faced fewer withdrawals than the other ones. Thus it can be suggested that innovative activities help decrease the likelihood of export withdrawals. This is especially clearly evidenced by product innovations. On the other hand, process innovations do not seem to contribute to a similar extent. This may at least partly explain the results presented above in Figure 5–firms concentrate their scarce resources on product innovations since the latter contribute to enhancing competitiveness considerably more than do other types of innovation.

The last figure about the differences in the share of export withdrawals among firms that assign different importance to cooperation with other network members does not allow us to draw satisfactory conclu-

FIGURE 7. Share of Firms (%) That Have Withdrawn from Foreign Markets Among the Firms with Different Innovative Activities

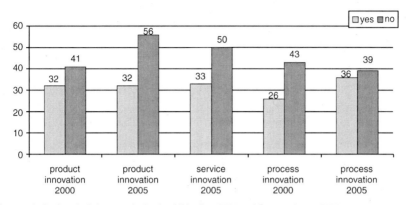

Source: Author's calculations on the basis of Wood. . . 2005 and Community. . . 2001.

sions about the role of cooperative activities in reducing the likelihood of withdrawals from foreign markets (see Figure 8). In the case of both intensive and no cooperation with educational institutions, consultants and organizations that provide R&D services, the share of export withdrawals is relatively low. However, Figure 6 suggests that these network members are often not considered to be important partners.

Figure 8 indicates that cooperation with other subsidiaries of the firm and suppliers is likely to reduce the probability of withdrawal. On the other hand, cooperation with competitors and other firms in the wood sector does not need to contribute in a similar manner since the share of withdrawals is smaller in those enterprises that have perceived cooperation to be unimportant.

CONCLUSION

The discussion in the theoretical part of this study indicated that there are three groups of reasons behind export withdrawals–lack of international experience, change in strategy, and poor performance or increase in production costs. Cooperation and innovation have direct and indirect effects on firms' international activities and can help them overcome several problems that may otherwise lead to export withdrawals. For example, cooperation with other network members may decrease the unfamiliarity of foreign markets, thereby enhancing international

FIGURE 8. Share of Firms (%) That Have Withdrawn from Foreign Markets Among the Firms That Have Different Perceptions About the Importance of Co-operation with Other Network Members

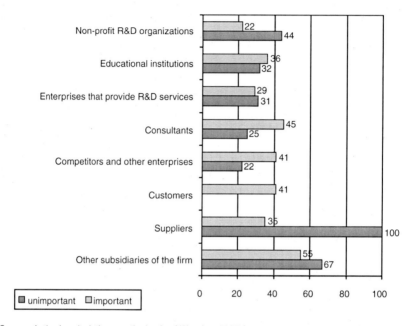

Source: Author's calculations on the basis of Wood. . . 2005.

operations and reducing the likelihood of withdrawals. Innovations, on the other hand, may help sustain competitive edge in the conditions of increasing production costs. Three potential effects of innovative and cooperative activities on export withdrawals were suggested on the basis of the discussion herein. This study concentrated on analyzing two of them–direct linkages between innovations and cooperation with the likelihood of withdrawals from the export markets.

The data from two different databases suggested that about 40% of the Estonian wood sector firms have faced export withdrawals. The main reason behind such developments in international markets is the termination of cooperation contracts with the existing partners. Lack of knowledge as a motivation was rated as the least important one.

The results of the analysis showed that Estonian wood sector firms have intensified their innovative activities, especially in the field of introducing new products. The need to introduce new products may, among other things, be determined by enhanced competitiveness in international markets. This kind of reasoning is supported by the low share of export withdrawals in the case of innovative firms, and especially in the case of those firms that have carried out product innovations.

On the other hand, our analysis of the influence of cooperative activities on the likelihood of export withdrawals provided mixed results. The share of withdrawals is relatively high both in the case when the firm cooperates with other subsidiaries, customers and suppliers and when it does not. However, the withdrawals are more characteristic of those enterprises that perceive cooperation as having low importance. Conversely, cooperative activities with competitors and other firms belonging to the wood industry present an opposite situation.

These preliminary results need validation by future studies. In-depth understanding of the experiences of Estonian exporting firms is needed to avoid blunders and promote international expansion and implementation of supportive policy measures. Promotion of innovative and cooperative activities may be instrumental in reducing the rate of withdrawals and guaranteeing success in international markets.

REFERENCES

Afuah, A. (2003). *Innovation Management: Strategies, Implementation, and Profits.* Oxford: Oxford University Press.

Aggregated data of the Estonian manufacturing industry (2004). Statistical Office of Estonia.

Anderson, V., S. Graham, & P. Lawrence (1998). Learning to Internationalize. *Journal of Management Development* 17: 7, 492-502.

Boddewyn, J. J. (1983). Foreign and Domestic Divestment and Investment Decisions: Like or Unlike? *Journal of International Business Studies* 14: 3, 23-35.

Bonaccorsi, A. (1992). On the Relationship between Firm Size and Export Intensity. *Journal of International Business Studies* 23: 4, 605-635.

Buckley, P. (2002). Is the International Business Research Agenda Running Out of Steam? *Journal of International Business Studies* 33: 2, 365-373.

Cavusgil, T. (1984). Differences Among Exporting Firms Based on Their Degree of Internationalization. *Journal of Business Research* 12: 2, 195-208.

Chiesa, V. & G. Toletti (2004). Network Collaborations for Innovation: The Case of Biotechnology. *Technology Analysis and Strategic Management* 16: 1, 73-96.

Community Innovation Survey 1998-2000 (2001).–Estonian Statistical Office.

Crick, D. (2002). The Decision to Discontinue Exporting: SMEs in Two U.K. Trade Sectors. *Journal of Small Business Management* 40: 1, 66-77.

Crick, D. (2004). U.K. SMEs' Decision to Discontinue Exporting: An Exploratory Investigation into Practices within the Clothing Industry. *Journal of Business Venturing* 19: 4, 561-587.

EFIA presentation (2004).–Estonian Forest Industries Association [http://www.emtl.ee/?id = 502].

Elango, B. (1998). An Empirical Examination of the Influence of Industry and Firm Drivers on the Rate of Internationalization by Firms. *Journal of International Management* 4: 3, 201-221.

Forsgren, M. (2002). The Concept of Learning in the Uppsala Internationalization Process Model: A Critical Review. *International Business Review* 11: 3, 257-277.

Hagedoorn, J. (1993). Understanding the Rationale of Strategic Technology Partnering: Interorganizational Modes of Cooperation and Sectoral Differences. *Strategic Management Journal* 14: 5, 371-385.

Hennart, J.-F. (2000). Transaction Costs Theory and the Multinational Enterprise. In: *The Nature of the Transnational Firm*, 72-118. Eds, Pitelis, C.N., Sugden, R. London: Routledge.

Jorde, T.M. & D.J. Teece (1990). Innovation and Cooperation: Implications for Competition and Antitrust. *Journal of Economic Perspectives* 4: 3, 75-96.

Koschatzky, K. (1999). Innovation Networks of Industry and Business-Related Services–Relations between Innovation Intensity of Firms and Regional Inter-Firm Cooperation. *European Planning Studies* 7: 6, 737-757.

Lindgren, U. & K. Spångberg (1981). Corporate Acquisitions and Divestments: The Strategic Decision-Making Process. *International Studies of Management and Organization* 11: 2, 24-47.

Luostarinen, R. (1989). *Internationalization of the Firm: An Empirical Study of the Internationalization of the Firms with Small and Open Domestic Markets with Special Emphasis on Lateral Rigidity as a Behavioral Characteristic in Strategic Decision Making.* Helsinki: The Helsinki School of Economics.

Luostarinen, R. & L. Welch (1997). *International Business Operations.* Helsinki: Helsinki School of Economics.

Madsen, T. K. & P. Servais (1997). The Internationalization of Born Globals: An Evolutionary Process? *International Business Review* 6: 6, 561-583.

Pauwels, P. & P. Mathyssens (1999). A Strategy Process Perspective on Export Withdrawal. *Journal of International Marketing* 7: 3, 10-37.

Peng, M. W. (2004). Identifying the big Question in International Business Research. *Journal of International Business Studies* 35: 2, 99-108.

Reiljan, E. (2005). *Reasons for De-internationalization: An Analysis of Estonian Manufacturing Companies.* Dissertationes Rerum Oeconomicarum Universitatis Tartuensis No. 11.

Sachdev, J. C. (1976). Disinvestment: A Corporate Failure or a Strategic Success. *International Studies of Management and Organization* 6: ½, 112-130.

Saetööstuse toodang 1998-2003 (2004). Eesti Metsatööstuse Liit [http://www.emtl.ee/?id = 612].

Trott, P. (2002). *Innovation Management and New Product Development.* Harlow: Prentice Hall.

Tödtling, F. (1999). Innovation Networks, Collective Learning, and Industrial Policy in Regions of Europe. *European Planning Studies* 7: 6, 693-697.

Vahlne, J.-E. & K.A. Nordström (1993). The Internationalization Process: Impact of Competition and Experience. *International Trade Journal* 7: 5, 529-548.

Wagner, H. (2004). Internationalization Speed and Cost Efficiency: Evidence from Germany. *International Business Review* 13: 4, 447-463.

Welch, D. E. & L. S. Welch (1996). The Internationalization Process and Networks: A Strategic Management Perspective. *Journal of International Marketing* 4: 3, 11-28.

Welch, L. S. & F. Wiedersheim-Paul (1980). Initial Exports–A Marketing Failure? *Journal of Management Studies* 17: 3, 333-344.

Wood Sector Survey (2005).–University of Tartu, Faculty of Economics and Business Administration.

doi:10.1300/J097v13n02_07

Index

Abcam, 26
Accounting, 198-199,207*t*,211*t*
Adaptation, shopping behavior and, 136
Administration. *see* Management
Administratively controlled (ADM)
    prices, 100
Advertising
    first mover advantages and, 48*t*
    shopping behavior and, 119
Agrana Group, 155-156*t*. *see also*
    Regionalization
Agrotorg, 74*t*
Aibe, 73
ANOVA analysis,
    202-203,204*t*,208*t*,212*t*
Arabia, 22,26,231-232
Asia, 22. *see also* First mover advantages
    (FMA); *specific countries*
Aspect, 22
    Asper Biotech, 20*t*,21*t*,22-23,26-28
    Atmosphere, store, shopping behavior
        and, 119,120*t*,131*t*,136*t*
Attitudes, shopping behavior and, 120*t*
Auchan, 74*t*
Australia
    Asper Biotech and, 26
    Mikromasch and, 24
Austria, 231-232
Axfood, Finnish/Swedish
    internationalization and, 74

Baltic markets. *see also specific*
    countries
    clusters and. *see* Cluster development
        process

Finnish/Swedish internationalization
    and. *see* Finland; Sweden
    overview of retailing in, 71-74
Bank Austria Creditanstalt, 155-156*t*. *see*
    also Regionalization
Banking industry, 155-156*t*. *see also*
    Regionalization
Baylor College of Medicine, 23
Belgium, 233-234
Bestseller, 76*t*,77
Biersdorf, 24
BIODATA, 25
Biotechnology. *see* Asper Biotech
Born globals, 2,14-15,219,222
Brand considerations, shopping behavior
    and, 117
Brazil, 24
BTG BiotecGen, 25
Bulgaria, 4,102*t*,103*t*
Buying process perception variables,
    shopping behavior and,
    119,120*t*

Canada, 24-26
CEE countries. *see* Central Europe;
    Eastern Europe; *specific*
    countries
Central Europe. *see also specific*
    countries
    early movers/followers and. *see* First
        mover advantages (FMA)
    export withdrawals and. *see* Export
        withdrawals
    foreign ownership of subsidiaries and.
        see Foreign ownership of
        subsidiaries

The Main Investors in the Seven CEE
   Countries, 96f
regionalization and. *see*
   Regionalization
role of German MNC subsidiaries in.
   see German MNC subsidiaries
Western multinational companies
   (WMC) in, 1
China
   Asper Biotech and, 26
   first mover advantages and, 49,57
   internationalization approaches and,
      22
   Krenholm Group and, 233-234
   Mikromasch and, 24
   TEA Language Center and, 26
   Top Emerging Markets in A.T.
      Kearney's Global Retail
      Development Index, 72t
   Wendre and, 234-235
Citymarket, 79-80,80t
Cluster Analysis and Clusters Profiles in
   the Evaluation of Store
   Atmosphere, 135t
Cluster development process
   discussion/conclusion and, 184-187
   Estonian companies in the Nordic
      wood and forestry cluster and,
      177-184
   introduction to, 168-169
   The Key Figures from Stora Enso
      Wood Processing Companies in
      the Baltic States, 179t
   The Key Financial Figures from
      Horizon Pulp & Paper, 181t
   methods/data and, 176-177
   networks and, 171-176,175f
   regional clusters/innovative
      development and, 169-171
   summary, 167-168
   A Summary of Case Studies and
      Survey Results, 186t
Columbia University, 23
Community Innovation Survey 2001,
   252-253

Conceptual Framework for the Analysis
   of Regionalization in CEE,
   153f
Conditional Logit Model,
   104-105,108t,110t
CONNECT network, 26
Consumer goods, 155-156t. *see also*
   Regionalization
Consumer involvement, shopping
   behavior and, 120t,128-129t
Consumer logistics, 130t
Controlling, value chain activities and,
   198-199
Controls, first mover advantages and,
   47,48t
Coop Norden, Finnish/Swedish
   internationalization and, 74
Cooperation, export withdrawals and. *see*
   Export withdrawals
Cultural considerations
   shopping behavior and,
      117,127-132,128-129t
   subsidiaries and, 201
Customer service, 198-199,207t,211t
Czeck Republic
   Descriptive Statistics for the
      Explanatory Variables, 103t
   introduction to, 7
   role of German MNC subsidiaries in.
      see German MNC subsidiaries
   The Sample Distribution of Firms in
      the Seven Countries, 102t
   Tesco and, 71

Demographics, shopping behavior and,
   126-127
Denmark, 7,24,231-232. *see also* Cluster
   development process
Development, value chain activities and,
   198-199
Dorinda, 74t
Dummies, first mover advantages and,
   48t,54-55

Early movers. *see* First mover
    advantages (FMA)
Eastern Europe. *see also specific*
    countries
    early movers/followers and. *see* First
        mover advantages (FMA)
    export withdrawals and. *see* Export
        withdrawals
    foreign ownership of subsidiaries and.
        see Foreign ownership of
        subsidiaries
    The Main Investors in the Seven CEE
        Countries, 96*f*
    regionalization and. *see*
        Regionalization
    Western multinational companies
        (WMC) in, 1
Economic clusters. *see* Cluster
    development process
Edeka, 74*t*
Eesti Uhispank. *see* SEB Eesti Uhispank
EF International Language Schools, 22
Efficiency-seeking subsidiaries, 200,203*t*
Ehitusmaailm, 80*t*
Ekovalda, 81*t*
EMT, 22
Enso, 178-180,179*t*,186*t*,251-252
Enterprise Estonia, 26
Entry mode, first mover advantages and,
    48*t*
Environment, first mover advantages
    and, 48*t*
Erste Bank, 155-156*t*. *see also*
    Regionalization
Estimation of the Base Model, 107-109
Estonia. *see also* Baltic markets
    case descriptions and, 19-26,20*t*,21*t*
    cluster development process and,
        177-184,179*t*. *see also* Cluster
        development process
    conclusions/implications and, 28-29
    discussion, 26-28
    export withdrawals and. *see* Export
        withdrawals

Finnish/Swedish internationalization
    and, 72
foreign ownership of subsidiaries and.
    see Foreign ownership of
    subsidiaries
ICA's Internationalization in the
    Baltic States, 81*t*
internationalization approaches and,
    13-17
introduction to, 1-2,9,12
The K Group's Internationalization in
    the Baltic States and Russia,
    80*t*
Krenholm Group and, 233-234
methodology and, 17-19
SEB Eesti Uhispank and,
    229-231,234-235
Stockmann and, 76*t*
summary, 11
Wendre and, 231-232
Estonian Biocentre, 26
Estonian Business School, 26
Estonian Genome Centre, 23
Estonian Innovation Foundation, 26
Estonian Nanotechnology Competence
    Centre, 24
Estonian Technology Agency, 26
Eurocoop, 78
Europe
    Central. *see* Central Europe
    Eastern. *see* Eastern Europe
    European Union. *see* European Union
European Union, 1,24
Evikon, 24
Exclusivity, first mover advantages and,
    40-41
Experience, international. *see*
    International experience
Explorative behavior, shopping behavior
    and, 120*t*,135*t*,137-138
Export intensity, first mover advantages
    and, 48*t*
Export withdrawals
    conclusions, 257-259

Export Share in the Turnover of
Different Industries in 1996 and
2002, 253*t*
Importance of Cooperation with
Other Network Members in the
Estonian Wood Industry, 256*f*
Influences on Initial Export
Marketing Behavior, 246*f*
innovative/cooperative activities and,
252-257
Introduction of Innovations in the
Estonian Wood Industry, 255*f*
introduction to, 8-9,244-245
main developments in the Estonian
wood sector and, 250-252
Main Indicators of the Estonian Wood
Sector, 251*t*
Reasons for Withdrawals from
Foreign Markets in the
Estonian Wood Industry, 255*f*
Share of Firms That Have Withdrawn
from Foreign Markets Among
the Firms That Have Different
Perceptions About the
Importance of Cooperation
with Other Network Members,
258*f*
Share of Firms That Have Withdrawn
from Foreign Markets Among
the Firms with Different
Innovative Activities, 257*f*
Share of Firms That Have Withdrawn
Some of Their Foreign
Activities, 254*f*
Sources of General and Market
Knowledge, 248*f*
summary, 243
theoretical framework and, 245-250

Factor Analysis on Consumer Shopping
Behavior by French, Italian and
Polish Consumers, 133-134*t*
Fast internationalization, 14-15,17*t*,18*f*.
see also Born globals

Felma, 74*t*
Fermentas, 26
Finance, value chain activities and,
198-199
Finland
The Baltic States and Russia as Target
Countries to Finnish and
Swedish Retailers, 69*t*
case descriptions and, 75-80,76*t*
Characteristics of the Finnish and
Swedish Food Retailer's
Domestic Markets, 66*t*
cluster development process and,
177-178. *see also* Cluster
development process
conclusions/implications and, 83-87
Hansabank Group and, 234-235
introduction to, 3-4,7,64-65
Krenholm Group and, 233-234
overview of retailing in Baltic
states/Russia and, 71-74,72*t*
Quattromed and, 25-26
retail internationalization and, 65-71
summary, 63
Summary of Case Companies
International Behavior in the
Baltic States and Russia, 85*t*
Wendre and, 231-232
Finnish internationalization model,
13-14,219,222
First mover advantages (FMA)
Average Market Share Distributed on
Host Country, 45*t*
Control Variables, 48*t*
defined, 36
discussion/conclusion and, 57-58
Entry Timing and Payoff in a Two
Player Game, 41*f*
introduction to, 36-37
model and, 47-49
Pearson Correlational Matrix, 56*t*
Regression Analysis for the Three
Models and, 50-51*t*
Regression Including Interaction
Links, 52-53*t*

results and, 49-57
summary, 35-36
survey and, 43-47
Variables Included in Industry
    Performance, 46*t*
Variables Included in Performance
    Satisfaction, 46*t*
FIT Biotech, 25
FMA. *see* First mover advantages (FMA)
Food retail. *see* Retail
    internationalization
Foreign direct investment (FDI)
    background information and, 95-97
    conclusions/implications and,
        109-111
    Conditional Logit Model, 108*t*
    The Conditional Logit Model:
        Comparison of Manufacturing
        and Service Firms, 110*t*
    The Correlational Matrix of the
        Explanatory Variables, 106*t*
    data/methodology and, 100-105
    Descriptive Statistics for the
        Explanatory Variables, 103*t*
    empirical results and, 105-109
    The Explanatory Variables and Their
        Expected Impacts, 101
    foreign ownership of subsidiaries and.
        see Foreign ownership of
        subsidiaries
    introduction to, 2,94-95
    literature review and, 97-100
    literature review/model formulation
        and, 97-100
    The Main Investors in the Seven CEE
        Countries, 96*f*
    The Sample Distribution of Firms in
        the Seven Countries, 102*t*
    summary, 93-94
Foreign ownership of subsidiaries
    case descriptions and, 227-234
    conclusions/future research directions
        and, 237-238
    discussion and, 234-237

The Internationalization Paths of
    Foreign-Owned Firms: A
    Conceptual Framework, 226*f*
    introduction to, 220-221
    literature review and, 221-225
    methodology and, 225-227
    summary, 219
Foreign subsidiaries. *see* German MNC
    subsidiaries
Forest industry. *see* Cluster development
    process; Export withdrawals
France
    internationalization approaches and,
        23
    introduction to, 5
    Mikromasch and, 24
    shopping behavior in. *see* Shopping
        behavior
    Wendre and, 231-232

Generali Vienna Holding, 155-156*t. see
    also* Regionalization
Geographic considerations
    first mover advantages and, 38
    as market seeking behavior,
        193-197,201,205,213*t*
    regionalization and, 149
German MNC subsidiaries
    conclusions/implications and,
        213-215
    effect of subsidiary's ownership
        structure and, 209-210
    influence of mode of market entry
        and, 210-213,211*t*
    influence of the subsidiary's host
        country and, 206-208
    introduction to, 192-193
    Market Entry Mode and Ownership
        Structure of German
        Subsidiaries..., 199*t*
    Most Frequent Value Chain Activities
        for Different Tasks Considered
        as "Important or Very
        Important", 203*t*

Most Frequent Value Chain Activities
for Subsidiaries Located in
Different Countries, 207*t*
The Response Rates of the Survey
Distributed by Countries Where
Subsidiaries Are Located, 199*t*
results and, 202-206
Results of ANOVA for the Number of
Value Chain Activities
Depending on Mode of Market
Entry, 212*t*
Results of ANOVA for the Number of
Value Chain Activities
Depending on the Degree of
Importance for Selected Tasks,
204*t*
Results of ANOVA for the Number of
Value Chain Activities
Performed Depending on
Subsidiary's Location, 208*t*
Sales, Number of Employees and
Balance Sheet Totals of the
Investigated Subsidiaries...,
199*t*
sample characteristics/operationaliza-
tion of variables and, 198-202
summary, 191-192
Test for Differences with Regard to
the Importance of Market
Seeking Between Greenfield
Subsidiaries and Acquisitions,
213*t*
theoretical background and, 193-197
Germany
Finnish/Swedish internationalization
and, 78
introduction to, 7
Krenholm Group and, 235-236
Mikromasch and, 24
MNC subsidiaries and. *see* German
MNC subsidiaries
Quattromed and, 25
SEB Eesti Uhispank and, 229-231
shopping behavior and, 124

Wendre and, 231-232
Great Britain. *see* United Kingdom
Greece, Mikromasch and, 24
Greenfield subsidiaries. *see* German
MNC subsidiaries

Hansabank Group, 227-229,234-235,
235*t*
Henkel CEE, 155-156*t*. *see also*
Regionalization
Hennes & Mauritz, Finnish/Swedish
internationalization and, 74
Hobby Hall, 76*t*
Holland, 24,95,231-234
Hong-Kong, 24,26
Horizon Pulp & Paper Ltd.,
180-182,181*t*,186*t*
Horizontal Clusters and Consumer
Nationality in the Perception of
Store Atmosphere, 136*t*
Host country, subsidiaries and,
206-208,207*t*,208*t*
Household goods, shopping behavior
and, 122-125
Human resource management, value
chain activities and, 198-199
Hungary
Descriptive Statistics for the
Explanatory Variables, 103*t*
early movers/followers and. *see* First
mover advantages (FMA)
introduction to, 2-3,7
role of German MNC subsidiaries in.
see German MNC subsidiaries
The Sample Distribution of Firms in
the Seven Countries, 102*t*
Tesco and, 71
Hyundai, 97

ICA, Finnish/Swedish
internationalization and,
74,80-82,81*t*,83-87,85*t*

IKEA, 74,77,82-87,83*t*,85*t*

I-model. *see* Innovation-related internationalization model

India, 26, 72*t*

Indonesia, 26

Industry performance, first mover advantages and, 45,46*t*,50-51*t*

Influences on Initial Export Marketing Behavior, 246*f*

Innovation, export withdrawals and. *see* Export withdrawals

Innovation-related internationalization model, 13,219,221-222,236

Institute for the Promotion of External Trade, 101

Institute of Molecular and Cell Biology, 26

In-store shopping behavior. *see* Shopping behavior

Insurance industry, 155-156*t*. *see also* Regionalization

Interaction effects, first mover advantages and, 42-43,47,49,55-57

International Cancer Research Centre, 23

International Cooperative Alliance, 78

International experience, export withdrawals and, 245,247

International scope and size, first mover advantages and, 48*t*

Internationalization process
  approaches to, 13-17
  case descriptions and, 19-26,20*t*,21*t*
  conclusions/implications and, 28-29
  discussion, 26-28
  in Finland/Sweden. *see* Finland; Sweden
  foreign ownership of subsidiaries and. *see* Foreign ownership of subsidiaries
  The Internationalization Paths of Foreign-Owned Firms: A Conceptual Framework, 226*f*
  introduction to, 1-2,12
  methodology and, 17-19

summary, 11
Two Types of Internationalization, 17*t*

Interprego, 81*t*

Investment motives, first mover advantages and, 48*t*

Israel, 24,26

IT infrastructure, value chain activities and, 198-199

Italy
  foreign direct investment location decisions and. *see* Foreign direct investment (FDI)
  introduction to, 4
  Krenholm Group and, 233-234
  Quattromed and, 25
  shopping behavior in. *see* Shopping behavior
  Wendre and, 231-232

Japan, 24-26

Jeol, 24

Joint ventures, German MNC subsidiaries and, 196-197

K Group, 74,78-80,80*t*,83-87,85*t*

Kesko. *see* K Group

Knowledge, sources of, 248*f*

Kopeika, 74*t*

Korea, 24,26

K-Rauta, 79

K-Rautakesko, 80*t*

Krenholm Group, 233-236,235*t*

K-TEK International, 24

Kvest Bank, 227-229

Language Center, TEA. *see* TEA Language Center

Latvia. *see also* Baltic markets
  cluster development process and, 179*t*
  Finnish/Swedish internationalization and, 72

Hansabank Group and,
227-229,234-235
ICA's Internationalization in the
Baltic States, 81*t*
The K Group's Internationalization in
the Baltic States and Russia,
80*t*
Krenholm Group and, 233-234
SEB Eesti Uhispank and, 234-235
Stockmann and, 76*t*
Top Emerging Markets in A.T.
Kearney's Global Retail
Development Index, 72*t*
Wendre and, 231-232
Lenta, 74*t*
Lithuania. *see also* Baltic markets
cluster development process and, 179*t*
early movers/followers and. *see* First
mover advantages (FMA)
Hansabank Group and, 234-235
ICA's Internationalization in the
Baltic States, 81*t*
introduction to, 2-3
The K Group's Internationalization in
the Baltic States and Russia,
80*t*
Krenholm Group and, 233-234
Quattromed and, 26
Stockmann and, 76*t*
Top Emerging Markets in A.T.
Kearney's Global Retail
Development Index, 72*t*
Wendre and, 231-232
Location decisions
background information and, 95-97
conclusions/implications and,
109-111
Conditional Logit Model, 108*t*
The Conditional Logit Model:
Comparison of Manufacturing
and Service Firms, 110*t*
The Correlational Matrix of the
Explanatory Variables, 106*t*
data/methodology and, 100-105

Descriptive Statistics for the
Explanatory Variables, 103*t*
empirical results and, 105-109
The Explanatory Variables and Their
Expected Impacts, 101
introduction to, 94-95
literature review/model formulation
and, 97-100
The Main Investors in the Seven CEE
Countries, 96*f*
The Sample Distribution of Firms in
the Seven Countries, 102*t*
summary, 93-94
Logistics, 130*t*,198-199
Logit Model, Conditional,
104-105,108*t*,110*t*

Magnit, 74*t*
Maico Metrics, 24
Management
alternate management models and,
162-163
influence of mode of market entry
and, 211*t*
regionalization and. *see*
Regionalization
shopping behavior and, 136-138
subsidiary, 198
value chain activities and,
198-199,207*t*
Market controlled prices, 100
Market development, regionalization
and, 150
Market entry, mode of,
210-213,211*t*,212*t*
Market growth, location decisions and,
107-109
Market size, 42,46,54-55,107-109
Market strategy, Finnish/Swedish
internationalization and, 67-69
Marketing strategies. *see also*
Advertising

efficiency-seeking subsidiaries and.
  see Efficiency-seeking
  subsidiaries
geographic-seeking subsidiaries and.
  see under Georgraphic
  considerations
influence of mode of market entry
  and, 211*t*
Influences on Initial Export
  Marketing Behavior, 246*f*
introduction to, 1
psychic market proximity seeking
  subsidiaries and. *see* Psychic
  market proximity seeking
  subsidiaries
resource-seeking subsidiaries and. *see*
  Resource-seeking subsidiaries
strategic asset seeking subsidiaries
  and. *see* Strategic asset seeking
  subsidiaries
value chain activities and,
  198-199,207*t*
Market-seeking subsidiaries,
  200-201,203*t*
Marketshare, first mover advantages and,
  44-45,45*t*,50-51*t*
MCI, 24
Medizintechnik, 25
Metro, 74*t*
Mexico, 24
Mikromasch, 20*t*,21*t*,23-25, 27
Mikros Turk, 74*t*
MNCs. *see* Western multinational
  companies (WMC)
Molecular diagnostics. *see* Quattromed
Multinational companies
  clusters and. *see* Cluster development
  process
  location decisions of. *see* Location
  decisions
  regionalization and. *see*
  Regionalization
  Western. *see* Western multinational
  companies (WMC)

Nanotechnology. *see* Mikromasch
Nature, 23
Network internationalization approach,
  16-17,171-176,175*f*,248
Network literature, introduction to, 2
New markets, early movers/followers
  and. *see* First mover advantages
  (FMA)
New Zealand, 24,26
NexTech Supply, 24
Nordic region. *see* Cluster development
  process
Norfos Mazmena, 73
Norway, 231-234
Novus Biologicals, 26

OLS regression analysis, introduction to,
  2-3
Olympus, 24
Operation strategy, Finnish/Swedish
  internationalization and, 70-71
Optimization, regionalization and, 151
Organizational perspective of
  regionalization, 145-148
Outlet, Stockmann, 76*t*
Ownership, foreign, introduction to, 8
Ownership structure, 209-210. *see also*
  Foreign ownership of
  subsidiaries

Palink, 73
Parent corporations. *see* Subsidiaries
Paterson, 74*t*
Perekriostok, 74*t*
Performance
  export withdrawals and, 245,247
  first mover advantages and,
    38,42-43,50-51*t*
  industry. *see* Industry performance,
    first mover advantages and
  regionalization and, 153*f*
  satisfaction, 45,46*t*

Personality variables, shopping behavior and, 119,120*t*
Personnel, shopping behavior and, 121-122
Petrovsky, 74*t*
PNAS, 23
Poland
    Descriptive Statistics for the Explanatory Variables, 103*t*
    early movers/followers and. *see* First mover advantages (FMA)
    introduction to, 2-7
    Mikromasch and, 24
    role of German MNC subsidiaries in. *see* German MNC subsidiaries
    The Sample Distribution of Firms in the Seven Countries, 102*t*
    shopping behavior and, 124
    shopping behavior in. *see* Shopping behavior
    Tesco and, 71
Portugal, 25
Price considerations, shopping behavior and, 118,120*t*
Price control, 100
PricewaterhouseCoopers Gene Technology Award, 25
Prisma, 78
Procurement, value chain activities and, 198-199,207*t*
Product space, first mover advantages and, 38
Production
    export withdrawals and, 245,247
    influence of mode of market entry and, 211*t*
    value chain activities and, 198-199,207*t*
Products
    first mover advantages and, 48*t*
    shopping behavior and, 119
Property rights protections, 100
PSA, 97

Psychic market proximity seeking subsidiaries, 203-204,203*t*,205-206,213*t*
Psychographic considerations, shopping behavior and, 120*t*,126-127
Purchased goods storage costs, shopping behavior and, 120*t*
Pyaterochka, 74*t*

Quality sensitivity, shopping behavior and, 120*t*
Quattromed, 20*t*,21*t*,25-28

Ramenka, 74*t*
Regionalization
    Advantages and Disadvantages of Regionalization, 149*t*
    clusters and. *see* Cluster development process
    concept of, 145-150
    Conceptual Framework for the Analysis of Regionalization in CEE, 153*f*
    conclusions/discussion and, 160-164
    findings and, 153-159
    introduction to, 144-145
    Overview of Selected Findings of the Study, 155-156*t*
    research design and, 150-153
    summary, 143-144
Research, value chain activities and, 198-199
Research evaluation costs, shopping behavior and, 120*t*
Resources, first mover advantages and, 48*t*
Resource-seeking subsidiaries, 200,203*t*
Retail internationalization
    The Baltic States and Russia as Target Countries to Finnish and Swedish Retailers, 69*t*
    Characteristics of the Finnish and Swedish Food Retailer's Domestic Markets, 66*t*
    in Finland/Sweden, 65-71

Rewe, 74*t*
Richard Lewis Communications, 22
Rimi, 73,80*t*,81*t*
Risk perception, shopping behavior and, 120*t*
Romania, 24,102*t*,103*t*
Russia
    clusters and. *see* Cluster development process
    Finnish/Swedish internationalization and. *see* Finland; Sweden
    Hansabank Group and, 227-229,234-235
    IKEA's Internationalization in Russia, 83*t*
    introduction to, 2-3
    The K Group's Internationalization in the Baltic States and Russia, 80*t*
    Krenholm Group and, 233-234
    Major Domestic and International Food Retailers in Russia, 74*t*
    Mikromasch and, 24,27
    overview of retailing in, 71-74
    SEB Eesti Uhispank and, 234-235
    Stockmann and, 76*t*
    TEA Language Center and, 22
    Top Emerging Markets in A.T. Kearney's Global Retail Development Index, 72*t*
    Wendre and, 231-232

S Group, Finnish/Swedish internationalization and, 74,77-78,83-87,85*t*
Saastumarket, 80*t*
Saint George International, 22
Sales, 198-199,207*t*,211*t*
Satisfaction, performance, 45,46*t*
Scandinavia. *see* Cluster development process
Scanning Probe Microscopy, 24
Schleswig-Holstein, 78
SEB Eesti Uhispank, 229-231,234-235
SEB Eesti Uhispank and, 235*t*
Sedmoy Continent, 74*t*

Segmentation, in-store, 132-136, 133-134*t*,135*t*,136*t*
Seiko, 24
Senukai, 79
Seppala, 76,76*t*,84
Service sector
    clusters and. *see* Cluster development process
    regionalization and, 163-164
Shopping activity perception variables, shopping behavior and, 119, 120*t*
Shopping behavior
    Cluster Analysis and Clusters Profiles in the Evaluation of Store Atmosphere, 135*t*
    conclusions/implications and, 136-138
    Consumer Involvement and In-Store Consumer Behavior, 128-129*t*
    Consumer Logistic, 130*t*
    distribution system for household goods and, 122-125
    Factor Analysis on Consumer Shopping Behavior by French, Italian and Polish Consumers, 133-134*t*
    findings and, 126-136
    Horizontal Clusters and Consumer Nationality in the Perception of Store Atmosphere, 136*t*
    introduction to, 116
    literature review and, 117-121
    Psychographic Variables and Shopping Behaviour, 120*t*
    research methodology and, 125-126
    The Role of Atmosphere, 131*t*
    summary, 115-116
SI, 24
Singapore, 24, 26
Skaninaviska Enskilda Banken. *see* SEB Eesti Uhispank
Slovak Republic, 71,102*t*,103*t*
Slovenia, 4, 72*t*,102*t*,103*t*
Socio-economic considerations, shopping behavior and, 126-127

SOK Corporation. *see* S Group,
      Finnish/Swedish
      internationalization and
Sokos, 78
South Korea, 23
Spain, 27,231-232
Spar, 74*t*
Standard of living, regionalization and, 150
Standardization, shopping behavior and,
      136
Stanford University, 23
Stockmann, Finnish/Swedish
      internationalization and, 75-77,
      76*t*,83-87,85*t*
Strategic asset seeking subsidiaries, 200,
      203*t*,212
Strategic perspective of regionalization,
      145-148
Strategy changes, export withdrawals
      and, 245,247
Stroymaster, 80*t*
Subsidiaries
   foreign ownership and. *see* Foreign
      ownership of subsidiaries
   German MNCs and. *see* German
      MNC subsidiaries
Sunergia Medical, 23
SuperNetto, 80*t*
Swedbank, 227-229
Sweden
   The Baltic States and Russia as Target
      Countries to Finnish and
      Swedish Retailers, 69*t*
   case descriptions and, 80-83
   Characteristics of the Finnish and
      Swedish Food Retailer's
      Domestic Markets, 66*t*
   cluster development process and. *see*
      Cluster development process
   conclusions/implications and, 83-87
   Hansabank Group and, 227-229
   introduction to, 3-4,7,64-65
   Krenholm Group and, 235-236
   Mikromasch and, 24
   overview of retailing in Baltic
      states/Russia and, 71-74,72*t*

   Quattromed and, 25
   retail internationalization and, 65-71
SEB Eesti Uhispank and, 229-231
   summary, 63
Summary of Case Companies
   International Behavior in the
      Baltic States and Russia, 85*t*
   Wendre and, 231-232
Switzerland, 24,231-232,233-234
Sylvester-Stora Enso, 178-180,179*t*,
      186*t*,251-252

Taiwan, 26
Tander, 74*t*
Tartu Biotechnology Park, 25
Tartu University, 24-26,252-253
TEA Language Center, 19-22,20*t*,21*t*,
      26,28
Technology, first mover advantages and,
      48*t*
Tesco, 71
Time factor, shopping behavior and,
      119-120,120*t*
Timing, first mover advantages and, 38,
      41*f*,42-43,46,49-54
Toftan sawmill, 177-178,186*t*
Trading House Scandinavia AB, 231-232
Traditional internationalization
      approach, 13-14,17*t*

Ukraine, 72*t*
U-model. *see* Uppsala
      internationalization model
UNIQA Group, 155-156*t*. *see also*
      Regionalization
United Arabian Emirates, 26,231-232
United Kingdom
   internationalization approaches and,
      23
   Krenholm Group and, 235-236
   Mikromasch and, 24
   Quattromed and, 25-26
   shopping behavior and, 124

Wendre and, 231-232
United States
  Asper Biotech and, 26
  internationalization approaches and, 23
  Krenholm Group and, 235-236
  Mikromasch and, 24,27
  Quattromed and, 25-26
  Wendre and, 231-232
University of North Carolina at Chapel Hill, 24
Uppsala internationalization model, 13, 219,221,236

Value chain activities
  defined, 198-199
  mode of market entry and, 210-211
  Most Frequent Value Chain Activities for Different Tasks Considered as "Important or Very Important", 203t
  Most Frequent Value Chain Activities for Subsidiaries Located in Different Countries, 207t
  Most Frequent Value Chain Activities with Regard to Ownership Structure and Mode of Market Entry, 211t
  overview of, 193-197
  Results of ANOVA for the Number of Value Chain Activities Depending on Mode of Market Entry, 212t

Results of ANOVA for the Number of Value Chain Activities Depending on the Degree of Importance for Selected Tasks, 204t
Results of ANOVA for the Number of Value Chain Activities Performed Depending on Subsidiary's Location, 208t
Viking Window Ltd., 182-183,186t
Vikonda, 81t
VitaMed, 25
Volkswagen, 97

Wal-Mart, 42
Wendre, 231-232,234-235,235t
Western multinational companies (WMC). *see also* Multinational companies
  introduction to, 1
  location decisions of. *see* Location decisions
Wood industry. *see* Cluster development process; Export withdrawals
Wood Sector Survey 2005, 252-253

Zara, 76-77,76t

BOOK ORDER FORM!

Order a copy of this book with this form or online at:
http://www.HaworthPress.com/store/product.asp?sku= 6001

Market Entry and Operational Decision Making in East-West Business Relationships

____ in softbound at $42.00 ISBN-13: 978-0-7890-3544-8 / ISBN-10: 0-7890-3544-8.
____ in hardbound at $75.00 ISBN-13: 978-0-7890-3543-1 / ISBN-10: 0-7890-3543-X.

COST OF BOOKS _____

POSTAGE & HANDLING _____
US: $4.00 for first book & $1.50
for each additional book
Outside US: $5.00 for first book
& $2.00 for each additional book.

SUBTOTAL _____

In Canada: add 6% GST. _____

STATE TAX _____
CA, IL, IN, MN, NJ, NY, OH, PA & SD residents
please add appropriate local sales tax.

FINAL TOTAL _____

If paying in Canadian funds, convert
using the current exchange rate,
UNESCO coupons welcome.

❑ BILL ME LATER:
Bill-me option is good on US/Canada/
Mexico orders only; not good to jobbers,
wholesalers, or subscription agencies.

❑ Signature _____

❑ Payment Enclosed: $_____

❑ PLEASE CHARGE TO MY CREDIT CARD:
❑ Visa ❑ MasterCard ❑ AmEx ❑ Discover
❑ Diner's Club ❑ Eurocard ❑ JCB

Account #_____

Exp Date_____

Signature_____
(Prices in US dollars and subject to change without notice.)

PLEASE PRINT ALL INFORMATION OR ATTACH YOUR BUSINESS CARD

Name	
Address	
City	State/Province ____ Zip/Postal Code
Country	
Tel	Fax
E-Mail	

May we use your e-mail address for confirmations and other types of information? ❑Yes ❑No We appreciate receiving
your e-mail address. Haworth would like to e-mail special discount offers to you, as a preferred customer.
We will never share, rent, or exchange your e-mail address. We regard such actions as an invasion of your privacy.

Order from your **local bookstore** or directly from
The Haworth Press, Inc. 10 Alice Street, Binghamton, New York 13904-1580 • USA
Call our toll-free number (1-800-429-6784) / Outside US/Canada: (607) 722-5857
Fax: 1-800-895-0582 / Outside US/Canada: (607) 771-0012
E-mail your order to us: orders@HaworthPress.com

For orders outside US and Canada, you may wish to order through your local
sales representative, distributor, or bookseller.
For information, see http://HaworthPress.com/distributors

(Discounts are available for individual orders in US and Canada only, not booksellers/distributors.)

Please photocopy this form for your personal use.
www.HaworthPress.com

BOF07